Macmillan/McGraw-Hill READING

 **Macmillan
McGraw-Hill**

New York   Farmington

Contributors

The Princeton Review, Time Magazine, Accelerated Reader

The Princeton Review is not
affiliated with Princeton
University or ETS.

learning through listening

Students with print disabilities may be eligible to obtain an accessible, audio version of the
pupil edition of this textbook. Please call Recording for the Blind & Dyslexic at 1-800-221-4792
for complete information.

Macmillan/McGraw-Hill

A Division of The McGraw-Hill Companies

Published by Macmillan/McGraw-Hill, a division of The McGraw-Hill Companies, Inc., Two Penn Plaza, NY, NY 10121

Macmillan/McGraw-Hill READING

Authors

James Flood

Jan E. Hasbrouck

James V. Hoffman

Diane Lapp

Donna Lubcker

Angela Shelf Medearis

Scott Paris

Steven Stahl

Josefina Villamil Tinajero

Karen D. Wood

Macmillan
McGraw-Hill

New York   Farmington

Computer Center

Managing the

Art Center

Working with Words Center

Phonics Center

Reading and Listening Center

Writing Center

Classroom

Math Center

1 2 3 4 5

Teacher Directed Small Group Instruction

Sample Management Plan

Group 1	Group 2	Group 3	Group 4
With Teacher	Phonics Center or Word Center	Writing Center or Reading Center	Cross-Curricular Center
Phonics Center or Word Center	**With Teacher**	Cross-Curricular Center	Writing Center or Reading Center
Writing Center or Reading Center	Cross-Curricular Center	**With Teacher**	Phonics Center or Word Center
Cross-Curricular Center	Writing Center or Reading Center	Phonics Center or Word Center	**With Teacher**

Creating CENTERS

Establishing independent Centers and other independent activities is the key to helping you manage the classroom as you meet with small groups.

Reading and Listening

Set up a classroom library that includes Theme Big Books, Leveled Books, and other independent reading titles on each group's independent reading level. Also, see the Theme Bibliography on pages T98 and T99 for suggested titles.

Children can use the Reading Center for:

- Self-selected reading
- Paired reading
- Listening to selections on audiocassette

Phonics

Children can practice the phonics skills they are learning. Phonics Center activities may include:

- Sorting picture cards by initial/final blends
- Writing blends
- Reading blends
- Substituting consonants to build words
- Sorting and classifying sounds

Writing

Children can practice their fine motor, handwriting, and writing skills.

Children can use the Writing Center for:

- Writing/drawing about their own experiences
- Practicing forming letters
- Responding to literature
- Journal writing

Working with Words

Children can practice reading and identifying high-frequency words. Place Word Building Manipulative Cards for the words *try, their, fall, would, old, grow, any, new, together, too, eat, now, where, know, why,* and *under* in the Center. Have pairs of children practice reading the words together.

Children can use the Working with Words Center for:

- Matching word cards
- Reading words
- Using words in sentences
- Playing word games

Cross-Curricular

CENTERS

Set up Cross-Curricular Centers to help extend selection concepts and ideas. Suggestions for Cross-Curricular Centers can be found throughout the unit.

Science

- Jumping Beans, 20
- Animal Homes, 68D
- Owls, 86
- Hot Snakes, 110
- The Night Sky, 126D

Math

- Bats, 22
- Shape Faces, 58
- Story Problems, 82
- Make a Snake, 98D
- Snake Facts, 104

Social Studies

- Friendly Sentences, 8D
- Forests, 16
- Career Notes, 38D
- Everday Emotions, 48
- My Family, 68D
- Child vs. Pet Care, 118
- What Do You See?, 126D

Music

- Music, 84

Additional Independent Activities

The following independent activities are offered as a means to practice and reinforce concepts and skills taught within the unit.

PUPIL EDITION: READER RESPONSE

Story Questions to monitor student comprehension of the selection. The questions are leveled, progressing from literal to more critical thinking questions.

Story Activities related to the selection. Four activities are always provided: one Writing activity, two Cross-Curricular activities, and a Research and Inquiry activity in the "Find Out More" project, which encourages students to use the Internet for research.

LEVELED PRACTICE

Each week, Reteach, Practice, and Extend pages are offered to address the individual needs of students as they learn and review skills.

McGraw-Hill Reading

Theme Chart

MULTI-AGE Classroom

Using the same global themes at each grade level facilitates the use of materials in multi-age classrooms.

GRADE LEVEL	Experience — Experiences can tell us about ourselves and our world.	Connections — Making connections develops new understandings.
Kindergarten	**My World** — We learn a lot from all the things we see and do at home and in school.	**All Kinds of Friends** — When we work and play together, we learn more about ourselves.
Subtheme 1	At Home	Working Together
Subtheme 2	School Days	Playing Together
1	**Day by Day** — Each day brings new experiences.	**Together Is Better** — We like to share ideas and experiences with others.
2	**What's New?** — With each day, we learn something new.	**Just Between Us** — Family and friends help us see the world in new ways.
3	**Great Adventures** — Life is made up of big and small experiences.	**Nature Links** — Nature can give us new ideas.
4	**Reflections** — Stories let us share the experiences of others.	**Something in Common** — Sharing ideas can lead to meaningful cooperation.
5	**Time of My Life** — We sometimes find memorable experiences in unexpected places.	**Building Bridges** — Knowing what we have in common helps us appreciate our differences.
6	**Pathways** — Reflecting on life's experiences can lead to new understandings.	**A Common Thread** — A look beneath the surface may uncover hidden connections.

Themes: Kindergarten – Grade 6

Expression	Inquiry	Problem Solving	Making Decisions
There are many styles and forms for expressing ourselves.	By exploring and asking questions, we make discoveries.	Analyzing information can help us solve problems.	Using what we know helps us evaluate situations.
Time to Shine We can use our ideas and our imagination to do many wonderful things.	**I Wonder** We can make discoveries about the wonders of nature in our own backyard.	**Let's Work It Out** Working as part of a team can help me find a way to solve problems.	**Choices** We can make many good choices and decisions every day.
Great Ideas	In My Backyard	Try and Try Again	Good Choices
Let's Pretend	Wonders of Nature	Teamwork	Let's Decide
Stories to Tell Each one of us has a different story to tell.	**Let's Find Out!** Looking for answers is an adventure.	**Think About It!** It takes time to solve problems.	**Many Paths** Each decision opens the door to a new path.
Express Yourself We share our ideas in many ways.	**Look Around** There are surprises all around us.	**Figure It Out** We can solve problems by working together.	**Starting Now** Unexpected events can lead to new decisions.
Be Creative! We can all express ourselves in creative, wonderful ways.	**Tell Me More** Looking and listening closely will help us find out the facts.	**Think It Through** Solutions come in many shapes and sizes.	**Turning Points** We make new judgments based on our experiences.
Our Voices We can each use our talents to communicate ideas.	**Just Curious** We can find answers in surprising places.	**Make a Plan** Often we have to think carefully about a problem in order to solve it.	**Sorting It Out** We make decisions that can lead to new ideas and discoveries.
Imagine That The way we express our thoughts and feelings can take different forms.	**Investigate!** We never know where the search for answers might lead us.	**Bright Ideas** Some problems require unusual approaches.	**Crossroads** Decisions cause changes that can enrich our lives.
With Flying Colors Creative people help us see the world from different perspectives.	**Seek and Discover** To make new discoveries, we must observe and explore.	**Brainstorms** We can meet any challenge with determination and ingenuity.	**All Things Considered** Encountering new places and people can help us make decisions.

Stories to Tell

Each one of us has a different story to tell.

Unit Planner 6C
Unit Resources 6E
Meeting Individual Needs 6F
Unit Assessment Resources 6G
Unit Opener 6I
"Something About Me" an anonymous poem 6

STAN'S STUNT 8A

written by **Lynne Plourde**
illustrated by **Pam Levy**

SKILLS			
Phonics	**Comprehension**	**Vocabulary**	**Study Skill**
• **Introduce/Apply** Blends	• **Introduce** Story Element: Setting	• **Introduce** Possessives	• Diagrams
• **Review** Blends			

A HUMOROUS STORY

GREG'S MASK 38A

written by **Ann McGovern**
illustrated by **Winky Adam**

SKILLS			
Phonics	**Comprehension**	**Vocabulary**	**Study Skill**
• **Introduce/Apply** Blends	• **Introduce** Compare and Contrast	• **Review** Possessives	• Diagrams
• **Review** Blends			

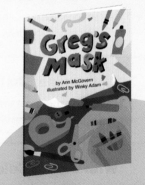

REALISTIC FICTION

SAM'S SONG 68A

written by **Alyssa Satin Capucilli**
illustrated by **Melissa Iwai**

SKILLS			
Phonics	**Comprehension**	**Vocabulary**	**Study Skill**
• **Introduce/Apply** *ch, wh, nk* • **Review** *ch, wh, nk*; Blends	• **Review** Compare and Contrast	• **Introduce** Contractions	• Diagrams

A FANTASY STORY

SNAKES 98A

written by **Francis Minters**

SKILLS			
Phonics	**Comprehension**	**Vocabulary**	**Study Skill**
• **Introduce/Apply** Long *a: a-e* • **Review** *a-e; ch, wh, nk*	• **Review** Story Elements: Setting	• **Review** Contractions	• Diagrams

A NONFICTION ARTICLE

TIME FOR KIDS LET'S CAMP OUT! 126A

SKILLS			
Phonics	**Comprehension**	**Vocabulary**	**Study Skill**
• **Review/Apply** *a-e; ch, wh, nk*; Blends	• **Review** Compare and Contrast • **Review** Story Elements: Setting	• **Review** Possessives • **Review** Contractions	• Diagrams

A SOCIAL STUDIES ARTICLE

Unit Closer 140

"You're an Author Now" a poem by *Kalli Dakos*

Reading Media 142A

Unit Assessment 144A

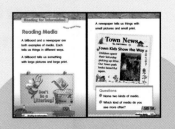

INFORMATIONAL TEXT

Unit Planner

	WEEK **1** Stan's Stunt	WEEK **2** Greg's Mask
Leveled Books	**Easy:** *Bat Helps Out* **Independent:** *Two Tests* **Challenge:** *Walking Through the Jungle*	**Easy:** *Kent and Glen* **Independent:** *Dig For Clams* **Challenge:** *Big Brother Little Brother*
☑ **Tested Skills**	☑ **Phonics** Introduce Blends, 8I–8J Review Blends, 37E–37F Review Blends, 37G–37H ☑ **Comprehension** Introduce Story Elements, 37I–37J ☑ **Vocabulary** Introduce Possessives, 37K–37L ☑ **Study Skills** Diagrams, 36	☑ **Phonics** Introduce Blends, 38I–38J Review Blends, 67E–67F Review Blends, 67G–67H ☑ **Comprehension** Introduce Compare and Contrast, 67I–67J ☑ **Vocabulary** Review Possessives, 67K–67L ☑ **Study Skills** Diagrams, 66
Minilessons	**Make Inferences,** 13 **Context Clues,** 15 **Phonics and Decoding:** Blends *fl, sn, sl,* 23 **Make Predictions,** 29 **Main Idea,** 31	**Context Clues,** 43 **Use Illustrations,** 47 **Make Inferences,** 51 **High-Frequency Words,** 49 **Cause and Effect,** 53 **Phonics and Decoding:** Blends, 57, 59 **Main Idea,** 61
Language Arts	**Writing:** Interactive Writing, 37M **Grammar:** Verbs, 37O **Spelling:** Words with Blends, 37Q	**Writing:** Interactive Writing, 67M **Grammar:** Present-Tense Verbs, 67O **Spelling:** Words with Blends, 67Q

Activities

Curriculum Connections	**Read Aloud:** "The Lion and the Mouse," 8G **Phonics Rhyme:** "Circus Stunts," 8/9 **Social Studies:** Friendly Sentences, 8D Forests, 16 **Science:** Jumping Beans, 20 **Math:** Bats, 22 **Art:** Animal Masks, 8D	**Read Aloud:** "Making Faces," 38G **Phonics Rhyme:** "Drips! Drops!" 38/39 **Social Studies:** Career Notes, 38D Everyday Emotions, 48 **Art:** Masks, 50 **Science:** Animal Facts, 38D Animal Groups, 56 **Math:** Shape Faces, 58
CULTURAL PERSPECTIVES	Rainforests, 14	Masks, 50

WEEK **3** Sam's Song	WEEK **4** Snakes	WEEK **5** Let's Camp Out!	WEEK **6** Review, Writing, Reading Information, Assessment
Easy: *What's New at the Zoo?* **Independent:** *What Can Meg Do?* **Challenge:** *The Cow that Went OINK*	**Easy:** *In the Lake* **Independent:** *The Cave* **Challenge:** *Great Snakes!*	Self-Selected Reading of Leveled Books	Self-Selected Reading

☑ **Phonics** Introduce *ch, wh, nk,* 68I–68J Review *ch, wh, nk,* 97E–97F Review *ch, wh, nk;* Blends, 97G–97H ☑ **Comprehension** Review Compare and Contrast, 97I–97J ☑ **Vocabulary** Introduce Contractions, 97K–97L ☑ **Study Skills** Diagrams, 96	☑ **Phonics** Introduce Long *a: a-e,* 98I–98J Review Long *a: a-e,* 125E–125F Review *a-e; ch, wh, nk,* 125G–125H ☑ **Comprehension** Review Story Elements, 125I–125J ☑ **Vocabulary** Review Contractions, 125K–125L ☑ **Study Skills** Diagrams, 124	☑ **Phonics** Review *a-e; ch, wh, nk;* Blends, 126I–126J ☑ **Comprehension** Review Compare and Contrast, 139E–139F Review Story Elements, 139G–139H ☑ **Vocabulary** Review Possessives, 139I–139J Review Contractions, 139K–139L ☑ **Study Skills** Diagrams, 138	☑ **Assess Skills** Blends *ch, wh, nk* Long *a: a-e* Story Elements Compare and Contrast Possessives Contractions Diagrams ☑ **Assess Grammar and Spelling** Review Verbs, 144A Review Spelling Patterns, 144B ☑ **Unit Progress Assessment** ☑ **Standardized Test Preparation** 📰 **Reading Media** 142A
Context Clues, 77 **High-Frequency Words,** 79 **Make Inferences,** 81 **Setting,** 89 **Main Idea,** 91	**Make Inferences,** 105 **Draw Conclusions,** 109 **Diagraph /ch/ ,** 111 **Cause and Effect,** 113 **Final Consonants,** 115 **Summarizing,** 119	**Context Clues,** 131 **Main Idea,** 133	

Writing: Interactive Writing, 97M **Grammar:** Past-Tense Verbs, 97O **Spelling:** Words with *ch, wh, nk,* 97Q	**Writing:** Interactive Writing, 125M **Grammar:** *Is* and *Are,* 125O **Spelling:** Words with Long *a: a-e,* 125Q	**Writing:** Interactive Writing, 139M **Grammar:** Contractions with *Not,* 139O **Spelling:** Words from Science, 139Q	

Read Aloud: "The Plumage of the Owl," 68G **Phonics Rhyme:** "Lunch Munch," 68/69 **Social Studies:** My Family, 68D What's In a Name?, 78 **Math:** Story Problems, 82 **Music:** Starry Song, 84 **Science:** Animal Homes, 68D Owls, 86 **Language Arts:** Owls and Crickets, 88 Family Names, 74	**Read Aloud:** "The Snake," 98G **Phonics Rhyme:** "Snake's Trip," 98/99 **Math:** Make A Snake, 98D Snake Facts, 104 **Science:** Snake Facts, 98D Hot Snakes, 110 **Social Studies:** Child vs. Pet Care, 118 **Social Studies:** ChiSnake Tales, 114	**Read Aloud:** "The Night We Slept Outside," 126G **Phonics Rhyme:** "Camp Out!" 126/127 **Social Studies:** What Do You See?, 126D **Science:** The Night Sky, 126D	👥 **Cooperative Theme Project Research and Inquiry:** GROUP Tell a Story, 6J

Unit Resources

LITERATURE

LEVELED BOOKS

📖 **Easy:**
- *Bat Helps Out*
- *Kent and Glen*
- *What's New at the Zoo?*
- *In the Lake*

📖 **Independent:**
- *Two Tests*
- *Dig For Clams*
- *What Can Meg Do?*
- *The Cave*

📖 **Challenge:**
- *Walking Through the Jungle*
- *Big Brother Little Brother*
- *The Cow That Went OINK*
- *Great Snakes!*

THEME BIG BOOK
Share *I Go with My Family to Grandma's* to set the unit theme and make content-area connections.

🔘 💾 LISTENING LIBRARY
For student book selections and poetry. Available on **compact disc** and **audiocassette.**

Macmillan/McGraw-Hill

ℹ️ **Intervention** ➡️

Skills Intervention Guide

Easy Leveled Books

SKILLS

LEVELED PRACTICE

Practice: Student practice for phonics, comprehension, vocabulary and study skills; plus practice for instructional vocabulary and story comprehension. Take-Home Story included for each lesson.

Reteach: Reteaching opportunities for students who need more help with each assessed skill.

Extend: Extension activities for vocabulary, comprehension, story, and study skills.

📋 TEACHING CHARTS
Instructional charts for vocabulary and tested skills. Also available as transparencies.

WORD BUILDING MANIPULATIVE CARDS
Letter and word cards to utilize phonics and build instructional vocabulary.

LANGUAGE SUPPORT BOOK
ESL Parallel lessons and practice for students needing language support.

PHONICS/PHONEMIC AWARENESS PRACTICE BOOK
Additional practice on key phonetic elements.

FLUENCY ASSESSMENT
Evaluation and practice for building reading fluency.

LANGUAGE ARTS

GRAMMAR PRACTICE BOOK
Provides practice for grammar and mechanics lessons.

SPELLING PRACTICE BOOK
Provides practice with the word list and spelling patterns. Includes home involvement activities.

DAILY LANGUAGE ACTIVITIES
Activities that provide reinforcement of grammar, mechanics, and usage skills. Available as blackline masters and transparencies.

HANDWRITING HANDBOOKS
Available for instruction and practice.

McGraw-Hill School
TECHNOLOGY

🔘 **Phonics** CD-ROM
Provides phonics support.

interNET CONNECTION Extend lesson activities through research and inquiry ideas. Visit **www.mhschool.com/reading.**

✏️ **Handwriting CD-ROM** Provides practice activities.

Resources for Meeting Individual Needs

	EASY	INDEPENDENT	CHALLENGE	LANGUAGE SUPPORT
BOOK 3				
Stan's Stunt	**Leveled Book:** *Bat Helps Out* **Reteach,** 85–92 **Alternate Teaching Strategies,** T64–T76 **Writing:** Draw Pictures, 37M–37N *Phonics* **CD-ROM** **Intervention**	**Leveled Book:** *Two Tests* **Practice,** 85–92 **Alternate Teaching Strategies,** T64–T76 **Writing:** Write a Story, 37M–37N *Phonics* **CD-ROM**	**Leveled Book:** *Walking Through the Jungle* **Extend,** 85–92 **Writing:** Journal Entry, 37M–37N *Phonics* **CD-ROM**	**Teaching Strategies,** 10A, 11, 13, 17, 24, 27, 37N Language Support, 91–99 **Alternate Teaching Strategies,** T64–T76 **Writing:** Make a Field Guide, 37M–37N *Phonics* **CD-ROM**
Greg's Mask	**Leveled Book:** *Kent and Glen* **Reteach,** 93–100 **Alternate Teaching Strategies,** T64–T76 **Writing:** Give Instructions, 67M–67N *Phonics* **CD-ROM** **Intervention**	**Leveled Book:** *Dig for Clams* **Practice,** 93–100 **Alternate Teaching Strategies,** T64–T76 **Writing:** New Story, 67M–67N *Phonics* **CD-ROM**	**Leveled Book:** *Big Brother Little Brother* **Extend,** 93–100 **Writing:** Write an Invitation, 67M–67N *Phonics* **CD-ROM**	**Teaching Strategies,** 40A, 41, 44, 46, 49, 55, 67N Language Support, 100–108 **Alternate Teaching Strategies,** T64–T76 **Writing:** Make a Chart, 67M–67N *Phonics* **CD-ROM**
Sam's Song	**Leveled Book:** *What's New At the Zoo?* **Reteach,** 101–108 **Alternate Teaching Strategies,** T64–T76 **Writing:** Draw Pictures, 97M–97N *Phonics* **CD-ROM** **Intervention**	**Leveled Book:** *What Can Meg Do?* **Practice,** 101–108 **Alternate Teaching Strategies,** T64–T76 **Writing:** New Story, 97M–97N *Phonics* **CD-ROM**	**Leveled Book:** *The Cow that Went OINK* **Extend,** 101–108 **Writing:** Journal Entry, 97M–97N *Phonics* **CD-ROM**	**Teaching Strategies,** 70A, 71, 79, 83, 85, 87, 97N Language Support, 109–117 **Alternate Teaching Strategies,** T64–T76 **Writing:** Make a Songbook, 97M–97N *Phonics* **CD-ROM**
Snakes	**Leveled Book:** *In the Lake* **Reteach,** 109–116 **Alternate Teaching Strategies,** T64–T76 **Writing:** Draw Pictures, 125M–125N *Phonics* **CD-ROM** **Intervention**	**Leveled Book:** *The Cave* **Practice,** 109–116 **Alternate Teaching Strategies,** T64–T76 **Writing:** New Story, 125M–125N *Phonics* **CD-ROM**	**Leveled Book:** *Great Snakes* **Extend,** 109–116 **Writing:** Journal Entry, 125M–125N *Phonics* **CD-ROM**	**Teaching Strategies,** 100A, 101, 102, 105, 107, 115, 117, 125N Language Support, 118–126 **Alternate Teaching Strategies,** T64–T76 **Writing:** Make a Mural, 125M–125N *Phonics* **CD-ROM**
Let's Camp Out!	**Review** **Reteach,** 117–124 **Alternate Teaching Strategies,** T64–T76 **Writing:** Draw Pictures, 139M–139N *Phonics* **CD-ROM** **Intervention**	**Review** **Practice,** 117–124 **Alternate Teaching Strategies,** T64–T76 **Writing:** New Story, 139M–139N *Phonics* **CD-ROM**	**Review** **Extend,** 117–124 **Writing:** Journal Entry, 139M–139N *Phonics* **CD-ROM**	**Teaching Strategies,** 128A, 129, 139N Language Support, 127–135 **Alternate Teaching Strategies,** T64–T76 **Writing:** Retell a Story 139M–139N

INFORMAL

Informal Assessment

- Phonics, 8J, 33, 37F, 37H; 38J, 63, 67F, 67H; 68J, 93, 97F, 97H; 98J, 121, 125F, 125H; 126J, 135
- Comprehension, 32, 33, 37J; 62, 63, 67J; 92, 93, 97J; 120, 121, 125J; 134, 135, 139F, 139H
- Vocabulary, 37L, 67L, 97L, 125L, 139J, 139L

Performance Assessment

- Research and Inquiry, 6J, 141
- Listening, Speaking, Viewing Activities, 8G, 8H, 10A, 10–37, 37D, 37M–N; 38G, 38H, 40A, 40–67, 67D, 67M–N; 68G, 68H, 70A, 70–97, 97D, 97M–N; 98G, 98H, 100A, 100–125, 125D, 125M–N; 126G, 126H, 128A, 128–139, 139D, 139M–N
- Portfolio, 37N, 67N, 97N, 125N
- Writing, 37M–N, 67M–N, 97M–N, 125M–N, 139M–N
- Fluency, 32, 62, 92, 120, 134

Leveled Practice

Practice, Reteach, Extend

- **Phonics and Decoding**
  Blends, 85, 89, 90, 93, 97, 98, 106, 117
  Digraphs *ch, wh, nk,* 101, 105, 106, 114, 117
  Long *a: a-e,* 109, 113, 114, 117
- **Comprehension**
  Story Elements, 91, 115, 122
  Compare and Contrast, 99, 107, 121
- **Vocabulary Strategies**
  Possessives, 92, 100, 123
  Contractions, 108, 116, 124
- **Study Skills**
  Diagrams, 88, 96, 104, 112, 120

FORMAL

Selection Assessments

- **Skills and Vocabulary Words**
  Stan's Stunt, 41–44
  Greg's Mask, 45–48
  Sam's Song, 49–52
  Snakes, 53–56
  Let's Camp Out! 57–58

Unit 3 Test

- **Phonics and Decoding**
  Blends
  Digraphs *ch, wh, nk*
  Long *a: a-e*
- **Comprehension**
  Story Elements
  Compare and Contrast
- **Vocabulary Strategies**
  Possessives
  Contractions

Grammar and Spelling Assessment

- **Grammar**
  Verbs, 69, 75, 81, 87, 93, 95–96
- **Spelling**
  Unit Assessment, 95–96

Fluency Assessments

- Fluency Passages, 14–17

Diagnostic/Placement Evaluation

- Phonemic Awareness Assessment
- Placement Tests
- Informal Reading Inventories
- Running Records

Test Preparation

- Test Power in Teacher's Edition, 37, 67, 97, 125, 139

Reading Test Generator

- Assessment Software

Assessment Checklist

Student .... **Grade** ....

Teacher ....

	Stan's Stunt	Greg's Mask	Sam's Song	Snakes	Let's Camp Out!	Assessment Summary
LISTENING/SPEAKING						
Participates in oral language experiences						
Listens and speaks to gain knowledge of culture						
Speaks appropriately to audiences for different purposes						
Communicates clearly						
READING						
Uses phonological awareness strategies, including						
• Identifying, segmenting, and combining syllables						
• Producing rhyming words						
• Identifying and isolating initial and final sounds						
Uses a variety of word identification strategies:						
• Phonics and decoding: blends						
• Phonics and decoding: digraphs *ch, wh, nk*						
• Phonics and decoding: long *a: a-e*						
• Possessives						
• Contractions						
Reads with fluency and understanding						
Reads widely for different purposes in varied sources						
Develops an extensive vocabulary						
Uses comprehension strategies: Compare and Contrast						
Responds to various texts						
Analyzes the characteristics of various types of texts:						
• Story Elements (Character, Setting, Plot)						
Conducts research using various sources: Diagrams						
Reads to increase knowledge						
WRITING						
Writes for a variety of audiences and purposes						
Composes original texts using the conventions of written language such as capitalization and penmanship						
Spells proficiently						
Composes texts applying knowledge of grammar and usage						
Uses writing processes						
Evaluates own writing and writing of others						

+ Observed   – Not Observed

Introduce the Theme

Stories to Tell

Each one of us has a different story to tell.

DISCUSS THE THEME Read the theme statement to children. Ask them to think of stories they have told about themselves, and which of those stories are their favorites. Encourage children to think of favorite stories they have read or have heard others tell. Ask:

- What did you enjoy about these stories?
- What kinds of stories do you like?

Help children think of the many ways that stories can be told—in books, or movies, or even in paintings or poems.

SHARE A STORY Have children preview the unit by reading the table of contents and paging through the selections. Use the Big Book *I Go With My Family to Grandma's* as an introduction to

the unit theme Stories to Tell. Discuss with children how each character in the book has her own story to tell.

PREVIEW UNIT SELECTIONS Have children preview the unit by reading the selection titles and looking at the illustrations. Have children work in small groups to brainstorm a list of ways that the stories, poems, and the *Time for Kids* magazine article relate to the theme Stories to Tell. Ask:

- How might these pieces relate to the theme Stories to Tell?
- How might these stories be alike?
- How might these stories be different?
- Do you think any of these selections are about real people and real events? How can you tell?

Have each group present their list to the class. Then encourage other groups to add any new ideas they heard to their lists.

THEME CONNECTIONS

Each of the five selections relates to the unit theme Stories to Tell as well as to the global theme Expression. These thematic links will help children make connections across texts.

Stan's Stunt A skunk and his friends express themselves through stunts.

Greg's Mask A boy expresses himself by making masks.

Sam's Song A baby owl learns to sing with her family.

Snakes We learn how a snake moves, eats, and grows.

Let's Camp Out! Camping out is a good way to enjoy nature.

Research *and* Inquiry

Theme Project: Tell a Story
Have children work in teams to brainstorm lists of people or places in their school or neighborhood they might want to know more about. They will then choose a person or place from the list that they want to research further. Encourage children to create a profile or history of that person or place.

List What They Know Once children have picked a person or place, have them list what they already know about it.

Ask Questions and Identify Resources Next, ask children to brainstorm some questions they would need to answer in order to prepare their presentations. Have them list possible resources. Remind children to take notes about any important details.

Create a Presentation When their research is complete, children will present what they have learned to the class. Encourage children to be creative. They can make a brochure or poster, or give a talk about what they have learned. Encourage children to use visuals to help them tell the story of the person or place.

QUESTIONS	POSSIBLE RESOURCES	ANSWERS
• What is special about this person or place? • Why is this person or place important in the school or neighborhood? • What are the important facts in the history of this person or place?	• Talk to the person • Visit the place • Talk to someone who is familiar with the person or place	

See **Wrap Up the Theme,** page 140.

Research Strategies

Encourage children to visit the person or place they have chosen. Have them find out for themselves what makes this person or place important to the community. Share these important tips with the children about visiting the person or place they chose.

• Call ahead to ask if and when you could come and talk with them.

• Tell the person you are doing research for a project.

• If visiting a person, ask him or her to tell you what he or she does.

• If visiting a place, make a list of five things you like about it.

 interNET **CONNECTION** Students can learn more about storytelling by visiting **www.mhschool.com/reading**

6J

Poetry

Read the Poem

READ ALOUD Tell children that poems are often about something that is happening to the poet. Read aloud "Something About Me."

- What does the poem tell you?
- What is this poem about?

LISTENING LIBRARY The poem is available on **audio-cassette** and on **compact disc.**

ECHO READING Read the poem aloud, line by line. Have children read each line aloud after you. Encourage them to track the words with their finger as they read them. Help children identify the exclamation mark at the end of the poem. Model the proper way to read this exclamation mark.

Learn About Poetry

FIRST PERSON

Explain the following features of first person:

- When a poem or story is written in *first person,* it is usually about the person who is writing the poem or telling the story. The "first person" is the poet or storyteller.

- A poem or story written in first person is likely to include the words *I'm* or *me.* These words show that the author of the poem is talking about himself or herself. When poets or storytellers write in first person, they are describing their own feelings and experiences.

6

MEET THE POET

ABOUT "ANONYMOUS" Point to the word "Anonymous" at the end of the poem. Explain that this is the word we use when we don't know the name of the person who wrote something.

Stories to Tell

Something About Me

There's something about me
That I'm knowing.
There's something about me
That isn't showing.

I'm growing!

Anonymous

7

Poetry

RAISE YOUR HAND FOR *I'M* OR *ME*
Read "Something About Me" to children. Then reread the poem, having children raise their hands each time they hear the words *I'm* or *me*. Explain that these words show that the poet wrote the poem as if the poet were talking about himself or herself.

Oral Response

SMALL-GROUP DISCUSSIONS Have 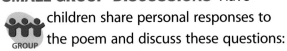 children share personal responses to the poem and discuss these questions:

- What is it about me that I'm knowing?
- The poet says that his growing isn't showing. Is that really true? How can you tell when a person has grown?
- What are three words from the poem that rhyme?
- As well as using rhyme, how is this poet using rhythm?

RESPONDING TO POETRY

Encourage children to think of a person, place, or thing that they know has changed a lot. Have the children draw "before" and "after" pictures showing how that person, animal, place, or thing has changed.

Encourage children to include details that have changed. Has a child grown taller? Are bushes around a house fuller? Is someone's hair longer?

Concept
- Woodland Animals

Comprehension
- Story Element: Setting

Phonics
- Blends

Vocabulary
- try
- fall
- their
- would

Reaching All Learners

Anthology

Stan's Stunt

Selection Summary In this tale of woodland animal friends, each character has a kind of "story" to tell. As the animals show off the stunts they can do, it's the skunk who has the last laugh.

by Lynn Plourde
illustrated by Pam Levy

Listening Library

INSTRUCTIONAL pages 10–37

Circus Stunts

Come to the tent!
Come and see the stunts!
Skunk can swing and swing on a ring.
Bat can jump and jump with a mask.
Cat can sing and sing and sing.
Frog can flip and flop and swing!

Rhyme applies to Phonics

About the Author Lynne Plourde grew up in Maine. She went to college there and she still lives there today. Ms. Plourde has written many books for children and adults. She also helps children who have trouble speaking. She thinks both of her jobs are very interesting and a lot of fun.

About the Illustrator When Pamela R. Levy was little she liked to draw. She did not think about becoming an artist until she went to college. Today she is the illustrator of many children's books. She also likes to dance, read, and garden.

Same Concept, Skills and Vocabulary!

Leveled Books

EASY
Lesson on pages 37A and 37D
`DECODABLE`

INDEPENDENT
Lesson on pages 37B and 37D

🏠 *Take-Home version available*
`DECODABLE`

CHALLENGE
Lesson on pages 37C and 37D

Leveled Practice

EASY
Reteach, **85–92** Blackline masters with reteaching opportunities for each assessed skill

INDEPENDENT/ON-LEVEL
Practice, **85–92** Workbook with Take-Home Stories and practice opportunities for each assessed skill and story comprehension

CHALLENGE
Extend, **85–92** Blackline masters that offer challenge activities for each assessed skill

Quizzes Prepared by ▲ **Accelerated Reader**

Center Activities

Social Studies	Friendly Sentences, *8D*
Science	Jumping Beans, *20*
Math	Bats, *22*
Art	Animal Masks, *8D*
Language Arts	Read Aloud, *8G*
Cultural Perspectives	Rainforests, *14*
Writing	About a Stunt, *34*
Research and Inquiry	Find Out More, *35*
🖥 **Internet Activities**	www.mhschool.com/reading

Center Activities

Each of these activities takes 15-20 minutes.

Phonics

MATERIALS
- Index cards

Blend and Sort

 Objective: Sort index cards according to their initial and final blend.
PARTNERS

◆ Provide pairs of children with index cards that each feature a word that begins or ends with a blend (*st, sk, mp, ft, nt, sp, nd*).

◆ Children sort the cards according to their beginning or ending blend sound.

Writing

MATERIALS
- Construction paper
- Crayons

Animal Antics

 Objective: Write and illustrate sentences about animals.
GROUP

◆ Have children draw a favorite animal doing a funny stunt.

◆ Children write a sentence that tells about their picture.

◆ Children can then share their pictures and sentences with others.

Reading and Listening

Independent/Self-Selected Reading

 Objective: Listen and use illustrations to understand a story.
ONE

Fill the Center with books and corresponding audiocassettes or CD-ROMs children have read or listened to this week. You can also include books from the Theme Bibliography on pages T98 and T99.

Leveled Readers

- *Bat Helps Out* by Ellen Dreyer
- *Two Tests* by Becky Gold
- *Walking Through the Jungle* by Debbie Harter

◆ Theme Big Book *I Go with My Family to Grandma's* by Riki Levinson

 ◆ *Stan's Stunt* by Lynn Plourde

◆ "Something About Me"—Anonymous

◆ Phonics Practice Reader, Vol. 1

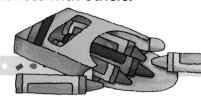

Working with Words

Word Hunt

Objective: Reinforce vocabulary words: *try, fall, their, would*.

◆ Have partners write each word on an index card.

◆ Children look through *Stan's Stunt* and find each word.

◆ Partners read the sentences to each other. They can make up other sentences for the words, too.

MATERIALS
- *Stan's Stunt* in the Student Anthology
- Index cards
- Pencil

try their would fall

Art

Animal Masks

Objective: Create masks to retell and dramatize a story.

◆ Have each child choose a character from *Stan's Stunt*.

◆ Each child can make a mask of that animal.

◆ Invite children to act out the story with their masks.

MATERIALS
- Paper plates
- Construction paper
- Scissors
- Glue
- Various art materials: glitter and yarn.

Social Studies

The Best Pet

Objective: Write and illustrate a sentence about friends.

◆ Have children think about how the animals in the story showed that they were friends.

◆ Invite children to draw a picture of things they like to do with their own friends.

◆ Children can write a sentence that tells about their picture.

MATERIALS
- Assorted animal pictures from magazines
- Paper
- Crayons

STAN'S STUNT
by Lynn Plourde
illustrated by Pam Levy

Suggested Lesson Planner

READING AND LANGUAGE ARTS	**DAY 1** Focus on Reading and Skills	**DAY 2** Read the Literature
● **Phonics Daily Routines**	Daily **Phonics** Routine: **Segmenting,** 8J **Phonics** CD-ROM	Daily **Phonics** Routine: **Blending,** 10A **Phonics** CD-ROM
● **Phonological Awareness** ● **Phonics** *Blends* ● **Comprehension** ● **Vocabulary** ● **Study Skills** ● **Listening, Speaking, Viewing, Representing**	**Read** **Read Aloud,** 8G "The Lion and the Mouse" ☑ **Develop Phonological Awareness,** 8H ☑ **Introduce Blends,** 8I–8J **Reteach, Practice, Extend,** 85 **Phonics/Phonemic Awareness Practice Book,** 117–120 **Read** **Apply Blends** "Circus Stunts," 8/9	**Build Background,** 10A Develop Oral Language **Vocabulary,** 10B–10C *try* *fall* *their* *would* **Word Building Manipulative Cards** **Teaching Chart 63** Reteach, Practice, Extend, 86 **Read** **Read the Selection,** 10–33 **Guided Instruction** ☑ **Read Words with Blends** **Genre: Story,** 11 **Cultural Perspectives,** 14
	ℹ️ Intervention Program	ℹ️ Intervention Program
● **Curriculum Connections**	**Link** Language Arts, 8G	**Link** Science, 10A
● **Writing**	✏️ **Writing Prompt:** Describe a stunt that you can do.	✏️ **Writing Prompt:** What if you were a frog? Write what you do and what you like about being a frog. 📓 **Journal Writing** Quick-Write, 33
● **Grammar**	**Introduce the Concept: Verbs,** 37O Daily Language Activity: Identify the word that shows action. **Grammar Practice Book,** 65	**Teach the Concept: Verbs,** 37O Daily Language Activity: Identify action words in sentences. **Grammar Practice Book,** 66
● **Spelling** *Blends*	**Introduce Spelling Words: Words with Blends,** 37Q **Spelling Practice Book,** 65–66	**Teach the Patterns: Words with Blends,** 37Q **Spelling Practice Book,** 67

 Intervention Program Available

Meeting Individual Needs

 = **Skill Assessed in Unit Test**

 Intervention Program Available

 **DAY 3** *Read the Literature*

DAY 4 *Build Skills*

DAY 5 *Build Skills*

Daily  **Routine:**
Fluency, 35

 CD-ROM

Daily  **Routine:**
Writing, 37F

 CD-ROM

Daily  **Routine:**
Letter Substitution, 37H

 CD-ROM

Reread for Fluency, 32

Story Questions, 34
  Reteach, Practice, Extend, 87

Story Activities, 35

Study Skill, 36
  ☑ **Diagrams**
  Teaching Chart 64
  Reteach, Practice, Extend, 88

Test Power, 37

 Read the Leveled Books, Guided Reading
  ☑ **Read Words with Blends**
  ☑ **High-Frequency Words**

 Intervention Program

 **Read the Leveled Books and the Self-Selected Books**

  ☑ **Review Blends,** 37E–37F
  Teaching Chart 65
  Reteach, Practice, Extend, 89
  Language Support, 96
  Phonics/Phonemic Awareness
    Practice Book, 117–120

  ☑ **Review Blends,** 37G–37H
  Teaching Chart 66
  Reteach, Practice, Extend, 90
  Language Support, 97
  Phonics/Phonemic Awareness
    Practice Book, 117–120

  Minilessons, 13, 15, 23, 29, 31

 Intervention Program

 Read Self-Selected Books

  ☑ **Introduce Story Elements,** 37I–37J
  Teaching Chart 67
  Reteach, Practice, Extend, 91
  Language Support, 98

  ☑ **Introduce Possessives,** 37K–37L
  Teaching Chart 68
  Reteach, Practice, Extend, 92
  Language Support, 99

  Listening, Speaking, Viewing, Representing, 37N
    Make Stick Puppets
    Perform Animal Stunts

  Minilessons, 13, 15, 23, 29, 31

 Intervention Program

 Social Studies, 8D, 16

Activity Science, 20

 Art, 8D Math, 22

 Writing Prompt: What kind of stunt would you teach? How would you teach it?

Writing Prompt: Write a thank-you note to a group of animals that performed for your class.

  Interactive Writing: Make a Field Guide, 37M
    Prewrite, Draft

  Meeting Individual Needs for Writing, 37N

Writing Prompt: Write about an animal you saw at the zoo. What did it do? What did you like about it?

  Interactive Writing: Make a Field Guide, 37M
    Revise, Publish

Practice and Write: Verbs, 37P
  Daily Language Activity: List verbs from *Stan's Stunt* and use them in sentences.

Grammar Practice Book, 67

Practice and Write: Verbs, 37P
  Daily Language Activity: Identify verbs and use them in sentences.

Grammar Practice Book, 68

Assess and Reteach: Verbs, 37P
  Daily Language Activity: Identify verbs in sentences.

Grammar Practice Book, 69–70

Practice and Extend: Words with Blends, 37R

Spelling Practice Book, 68

Practice and Write: Words with Blends, 37R

Spelling Practice Book, 69

Assess and Reteach: Words with Blends, 37R

Spelling Practice Book, 70

Read Aloud

The Lion and the Mouse

from a fable by Aesop
Here is one of the oldest and best-loved stories of kindness paid and repaid. From it we learn that compassion lies within the power of both the mighty and the meek. Kindness is not a feeble virtue.

One day a great lion lay asleep in the sunshine. A little mouse ran across his paw and wakened him. The great lion was just going to eat him up when the little mouse cried, "Oh, please, let me go, sir. Some day I may help you."

The lion laughed at the thought that the little mouse could be of any use to him. But he was a good-natured lion, and he set the mouse free.

Not long after, the lion was caught in a net. He tugged and pulled with all his might, but the ropes were too strong. Then he roared loudly. The little mouse heard him, and ran to the spot.

"Be still, dear Lion, and I will set you free. I will gnaw the ropes."

With his sharp little teeth, the mouse cut the ropes, and the lion came out of the net.

"You laughed at me once," said the mouse. "You thought I was too little to do you a good turn. But see, you owe your life to a poor little mouse."

Oral Comprehension

LISTENING AND SPEAKING Encourage children to listen for the words that describe the animals in this story. Reread the first two sentences. Ask children to tell you what kind of lion lay asleep in the sunshine. (a *great* lion) What kind of mouse ran across the lion's paw? (a *little* mouse)

Activity Have children look around the room and find one thing they can do to help someone or something. Suggest that perhaps they can hang up all the jackets that have fallen off hooks, or push in the chairs, or pick up any papers on the floor.

▶ **Visual/Kinesthetic**

GENRE STUDY: FABLE Explain to children that a fable is a short story that teaches a moral or a lesson. The characters are often animals, but they speak and act like people. Ask: What is the moral of this story? What did you learn from it? Why would we expect that the mouse can't help the lion? (because he is so much smaller than the lion) "The Lion and the Mouse" teaches us that there are many ways one person can help another person, whether they are big or small.

Develop Phonological Awareness

Blend Sounds

Phonemic Awareness

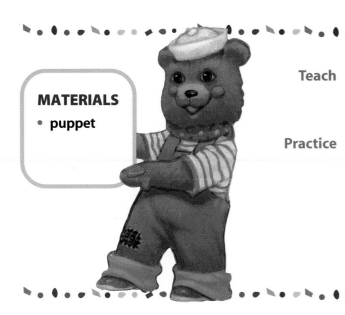

MATERIALS
- puppet

Teach   Have the puppet say: /j/-/u/-/m/-/p/. *Now, listen as the puppet says these sounds together:* /jump/. Have children repeat the sounds: /j/-/u/-/m/-/p/. Have them say them together: *jump.*

Practice   Use the following words to have children practice their blending. For each word, say the sounds, for example: /l/-/u/-/m/-/p/. Then have children blend the sounds to form the word, *lump.* Choose from these words: *lump, bump, went, lint, bend, hand, spill, spin, best, stop, bang, ring, flop, flip.*

Segment Sounds

Phonemic Awareness

MATERIALS
- four colored blocks

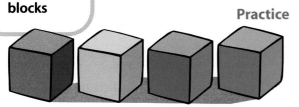

Teach   Ask children to listen as you say the word *mask.* Have them identify the four sounds in the word: /m/-/a/-/s/-/k/. Then display a block to represent each sound in the word. Have children repeat the sounds. Say *mask* and have children repeat the word with you.

Practice   Have children practice segmenting sounds. First have them say a word. Then have children say the individual sounds in the word. Use the following words: *camp, dust, ramp, wing, stop.*

Substitute Sounds

Phonemic Awareness

/s/-/l/-/i/-/p/

Teach   Say the word *flip.* Have children identify the four sounds in the word: /f/-/l/-/i/-/p/. Then explain that you are going to remove the /f/ from *flip* and replace it with /s/. Ask children to identify the new word. *(slip)* Repeat with *skunk* and *bunk.*

Practice   Using the following word sets, have children make new words by changing the beginning sounds. Say the first word in the set, and then give children the beginning sounds for the other words. Have them say the new words with you: *bent (sent, tent, went); dust (just, must, rust); hang (bang, rang, sang).*

INFORMAL ASSESSMENT   Observe children as they blend sounds, segment sounds, and substitute initial sounds. If children have difficulty, see Alternate Teaching Strategies on page T64.

OBJECTIVES

Children will:

- identify continuant/stop blends.
- form and read words with blends.
- review short vowels; consonants; digraphs.
- learn strategies for decoding multisyllabic words.

MATERIALS

- letter cards from the **Word Building Manipulative Cards**

Skills Finder

Blends	
Introduce	B2: 96I-J; B3: 8I-J, 38I-J
Review	B3: 37E-F, 37G-H 67E-F, 67G-H, 97G-H
Test	Book 2, Book 3
Maintain	B3: 23, B4: 13

SPELLING/PHONICS CONNECTIONS

Words with continuant/stop blends: See the 5-Day Spelling Plan, pages 37Q–37R

TEACHING TIP

MULTISYLLABIC WORDS Write and say *wiggle*. Model clapping out the parts, or syllables, in the word. Have children say the word and clap out the syllables. Point out that many words end in the syllable *-gle*. Say that *–le* at the end of the word stands for the sound /əl/. Write the words *waggle* and *giggle* on the chalkboard. Read each word with children.

Introduce Blends

Identify Continuant/Stop Blends

Let children know they will learn to read some more words with consonants that blend together.

- Display the *m* letter card and say /m/. Repeat with the *p* letter card. Have children repeat after you.

- Then blend the sounds together while running your hand under the cards to read /mp/. Have children repeat after you.

- Repeat with letter cards for the blends *st, sp, sk, ng, nt, nd, ft.*

BLENDING Model and Guide Practice with Continuant/Stop Blends

- Point to the *m* and *p* letter cards and say /mp/. Have children repeat after you.

- Place the *u* letter card in front of the *m* letter card.

- Blend the sounds together and have children repeat after you.

- Place the *j* letter card in front of the *u* letter card.

- Run your hand under the cards and blend the sounds together to read *jump*. Have children repeat after you.

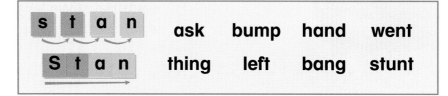

Use the Word in Context

Use the word in context to reinforce its meaning. Example: *The frog can jump far.*

Repeat the Procedure

Use the following words to continue modeling and guided practice with continuant/stop blends:

s t a n	ask	bump	hand	went
S t a n	thing	left	bang	stunt

PRACTICE

LETTER SUBSTITUTION Build Words with Continuant/Stop Blends with Letter Cards

Use letter cards to build the word *fast*, asking children to repeat after you. Change the word to *fist* by replacing the *a* with *i*. Have children repeat after you. Next, ask children to build and write the following words, substituting the appropriate letters: mask→task; jump→dump; fast→fist; left→lift. ▶ **Kinesthetic**

GROUP

ASSESS/CLOSE

Read Words with Blends

To assess children's ability to identify and read words with continuant/ stop blends, observe them as they build words in the Practice activity.

ADDITIONAL PHONICS RESOURCES

Phonics/Phonemic Awareness Practice Book, pages 117–120

PHONICS KIT
Hands-on Activities and Practice

McGraw-Hill School
TECHNOLOGY

Phonics CD-ROM
activities for practice with Blending and Segmenting

Meeting Individual Needs for Phonics

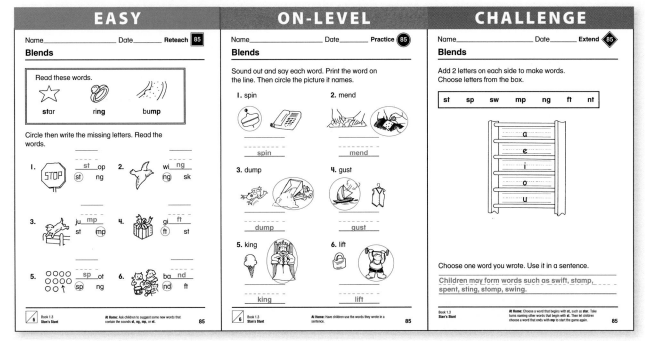

Reteach, 85   Practice, 85   Extend, 85

Daily Routines

DAY 1 **Segmenting** Distribute letter boxes. Say a blended word aloud. Have children write the spelling of each sound in the appropriate box. (Use *went, jump, spill, send, sing, lift*)

DAY 2 **Blending** Write the spelling of each sound in *bump* as you say it. Ask children to blend the sounds as they read the word. Repeat with *spin* and *stand*.

DAY 3 **Fluency** Write a list of words using continuant/ stop blends. Examples: *stunt, must, hang, went, bump*. Point to each word, asking children to blend the sounds silently. Ask a volunteer to read each word.

DAY 4 **Writing** Have children choose two words using continuant/stop blends and create a rhyming couplet with the words. Children can illustrate their rhymes.

DAY 5 **Letter Substitution** Using the letter cards, have pairs of children build *bend*. Taking turns, one child is to change a letter to build a new word, asking the partner to read it.

OBJECTIVES

Children will read a poem with words containing blends.

Apply Blends

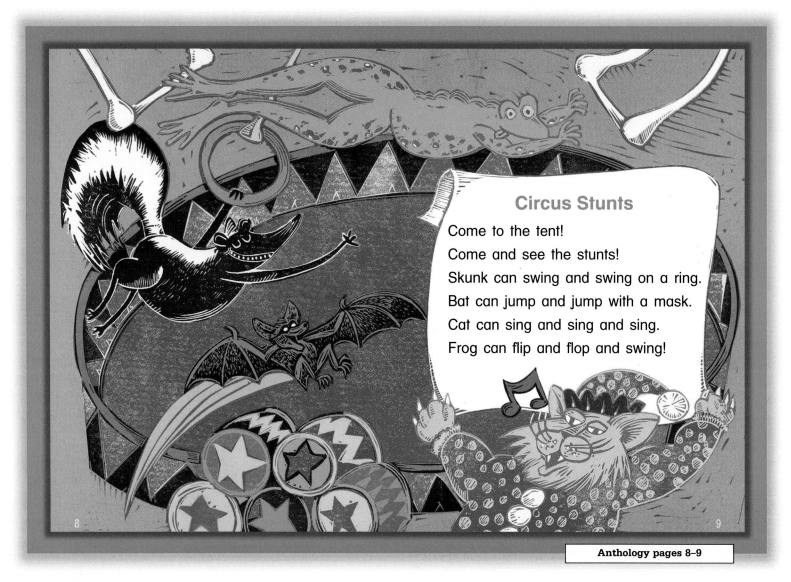

Circus Stunts

Come to the tent!
Come and see the stunts!
Skunk can swing and swing on a ring.
Bat can jump and jump with a mask.
Cat can sing and sing and sing.
Frog can flip and flop and swing!

Anthology pages 8–9

Read and Build Fluency

READ THE POEM Tell children they will read a poem called *Circus Stunts*. Model reading as you stress the alliterative words *flip* and *flop*. Have children listen for words with blends. Have children read along with you.

REREAD FOR FLUENCY Have children pretend they are circus leaders. Have them do repeated readings of the poem until they achieve fluency.

ONE

READ A DECODABLE STORY For additional practice reading and to develop fluency, ask children to read *Bang, Thump, Ping!* from **Phonics Practice Reader, Vol. 1.**

Dictate and Spell

DICTATE WORDS Say the word frog. Then segment it into its four individual sounds. Repeat the word aloud and use it in a sentence: *Frog can flip and hop.* Then have children say the word and write the letter or letters that represent each sound until they make the entire word. Repeat with *stunt, tent, skunk, swing, ring, jump, mask, flip,* and *flop* from the poem. Then repeat with words not from the poem, such as *bang, dent, camp, fast, king, nest, skit, slant, trust,* and *west.*

JOURNAL

Intervention Skills Intervention Guide, for direct instruction and extra practice in Blends

Build Background

Science

Concept: Woodland Animals

Evaluate Prior Knowledge

CONCEPT: WOODLAND ANIMALS Ask children to name and describe some animals that might live in a forest. Use the following activities if children need more information about forest-dwelling creatures.

MAKE AN ANIMAL CHART Work with children to create a chart that lists forest-dwelling animals and shows the kind of things they might do. ▶ **Linguistic**

FOREST ANIMALS	
bird	flies, looks for worms, builds nests
fox	cares for babies, looks for food
deer	eats plants, sleeps in the grass

Graphic Organizer 51

MAKE AN ANIMAL PICTURE Encourage children to draw a picture of an animal they might expect to see in a forest. Suggest that they use the animal chart for ideas. Have children write a sentence describing their picture.

WRITING

Develop Oral Language

CONNECT WORDS AND ACTIONS Have

ESL children pretend to be a forest animal. Encourage them to show some things animals do. If possible, hold up pictures of appropriate animals. Give directions such as :

- Fly *like* a bird.
- Hop *like* a rabbit.
- Hoot *like* an owl.

▶ **Kinesthetic/Linguistic**

DAILY **Phonics** ROUTINES

DAY 2 **Blending** Write the spelling of each sound in *bump* as you say it. Ask children to blend the sounds as they read the word. Repeat with *spin* and *stand*.

Phonics CD-ROM

LANGUAGE SUPPORT

To build more background, see pages 91-94 in the **Language Support Book.**

OBJECTIVES

Children will:

- identify high-frequency words *try, their, fall,* and *would.*

MATERIALS

- Teaching Chart 63
- Word Building Manipulative Cards *try, their, fall, would*

TEACHING TIP

The following chart indicates words from the upcoming story that children have learned to decode and high-frequency words that have been taught in this lesson.

Decodable		High-Frequency
asked	Stan	try
bump	stunt	fall
held	thing	their
jump	went	would

SPELLING/VOCABULARY CONNECTIONS

The words *try, fall, their,* and *would* are Challenge Words. See page 37Q for Day 1 of the 5-Day Spelling Plan.

---

try

fall

their

would

Vocabulary
High-Frequency Words

Stunts

Frogs on a stump will jump.
Bugs in the sun will run.
Rats on a log will jog.
Ducks in the slush will rush.
Bats in a loft will hang and flap (their) wings.
Cats that are soft will do a lot of things.
Could you, (would) you like to (try) them all?
Could you, (would) you? Look out! Do not (fall)

Teaching Chart 63

Auditory

LISTEN TO WORDS Without displaying it, read aloud "Stunts" on **Teaching Chart 63**. Then ask volunteers to pantomime the different animals as you read the poem again.

FIND HOMONYMS FOR HIGH-FREQUENCY WORDS Tell children that some words sound the same as other words but mean different things and are spelled differently. (Examples: *would* and *wood, their* and *there*)

- Read a line of the poem where a high-frequency word appears. Ask: *Does the word sound like another word that means something different?* If it does, have children use each word in a sentence.
- Repeat with each high-frequency word.

Visual

TEACH WORDS Display "Stunts" on **Teaching Chart 63**. Read the poem, tracking the print with your finger. Next, point to and say the word *try*. Ask them to hold up the vocabulary card for *try* and say the word. Repeat this procedure for *their, fall,* and *would.*

Hold up vocabulary cards for *try, their, fall,* and *would* one at a time. Have volunteers read the words and then circle them on the chart.

Word Building Manipulative Cards

WRITE A STUNT Have children pick one of the stunts in the poem. Then, have them write a sentence using this language pattern: *I would like to try to run in the sun with the bug.*

Word Wall

I Spy Tell children that you are going to play a game called "I Spy." Give children clues about each word wall word such as, "I spy with my eye, a word that rhymes with *bear*." Children should use the clues to guess which word you are describing. Continue with the rest of this week's word wall words.

Bumpy Words Give children macaroni, glue, and paper. They can practice spelling the word wall words using these materials. After spelling the words with macaroni, have children spell each word wall word out loud.

LANGUAGE SUPPORT

To help children develop understanding and recognition of high-frequency words, see page 91 in the **Language Support Book.**

Assess

Write Sentences Observe children during the activities to be sure that they are comfortable spelling the word wall words. Then ask children to write the words on a piece of paper. Have them use each one in a sentence.

Meeting Individual Needs for Vocabulary

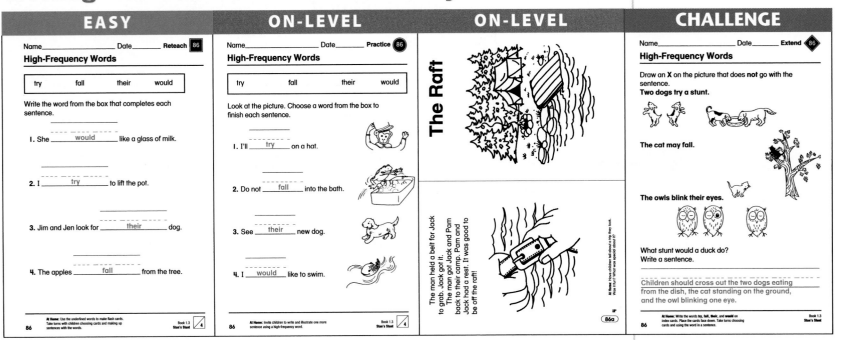

EASY	ON-LEVEL	ON-LEVEL	CHALLENGE
Reteach, 86	Practice, 86	Practice, 86a Take-Home Story	Extend, 86

10C

Comprehension

Prereading Strategies

PREVIEW AND PREDICT Point to and read aloud the names of the author and the illustrator. Then take a **picture walk** through the illustrations, stopping at page 17. Have children discuss what they think the animals might be doing. Then have children make predictions about the story. Ask questions such as:

- Where do you think the story might take place?
- Who do you think the main characters in the story might be?
- What will the story most likely be about?

Record their predictions about the story and the characters.

SET PURPOSES Ask children what they want to find out by reading the story. For example:

- Why is the story called *Stan's Stunt?*
- What are the characters in the story trying to do?

READ TOGETHER

Meet Lynn Plourde

Lynn Plourde lives in Maine. She has written many books for children. She also helps school children who have trouble speaking. She thinks both of her jobs are a lot of fun.

①

Meet Pamela R. Levy

When Pamela R. Levy was little she liked to draw. She did not think about becoming an artist until she went to college. Today she is the illustrator of many children's books. She also likes to dance, read, and garden.

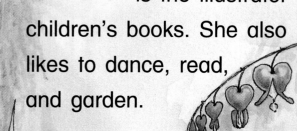

10

Meeting Individual Needs • Grouping Suggestions for Strategic Reading

EASY	ON-LEVEL	CHALLENGE
Shared Reading Read the story aloud as you track print and model directionality. As you read with children, model using the strategy of paying attention to the sequence of events to better understand what is happening in the story.	**Guided Instruction** Read the selection with children, using the Comprehension questions. Monitor any difficulties in reading that children may have in order to determine which numbered prompts to use. After reading the story with children, have children reread it, using the rereading suggestions on page 32.	**Independent Reading** Have children set purposes before they read. Remind children that, as they read, observing the details in the illustrations can help them link all the story ideas together. After reading, have children retell the story. Children can also use the questions on page 34 for a group discussion.

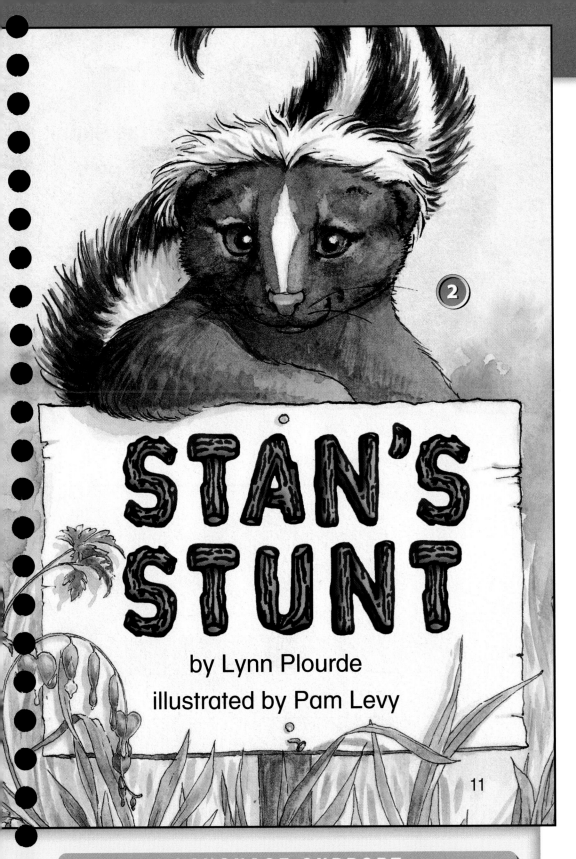

STAN'S STUNT

by Lynn Plourde

illustrated by Pam Levy

11

LANGUAGE SUPPORT

A blackline master for making stick puppets can be found in the **Language Support Book.** This will help children focus on characters.

For ESL children, a picture walk is important to introduce and build vocabulary. Talk about the pictures and story line using story vocabulary and synonyms. Check for comprehension by inviting children to point to pictures or answer yes/no questions.

LANGUAGE SUPPORT, 95

Comprehension

☑ **Phonics Blends**

STRATEGIC READING Tell children that paying attention to the characters and the things they do in *Stan's Stunt* will help them understand the story. Explain that they can make and use stick puppets to reenact the story events. Children will use the puppets of Stan the Skunk, Frog, Bat, and Owl to hold up as they pantomime each character's special stunt.

① **SETTING** We are going to read *Stan's Stunt.* Let's make sure we have our stick puppets ready to help us as we read. *Story Props*

Point to the top picture on page 10. This is the author, Lynn Plourde. Do you think teaching children has given her ideas for her books? Now look at the other picture. This is Pamela R. Levy. She drew the pictures in this story. *Concept of a Book: Author/Illustrator*

② What animal is on page 11? (a skunk) Where do skunks usually live? (the forest, wooded areas) *Use Illustrations*

Genre

Story

Remind children that a story:

- is a fictional piece telling about a series of events.
- contains the elements of character, plot, and setting.
- focuses on several characters that are presented with a problem they must solve.

Activity Encourage children to speculate on the ways the story might be different if it were a nonfiction piece. In what ways might these animals act differently if this were nonfiction?

11

Comprehension

TRACKING PRINT Point to the word in the first sentence where we will start reading. *(I)* Now let's read the sentence together. *Syntactic Cues*

3 **Phonics** **BLENDS** *"I can do a ... "* I'm not sure what this word is. Let's blend the sounds of the letters together and read it: s t u n t stunt. Let's read the word after *said* the same way: S t a n Stan. *Graphophonic Cues*

3 "I can do a stunt," said Stan the Skunk. "What is a stunt?" asked Stan's pals. "A stunt is a good trick!" said Stan.

12

Fluency

GROUP READING

Encourage children to imagine the sounds they might hear if they were in the forest with Stan and his pals.

Have children slowly read aloud together, using expression and feeling in their voices.

PREVENTION/INTERVENTION

TRACKING PRINT Have children use self-stick notes or self-adhesive dots to mark the first word in each sentence in their books. Tell them to look for capital letters to find the starting place for each sentence. *Syntactic Cues*

Up went Stan's tail.
"No! Stop! Stop!" yelled Stan's pals. ⑥

⑤

④

13

ESL Blends may be difficult for ESL children to distinguish. *S* blends will be especially difficult for Spanish speakers. To reinforce hearing the *st* blend, point out that it appears in three different words on pages 12 and 13 (*Stan, stunt,* and *stop*). Ask volunteers to identify those three words. Invite the children to read the text with you to practice pronouncing the *st* blend.

Comprehension

④ How does Stan's tail look? (It is all the way up.) Why do you think this is causing his friends to yell "stop"? (because they are afraid he might spray them) What do you think will happen next? *Use Illustrations/ Make Predictions*

⑤ Point to the words that Stan's pals yell. Read them with me. Remember to blend the sounds of the letters together if you need to: s t o p stop. *Graphophonic Cues*

⑥ Let's read what Stan's pals yell: *"No! Stop! Stop!"* What do you see after each of these three words? (an exclamation mark) The exclamation mark tells us to read each word with emotion to show that Stan's pals are excited. Let's read these three words again, with an excited voice. *Concepts of Print*

Minilesson
REVIEW/MAINTAIN
Make Inferences

Remind children that an author can show how characters feel by showing what they say or do.

• Have children act out the behavior of Stan's pals in the picture on page 13.

• Then ask them to brainstorm a list of words telling how Stan's pals might feel.

• Discuss why they might feel that way.

Activity Have children look back at the picture of Stan's pals on the previous page. Have them draw or write about how their feelings seem to have changed, and why.

Comprehension

7 Let's use our stick puppets to show what Owl's stunt is. *Story Props*

SINGULAR POSSESSIVE PRONOUNS
Let's read the first sentence. The words *Look at my stunt* are said by Owl. Whose stunt is described by the word *my*? (Owl's stunt) Now look ahead to the first sentence on page 17. Who says this sentence? (Stan) Whose stunt is described by the word *my* in this sentence? (Stan's stunt) Explain to children that *my* is used to tell that something belongs to the speaker.

8 Now let's read all the sentences on this page. Can you find two words on this page that are opposite in meaning? *(up, down)* Let's stand up and sit down to show what those words mean. *Pantomime/ Semantic Cues*

8 "Look at *my* stunt," said Owl. Up and down went Owl's lids.

14

CULTURAL PERSPECTIVES

RAINFORESTS Ask children what they know about rainforests. Then share:

- Rainforests are usually in tropical areas.
- They can get more than 80 inches of rain each year.
- Many unique plants and animals grow in them.

RESEARCH AND INQUIRY Have children use nonfiction books to research plants and animals found in the Amazon rainforest. ▶**Visual/Linguistic**

inter NET CONNECTION For more information on rainforests, go to **www.mhschool.com/reading**.

Owl's lids went wink blink.
Then his lids went blink wink.
"Stan, | try | Owl's stunt," said Stan's pals.

15

Comprehension

9 Why do you think Bat, Stan, and Frog are watching Owl? (because he is performing his stunt) *Using Picture Clues*

10 **Phonics** **BLENDS** Look at the first sentence on this page. Now point to the third word. Read this word aloud with me. Use your finger to help you blend the sounds of the letters together.
w e n t, went *Graphophonic Cues*

CONCEPTS OF PRINT How many sentences do you see on this page? (3) Use your fingers to count the number of sentences. *Syntactic Clues*

Minilesson
REVIEW/MAINTAIN
Use Context Clues

Remind children that they can sometimes use the other words in a sentence to figure out unfamiliar words.

• Point to the word *lids* in the first two sentences on page 15.

• Ask children what clues they might use to figure out what the word means. (look at the pictures; look at the other words on the page)

• Read the words *wink* and *blink*. Ask children what *wink* and *blink* could have to do with the word *lids*. (Owl could be winking and blinking his eyelids.)

Activity Ask children to wink and blink. Then ask what part of their body moved.

PREVENTION/INTERVENTION

CONCEPTS OF PRINT Write the sentence *A stunt is a good trick* on the chalkboard and read it with children. Guide children to tell you that this is a *sentence* because it tells a complete thought. Remind children that sentences are made up of words, and that words have spaces between them. Have volunteers come up to the chalkboard and use their index fingers to frame each word in the sentence. Then have children count the number of words in the sentence. (6) *Syntactic Cues*

15

Comprehension

 Phonics **BLENDS** Point to the word *stunt* on page 16. Have you seen this word before? (yes) Let's look back to see where we've seen this word before. (on pages 11, 12, 14, 15) Read it with me again. If you need to, you can use your finger to help you remember to blend the sounds of the letters together. s t u n t, stunt
Graphophonic Cues

TEACHING TIP

MAKE CONNECTIONS If children are having difficulty understanding the word *stunt*, you might want to bring in a news story that would expand this word into the "real" world. For example, you could pass around a news clip about a professional stuntman or stuntwoman who doubles for a famous actor or actress. Have children talk about what kinds of stunts this person might do. Remind them that a *stunt* is a good trick (as stated at the beginning of the story, page 12).

"I like Owl's stunt," said Stan.
"And I can do his stunt," said Stan.
Stan went wink blink.
Then Stan went blink wink.

16

Activity

Cross Curricular: Social Studies

FORESTS Forests are very important to human and animal life. Trees in the forests give off oxygen and provide wood to make paper and lumber for homes. Forests provide homes to many plants and animals. Have children draw a scene from a forest. ▶ **Linguistic/Visual**

RESEARCH AND INQUIRY Invite children to look through non-fiction books and magazines to learn more about forests. Have volunteers share what they have learned with their classmates.

"But I would like to do *my* stunt,"
said Stan.
Up went Stan's tail again.
"No! Stop! Stop!" yelled Stan's pals.

17

Comprehension

12 Let's look at the expressions on the faces of Stan's pals on page 17. How do you think they feel? (worried) How can you tell? *Use Picture Clues*

13 What is the owl doing with his wings on this page? (flapping them) Let's hold up our Owl puppet and act out what he is doing. *Story Props*

14 **Phonics** BLENDS Let's look at what Stan's friends are yelling. Can you find the words in the last line on this page with the /st/ sound? Let's read the words together. *(Stop, Stan's) Graphophonic Cues*

Comprehension

15 What is Frog doing? (He is jumping.)
What do you think will happen next?
Why do you think that? (Answers will vary.)
Make Predictions/Use Illustrations

16 Let's see what else we can find in the
forest besides trees and animals. What
do you see? (a pond, lily pads, reeds) *Use
Illustrations*

Ｓelf-monitoring
STRATEGY

RELATE TO PERSONAL EXPERIENCES
It's easier to understand a story you are
reading if you can connect what happens
in the story with something that has happened in your own life.

- Have you ever tried to stop a friend from
  doing something he or she wanted to
  do? How did you try? Did it work?

- Has anyone ever tried to trick you into
  acting differently from the way you
  wanted to act?

- Do you have a favorite trick or stunt you
  like doing for friends or family members?

"Take a look at *my* stunt," said Frog.
Up and down went Frog's legs.

18

Frog went jump bump.

Then Frog went bump jump.

"Stan, try Frog's stunt," said Stan's pals.

19

Comprehension

17 Let's use our stick puppets to show Frog's stunt. Where is he leaping? *(across the water)* **Story Props**

18 **Phonics** **BLENDS** Does anyone see any rhyming words on this page? *(jump, bump)* Find the third word in the first sentence and point to it with your finger. Now read the word with me, using your finger to help you remember to blend the sounds of the letters together: j u m p jump. Now let's do the same with the next word: b u m p bump. *Graphophonic Cues*

PHONOLOGICAL AWARENESS Say the sentence: *"Stan, try Frog's stunt," said Stan's pals*. I hear one word that ends with the same sound as *had*. Does anyone know what word it is? *(said)*

PREVENTION/INTERVENTION

PHONOLOGICAL AWARENESS
Say the sentence *"I like to read in bed," said Ned*.

- Ask children to count the number of words they hear in the sentence. (8)

- Say the sentence again. Then ask children to raise their hands when they hear a word that that ends like *had* or *said*.

- Read the sentence again, and ask children to name the words they hear that end with the /d/ sound. *(read, bed, said, Ned)*

Comprehension

19 Let's think back to the pages we've already read. Every time Stan does one of his pal's stunts, what does he say next? (that he wants to do his stunt) **So, what do you think Stan is going to say on the next page?** *("I would like to do my stunt.")* **Make Predictions/Critical Thinking**

19

"I like Frog's stunt," said Stan.

"And I can do his stunt," said Stan.

Stan went jump bump.

Then Stan went bump jump.

20

Activity

Cross Curricular: Science

JUMPING BEANS Tell children that jumping beans grow in Central and South America. Each bean contains a tiny caterpillar. When the caterpillar snaps its body, the bean jumps and rolls!

- People in the United States usually call them *Mexican jumping beans*.

- In the Southwest, these lively beans are sometimes called *bronco beans*.

- In Mexico, they're called *leapers*.

Activity If possible, clear enough space in the room, and have children hop like jumping beans. ▶ **Kinesthetic**

"But I would like to do *my* stunt,"
said Stan.
Up went Stan's tail again.
"No! Stop! Stop!" yelled Stan's pals.

20

21

Comprehension

20 Let's read page 21 together. Did Stan say what you thought he was going to say? (yes) *Confirm Predictions*

21 Let's look closely at the background in the picture on this page. What do you notice in the pond? (a mother duck with her ducklings) *Use Illustrations*

 RHYMING WORDS Say the word *tail*. What are some words that rhyme with *tail*? (mail, snail, nail) How many syllables do you hear in each word? (one)

TEACHING TIP

ALLITERATION Have children find the name of the central character on this page. *(Stan)* Write the word on the chalkboard and have a volunteer circle the first two letters in the word. What sound does this blend make? *(/st/)* Have children identify the other *st* words on this page. *(stunt, stop)* Explain that an author often chooses to match beginning sounds in several words on purpose. Elicit from children simple sentences with words with the same beginning sounds—for example *Meg makes mud pies.*

---

p/i PREVENTION/INTERVENTION

RHYMING WORDS Put the letter cards *t, a, i, l* on the chalkboard ledge. Place the letter cards *f, h, j, m, n, p, r,* and *s* in a bag. Invite volunteers to choose a letter from the bag and place it over the *t* to create a new word that rhymes with *tail*. Have children take turns reading the word and using it in a sentence. *Graphophonic Cues*

Comprehension

22 Let's use our stick puppets to focus our attention on Bat's wonderful stunt. Who can tell me what Bat is hanging from? (a tree branch) *Story Props*

23  **BLENDS** Point to the word *stunt*. Have you seen this word before? (yes) Does anyone see another word that ends with the /n/ /t/ sounds? *(went)* Point to the word *went* with your finger to read it with me: w e n t went. *Graphophonic Cues*

22

23 "Take a look at *my* stunt," said Bat. Upside down went Bat.

22

Cross Curricular: Math

BATS Bats are the only mammals that can fly. Most bats help people by eating harmful insects.

- The common brown bat has a body 4 inches long and a wingspan of 14 inches.
- The flying fox (a kind of bat) has a one-foot-long body and a wingspan of 5 feet.

Draw pictures on the chalkboard to show the size and wingspan of the two bats.

RESEARCH AND INQUIRY Have children search through nonfiction books or on the Internet for more facts about bats.

▶ **Linguistic**

Bat went flip flop.

Then Bat went flop flip.

"Stan, try Bat's stunt," said Stan's pals.

23

Comprehension

24 Let's think back to the pages we've already read in the story. Which characters have already shown their own stunts? (Owl, Frog, Bat) Which character has not done his own stunt yet? (Stan) *Sequence of Events*

25 What do you think Stan is going to do on the next page? (He will try out Bat's stunt.) Let's turn the page to find out. *Make Predictions*

Minilesson

REVIEW/MAINTAIN

Blends *fl, sn, sl*

Emphasize the beginning sound of the word *flip* as you read page 23. Write the letters *fl* on the chalkboard. Ask children to:

- find the words on page 23 that begin with the sound /fl/ and the letters *fl*.
- name other words that start with the sound they hear at the beginning of *flip*.

Activity Write the following letters on index cards: *fl, sn, sl, ap, ip*. Place the blends in one bag and the endings in another. Have volunteers choose one card from each bag, blend and say the word formed, and then return the cards for the next volunteer.

Phonics CD-ROM Have children use the interactive phonics activities for more reinforcement with blends.

Comprehension

26 Raise your hand if you guessed that Stan was going to try Bat's stunt on this page. *Nonverbal Response*

27 What kind of animals are better at hanging upside down from tree branches, bats or skunks? (bats) *Make Inferences*

TEACHING **TIP**

SUMMARIZE After children have read *Stan's Stunt,* have them make use of their stick puppets by summarizing the main events of the story. Have small groups take turns presenting their version to the rest of the class.

Fluency

READ WITH EXPRESSION

 Have partners take turns reading page 24. Remind children to:
PARTNERS

• think about how Stan is feeling when he sees Bat.

• pause at the end of sentences and at commas.

• change the speed of reading depending on the passage.

26 "I like Bat's stunt," said Stan. "And I can do his stunt," said Stan.

24

LANGUAGE SUPPORT

ESL Add to the Animal Chart you started in Build Background on page 10A. Ask children to recall the animals from the story up to this point and orally talk about their characteristics. Allow children to point to the illustrations if they do not have the English vocabulary to describe. Be sure to restate their intent providing the English words.

Stan went flip flop.

Then Stan went flop flip.

"Do not fall!" yelled Stan's pals. **(29)**

25

Comprehension

(28) Let's look at the picture on page 24. Was Stan good at doing Bat's stunt? (no) How do you know? (He almost fell from the tree.) *Use Illustrations*

(29) Let's read what Stan's pals say in the last line on this page. This time, they say something different. Do you know what it is? (Do not fall!) Do they say this quietly or loudly? (loudly) How do you know? (the exclamation mark) Let's read the sentence again, with a worried voice. *Concepts of Print*

(p/i) BLENDING WITH SHORT *a* Point to the last word on the page. Now let's blend and read the word with me. *(pals) Graphophonic Cues*

(p/i) PREVENTION/INTERVENTION

BLENDING WITH SHORT *a* Write the following letters on squares of paper and put them in paper bags. Bag 1: *st, fl, m, s*; Bag 2: *a*; Bag 3: *n, nd, t, p*. Have a child pull one letter from each bag and place them in order on a desk. Ask the child to blend the letters together to read the word. Correct any miscues the child may make and model blending. If the letters make a nonsense word, have the child choose a new initial or final letter and blend again. Repeat, alternating volunteers. *Graphophonic Cues*

Comprehension

 30 Let's review which characters have done stunts, and what kind of stunts they have done. Who did the first stunt? (Owl) What did Owl do? (It went wink blink.) Who did the second stunt? (Frog) What did Frog do? (It went jump bump.) Who did the last stunt? (Bat) What did Bat do? (It went flip flop.) *Sequence of Events*

31 Do you think Stan is finally going to do a stunt? What do you think it's going to be? *Make Predictions*

TEACHING TIP

QUOTATION MARKS Read the first sentence on page 26. Point to the quotation marks and explain to children that quotation marks tell us that someone is speaking. Elicit from children that the quotation marks show that Stan is speaking. Direct children's attention to the previous page and ask if anyone sees quotation marks there. Which words appear in quotation marks? (*Do not fall!*) Who is speaking? (Stan's pals)

"Now I will do *my* stunt," said Stan.
Up went Stan's tail again.
Stan's pals had run out of stunts.

30

31

26

Stan's pals held their noses.
"Do it!" said Stan's pals.
"Do your stunt."

27

Comprehension

32 What are Stan's pals doing on page 27? (holding their noses) Why? (They think Stan is going to spray.) *Make Inferences*

33 Let's read what Stan's pals say on this page: "Do it! Do your stunt." Is this very different from what they have said before? (yes) How? (Before they said, "No! Stop! Stop!") *Compare and Contrast*

34 Have children stand and model the behavior of Stan's pals. Ask them to repeat the words spoken by Stan's pals while holding their noses. Remind children that the exclamation mark means that the words are spoken with emotion. *Pantomime*

Comprehension

35 What do you see in the picture on page 28? (Stan's tail) What do you think is going to happen next? (Stan will spray.) *Make Predictions*

And Stan did.

28

Back and forth went Stan's tail.
Stan went wiggle waggle.

29

Comprehension

36 Does Stan look happy on page 29? (yes) Why do you think he's so happy? (He's finally doing his stunt.) *Make Inferences*

37 Let's do Stan's stunt with him. Hold up your stick puppet for Stan and go *wiggle waggle* like he does. *Story Props*

PHONOLOGICAL AWARENESS
Listen as I say these two words aloud: *wiggle, waggle*. What is the difference in the way they sound? (One has an /i/ sound; one has an /a/ sound.) How many syllables do you hear in each word? (2) *Discriminating*

Minilesson

REVIEW/MAINTAIN

Make Predictions

Review that better readers use story clues and what they already know to predict events and then confirm or revise predictions as they get more information.

- Ask children to look back at the prediction they made on page 28. Does the information on page 30 confirm their prediction?

Activity Have children revise their predictions if necessary and then predict what will happen next.

PREVENTION/INTERVENTION

PHONOLOGICAL AWARENESS
Say the word *wiggle*. Then say the following words and have children raise a hand when a word has an /i/ sound: *did, hid, mad, big, cup, lip, sip, yes*. Next, say the word *waggle*.

Then say the following words and have children raise a hand when a word has an /a/ sound: *bag, sad, pin, ran, not, cat, hat*.

Comprehension

38 Let's look closely at the picture on page 30. Where are Stan's pals? (far away, sitting on the rock) Why are they far away? (They don't want to be near Stan when he sprays because it might smell bad.) *Critical Thinking*

39 Now let's read this page. What do Stan's pals smell? (not a thing) Do you think they are surprised? *Make Inferences*

39 Stan wagged and wagged his tail. Stan's pals sniffed and sniffed. But they did not smell a thing.

30

"What a good stunt!" said Stan's pals.

31

Comprehension

40 Who is speaking on page 31? (Stan's pals) How do we know that someone is speaking? (the quotation marks and the word *said*) How do we know that Stan's pals are speaking with emotion? (the exclamation mark) Let's read this sentence together with the same emotion that Stan's pals are feeling. *Concepts of Print*

Minilesson
REVIEW/MAINTAIN
Main Idea

Remind children that the main idea

• tells what a story is about.

• can be told in one or two sentences.

Work with children to write a sentence that tells the main idea of this story. Have them

• reread the title of the story.

• look through the story and notice how the words and facial expressions of Stan's pals change from the beginning of the story to the end.

• think about what Stan's pals expect to happen and what really happens.

Activity Write the main idea of the story on the chalkboard. Then have children make posters to illustrate the lesson learned by Stan's pals in the story.

31

Comprehension

41 Let's look at Stan and his pals on pages 32 and 33. Who can name the four animals in this story? (Stan, Owl, Frog, Bat) What are they all doing? (going *wiggle waggle* like Stan) *Use Illustrations*

RETELL THE STORY Ask children to work in groups of three to retell the story. They may want to use their stick puppets to show which character is speaking or doing the action. After children decide on what they will say in their retelling, encourage them to choose roles and act out the story.

STUDENT SELF-ASSESSMENT

Have children ask themselves the following questions to assess how they are reading:

- How did I use what I know about doing stunts with friends to help me understand the events in this story?

- How did I use the illustrations to help me understand the setting of this story?

- How did I use the pictures and the letters and sounds I know to help me read the words in the story?

TRANSFERRING THE STRATEGIES

- How can I use these strategies to help me read other stories?

41

"Will you try *my* stunt now?" asked Stan.
"Yes! Yes!" said Stan's pals.

32

REREADING FOR *Fluency*

ONE Children who need fluency practice can read along silently or aloud as they listen to the story on audiocassette.

READING RATE When you evaluate reading rate, have children read aloud from the story for one minute. Place a stick-on note after the last word read. Count words read. To

evaluate children's performance, see the Running Record in the **Fluency Assessment** book.

i Intervention For leveled fluency lessons, passages, and norms charts, see **Skills Intervention Guide**, Part 5, Fluency.

Stan and his pals went waggle wiggle.
Then Stan and his pals went giggle
giggle.

33

Comprehension

Return to Predictions and Purposes

Reread children's predictions about the story. Discuss the predictions, noting which needed to be revised. Then ask children if the story answered the questions they had before they read it.

Have children talk about the strategy of using the story puppets. Did they feel that using the puppets helped them to understand the story?

INFORMAL ASSESSMENT

HOW TO ASSESS

Phonics **BLENDS** Write the word *stop* on the chalkboard and have children read it aloud. Then repeat with the word *held*.

FOLLOW UP

Phonics **BLENDS** Continue to model continuant/stop blends for children who are having difficulty.

LITERARY RESPONSE

QUICK-WRITE Have children draw a picture of their favorite character from the story and write why they liked that character best.

ORAL RESPONSE Have children use their journal entries to discuss these questions:

- Do you think Stan's pals were right to be worried about Stan's stunt?

- Which stunt did you like best? Why?
- If you were one of Stan's pals, which stunt would you do?

SENTENCE STRIPS Children can use strips 1–58 to retell *Stan's Stunt*.

> 1
> "I can do a stunt," said Stan the Skunk.

> 2
> "What is a stunt?" asked Stan's pals.

33

Story Questions

Tell children that now they will read some questions about the story. Help children read the questions. Discuss possible answers.

Answers:

1. Owl blinks his eyes. *Literal/Plot*

2. They thought Stan was going to spray. *Inferential/Make Inferences*

3. Owl could blink; Frog could jump; Bat could hang upside down; Stan could wag his tail. *Inferential/Compare and Contrast*

4. Answers will vary. *Critical/Summarize*

5. Answers will vary. *Critical/Reading Across Texts*

Write About a Stunt Have children read the directions in their anthologies. Ask children to brainstorm various stunts they might want to try. List their ideas on the chalkboard.

Story Questions & Activities

READ TOGETHER

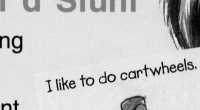

1 What does Owl do?

2 Why did Stan's pals yell, "Stop!"?

3 What other stunts could the animals do?

4 Tell the story in your own words.

5 Name animals you have read about.

Write About a Stunt

Draw yourself doing a stunt.

Tell about the stunt.

Then write about it.

I like to do cartwheels.

Meeting Individual Needs

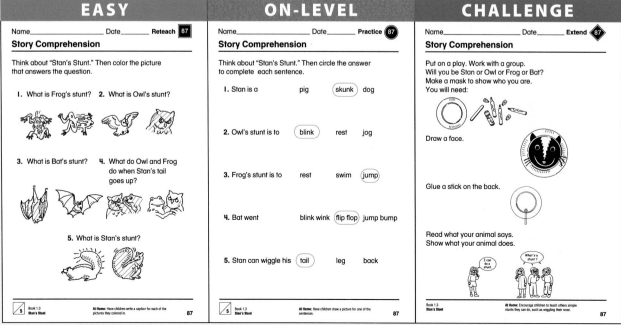

EASY	ON-LEVEL	CHALLENGE
Reteach, 87	Practice, 87	Extend, 87

Make a Forest Mural

Draw a picture of a forest.

Name an animal that lives in the forest.

Draw a picture of this animal.

Glue your picture in the forest.

35

Find Out More

Have you ever seen a skunk?

Find out more about this animal.

Share what you learn.

DAILY **Phonics** ROUTINES

DAY 3 Write a list of words using continuant/stop blends. Examples: *stunt, must, hang, went, bump.* Point to each word, asking children to blend the sounds silently. Ask a volunteer to read each word.

Phonics CD-ROM

Story Activities

Make a Forest Mural

Materials: large sheets of paper and crayons

Read the directions aloud. Help children who have questions. First, ask children what kinds of trees, plants, and animals they might expect to find in a forest. Do they know the names of some trees and plants? Can they think of other animals they might find in the forest, besides the ones in the story?

GROUP Have children work together in small groups to draw their pictures and glue them onto the mural. Encourage them to draw their animals in a detailed scene with foliage.

Find Out More

RESEARCH AND INQUIRY Ask if children have had any personal experiences with skunks. Encourage them to talk to family members or look in the library to learn more about skunks. Invite children to share any interesting facts orally with the class and to raise any unanswered questions.

ONE

*inter***NET** To access sites about
CONNECTION animals, children can go to
www.mhschool.com/reading.

FORMAL ASSESSMENT

After page 35, see the Selection Assessment.

Study Skills

DIAGRAMS

OBJECTIVES

Children will:

• learn to read a diagram, a type of picture with labels, to gather information.

Remind children that they have just read a story about a skunk. Tell them that they will read a diagram to learn more about skunks.

Display **Teaching Chart 64**. Have children read the sentence and the title of the diagram with you. Then invite children to describe what they notice about the diagram. Ask children what they think the words in the diagram might mean. Together, read the words using picture clues. Point to each part of the skunk and ask children to name it. Have them suggest how the skunk uses each part. Help children read the questions below the diagram, encouraging them to identify the labels that answer each question.

STUDY SKILLS

READ TOGETHER

Skunk

This diagram shows the parts of a skunk.

tail

body

head

paw

claws

nose   eyes

Look at the Diagram

❶ What color is the skunk's tail?

❷ Count the claws on a paw.

Meeting Individual Needs

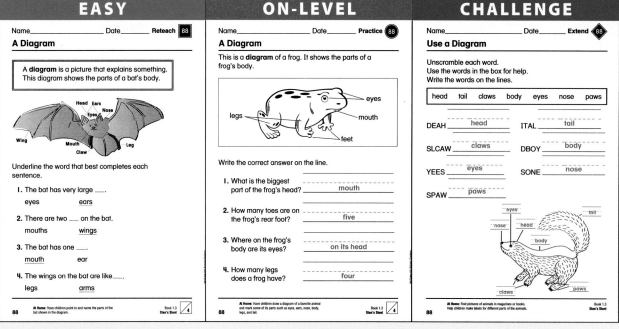

EASY

A Diagram

A **diagram** is a picture that explains something. This diagram shows the parts of a bat's body.

Underline the word that best completes each sentence.

1. The bat has very large ___.
   eyes   ears

2. There are two ___ on the bat.
   mouths   wings

3. The bat has one ___.
   mouth   ear

4. The wings on the bat are like ___.
   legs   arms

Reteach, 88

ON-LEVEL

A Diagram

This is a **diagram** of a frog. It shows the parts of a frog's body.

eyes
legs
mouth
feet

Write the correct answer on the line.

1. What is the biggest part of the frog's head?   mouth

2. How many toes are on the frog's rear foot?   five

3. Where on the frog's body are its eyes?   on its head

4. How many legs does a frog have?   four

Practice, 88

CHALLENGE

Use a Diagram

Unscramble each word.
Use the words in the box for help.
Write the words on the lines.

| head | tail | claws | body | eyes | nose | paws |

DEAH   head   ITAL   tail

SLCAW   claws   DBOY   body

YEES   eyes   SONE   nose

SPAW   paws

eyes   tail
nose   head
body
claws   paws

Extend, 88

TEST POWER

Flo the Pig

Flo is a pink pig.

She lives on a farm in a pigpen.

There are many other pigs.

Flo likes to play games.

Her favorite game is piggyback.

When Flo plays, she likes to win.

But win or lose, Flo has fun.

Where does this story take place?

○ In the forest

◉ On a farm

Look for clues in the story to help answer the question.

37

Test Power

THE PRINCETON REVIEW

Read the Page

Explain to children that you will be reading this story as a group. You will read the story, and they will follow in their books.

Request that children put pens, pencils, and markers away, since they will not be writing in their books.

Discuss the Question

Discuss with children the kinds of words that describe places. Then have them read the story, looking for words that describe places. Have children read aloud the words they have found.

Test-Tip

Look for key words to help you locate the answer to a question. In this case, look for words that describe places.

Leveled Books

Bat Helps Out

by Ellen Dreyer
illustrated by Judy Pfeiffer

EASY

Bat Helps Out

☑ **Blends**

High-Frequency Words:
try, fall, their, would

Guided Reading

PREVIEW AND PREDICT Discuss each illustration up to page 5, using the high-frequency words. As you take the **picture walk,** have children predict what the story is about. Chart their ideas.

SET PURPOSES Have children write or draw why they want to read *Bat Helps Out.* For example: *I want to find out how the bat helps the frog.*

READ THE BOOK Use the following questions to guide children's reading or to ask after they have read the story independently.

Pages 2–3: Who sees some high-frequency words we just learned? *(would, fall, try)* Model: I'm not sure what this word is, but I can blend the sounds of the letters together to read it: w e n t went. The word is *went. Phonics and Decoding*

Pages 4–5: What happened when Frog jumped? (He got stuck in mud.) *Cause and Effect*

Pages 6–7: How does Bat pull Frog out of the mud? (He pulls Frog out of the mud with his legs; he flaps his wings to lift him up.) *Use Illustrations*

Page 8: Why does Bat say, "Glad to help"? (It makes Bat feel good to help his friend.) *Make Inferences*

RETURN TO PREDICTIONS AND PURPOSES Discuss children's predictions and purposes for reading.

LITERARY RESPONSE The following questions will help focus children's responses:

• How did Frog get stuck?

• Have you ever helped somebody out? Tell about it.

Also see the story questions and activity in *Bat Helps Out.*

See the **Phonics CD-ROM** for practice with blends.

Answers to Story Questions
1. Frog
2. Answers will vary. They are friends.
3. Answers will vary: In a lake or pond.
4. Answers will vary.
5. Answers will vary.

The Story Questions and Activity below appear in the Easy Book.

Story Questions and Activity
1. Who got stuck in the mud?
2. Why did Bat help Frog?
3. Where does the story take place?
4. Tell the story in your own words.
5. Name another story where animals help out.

Make Stick Puppets
Draw Bat and Frog. Cut them out. Glue them onto craft sticks. Use your puppets to tell the story.

from Bat Helps Out

Leveled Books

INDEPENDENT

Two Tests

☑ **Blends**

High-Frequency Words: *try, fall, their, would*

by Becky Gold
illustrated by Mariano Gil

Guided Reading

PREVIEW AND PREDICT Discuss each illustration up to page 4, using the High-Frequency Words. As you take the **picture walk**, have children predict what will happen in the story.

SET PURPOSES Have children write or draw why they want to read *Two Tests*. For example: *I want to find out who is faster, Bat or Owl.*

READ THE BOOK Use questions like the following to guide children's reading or after they have read the story independently.

Page 2: I'm not sure what this word is, but I can blend the sounds together: s p e d sped. The word is *sped*. *Phonics and Decoding*

Page 3: Does Owl think he is faster than Bat? (No.) *Analyze Character and Plot*

Pages 4–5: Who sees high-frequency words that we just learned? *(would, try)* Let's read these pages together. What word has the letters *mp* in it on page 5? *(pumped) High-Frequency Words/Phonics and Decoding*

Pages 6–7: Look at Owl's and Bat's eyes. What are they doing? (closing) Why? (They are tired; they are going to sleep.) *Use Illustrations*

Page 8: Look at the sun in the picture. What does this tell you? (It is daytime.) When do you think bats and owls sleep? (during the day) *Make Inferences*

RETURN TO PREDICTIONS AND PURPOSES Discuss children's predictions. Ask which were close to the story and why. Have children review their purposes for reading. Did they find who is faster?

LITERARY RESPONSE The following questions will help focus children's responses:

- What are you able to do fast? Tell about it.

- What are the two tests? What other stories have you read testing who could do something faster? What happened?

Also see the story questions and writing activity in *Two Tests*.

See the **Phonics** **CD-ROM** for practice with blends.

Answers to the Story Questions

1. Bat
2. It was a tie.
3. Answers will vary: In the woods or forest.
4. The first test was about whose wings were faster. The second test was about who could fall asleep first.
5. Answers will vary.

The Story Questions and Activity below appear in the Independent Book.

Story Questions and Activity

1. Who could fly faster, Bat or Owl?
2. Who won the second test?
3. Where does this story take place?
4. Tell about the two tests Bat and Owl had.
5. Tell about a contest you have been in.

Write a Story

Think about an animal that can move fast.

Write about it.

Tell how being fast helps the animal be safe.

from Two Tests

Leveled Books

CHALLENGE

Walking Through the Jungle

☑ **Blends**

Guided Reading

The Story Questions and Activity below appear in the Challenge Book.

Story Questions and Activity

1. What does the girl see in the river?
2. What happens wherever the girl goes?
3. What other animals live in the ocean?
4. Tell all the places where the story happens.
5. What is the same about this story and *I Went Walking*?

Where Do You Want to Go?

Pick a place from the story you like best. What will you do there? Draw a picture. Write a few sentences about your picture.

from *Walking Through the Jungle*

PREVIEW AND PREDICT Discuss each illustration up to page 19. As you take the **picture walk**, have children predict what the story is about. Chart their ideas.

SET PURPOSES Have children write or draw why they want to read *Walking Through the Jungle*. For example: *I want to find out what else she sees in the jungle.*

READ THE BOOK Use the following questions to guide children's reading or to ask after they have read the story independently.

Pages 4–15: How does the girl look on page 4? (happy) How does she look on page 7? (scared) Why? (There's a big lion chasing her.) Where does she go next? (to the ocean) What chases her there? (a whale) Then what chases her? (a wolf) *Use Illustrations/ Sequence of Events*

Page 19: There's a word that appears two times on this page that has the /ft/ sound. Point to it. Now read it aloud with me. (*after*) Which letters blend together to make the /ft/ sound? (*f* and *t*) *Phonics and Decoding*

Pages 26–29: What happens at the end of the story? (The girl and all the animals run home for supper.) How are the animals different in the picture on pages 28–29? (They look friendly, not wild.) *Analyze Character and Plot*

RETURN TO PREDICTIONS AND PURPOSES Have children review their predictions and purposes for reading. Did they find out what the girl saw in the jungle?

LITERARY RESPONSE Have children discuss questions like the following:

- Have you ever traveled to someplace new? How was it different from where you live?

Also see the story questions and writing activity in *Walking Through the Jungle*.

See the 🔘 **Phonics CD-ROM** for practice with blends.

Bringing Groups Together

Anthology and Leveled Books

Connecting Texts

CLASS DISCUSSION
Lead a discussion of the various ways in which animals are able to move. Be sure to include *hop/jump* and *slither*. Guide children to recognize that many animals can move in more than just one way.

- Name some animals from the stories that can swim. Name some that fly.

- Can you think of an animal that can move in more than one way?

MOVEMENT CHART List the different ways in which animals move across the top of the chart. Call on volunteers from all reading levels to name the animals they read about and tell how the animals moved. Have children decide under which column(s) the names should be listed. Animals capable of moving different ways may be listed on the chart in each applicable column. Example: *squirrel* would be listed under *hop/jump* and *walk/run*.

How Animals Move				
Fly	Swim	Walk/Run	Slither	Hop/Jump
owl bat	frog whale crocodile polar bear	squirrel monkey lion wolf polar bear crocodile	snake	frog squirrel monkey

Viewing/Representing

GROUP PRESENTATIONS Divide the class into groups, one for each of the four books. (For *Stan's Stunt,* combine children of different reading levels.) Have each group draw pictures of the main events and orally summarize the book. Have each group present its pictures and summary.

AUDIENCE RESPONSE
Ask children to pay attention to each group's presentation. Allow time for questions after each group presents.

Research and Inquiry

MORE ABOUT ANIMALS Have children ask themselves: What else would I like to know about woodland and other wild animals? Then invite them to do the following:

- Bring in pictures of different woodland or wild animals.

- Take a class trip to a park or wooded area to see where woodland animals live.

- Choose an animal you know and tell about it.

interNET CONNECTION Have children log on to **www.mhschool.com/reading** for links to Web pages about woodland animals.

Children will:

- identify continuant/stop blends.
- blend and read words with continuant/stop blends.
- review initial and final consonants, short vowels.

MATERIALS:
- Teaching Chart 65

Skills Finder

Blends	
Introduce	B2: 96I-J; B3: 8I-J, 38I-J
Review	B2: 123G-H, B3: 37E-F, 67E-F, 67G-H, 97G-H
Test	Book 2, Book 3
Maintain	B3: 23; B4: 13

LANGUAGE SUPPORT

ESL ESL children may not recognize some English vocabulary words. You may wish to introduce the vocabulary they will need in order to do the lesson prior to your asking them to work with the teaching chart so they will be familiar with the words *stop, spot, stand* and *stamp*.

Review **Blends**

PREPARE

Listen for Blends Read the following sentences aloud and have children raise a hand whenever they hear a word with a blend:

- The <u>skunk</u> and the <u>spider</u> are pals. They <u>jump</u> and <u>sing</u> all day.

TEACH

Review Blends
- Tell children they will review the sounds that some blends make.
- Say /sp/. Have children say and write the letters that stand for /sp/.

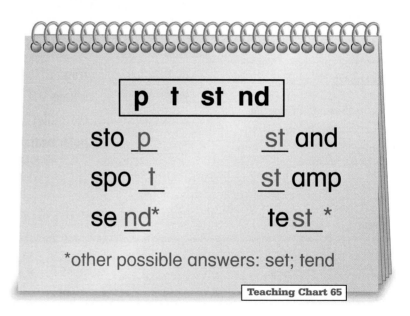

BLENDING Model and Guide Practice with Blends
- Display **Teaching Chart 65**.
- Ask children to suggest a letter from the box that you could write in the first blank space to make a word. (p) Write the letter *p* in the blank space. Then run your hand under the letters, blending them to read the word *stop*. s t o p stop
- Repeat, having children read the word with you.

Use the Word in Context Have volunteers use the word in context to reinforce its meaning. Example: *Cars stop when the light turns red.*

Repeat the Procedure Repeat the activity with the other incomplete words. Ask volunteers to choose letters to complete the words and blend the sounds together.

PRACTICE

Build and Sort Words with Letter Banks

PARTNERS

Write the following letter banks on the chalkboard, as shown:

st h l	a e i o u	ng nd mp ft nk nt

Have a volunteer choose a letter from the second bank. Write it on the chalkboard. Then ask another child to choose letters from the first and third banks to form a word. Ask children to read the word. Have pairs repeat the activity, keeping a list of words formed. Then have children sort their list of words into groups according to vowel sounds.

▶ **Visual/Linguistic**

ASSESS/CLOSE

Read Words with Blends

To assess children's mastery of reading words with blends, observe them as they form and read words in the Practice activity.

ADDITIONAL PHONICS RESOURCES

Phonics/Phonemic Awareness Practice Book
pages 117–120

PHONICS KIT
Hands-on Activities and Practice

McGraw-Hill School
TECHNOLOGY

Phonics CD-ROM
activities for practice with
Blending and Segmenting

DAILY Phonics ROUTINES

DAY 4
Writing Have children choose two words with continuant/stop blends and create a rhyming couplet with the words. Children can illustrate their rhymes.

Phonics **CD-ROM**

SPELLING/PHONICS CONNECTIONS

Words with continuant/stop blends: See 5-Day Spelling Plan, pages 37Q–37R.

i **Intervention** ▶ **Skills**
Intervention Guide, for direct instruction and extra practice in Blends

---

Meeting Individual Needs for Phonics

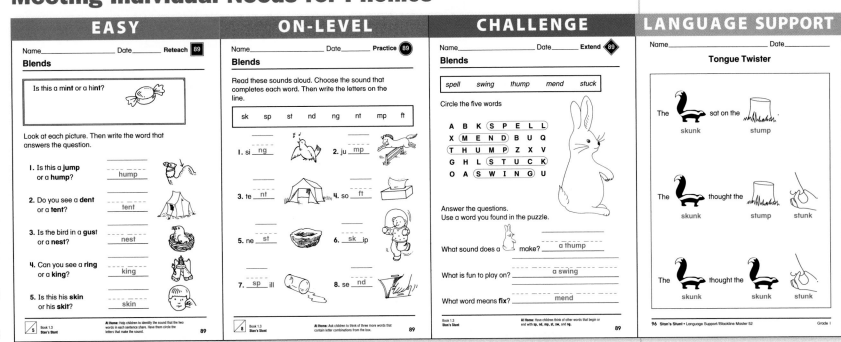

Reteach, 89   Practice, 89   Extend, 89   Language Support, 96

37F

Review **Blends**

OBJECTIVES

Children will:

- review continuant/stop blends: *sk, sp, st, ng, nd, mp.*
- review initial and final continuant/continuant blends and double consonants: *sm, sn, fl; ll, ff.*
- cumulative review: **initial and final consonants, short vowels.**

MATERIALS

- letter cards from the **Word Building Manipulative Cards**
- **Teaching Chart 66**
- **Phonics Practice Reader, Volume 1**

Skills Finder

Blends	
Introduce	B2: 96I-J; B3: 8I-J, 38I-J
Review	B2: 123G-H, B3: 37G-H, 67E-F, 67G-H, 97G-H
Test	Book 2, Book 3
Maintain	B3: 23; B4: 13

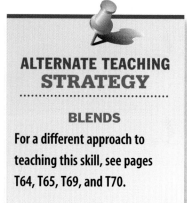

ALTERNATE TEACHING STRATEGY

BLENDS

For a different approach to teaching this skill, see pages T64, T65, T69, and T70.

PREPARE

Identify the Blend *fl* as the Symbol for /fl/ and the Blend *mp* as the Symbol for /mp/

Remind children that two letters together sometimes make a blend. Write the blends *fl* and *mp* on the chalkboard, saying them aloud. Tell children to repeat the sounds after you as you point to them. Ask children to suggest words using these blends. (Examples: *flat, camp*)

TEACH

BLENDING Model and Guide Practice with Blends and Double Consonants

- Display **Teaching Chart 66**. Explain to children that they can make words by writing one of the two blends or a double consonant in the blank space. Tell children that the other set of letters will not make a real word.

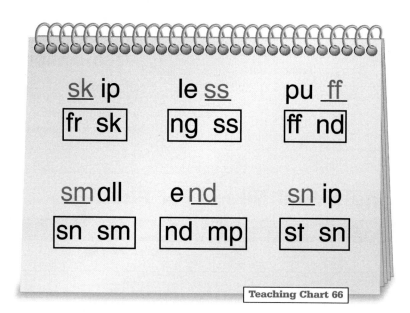

Teaching Chart 66

- Blend the first two possible words on the chart with children.

  f r i p   frip   s k i p   skip

- Ask children which is the real word. (skip)
- Have a volunteer write the blend *sk* in the blank and read the word *skip.*

Use the Word in Context

- Ask a volunteer to use the word *skip* in context to reinforce its meaning. Example: *I like to run and skip.*

Repeat the Procedure

- Continue with **Teaching Chart 66**. Have children blend the sounds aloud and tell which letters make a real word.

PRACTICE

**BLENDING
Build and Sort
Words with
Blends**

GROUP

Have children work in small groups. Have each group build as many words with *st* as possible. Repeat with *ng* and *fl*. Have groups choose two words for each blend to put on a class bulletin board under *st, ng,* or *fl.* Children should read the words they chose to check their sorting.

▶ **Visual/Linguistic**

ASSESS/CLOSE

**Draw and Label
a Picture**

Use your observations from the Practice activity to determine if children need more reinforcement with blends. Have children choose a word with *st, ng,* or *fl* and draw and label its picture.

**Read A
Decodable Story**

For additional practice reading words with continuant/stop blends and double consonants, and to develop fluency, direct children to read the story *I Would If I Could* from the **Phonics Practice Reader, Volume 1.**

DAY **5** **Letter Substitution**
Using the letter cards, have pairs of children build *bend.* Taking turns, one child is to change a letter to build a new word, asking the partner to read it.

Phonics CD-ROM

i **Intervention** ▶ **Skills**
Intervention Guide, for direct instruction and extra practice in Blends

ADDITIONAL PHONICS RESOURCES

**Phonics/Phonemic Awareness
Practice Book
pages 117–120**

PHONICS KIT
Hands-on Activities and Practice

McGraw-Hill School
TECHNOLOGY

Phonics **CD-ROM**
activities for practice with
Blending and Segmenting

Meeting Individual Needs for Phonics and Decoding

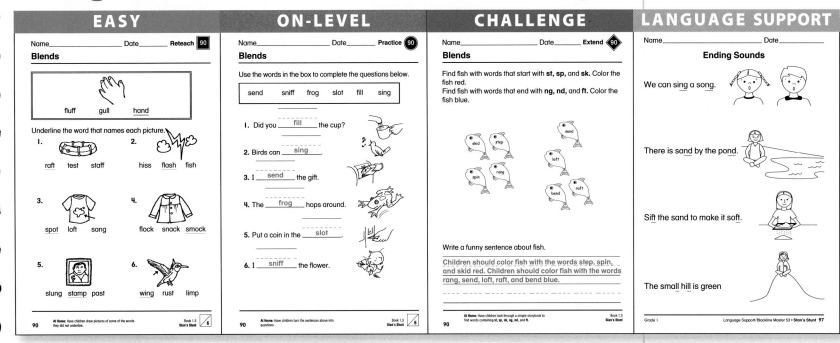

EASY	ON-LEVEL	CHALLENGE	LANGUAGE SUPPORT
Reteach, 90	Practice, 90	Extend, 90	Language Support, 97

OBJECTIVES

Children will make inferences about setting to help them better understand the story.

MATERIALS:
• **Teaching Chart 67**

Skills Finder

Story Elements

Introduce	B2: 351-J
Review	B2: 651-J, B3: 3711-J, 1251-J, 139G-H
Test	Book 2, Book 3
Maintain	B3: 89; B4: 25, 107, 109

TEACHING TIP

MANAGEMENT If children decide to draw a scene from their favorite story in the Assess/Close Activity, you might want to help them find the story book. Suggest that children work in pairs, looking through a story book together to get more ideas for their illustrations.

SELECTION CONNECTION
Reading

Children may choose from the following titles.

ANTHOLOGY

• *Stan's Stunt*

LEVELED BOOKS

• *Bat Helps Out*

• *Two Tests*

• *Walking Through the Jungle*

Bibliography, page T98–T99

371   *Stan's Stunt*

Introduce Story Elements

PREPARE

Introduce the Concept   Tell children that the setting of a story is where and when a story takes place. Explain that the setting often affects what happens in the story and how the characters feel and act.

TEACH

Identify Setting   Display **Teaching Chart 67**. Allow children to comment on the picture. Then read the chart aloud.

The leaves are falling in the forest.
Owl was sleeping.
Squirrel was busy looking for nuts.

Teaching Chart 67

MODEL   From the pictures, I know that this story is set somewhere with trees. If I read the first sentence I can tell where the story takes place—in the forest. But setting also tells about when a story takes place. I see leaves in the picture and read that they are falling, so it must be fall. I also know that the setting can affect the characters. I see and read that Squirrel is looking for nuts, which is something it must do to have enough food before winter comes.

Have children point to pictures on the **Teaching Chart** that give clues about the setting of the story.

PRACTICE

Add to the Chart

GROUP

Have children use **Teaching Chart 67** to continue drawing inferences from the setting. Suggest other topics to include in the chart, such as characters and how the setting affects them. Prompt children with questions such as:

- What time do you think it is in the story, day or night?
- What is Owl doing at this time? When do owls usually sleep?
- What other kinds of characters do you think Owl and Squirrel might meet?

Add children's answers to the chart. ▶ **Linguistic**

ASSESS/CLOSE

Story Settings Invite children to draw a scene from a favorite story, movie, or television show. Ask them to write a sentence about the setting of the story that they have chosen to illustrate.

ALTERNATE TEACHING STRATEGY

STORY ELEMENTS

For a different approach to teaching this skill, see page T67.

 **Intervention** ▶ Skills

Intervention Guide, for direct instruction and extra practice in Story Elements

---

Meeting Individual Needs for Comprehension

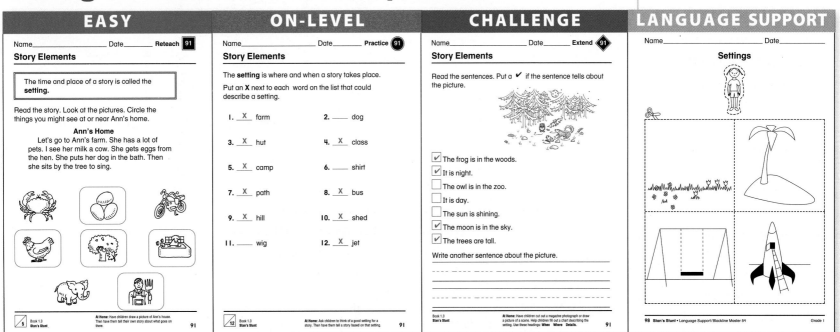

Reteach, 91   Practice, 91   Extend, 91   Language Support, 98

37J

OBJECTIVES

Children will identify and use possessive nouns, pronouns and singular possessive pronouns.

MATERIALS
• Teaching Chart 68

Skills Finder

Possessives

Introduce	B3: 37K-L
Review	B3: 67K-L, 139I-J
Test	Book 3

LANGUAGE SUPPORT

ESL For children having difficulty with possessive nouns and pronouns, expand the Practice activity by having a small group pass around a pencil or another classroom object. Have the first child say, *This is my pencil.* Then ask this child to pass the pencil to the child on his or her right and say, *This is Victor's pencil.* Ask each child to repeat both sentences as he or she passes the object.

TEACHING TIP

SINGULAR POSSESSIVE PRONOUNS Reinforce the concept of singular possessive pronouns by reminding children that a pronoun takes the place of a person, place or thing. A possessive noun tells who or what owns something. Explain that *mine, yours, hers,* and *his* are singular possessive pronouns. Point out that unlike possessive nouns, these words do not have an apostrophe.

Introduce Possessives

PREPARE

Introduce the Concept of Possessives

Have a volunteer hold up a pencil. Ask the volunteer: *Whose pencil is this?* (my pencil) Then ask the class: *Whose pencil is that?* (Maria's pencil) Write the words *my pencil* and *Maria's pencil* on the chalkboard.

TEACH

Identify Possessive Forms

Explain to children that words like *my* and *Maria's* are used to show that something belongs to someone. Display **Teaching Chart 68**. Have children identify the characters from the story before you model the use of possessive nouns and pronouns.

Teaching Chart 68

MODEL Who remembers what Stan's stunt was? Which picture shows Stan's tail? Which picture shows Bat's stunt? Let's point to the mark before the s in *Stan's* and *Bat's.* This mark is called an apostrophe. Sometimes we show that something belongs to someone by adding an apostrophe and an s after the person's name. What are Owl and Frog doing in this picture? We can also use words like *their* or *his* or *my* to show that something belongs to someone.

PRACTICE

Use of Possessives

GROUP

Have children work together in small groups. Ask them to take turns pointing at various articles of clothing they are wearing. Group members should suggest different ways of telling who owns the object or piece of clothing. Examples: Tricia's shoe, my shoe, her shoe, or your shoe. ▶ **Linguistic/Kinesthetic**

ASSESS/CLOSE

Apply the Concept of Possessives

Point at various objects in the room and ask children to identify them in various ways by using possessives. Examples: teacher's desk, Robert's thumb, her crayons. Write some of the responses on the chalkboard. As you point to examples on the chalkboard, encourage children to practice saying apostrophe -*s*.

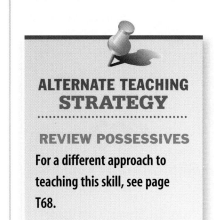

ALTERNATE TEACHING STRATEGY

REVIEW POSSESSIVES

For a different approach to teaching this skill, see page T68.

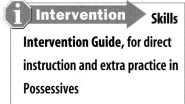

i **Intervention** ▶ **Skills Intervention Guide,** for direct instruction and extra practice in Possessives

Meeting Individual Needs for Vocabulary

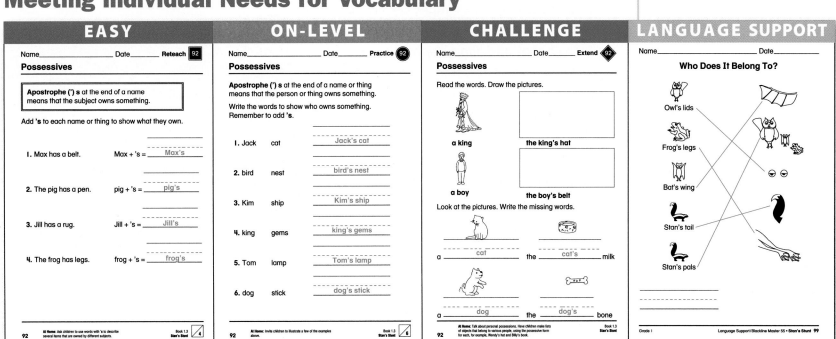

Reteach, 92   Practice, 92   Extend, 92   Language Support, 99

Handwriting CD-ROM

TEACHING TIP

Technology
If children are using computers, suggest that they proofread their work on the computer screen. That way, they can make corrections before printing out their work.

Interactive Writing

Make a Field Guide to Animal Stunts

Prewrite

LOOK AT THE STORY PATTERN Have children revisit *Stan's Stunt* and guide them to notice the language pattern of the story again. Then tell them that the class will create a field guide of animal stunts. The field guide will compare things that different animals can do. For example, children might want to write about a bee who can hum "bizz buzz, buzz bizz." List children's ideas for animals and their stunts.

Draft

WRITE ABOUT THE ANIMALS' STUNTS Help children choose one of the animals from the board list. Guide them to create a sentence about that animal's stunt, using the language pattern of *Stan's Stunt.* Use the present tense for this process.

- Begin by saying, for example, *Let's write about the rabbit. We can say that he goes hippy hoppy and hoppy hippy. Can anyone include this and tell some sentences to inform us about a rabbit's stunt?* As you say familiar sounds and patterns, challenge children to come up and write the word. Write all unfamiliar words yourself.

- Continue this process for all the animals. Guide children to compare each stunt the animals can do. (Example: *The rabbit can go hippy hoppy and hoppy hippy. But the horse can go even faster, clippety cloppety and cloppety clippety.*)

Revise

PUNCTUATION Invite children to reread their animal sentences. Remind them that every sentence must begin with a capital letter and end with the appropriate punctuation, either a period, or a question mark, or an exclamation point. Have children check to see that each sentence begins with a capital letter and has the correct punctuation.

Publish

CREATE THE FIELD GUIDE Have children take turns rereading the sentences aloud. Then have children work in groups to assemble a class book. Have children create illustrations. Then have them copy the appropriate text onto each page.

The rabbit can go hippy hoppy. The rabbit can go hoppy hippy.

Presentation Ideas

MAKE STICK PUPPETS Invite children to choose animals from the class field guide to make into stick puppets. Have them show each animal doing specific things described in the guide. ▶ **Representing/Viewing**

PERFORM ANIMAL STUNTS Have children act out different animal stunts from their guide, introducing each stunt by saying: *I can go. . . .* Then have the other children guess what animal is being represented.
▶ **Speaking/Viewing**

Meeting Individual Needs for Writing

EASY

Draw Pictures Children can draw pictures of themselves performing stunts. Have them label their pictures, following language patterns from *Stan's Stunt.*

ON-LEVEL

Write a Story Using Comparison Children can work in pairs to compare animals and tell what happens when they perform each other's stunts. Have them follow the language pattern of *Stan's Stunt.*

CHALLENGE

Journal Entry Children can write a journal entry about the usefulness of different animals' stunts. Have them compare two animals and write about what would happen if they switched stunts.

5 Day Grammar and Usage Plan

DAY 1 — Introduce the Concept

Oral Warm-Up Write the following words on the chalkboard and read them aloud with the children: *run, nap, jump, kick, blink.*

Introduce Verbs Remind children that a sentence is a group of words that tells a complete thought. These words have special names. One kind of word is called a *verb.* Discuss with children:

> **Verbs**
>
> A **verb** is a word that shows action.

Daily Language Activity Write the following sentence on the chalkboard: *Stan runs to the bus.* Ask children to find the word that shows action. (*runs*)

Write the following sentence and have children find the action word and identify it as a verb: *Owl hugs the doll.* (*hugs*)

WRITING Assign daily Writing Prompt on page 8E.

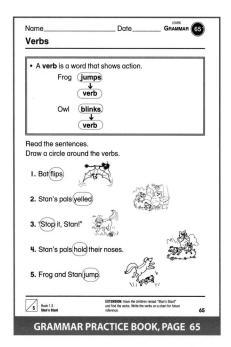

GRAMMAR PRACTICE BOOK, PAGE 65

DAY 2 — Teach the Concept

Review Verbs Remind children that yesterday they learned about words that show action. Write the following sentence on the chalkboard: *Frog jumps on the log.* Read the sentence aloud, asking children to read with you. Ask children to find the verb. (*jumps*)

Daily Language Activity Write the following on the chalkboard: *Frog swims to the stump. Bat packs for the trip.* Read aloud with children and have them identify the action word in each sentence.

WRITING Assign the daily Writing Prompt on page 8E.

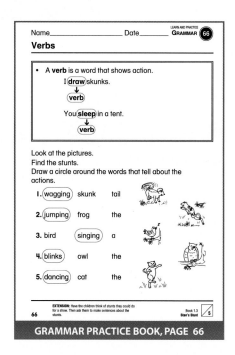

GRAMMAR PRACTICE BOOK, PAGE 66

Verbs

DAY 3 — Review and Practice

Learn from the Literature Review with children what verbs are. Write the following sentences from *Stan's Stunt* on the chalkboard:

> Stan wagged and wagged his tail.
>
> Stan's pals sniffed and sniffed.

Ask children to identify the action words. (*wagged, sniffed*)

Daily Language Activity Have children brainstorm a list of verbs from *Stan's Stunt*, and record their answers on the chalkboard. Then have them write a sentence containing one of the verbs.

 Assign the daily Writing Prompt on page 8F.

GRAMMAR PRACTICE BOOK, PAGE 67

DAY 4 — Review and Practice

Review Verbs Write the following sentence on the chalkboard: *Pig digs and kicks.* Ask children to identify the action words. (*digs, kicks*)

Daily Language Activity Ask children to come to the chalkboard and underline the verbs in the following sentence: *Pig taps and naps.* (*taps, naps*) Then have children use the verbs to form sentences orally.

Mechanics and Usage Before children begin the daily Writing Prompt on page 8F, review and discuss comma placement in a letter.

> **Commas**
> - Use a comma after the greeting in a letter.
> - Use a comma after the closing in a letter.

 Assign the daily Writing Prompt on page 8F.

GRAMMAR PRACTICE BOOK, PAGE 68

DAY 5 — Assess and Reteach

Daily Language Activity Write these sentences on the chalkboard. Read them with children. Have children identify the verbs in each sentence.

1. Mack packs the van. *packs*

2. Jack hits the ball. *hits*

3. The little cat sits. *sits*

Assess Use page 69 of the **Grammar Practice Book** for assessment.

Reteach Prepare word cards for each sentence presented on Days 1 through 5. Give each group one set. Have them identify the verbs in each sentence.

Use page 70 of the **Grammar Practice Book** for additional reteaching.

Assign the daily Writing Prompt on page 8F.

GRAMMAR PRACTICE BOOK, PAGE 69

5 Day Spelling Plan

DAY 1 — Introduce Spelling Words

Assess Prior Knowledge Write the word *jump* on the chalkboard. Circle the *m* and the *p* and ask children what sound each letter makes. Point out that the two sounds come together at the end of the word. Pronounce the word slowly and have children repeat it. Then repeat the exercise with the other Spelling Words, focusing on the final /mp/, final /nt/, or initial /sp/ in each word.

Write the Challenge Words on the chalkboard and read them aloud, having children repeat after you. Invite children to use the words in sentences.

Spelling Words		Challenge Words	
1. **bump**	4. spill	7. try	9. their
2. **jump**	5. tent	8. fall	10. would
3. **went**	6. spell		

*Note: Words in **dark type** are from the story.*

Word Study On page 66 of the **Spelling Practice Book** are word study steps and an at-home activity.

Name_____ Date_____ SPELLING 65

Words with Blends

Complete each word by writing the letters **mp**, **nt**, or **sp** on the line.

1. bu **mp**   2. we **nt**

3. **sp** ill   4. ju **mp**

5. te **nt**   6. **sp** ell

Directions (to teacher)

Write the word *bump* on the chalkboard or form the word with letter cards. Say the word aloud and have children repeat it. Have them listen for the sounds /m/ and /p/ together at the end of the word. Then have them look at the first example. Point out that *mp* has been filled in.

Display the word *went*. Say the word and have children repeat it. Ask them to listen for the two sounds at the end of the word (/n/ and /t/). Have them complete the second example.

Display the word *spill* and repeat the process above, having students listen for the sounds at the beginning of the word (/s/ and /p/). Have them complete the third example.

Then display the words *jump, tent,* and *spell.* Say the words and have children repeat them. Have children listen for /mp/, /nt/, or /sp/ in each word. Then have them complete the page.

Book 1.3
Stan's Stunt

65

SPELLING PRACTICE BOOK, PAGE 65

WORD STUDY STEPS AND ACTIVITY, PAGE 66

DAY 2 — Teach the Pattern

Match the Patterns Write two columns of words on the chalkboard, the first containing *bump, went, spill,* the second *jump, spell, tent.* Invite children to draw lines connecting words that have the same sound either at the end or at the beginning. Ask children to say and circle the sound that is the same.

To extend the activity, display the following word cards and have volunteers put them in the group that shows the same pattern: *lamp, hint, spent, pump, spot, spin.* Ask them to identify a word that shows two of the patterns.

Name_____ Date_____ SPELLING 67

Words with Blends

Look at the spelling words in the box.

tent bump spell jump spill went

Write the words that end with **mp**.

1. bump   2. jump

Write the words that end with **nt**.

3. went   4. tent

Write the words that begin with **sp**.

5. spill   6. spell

Book 1.3
Stan's Stunt

67

SPELLING PRACTICE BOOK, PAGE 67

Words with Blends

Word Meaning: Endings Write the words *bump, jump, spill, spell* on the chalkboard. Read the words and have children repeat them after you. Tell them that these are action words and that sometimes an *-s* ending is added to them. Have students write each word, adding the *-s* ending. Then have them use the new words in sentences. Give an example such as, *The boy bumps his head.*

Identify Spelling Patterns Write this sentence on the chalkboard: *Would you like to try to sleep in their tent?* Ask children to read the sentence aloud, raising their hands when they read a word with the spelling pattern *nt* and snapping their fingers when they hear a **Challenge Word**. Repeat for the sentence, *She would try not to bump her head when she went into the tent.*

Match the Pattern Make a list of words on the chalkboard: *went, spell, bump, spill, tent, jump.* Ask children to repeat the words as you read them, and to listen to ending sounds of each word. List spelling patterns *-mp, -nt, sp* beside the words and ask children to say the words that match each pattern. Invite volunteers to draw lines to match patterns with words.

Have children use as many spelling words as possible in the daily Writing Prompt on page 8D. Remind them to check their writing for errors in spelling, grammar, and punctuation.

Optional Spelling Test You may wish to give children a spelling test. You may administer it in the following manner: (1) Read the word. (2) Give a simple sentence containing the word. (3) Say the word again. Or you may use page 70 of the **Spelling Practice Book** for the posttest. If you wish, you may create additional sentences for the Challenge Words.

Personal Word List Have children add the words they still find difficult to their lists of troublesome words in their journals. Have children draw and label an illustration for each word. Children should refer to these word lists during later writing activities.

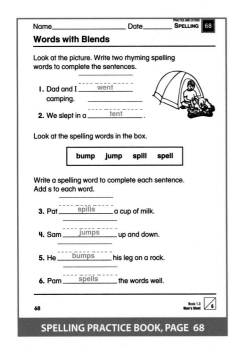

SPELLING PRACTICE BOOK, PAGE 68

SPELLING PRACTICE BOOK, PAGE 69

SPELLING PRACTICE BOOK, PAGE 70

37R

Concept
- **Sibling Relations**

Comprehension
- **Compare and Contrast**

Phonics
- **Blends**

Vocabulary
- **any**
- **new**
- **old**
- **grow**

Anthology

Greg's Mask

Selection Summary Relations between Greg and his sister Tam break down when she lets a bad mood get the best of her. As these siblings work out their differences, children may find they have similar stories to share from their own lives.

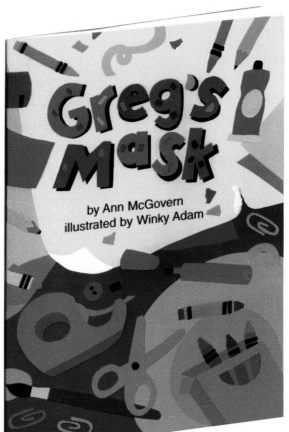

by Ann McGovern
illustrated by Winky Adam

Listening Library

Drips! Drops!

Drip, drop, it is wet.
The drops are small and big.
Brett and Glen slip and slop
As they play and dig.

Drip, drop, it is wet.
The drops are big and loud.
Brett and Glen wait for the sun
To drag away the cloud.

Rhyme applies to Phonics

INSTRUCTIONAL pages 40–67

About the Author   When Ann McGovern was a little girl, she was so shy that she never raised her hand in class. "I became a writer to express the feelings that I couldn't speak out," she says. Ms. McGovern is now the well-known author of several children's books.

About the Illustrator   Winky Adam is an author and illustrator of children's books. "I knew I wanted to create children's books since I was in the third grade," she says. Ms. Adam spends a lot of time with children, because they give her ideas for her drawings.

Leveled Books

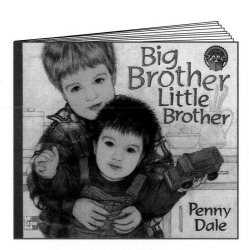

EASY
Lesson on pages 67A and 67D
DECODABLE

INDEPENDENT
Lesson on pages 67B and 67D
🏠 *Take-Home version available*
DECODABLE

CHALLENGE
Lesson on pages 67C and 67D

Leveled Practice

EASY
Reteach, 93-100 Blackline masters with reteaching opportunities for each assessed skill

INDEPENDENT/ON-LEVEL
Practice, 93-100 Workbook with Take-Home Stories and practice opportunities for each assessed skill and story comprehension

CHALLENGE
Extend, 93-100 Blackline masters that offer challenge activities for each assessed skill

Quizzes Prepared by 📊 **Accelerated Reader**

Center Activities

Social Studies . . . Career Notes, *38D*

Everyday Emotions, *48*

Science . . . . Animal Facts, *38D*

Animal Groups, *56*

Math . . . . Shape Faces, *58*

Language Arts . . Read Aloud, *38G*

Cultural Perspectives . . . . . Masks, *50*

Writing . . . . A Poster, *64*

Research and Inquiry . . . . . . Find Out More, *65*

Internet Activities . . . . www.mhschool.com/reading

 # Center Activities

 Each of these activities takes 15–20 minutes.

Phonics

Blend Search

PARTNERS **Objective:** Write words with *pl*, *dr*, *sl*, and *cl*.

◆ Have partners write *pl*, *dr*, *sl*, *cl* and look through *Greg's Mask* for words that begin with each blend.

◆ Then children write the word, say it, and underline the two letters that make up the blend.

MATERIALS
- *Greg's Mask* in the Student Anthology
- Pencil

Writing

Cast of Characters

GROUP **Objective:** Write names for the characters in a skit.

◆ Have children look at the picture on pages 56 and 57 that shows all seven animal masks.

◆ Encourage children to identify each animal and make up funny names for them, such as Pinky Pig.

◆ Children may write their funny names.

MATERIALS
- *Greg's Mask* in the Student Anthology
- Paper
- Pencil

Reading and Listening

Independent/Self-Selected Reading

ONE **Objective:** Listen and use illustrations to understand a story.

Fill the Center with books and corresponding audiocassettes or CD-ROMs children have read or listened to this week. You can also include books from the Theme Bibliography on pages T98 and T99.

Leveled Readers

◆ *Kent and Glen* by Anne Miranda
◆ *Dig for Clams* by Della Cohen
◆ *Big Brother LIttle Brother* by Penny Dale

◆ Theme Big Book *I Go with My Family to Grandma's* by Riki Levinson

◆ *Greg's Mask* by Ann McGovern

◆ "Something About Me"—Anonymous

◆ Phonics Practice Reader, Vol. 1

Working with Words

Find It and Read It

ONE **Objective:** Reinforce vocabulary words: *any, new, grow, old*.

- Have children use sticky notes to mark sentences in the story that include the vocabulary words.

- Children can then record themselves reading the story sentences.

MATERIALS
- *Greg's Mask* **in the Student Anthology**
- **Sticky notes**
- **Tape recorder**

Social Studies

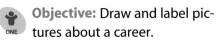

Career Notes

ONE **Objective:** Draw and label pictures about a career.

- Write this story sentence on mural paper: *I just may do this when I grow up!*

- Have children draw pictures of themselves in jobs they'd like to do when they grow up.

- Children can write a sentence about their picture.

MATERIALS
- **Mural paper**
- **Crayons**

Science

Animal Facts

PARTNERS **Objective:** Write facts about an animal.

- Have partners work together to draw a picture of one of the animals in *Greg's Mask*.

- Then the partners write a sentence that gives information about that animal.

- Suggest that children write the sentence from the animal's point of view—something that the animal would tell about itself!

MATERIALS
- **Drawing paper**
- **Crayons**

I like to swim in a pond.

Greg's Mask
by Ann McGovern
illustrated by Winky Adam

Suggested Lesson Planner

READING AND LANGUAGE ARTS	DAY 1 — Focus on Reading and Skills	DAY 2 — Read the Literature
Phonics Daily Routines	Daily **Phonics** Routine: **Rhyming, 38J** **Phonics** CD-ROM	Daily **Phonics** Routine: **Blending, 40A** **Phonics** CD-ROM
Phonological Awareness **Phonics** *Blends* **Comprehension** **Vocabulary** **Study Skills** **Listening, Speaking, Viewing, Representing**	**Read** **Read Aloud,** 38G "Making Faces" ☑ **Develop Phonological Awareness,** 38H ☑ **Introduce Blends,** 38I–38J **Reteach, Practice, Extend,** 93 **Phonics/Phonemic Awareness Practice Book,** 121–124 **Read** **Apply Blends** "Drips! Drops!" 38/39 ℹ️ Intervention Program	**Build Background,** 40A Develop Oral Language **Vocabulary,** 40B–40C any · new grow · old **Word Building Manipulative Cards** **Teaching Chart 69** **Reteach, Practice, Extend,** 94 **Read** **Read the Selection,** 40–63 **Guided Instruction** ☑ Blends ☑ Story Elements **Genre: Story,** 41 **Cultural Perspectives,** 50 **Writer's Craft,** 60 ℹ️ Intervention Program
Curriculum Connections	**Link** Language Arts, 38G	**Link** Social Studies, 40A
Writing	✏️ **Writing Prompt:** Write about a brother or a sister. The brother or sister may be real or imaginary. Tell what you like about him or her.	✏️ **Writing Prompt:** Imagine that you are putting on a play in school. Tell what the play is about and who your characters are. 📔 **Journal Writing** Quick-Write, 63
Grammar	**Introduce the Concept: Present Tense,** 67O Daily Language Activity: Identify the word that shows present action. **Grammar Practice Book,** 71	**Teach the Concept: Present Tense,** 67O Daily Language Activity: Identify present-tense verbs. **Grammar Practice Book,** 72
Spelling *Blends*	**Introduce Spelling Words: Words with Blends,** 67Q **Spelling Practice Book,** 71–72	**Teach the Patterns: Words with Blends,** 67Q **Spelling Practice Book,** 73

Meeting Individual Needs

 = Skill Assessed in Unit Test

 Intervention Program Available

Read EVERY DAY

DAY 3 — *Read the Literature*

DAY 4 — *Build Skills*

DAY 5 — *Build Skills*

DAY 3

Daily **Phonics** Routine:
Writing, 65

 **Phonics CD-ROM**

Reread for Fluency, 62

Story Questions, 64
Reteach, Practice, Extend, 95

Story Activities, 65

Study Skill, 66
☑ Diagrams

Teaching Chart 70
Reteach, Practice, Extend, 96

 Read the Leveled Books, Guided Reading
☑ Blends
☑ Story Elements
☑ High-Frequency Words

 Intervention Program

Activity Social Studies, 38D, 48

 Writing Prompt: Pretend you are wearing a mask. Write about how your friends act when they see you.

Journal Writing, 67D

Practice and Write: Present Tense, 67P
Daily Language Activity: Identify present-tense verbs in sentences.

Grammar Practice Book, 73

Practice and Extend: Words with Blends, 67R

Spelling Practice Book, 74

DAY 4

Daily **Phonics** Routine:
Letter Substitution, 67F

 **Phonics CD-ROM**

 Read the Leveled Books and the Self-Selected Books

☑ **Review Blends,** 67E–67F
Teaching Chart 71
Reteach, Practice, Extend, 97
Language Support, 105
Phonics/Phonemic Awareness
Practice Book, 121–124

☑ **Review Blends,** 67G–67H
Teaching Chart 72
Reteach, Practice, Extend, 98
Language Support, 106
Phonics/Phonemic Awareness
Practice Book, 121–124

Minilessons, 43, 47, 49, 51, 53, 57, 59, 61

Intervention Program

Activity Science, 38D, 56

Writing Prompt: Write about a book you have read with a brother and sister in it.

Interactive Writing: Make a Chart, 67M
Prewrite, Draft

Meeting Individual Needs for Writing, 67N

Practice and Write: Present Tense, 67P
Daily Language Activity: Identify present-tense verbs in sentences.

Grammar Practice Book, 74

Practice and Write: Words with Blends, 67R

Spelling Practice Book, 75

DAY 5

Daily **Phonics** Routine:
Fluency, 67H

 **Phonics CD-ROM**

 Read Self-Selected Books

☑ **Introduce Compare and Contrast,** 67I–67J
Teaching Chart 73
Reteach, Practice, Extend, 99
Language Support, 107

☑ **Review Possessives,** 67K–67L
Teaching Chart 74
Reteach, Practice, Extend, 100
Language Support, 108

Listening, Speaking, Viewing, Representing, 67N
Make the Masks
Perform an Animal Pantomime

Minilessons, 43, 47, 49, 51, 53, 57, 59, 61

 Intervention Program

Activity Math, 58

Writing Prompt: Pretend you are having an argument with your brother, sister, or a friend. Write about how you solve it.

Interactive Writing: Make a Chart, 67M
Revise, Publish

Assess and Reteach: Present Tense, 67P
Daily Language Activity: Identify and use present-tense verbs.

Grammar Practice Book, 75–76

Assess and Reteach: Words with Blends, 67R

Spelling Practice Book, 76

Link
Language Arts

Read Aloud

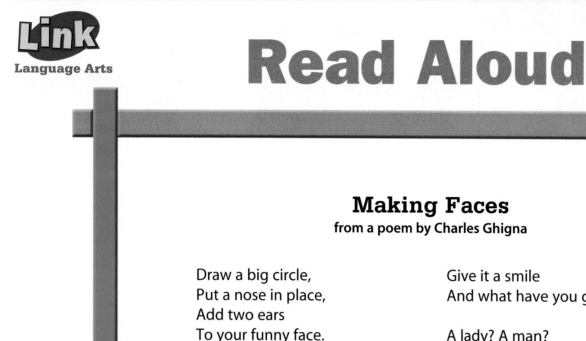

Making Faces
from a poem by Charles Ghigna

Draw a big circle,
Put a nose in place,
Add two ears
To your funny face.

Long hair, short hair
On its head?
Black hair, blond hair,
Brown or red?

Blue eyes, brown eyes,
Glasses or not,

Give it a smile
And what have you got?

A lady? A man?
A boy or a girl?
A bald-headed daddy?
A baby with a curl?

Look at the face
That you drew.
Now look in the mirror—
Is it you?

Oral Comprehension

LISTENING AND SPEAKING Motivate children to think about imagery by reading this poem about faces. Have children picture the faces as you read. When you are done, ask: "What is the poem about? Are there any things about faces that were left out of the poem?" Then have children think about the end of the poem. Say: "Suppose you drew a face without thinking. Do you think it would look like you? Why or why not?"

Activity Have children work in small groups to make a poster of faces. Ask children to take turns drawing parts of each face. Remind children that they can use the poem to think of ways that they can make each face different.
▶ **Visual**

GENRE STUDY: POEM Point out how poems are often organized into stanzas, or parts. Discuss with children how the lines of this poem are arranged. Ask volunteers to name the rhyming words at the end of the lines in each stanza. Point out the rhyming pattern. The second and fourth lines in each stanza rhyme. Explain that the rhyming words in the poem help create a rhythm. Read the poem aloud again, emphasizing the rhythm and stressing the rhyming words.

Develop Phonological Awareness

Blend Sounds

MATERIALS
- classroom objects

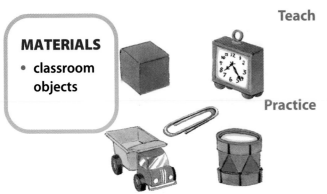

Teach Tell children you will point to an object and say the sounds that make up its name. Point to the block and say: *Listen carefully to these sounds—/b/-/l/-/o/-/k/.* Ask children to blend the sounds together to form the word. (*block*) Repeat with the word *drum*.

Practice Say the sounds for the names of the other classroom objects: *clock, clip, truck.* Have children blend the sounds to say each word. Repeat with additional words: *last, bend, clack, cliff, raft, drag, dress, plot, hint, trap, trick,* and *flag.*

Segment Sounds

MATERIALS
- four colored blocks

Teach Say the word *trap.* Then ask children to listen as you say each of the four sounds: /t/-/r/-/a/-/p/. Point to a block for each sound. Have children say the word and the sounds with you.

Practice Distribute four blocks to each child. Have children practice segmenting sounds in the following words: *plot, end, clam, list, grab, trim, plum, trick, slam,* and *sent.* First, have children say the word. Then have them point to a block as they say each sound in the word. Then have them say the number of sounds in the word.

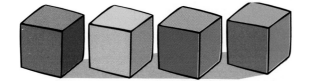

Substitute Sounds

MATERIALS
- puppet

Teach Tell children to listen as the puppet says a word and then makes a new word by changing the ending sound. Have the puppet say: *Listen to this word—*trick. *I can take the /k/ sound off the end of* trick *and add the /p/ sound: /t/-/r/-/i/-/p/. What is the new word?* (trip)

Practice Continue working with the puppet to create more new words. Use the following word sets: *clam, clap; drill, drip; plug, plum; track, trap; grin, grill.*

INFORMAL ASSESSMENT Observe children as they blend sounds, segment sounds, and substitute final sounds. If children have difficulty, see Alternate Teaching Strategies on page T69.

38H

ⓋBJECTIVES

Children will:

- identify stop/continuant blends: *bl, cl, cr, dr, gl, pl, tr,* and *tw.*

- blend letters and read words with blends.

- review short *a, i, o, u;* digraphs *sh, ck;* double consonants *ss.*

MATERIALS

- letter cards from the **Word Building Manipulative Cards**

Skills Finder

Blends

Introduce	B2: 96I-J, B3:8I-J, 38I-J
Review	B2: 123G-H; B3: 37E-F, 67E-F, 67G-H, 97G-H
Test	Book 2, Book 3
Maintain	B3: 23; B4: 13

SPELLING/PHONICS
CONNECTIONS

Words with blends: see 5-Day Spelling Plan, pages 67Q–67R.

TEACHING **TIP**

MULTISYLLABIC

WORDS Say the words *ship, putting, having,* and *worked.* Ask children how many syllables or parts each word has. Help children understand that a syllable is a part of a word that includes a vowel sound. Write each word on the board and put a dot under the vowels. Continue with other words.

Introduce Blends

Identify Stop/Continuant Blends Explain to children that they are going to blend the letters *d* and *r*.

- Display the *d* and *r* letter cards.

d r

BLENDING Model and Guide Practice with Stop/Continuant Blends

- Blend the sounds /d/ and /r/ and have children repeat the sounds after you.

d r   d r

- Point to the letters *d* and *r* and say /dr/. Have children repeat after you.

- Place the *i* and *p* letter cards after the *d* and *r* letter cards.

- Using the short vowel /i/ sound and the /p/ sound, blend the sounds together and say *drip*. Have children repeat after you.

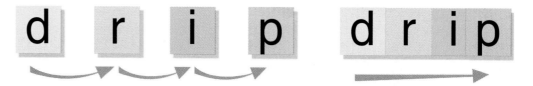

Use the Word in Context
- Use the word in context to reinforce its meaning. Example: *Did the paint drip?*

Repeat the Procedure
- Use the following words to continue modeling and guided practice with stop/continuant blends.

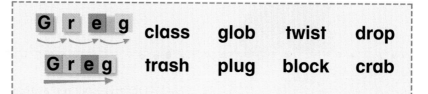

G r e g	class	glob	twist	drop
G r e g	trash	plug	block	crab

38I   *Greg's Mask*

PRACTICE

LETTER SUBSTITUTION Build Words with Stop/Continuant Blends

PARTNERS

Replace the *i* letter card with *o* to build the word *drop*. Blend the sounds together. Have children repeat after you. Encourage children to build *cl, gl, pl, tr,* and *dr* words with their letter cards. Have children make a list of the words they form. ▶ **Linguistic/Kinesthetic**

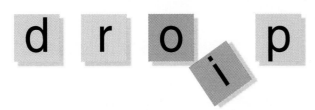

ASSESS/CLOSE

Read and Write Words with Blends

To assess children's ability to blend and read words with stop/continuant blends, have them point to and read two of the words from the Practice activity.

ADDITIONAL PHONICS RESOURCES

Phonics/Phonemic Awareness Practice Book, pages 122–124

PHONICS KIT
Hands-on Activities and Practice

McGraw-Hill School **TECHNOLOGY**

Phonics CD-ROM
activities for practice with Blending and Segmenting

Meeting Individual Needs for Phonics

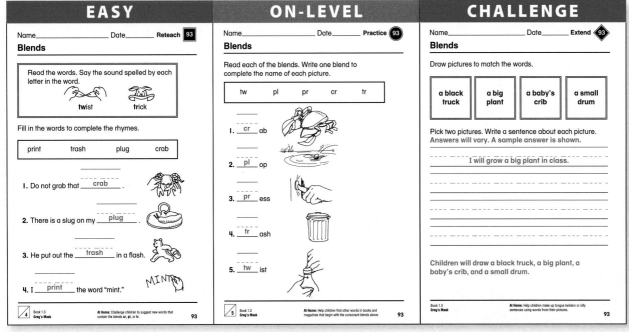

Reteach, 93   Practice, 93   Extend, 93

Daily Routines

DAY 1
Rhyming Say the word *slip*. Ask children to say other words that rhyme with *slip*. Continue with the word *drop*.

DAY 2
Blending Write the word *snap*. Say it aloud asking children to repeat after you. Ask children to blend the sounds as they read the word. Repeat with the words *clap, twist, trash*.

DAY 3
Writing Invite children to write two short sentences in which they use words with *dr, gr, cl, bl,* and *tr*. Examples: *Drop the ball. Clap your hands.*

DAY 4
Letter Substitution Have children substitute blends to make a new word. For example: *drip/flip, clap/snap,* and *drop/plop*.

DAY 5
Fluency Write the words *trick, plum, blot, crash* on the chalkboard. Point to each word and ask children to blend the sounds silently. Then have children read each word aloud.

38J

TESTED
OBJECTIVES

Children will read a poem
with words containing
blends.

Apply **Blends**

Drips! Drops!

Drip, drop, it is wet.
The drops are small and big.
Brett and Glen slip and slop
As they play and dig.

Drip, drop, it is wet.
The drops are big and loud.
Brett and Glen wait for the sun
To drag away the cloud.

38   39

Anthology pages 38–39

Read and Build Fluency

READ THE POEM Tell children they will read a poem
called *Drips! Drops!* Model reading as you stress the alliterative words *drips* and *drops*. Use your finger to track print.
Show that a period signals a pause. Then have children
read with you.

REREAD FOR FLUENCY Have children work in pairs to
reread the poem. Have them alternate reading
each stanza. Tell them to read their
PARTNERS lines with lots of expression.

READ A DECODABLE STORY For
additional practice reading and to develop
fluency, have children read the story *The
Twins' Tricks* from **Phonics Practice Reader, Vol. 1.**

Dictate and Spell

DICTATE WORDS Segment the word *drips* into its five
individual sounds. Emphasize the consonant blend
JOURNAL *dr.* Repeat the word aloud and use it in a sentence:
The rain drips on the ground. Then have children say the
word and write the letter or letters that represent each
sound until they make the entire word. Repeat with *drag,
drop, Brett,* and *Glen* from the poem. Then repeat with
other words such as *clap, click, clock, club, drill, drum, dress,
plug,* and *plus.*

i Intervention ▶ **Skills Intervention Guide,** for
direct instruction and extra practice in Blends

Build Background

Link

Social Studies

Concept: Sibling Relations

Evaluate Prior Knowledge

CONCEPT: SIBLING RELATIONS Ask children if they have sisters or brothers, or if they have friends with sisters and brothers. Invite children to talk about what it is like to have sisters and brothers.

MAKE A WORD WEB FOR SIBLINGS

Work with children to develop a word web that records aspects of sibling relationships. Children will probably answer a question such as, "Do you and your sister or brother go places together?" with specifics such as, "My sister and I went to the park." Help them generalize their answers by asking questions such as, "Where else have you and your sister gone?" "Are you saying that you go places together? Should I write that in the web?"

▶ **Linguistic**

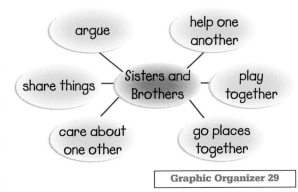

argue

help one another

share things

Sisters and Brothers

play together

care about one other

go places together

Graphic Organizer 29

DRAW A PICTURE OF SIBLINGS

WRITING **ONE** Encourage children to draw a picture of two siblings doing something together. Ask children to write a word or phrase to tell about their picture.

Develop Oral Language

CONNECT WORDS AND ACTIONS

ESL Encourage children to act out the elements listed on the word web to better understand the relationship between brothers and sisters. If possible, try to pair children with lower English proficiencies with partners of native or near native fluency. Ask questions such as:

• What are you doing?

• Are you angry or happy?

• Are you excited?

▶ **Kinesthetic/Linguistic**

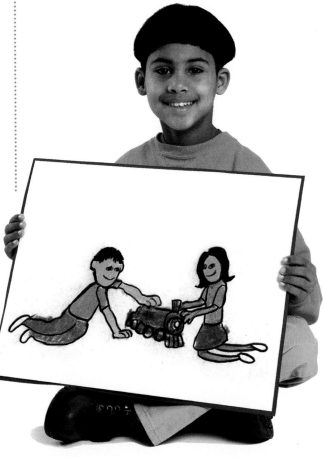

LANGUAGE SUPPORT

To build more background, see pages 100–103 in the **Language Support Book.**

DAILY Phonics ROUTINES

DAY 2 **Blending** Write the word *snap*. Say it aloud, asking children to repeat after you. Ask children to blend the sounds as they read the word. Repeat with the words *clasp*, *twist*, and *trash*.

Phonics CD-ROM

40A

Children will:

- identify high-frequency words *old*, *any*, *grow*, and *new*.

MATERIALS

- Teaching Chart 69
- Word Building Manipulative Cards *old*, *any*, *grow*, *new*

TEACHING TIP

The following chart indicates words from the upcoming story that children have learned to decode, as well as the high-frequency words that have been taught in this lesson. As children read, observe any difficulty they may have in reading the words.

Decodable		High-Frequency
Greg	twist	any
Greg's	drip	new
class	drop	old
glob	clip	grow
trash		

SPELLING/VOCABULARY CONNECTIONS

The words *old*, *grow*, *any*, and *new* are Challenge Words. See page 67Q for Day 1 of the 5-Day Spelling Plan.

---

old

any

grow

new

Vocabulary
High-Frequency Words

My Brothers

I am not as (old) as Brad.

And that gets me very mad.

I am not a tot like Ken.

And that gets me mad again.

I wish to (grow) up big and tall.

Or I wish to be so small.

(Any) size at all will do,

Just as long as it is (new.)

Teaching Chart 69

Auditory

LISTEN TO WORDS Without displaying it, read aloud "My Brothers" on **Teaching Chart 69**. Ask children to imagine how the child in the poem felt. Discuss their ideas.

TELL STORIES WITH HIGH-FREQUENCY WORDS

- Say aloud a high-frequency word. Read the line of the poem where the word appears.

- Ask volunteers to pretend they're Brad or Ken. Have them make up a sentence using the high-frequency word. They may tell how they feel about the child in the poem, or how they feel about each other.

- Repeat this activity with each of the high-frequency words.

Visual

TEACH WORDS Display "My Brothers" on **Teaching Chart 69**. Read the poem, tracking the print with your finger. Next, point to and say the word *old*. Ask them to hold up the vocabulary card for *old* and say the word. Repeat this procedure for *any*, *grow*, and *new*.

Hold up vocabulary cards for *old*, *any*, *grow*, and *new* one at a time. Have volunteers read the words and then circle them on the chart.

Word Building Manipulative Cards

READ AND ACT Divide the class into groups of three. Have one member of each group be the "middle" child. Have the "older" and "younger" siblings write the high-frequency words on the chalkboard, as the "middle" child reads the poem.

 **Activities**

Word Wall

Listen for the First Letter
Tell children that you are going to say sentences in which the first word of each sentence begins with the same letter(s) and sound as one of their word wall words. Encourage children to write the correct word on a piece of paper.

Anyone can come to my party. (any)

Open the milk carefully. (old)

Grapes are a tasty snack. (grow)

Nuts can be a crunchy treat. (new)

Be a Cheerleader
Say a cheer for each word wall word, such as: Give me an "A." (a) Give me an "n." (n) Give me an "y." (y) What word do you have? (any) Repeat for each word wall word.

LANGUAGE SUPPORT

To help children develop understanding and recognition of high-frequency words, see page 100 in the **Language Support Book.**

Assess

Write the Missing Word
Read aloud the following sentences. Ask children to write the word wall word that completes the sentence on a piece of paper.

1. *My _____ shoes are dirty.* (old)

2. *This tree will _____ to be taller than our house.* (grow)

3. *We went shopping for a _____ shirt.* (new)

4. *Do you have _____ sharp pencils?* (any)

Meeting Individual Needs for Vocabulary

EASY	ON-LEVEL	ON-LEVEL	CHALLENGE

EASY

Name_____ Date_____ Reteach **94**

High-Frequency Words

Read the story. Then circle the word that completes each sentence.

Jan's dog is very old.
He sits in the garden.
Jan just got him a new hat.
He watches the plants grow.
Are there any dog snacks left?
Jan wants to bring him one.

The dog is very ___ .
young (old) sick

He just got a ___ hat.
(new) bad pink

The dog likes to watch the plants ___ .
lick run (grow)

Jan asks if there are ___ snacks.
(any) old from

94 At Home: Invite children to write new sentences for each of the words. Book 1.3 Greg's Mask

ON-LEVEL

Name_____ Date_____ Practice **94**

High-Frequency Words

Read each sentence. Circle the word that completes the sentence. Then write the word.

| new | old | any | grow |

_____

1. I need __new__ pants. (new) any

2. Do you have __any__ red pants? (any) grow

3. My __old__ pants have a rip. any (old)

4. I want to __grow__ very tall. new (grow)

94 At Home: Ask children to write sentences using each of the high-frequency words. Book 1.3 Greg's Mask

ON-LEVEL

The Trash Plant

Bob put a new bat in the plant. "No," said the man. "New things are still good. We can use them again."
"Good idea!" said Bob.

At Home: Have children name other things that might end up in a trash plant.

94a

CHALLENGE

Name_____ Date_____ Extend **94**

High-Frequency Words

Work with a partner.
Open a toy shop.
Make signs for your shop.
Use words from the box.

| any | new | old | grow |

Signs will vary. Samples are shown.
Write your signs here.

Any toy pig in shop 25¢

New Doll 50¢

Old Truck 10¢

Toy Dog That Grows 60¢

You will need: card , glue , sticks ,
markers . Write one sign on each card.
Glue a stick to the back of each card.

94 At Home: Encourage children to make storage labels for shelves and drawer fronts using the words on this page and others. Book 1.3 Greg's Mask

Reteach, 94   **Practice, 94**   **Practice, 94a** **Take-Home Story**   **Extend, 94**

40C

Comprehension

Prereading Strategies

PREVIEW AND PREDICT Point to the author's name, Ann McGovern, and read it aloud. Ask children what the author does. Then point to the illustrator's name, Winky Adam. Ask what the illustrator does. Next, take a **picture walk** with children. Flip through the pages of the story and discuss the illustrations, looking for clues about the plot and the characters. After discussing the illustrations, have children make predictions about what will happen in the story. Record children's predictions about the plot, characters, and setting.

PREDICTIONS	WHAT HAPPENED
Greg will make a mask.	
Greg is angry at his sister.	

SET PURPOSES Ask children what they want to find out as they read the story. For example:

• What kind of mask does Greg make?

• Why is he angry?

• What happens at school?

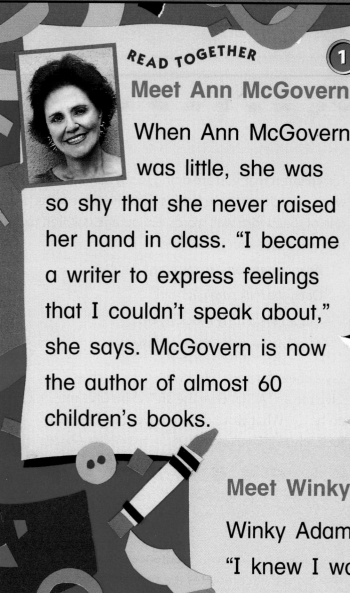

READ TOGETHER ①

Meet Ann McGovern

When Ann McGovern was little, she was so shy that she never raised her hand in class. "I became a writer to express feelings that I couldn't speak about," she says. McGovern is now the author of almost 60 children's books.

Meet Winky Adam

Winky Adam says, "I knew I wanted to create children's books since I was in the third grade." Today, she writes and illustrates children's books.

40

Meeting Individual Needs · Grouping Suggestions for Strategic Reading

EASY

Shared Reading Read the story aloud as you track print and model correct directionality. Invite children to read along with you. Talk about the plot and setting as you read each page.

ON-LEVEL

Guided Instruction Read the selection with children. Monitor any difficulties in reading that children may have in order to determine which Comprehension questions to emphasize. After reading the story with children, have children reread it, using the rereading suggestions on page 62.

CHALLENGE

Independent Reading Have children set purposes before they read. Remind them to look at the illustrations for clues about what is happening, where the story takes place, and how the characters feel. After reading the story, ask children to retell it.

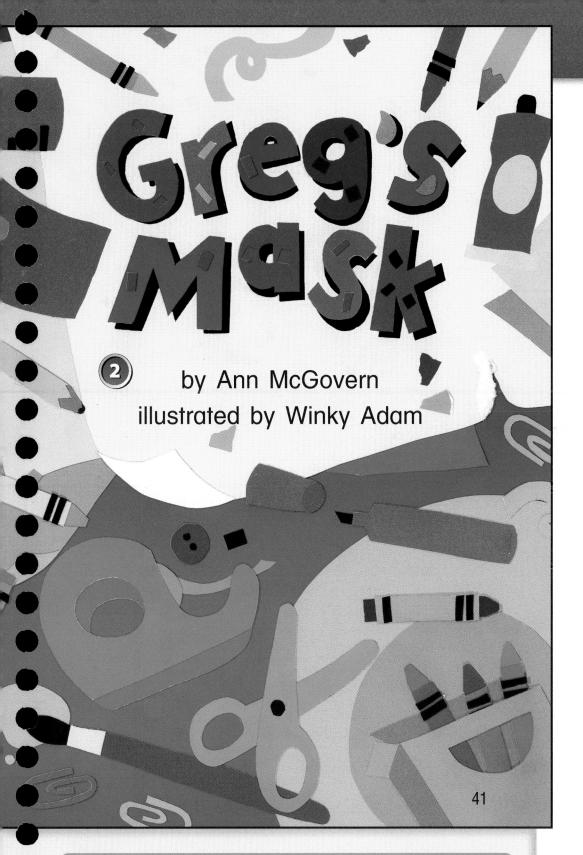

Greg's Mask

② by Ann McGovern

illustrated by Winky Adam

41

Comprehension

☑ **Phonics** Blends
☑ **Apply Setting**

STRATEGIC READING Explain to children that thinking about where the action takes place can help them understand the story. Sometimes the setting of a story changes. Let children know that they will be using their setting pictures to better understand where and when each part of the story takes place. Keep a running list visible to the class of what is happening where.

① We are going to read *Greg's Mask*. Let's look at the top picture on page 40. This is a picture of the author, Ann McGovern. Let's read about her. How do you think she expresses her feelings when she writes a book? Now let's read about Winky Adam. How do you think an illustrator expresses her feelings when she creates the pictures for a book? *Concept of a Book: Author/Illustrator*

② Look at the picture on page 41. What do you see? (art supplies) What do you think that means? (Someone is going to make something.) *Use Illustrations/Make Predictions*

Genre

Story

Remind children that a story is a fictional piece about a series of events. It focuses on characters who must deal with a problem. Ask children to look, as they read this story, for characters who may have a problem.

Activity Have children draw a picture of a mask they might like to make. What colors would the children use? Would the mask be happy, mad, or sad? Encourage volunteers to tell more about their mask.

LANGUAGE SUPPORT

Blackline masters for making the setting pictures can be found in the **Language Support Book**. Have children cut along the dotted line to separate the setting scenes. Have them paste each scene to a sheet of construction paper.

LANGUAGE SUPPORT, 104

Comprehension

3 Point to where we will start reading. Why does the word begin with a capital letter? (It is the first word in the sentence; it is a name.) *Concepts of Print*

4 **Phonics** **BLENDS** Let's blend the sounds together to read the first word in the second sentence. Read the first two letters G r. Now read the rest of the word: G r e g Greg. Look at the last word in the first sentence. Read the first two letters s k. Read the whole word s k i t skit. *Graphophonic Cues*

Fluency

GROUP READING

 Model tracking print and rereading to achieve fluency.

- Point to and read aloud the first word in the sentence.

- Run your finger under each word as you read the rest of the sentence without pausing.

- Then have children repeat this process, pointing to each word as they read. Repeat until children achieve fluency.

3 Greg's class was putting on a skit.
4 Greg had to make a mask for it.

42

Greg sang as he worked.
"Snip it here.
Clip it there.
Clip. Snip. Snip. Clip."

⑤

43

Comprehension

BLENDING When I say *snip, clip, snip, clip,* I hear rhyming sounds. Can anyone tell me which are the rhyming words? (*snip* and *clip*) Which part of the words rhyme? (The end of the words, *ip.*) Write the words *snip* and *clip* on the chalkboard. Blend the sounds aloud slowly as you draw the arrows as shown: s n i p c l i p. Point out the same ending in each word. *Graphophonic Cues*

⑤ ANALYZE SETTING Look at the pictures on these pages. Where is Greg making his mask? (in his kitchen; at home) How can you tell? (His mother and cat are there; there is a refrigerator.) Hold up the setting picture that tells where this part of the story is taking place. *Using Picture Clues/ Story Props*

Minilesson
REVIEW/MAINTAIN

Use Context Clues

Ask children to point to the word *skit* on page 42 and read it together.

- Encourage children to use context clues and personal experience to understand the meaning of the word *skit* by asking: When do people wear masks? When would children in school make and wear masks?

- Elicit that a *skit* is a short play.

Activity Have children talk about plays and skits they have seen. Make a list on the chalkboard.

P/i PREVENTION/INTERVENTION

BLENDING Write the words *snip* and *clip* on the chalkboard. Point to the letters *ip,* and have children read the /ip/ sound. Then read each complete word slowly as you draw the arrows as shown:

s n i p
c l i p

Ask children to read the words with you.

Have children take turns saying other words that rhyme with *snip* and *clip* (for example: *dip, flip, sip, trip, drip*). *Graphophonic Cues*

Comprehension

6 What marks do you see before the word *drip*? (quotation marks) What do the marks tell you? (Someone is speaking.) Who is speaking? (Greg) *Concepts of Print*

7 **Phonics** **BLENDS** Let's read the last line together *Drip. Drop. Drop. Drip.* What are the two sounds you hear at the beginning of each word? (/dr/) *Graphophonic Cues*

TEACHING TIP

VOWEL DISCRIMINATION Have children point to the words as they read the last line. Encourage them to follow along with their fingers to notice the "vowel" difference between *drip* and *drop* as they read the words with you. Ask how these words are different.

6 "Drip a drop of this.
Drop a glob of that.
7 Drip. Drop. Drop. Drip."

44

LANGUAGE SUPPORT

ESL Tell children you want to talk about a part of the story that deals with the question of "how much." Tell them that in the story when Greg paints his mask, he drips a drop at first and then he drops a glob. Ask them "How much is a drip?" Tell them you want them to draw a drip. Then ask "And if that's a drip, how much do you think a glob might be?" Ask them to draw it and show you by holding up their drawing. Repeat the questions: Can you show me a drip? And now can you show me a glob?

"Rip it here.
Nip it there.
Rip. Nip. Nip. Rip."

8

9

10

45

Comprehension

8 What is Greg doing? (ripping paper) Why is he doing that? (He could be making eyes, ears, and other things for the mask.) *Make Inferences*

BLENDING Let's look at the word *rip*. Write the first letter in your journal, and then say the sound aloud. Now write the second letter *i*. The sound is /i/. Let's blend the two together. The last letter is *p*, and that sounds like /p/. Put your finger on top of the *r*. We're going to change this word now to make another word, *nip*. I want you to make the /n/ sound and add the /ip/ sound. Now let's read the two words again. How are these words the same? (They both have the /ip/ sound.) *Graphophonic Cues*

9 **ANALYZE SETTING** Where is Greg working on his mask? (at home) How do you know? (His cat is there.) Hold up the setting picture that shows where Greg is. *Use Picture Clues/Story Props*

10 What is Greg doing as he makes his mask? (singing and dancing) How do you think he feels? (He is happy.) *Analyze Character*

PREVENTION/INTERVENTION

BLENDING Have children blend other short *i* words with you. Write the following words on the chalkboard: *did, sit, pin, big, six, zip*. Blend sounds of the letters of each word together, and have children repeat after you. Then ask children to use each word in a sentence. *Graphophonic Cues*

Comprehension

11 **Phonics** **BLENDS** Look at the first word on page 46. The word looks long, but we can use what we know about blending to read it. Help me blend this word aloud: t w i s t, twist. *Graphophonic Cues*

12 What is Greg twisting? (pipe cleaner) *Use Illustrations*

TEACHING TIP

MANAGEMENT Tell children to do the twist dance at least two feet away from each other to avoid collision. Once they've twisted, ask them if they know the meaning of *twist* now.

---

11 "Twist it here.

Tape it there.

12 Twist. Tape. Tape. Twist."

46

LANGUAGE SUPPORT

ESL If childen do not comprehend the vocabulary *twist* and *tape,* model twisting a piece of paper, as Greg is doing. Then, model taping the twisted paper onto another piece of paper. Children can work with twisting paper and taping it down at the Art Center.

(13) Greg's mask was done.
He put it on.

(14)

(15)

47

Comprehension

(13) Look at the first word on the page. How does the word end? (apostrophe and *s*) What does the apostrophe and *s* tell you? (Something belongs to Greg.) What belongs to Greg? (the mask) *Semantic Cues*

(14) What kind of mask did Greg make? (pig) How can you tell? (It has a pink face, snout, and ears like a pig.) *Use Illustrations*

(15) What is Greg doing with the mask? (He is trying it on his face.) How do we know this? (because we can see the back of his head looking toward the mirror and his reflection in the mirror) *Use Picture Clues/ Make Connections*

(p/i) **TRACKING PRINT** Point to the beginning of the first sentence. Let's read the two sentences on this page together. We'll start with the top line, follow it across from left to right, then sweep down to the second line and read it from left to right. As we read, use your finger to help you follow along. *Syntactic Cues*

Minilesson
REVIEW/MAINTAIN
Use Illustrations

Remind children that illustrations can give us clues about the story.

- Have children look at the illustrations showing Greg at work and make a list of all the supplies, people, and animals they see.

- Ask what Greg does with all of his supplies? (drips drops, drops globs, twists paper and pipe cleaners, tapes things onto the paper plate)

Activity Have children draw a mask they might like to wear.

(p/i) **PREVENTION/INTERVENTION**

TRACKING PRINT Ask children to work together with a partner. Begin on page 42. As you read, have children follow the text with their fingers moving in a left-to-right direction. Encourage children to pause at the period before continuing to read the next sentence. Continue rereading pages until all children are tracking print successfully. *Syntactic Cues*

47

Comprehension

16 Let's look at the picture of Greg. Let's read the words. How does Greg feel? (proud, happy, excited) How can you tell? (He's smiling; waving his hands.) Now look at the picture of Tam on page 49. Let's read the words. How does Tam feel? (angry) How can you tell? (Her face looks angry.)
Use Illustrations/Make Inferences

17 **ANALYZE SETTING** Using the clues in the two pictures on page 48 and 49, where are the two children? (in the same house, but now in Tam's bedroom.) How do you know?

18 Point to the marks at the beginning of the second sentence. What do they show? (that someone is speaking) Notice where they appear again. What does that tell you? (The person stops speaking.) Who is speaking? (Greg) *Concepts of Print*

16

17

18

Greg went to see his sister.

"Do you like my new mask?" he asked Tam.

48

Activity

Cross Curricular: Social Studies

EVERYDAY EMOTIONS Explain that everyone has bad days. Tell children that if something is bothering them, it's good to talk about it and bad to take it out on a sibling. Ask children: What's wrong with the way Tam acted? What do the words *I'm sorry* do?

Activity Have children form small groups or conduct a whole-class discussion. Talk about how to deal with hurt feelings, and where to get help.
▶ **Linguistic**

Tam was having a bad day. ⑲
"I do not want to look at
any old mask," she said. ⑳

49

Comprehension

⑲ What is different about the way the brother and sister look in these pictures? (Greg is excited and Tam looks angry, waving him away.) Tell me how to describe the look on Tam's face. (sour, angry, annoyed) Greg is standing there; what is Tam doing? (waves him away without looking up) *Make Inferences/Use Illustrations*

⑳ We all have good days and bad days. Who is having a bad day? (Tam) What kind of day do you think everyone will have? (a bad day) What happened? What caused this perfectly good day to become a bad day? (Tam has been mean to her brother.) *Cause and Effect*

Minilesson
REVIEW/MAINTAIN
High-Frequency Words

Write the following high-frequency words from kindergarten on two index cards each: *was, a, do, to, she, said.* Mix up the cards. Have children read the words. Then have them find the words in the sentences on page 49.

Activity Place the 12 cards face down in a grid. Have children play a matching game in which they flip the cards over to match pairs of words.

LANGUAGE SUPPORT

ESL Point to the illustration of Tam. Ask children what her facial expression tells them about how she feels. Elicit that she looks angry or upset. Ask them to predict how she might answer her brother. Then, read the page. Explain further what it means to have a bad day by using examples from the children's classroom experience, if necessary.

Comprehension

 **21** **BLENDS** Point to the last word on this page. Read the word with me, using your finger to help you blend the sounds of the letters together.

t r a sh trash *Graphophonic Cues*

Greg felt very sad. "My new mask is not any good," he said. And he tossed it into the trash. **21**

50

CULTURAL PERSPECTIVES

MASKS Explain that masks are used around the world. In Japanese *Kabuki* plays, actors wear masks instead of make-up. The word *Kabuki* suggests its meaning: *ka*: singing; *bu*: dancing; *ki*: acting.

Activity Invite children to create *Kabuki* masks. ▶ **Kinesthetic/Visual**

RESEARCH AND INQUIRY Have children find additional facts by looking in nonfiction books about masks.

*inter*NET **CONNECTION** For more information about masks, help children log onto **www.mhschool.com/reading**.

Greg was still mad at Tam the next day. He left before her.

51

Comprehension

22 Look at the expressions on the two faces. How do you think Greg is feeling? (Greg looks angry and hurt.) *Make Inferences/Analyze Character*

23 What is Greg doing? (He is leaving without Tam.) **How do we know this?** (He has his backpack on and is walking out the door while Tam is still gathering her things.) *Use Picture Clues/Draw Conclusions*

24 Why do you think Greg is still angry? (He feels sad about his mask and because his older sister is mean to him.) *Make Connections*

SENTENCES How many sentences are on this page? (2) What must each sentence tell? (a complete thought) How many words are in the first sentence? (9) *Syntactic Cues*

PREVENTION/INTERVENTION

SENTENCES Review with children that a sentence is a group of words that tells a complete thought. Read these word groups to children. Ask them to raise their hands when they hear a sentence.

• putting on a skit
• Greg's class
• Greg's class was putting on a skit.
• was done
• Greg's mask
• Greg's mask was done.

Encourage children to tell their own sentences and have other children indicate if each sentence tells a complete thought. *Syntactic Cues*

Minilesson
REVIEW/MAINTAIN

Make Inferences

Remind children that they can use clues in words and pictures to understand how characters are feeling.

• Have children describe Tam's expression in the illustration on page 51. Ask them to note where Tam is looking.

• Brainstorm a list of words that describe how Tam might be feeling.

Activity Invite children to compare and contrast how Tam and Greg are feeling. Encourage them to describe which feelings might be the same and which feelings might be different.

Comprehension

25 **ANALYZE SETTING** Where is the story taking place now? (at school, in the classroom) How can you tell it's the classroom? (teacher; chalkboard; it's time for the skit and the skit is at school.) Let's use our setting picture to show where Greg is. *Story Props*

P/I **CONCEPTS OF PRINT** Which words on this page begin with capital letters? (*It, Where, Miss, Wills, Greg, But*) Why do these words begin with capitals? (They begin a sentence or they name someone.) *Syntactic Cues*

26 Who is Miss Wills? (teacher) *Make Inferences*

GROUP READING

PARTNERS Have pairs of children take turns reading the sentences on page 52. Remind them to:

- think about how Greg is feeling.
- pause briefly at the periods.
- listen carefully to the words Tam speaks.

25 It was time for the skit.

26 "Where is your mask?" Miss Wills asked Greg. But Greg did not have it.

52

P/I **PREVENTION/INTERVENTION**

CONCEPTS OF PRINT Write *My name is _____.* on the board. Ask children to help you fill in their names. Point out that first and last names begin with a capital letter. Write *Miss Wills* and read it aloud. Ask children to find the capitals. Point out to children that titles, such as Miss, Mrs., or Mr., also begin with a capital letter. *Syntactic Cues*

Just then Tam ran into Greg's class. "Greg, you forgot your mask!" she yelled.

27

28

Class Skit Today!

53

Comprehension

27 Why do you think Tam brought the mask to Greg? (to make up with him) *Draw Conclusions*

28 How do you think Greg feels when he sees Tam with his mask? (happy to see his mask and to see Tam cares enough to bring it to him) *Make Inferences*

SELF-MONITORING STRATEGY

ASK QUESTIONS Ask yourself questions to help you understand the story.

- Why does Greg feel bad?
- How would I feel if I were Greg?
- Why didn't Greg bring the mask to school?

Minilesson
REVIEW/MAINTAIN
Cause and Effect

Explain to children one thing almost always leads to another. When something happens in a story or in real life, it will probably cause something else to happen.

- Have children look at pages 52–53. Ask them what might happen to the class skit because Greg doesn't have his mask.

Activity Write the following chart on the chalkboard. Supply causes and elicit the effects from children.

Cause	Effect
It's raining.	

Comprehension

(29) What do you think Greg will do now?
Make Predictions

> **TEACHING TIP**
>
> **ANALYZE CHARACTER**
> Have children focus on the character's emotions by rereading Tam's statement, saying the words with feeling.

(29) Then Tam said, "Do not be mad at me. I take back what I said. Your mask is good!"

54

Greg put on his mask. He was ready **30** **31**
for the skit.

55

30 How do you know Greg is ready for the skit? (He put his mask on.) How do you think he feels about his mask now? *Use Picture Clues/Make Inferences*

31 **BLENDS** Listen as I read the sentences on this page. Which word begins with the /sk/ sounds? *(skit)* Say it with me as I write it on the board. Which word ends with the /sk/ sounds? *(mask)* Let's read it together as I write it up here. Look at the board. How are these two words the same? (They both are spelled with *sk.*) *Graphophonic Cues*

LANGUAGE SUPPORT

ESL Help children use context clues to understand phrases. Reread the second sentence on page 54 together. Ask: *Can you really "take back" something you say?* (no) What did Tam mean when she wanted to take back what she said about his mask? (She didn't mean what she said to Greg, and she was sorry.)

Invite children to role-play the apology between Greg and Tam.

Comprehension

32 **ANALYZE SETTING** Where is the story happening now? (at school, in the classroom) Hold up your story prop that shows the school. *Story Props*

33 Look at the masks in the illustration. How are some of the masks alike? (all animal masks) How are they different? (Some cover the whole face, some don't.) *Compare and Contrast*

56

TEACHING TIP

MANAGEMENT Have children work in small groups. Assign each group one of the masks on pages 56 and 57 to look at and describe. Then have the groups compare and contrast masks.

Activity

Cross Curricular: Science

ANIMAL GROUPS List: duck, frog, fish, dog, and cat. Then make a list of the characteristics of mammals: They have hair or fur. They feed their young on milk. They give birth instead of laying eggs.

Activity Have children identify the animals on the list that are mammals.
▶ **Linguistic/Logical**

RESEARCH AND INQUIRY Invite children to find out about other mammals and share their information with the class.

(34)

(35)

There were masks of a duck, a frog, a fish, a dog, a mouse, and a cat. But Tam said Greg's mask was the best!

57

Comprehension

(34) Why do you think Tam is cheering? (She is happy for Greg.) *Make Inferences*

(35) What mark do you see after the word *duck?* (comma) Point to each comma in the sentence. How many commas did you count? (5) Let's read the sentence and pause at each comma. *Concepts of Print*

Minilesson

REVIEW/MAINTAIN

Blends

Tell children to look at the last word in the first line. *(frog)*

- Write the first two letters on a card, hold it up, and ask children to read it aloud.
- Write the last two letters on another card, hold it up and ask them to read it.
- Hold both cards up and ask them to put the two together.
- Apply this exercise with the last word on the page, *best*.

Activity Have children write the words in their journal.

Phonics CD-ROM Have children use the interactive phonics activities for reinforcement on blends.

Comprehension

(36) **ANALYZE SETTING** Where is the story happening now? (Greg and Tam are at a table in their house.)

(37) What is the look on Greg's face? (surprised) How is it different from the look he had when he and his sister were fighting? (happier) *Compare and Contrast*

(38) What word is in a different kind of type on this page? *(my)* Point to it. Do you think we should read this word with a special tone in our voices? Why? (to show that now Tam is asking about her skit) Let's read it together. *Concepts of Print*

(36)

(37) When Tam got home, she asked Greg,
(38) "Will you help me make a mask for *my* class skit?"

58

Cross Curricular: Math

SHAPE FACES Cut out small circles, squares, triangles, and rectangles from construction paper. Review characteristics of each shape with children.

Activity Give each child a paper plate and invite him or her to use the shapes to make a mask. You may also wish to provide yarn, string, buttons, and other craft items. When the masks are completed, have each child tell what shapes he or she used and tell you about the mask. Display the masks.

▶ **Visual/Kinesthetic**

Greg and Tam sang.

"Snip it here.

Clip it there.

Clip. Snip. Snip. Clip."

39

59

Comprehension

39 Who wants to show me what the children are doing on this page? *Role-Play*

Comprehension

BLENDING Are there words on this page that you recognize from the beginning of the story? Which are they? (*drip* and *drop*) How are these words the same? (Both begin with /dr/*dr* and end with /p/*p*.) *Graphophonic Cues*

"Drip a drop of this. Drop a glob of that. Drip. Drop. Drop. Drip."

60

Writer's Craft

RHYTHMS IN WRITING

Explain to children how writers create rhythms in a story by using patterns of sounds. Have children reread page 61. Encourage children to notice the similarities of the first two sentences: *Rip it here. Nip it there.* Why do they sound so similar? (The first words rhyme. Both sentences have the same number of syllables.)

Have children clap to the rhythm of the sentences on page 61. See if children can find other pages in the story with a rhythm with which they can clap along. Vary the tempo, if you wish, by having children clap faster or slower.

PREVENTION/INTERVENTION

BLENDING Write the word *drip* on chart paper. Frame the *i* and make the /i/ sound. Have children repeat, and then blend the sounds and read the word. Cover the letter *i* with an *o* written on a self-stick note.

Blend the sounds: d r o p drop. Repeat with *clip* and *clop, flip* and *flop,* and *tip* and *top.* *Graphophonic Cues*

60   *Greg's Mask*

"Rip it here. Nip it there.
Rip. Nip. Nip. Rip.
Twist it here. Tape it there.
Twist. Tape. Tape. Twist."

61

Comprehension

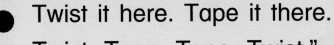 I'd like two volunteers to pretend to be Greg and Tam. Show me how you sing and make a mask. I'll sing first, then you sing after me. This part of the story can be made into a song. I'll read the first two lines, and then I want you to repeat it after me. *Role-Play*

Minilesson
REVIEW/MAINTAIN
Main Idea

Explain to children that the main idea tells what the story is about. Help focus children's ideas by asking:

- How did Greg and Tam feel at the beginning?
- What happened when Greg got to school?
- How did Greg and Tam feel at the ending?

Activity Fold a sheet of drawing paper in thirds. Have children draw a picture in each section to answer the questions above. Then have them write sentences to tell the main idea.

Comprehension

(41) What kind of mask did Tam make?
(dinosaur) *Use Illustrations*

RETELL THE STORY Have pairs of children work together to retell the story. Tell them they should include only the most important events in their summary. You may wish to have children use their setting pictures to retell the story. Children can take turns telling the story aloud while others in the group use props to act out the events.
Story Props

Tam's mask was done. She put it on. "What a good mask!" Greg said.

62

REREADING FOR *Fluency*

PARTNERS Have partners reread the story, alternating pages or reading the parts of Greg and Tam. Encourage them to read with expression.

READING RATE When you evaluate reading rate, have children read aloud from the story for one minute. Place a stick-on note after the last word read. Count words read. To evaluate children's performance, see the Running Record in the **Fluency Assessment** book.

(i) Intervention For leveled fluency lessons, passages, and norms charts, see **Skills Intervention Guide**, Part 5, Fluency.

"That was fun!" said Greg.

"I just may do this when I grow up!"

41

63

Comprehension

Return to Predictions and Purposes

Reread children's predictions about the story. Ask if the story answered all their questions.

PREDICTIONS	WHAT HAPPENED
Greg will make a mask.	Greg made a pig mask for a skit.
Greg is angry at his sister.	Tam doesn't like Greg's mask. Greg is sad.

Have children discuss the strategy of using the setting pictures to understand the story. Did they feel it was helpful to use the setting pictures to remember where the story was happening? Why?

INFORMAL ASSESSMENT

HOW TO ASSESS

Phonics BLENDS Turn to page 50. Have children read the sentences.

SETTING Have children talk about where the story takes place. Elicit the idea that the story setting changes.

FOLLOW UP

Phonics BLENDS Use repetitive words and phrases in the story to model blending.

SETTING Ask children to describe a classroom and a house or apartment. Then have them use the pictures in the story to figure out where Greg is.

LITERARY RESPONSE

QUICK-WRITE Have children focus on the brother–sister relationship between Greg and Tam. Ask them if Greg and Tam's relationship reminds them of their own sibling relationships. How? Ask them to use their journals to make a list of the differences and the similarities.

ORAL RESPONSE

• Why do arguments happen?

• Why is it important to work things through?

SENTENCE STRIPS Children can use strips 1–86 to retell *Greg's Mask*.

> 1
> Greg's class was putting on a skit.

> 2
> Greg had to make a mask for it.

Story Questions

Tell children that now they will read some questions about the story. Help children read the questions. Discuss possible answers.

Answers:

1. Answers will vary. Accept appropriate responses listing materials. *Literal/Details*

2. Answers will vary. Accept appropriate responses, including that Tam felt bad. *Inferential/ Characters*

3. The class skit was about animals. *Inferential/ Make Inferences*

4. Answers will vary. Accept appropriate summaries. *Critical/Summarize*

5. Answers will vary. *Critical/ Reading Across Texts*

Make a Poster Help children read the directions in their anthologies. You may want to bring in an ad or a poster advertising a show. What does it look like? What does it say?

Story Questions & Activities

READ TOGETHER

❶ How did Greg make his mask?

❷ Why did Tam bring the pig mask to Greg?

❸ What was the class skit about?

❹ Tell the story in your own words.

❺ How is Greg like Max the Cat?

Make a Poster

Draw a picture about Greg's skit.

Write a title for it.

Tell where the skit will be.

Tell when the skit will be.

Please come to see Pig and His Friends.
Time: 2:00 P.M. Place: Cafeteria

Meeting Individual Needs

EASY	ON-LEVEL	CHALLENGE

EASY

Name_____ Date_____ Reteach **95**

Story Comprehension

Think about what happened first, next, and last in "Greg's Mask." Then draw the pictures in the right order.

1. FIRST Drawing of Greg making mask
2. NEXT Drawing of Greg wearing mask
3. NEXT Drawing of Greg throwing out mask
4. LAST Drawing of Tam and Greg making dinosaur mask

Book 1.3
Greg's Mask
At Home: Invite children to make masks using paper bags or pie plates and string.
95

Reteach, 95

ON-LEVEL

Name_____ Date_____ Practice **95**

Story Comprehension

Read each sentence about "Greg's Mask." Write the name of the person it describes.

Miss Willis	Greg	Tam

1. Her class did a skit. _____ Miss Willis

2. He made a mask. _____ Greg

3. She did not like the mask. _____ Tam

4. He put the mask in the trash. _____ Greg

5. She said, "Where is your mask?" _____ Miss Willis

6. She came to school with the mask. _____ Tam

Book 1.3
Greg's Mask
At Home: Have children draw pictures of animal faces that would make good masks.
95

Practice, 95

CHALLENGE

Name_____ Date_____ Extend **95**

Story Comprehension

Write a letter to Greg. Tell him why you like his mask. Tell him about a mask you would like to make.
Dear Greg,

Letters will vary. They should say something positive about Greg's mask and describe or name another kind of mask.

Your friend,

Book 1.3
Greg's Mask
At Home: Have children create simple masks using materials such as paper plates, paint, tissue paper, yarn, and pipe cleaners.
95

Extend, 95

Make a Mask

Use a paper plate.

Make an animal mask.

Then use your mask for a class skit.

What will it be about?

Find Out More

There are many kinds of masks.

Look for pictures of masks.

What are they made of?

65

Story Activities

Make a Mask

Materials: paper plates, paint, materials such as yarn and tissue paper, glue

Read the directions aloud. Help children who have questions. First, have children choose a character they would like to be. You might ask children what their favorite animal is. Is this animal furry? Does it have large eyes and pointy ears? Have children discuss what materials they might use to make a mask for this character.

GROUP After the children have made their masks, you may wish to divide them into groups to come up with skits using their masks. Have each group perform its skit for the class.

Find Out More

RESEARCH AND INQUIRY Again, read the directions aloud, and help children who have questions. Then have them work in pairs.

PARTNERS

Have partners look through books and magazines to find a picture of a mask together. Have them notice the kind of materials used to make the mask. Which part of the world do they think this mask came from? Invite children to be descriptive in their responses.

interNET CONNECTION Have children log on to *www.mhschool.com/reading*, where they can access sites about masks.

FORMAL ASSESSMENT

See the Selection Progress Assessment Test for Book 3.

DAILY **Phonics** ROUTINES

DAY 3 **Writing** Invite children to write two short sentences in which they use words with stop/continuant blends. Examples: *Drop the ball. Clap your hands.*

Phonics CD-ROM

Study Skills

DIAGRAMS

OBJECTIVES

Children will learn about the materials in an art center.

Remind children that they have just read a story in which a child made a mask. Tell children that now they will look at a photo of an art center, a place with many kinds of art supplies.

Display **Teaching Chart 70.** Have children look at the photo of the table with the supplies. Invite them to describe what they see. Read the labels together. Have children suggest how each supply might be used to make a mask. Then help children read the questions below the photo, encouraging them to identify the labels that answer each question.

STUDY SKILLS

Art Center

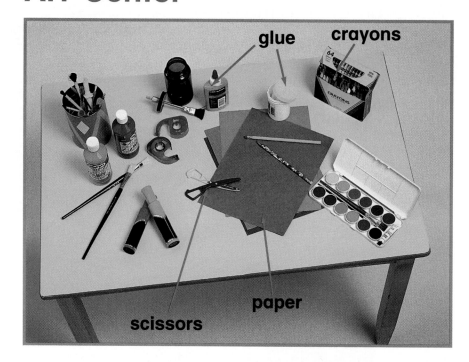

glue   crayons

scissors   paper

Look at the Art Center

1 What do you use to cut?

2 Tell what you would do with glue.

Meeting Individual Needs

EASY	ON-LEVEL	CHALLENGE

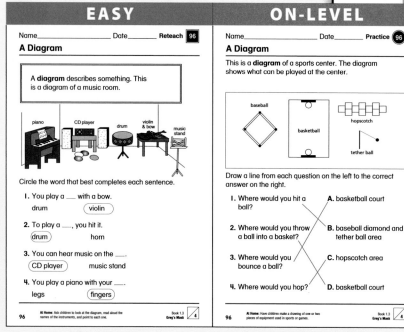

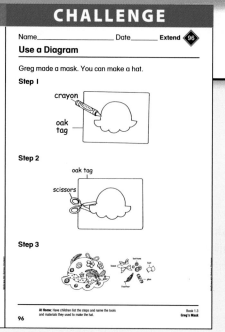

Reteach, 96   Practice, 96   Extend, 96

TEST POWER

Test Power

THE PRINCETON REVIEW

Bart's House of Snow

Bart got out of bed.

He went out to play in the yard.

He made a house in the snow.

Bart showed it to his sister.

At first, she did not like it.

But then, they started to play.

They played outside for a long time.

Then, they went in to have lunch.

Where does this story take place?

○ At Bart's school

◉ In Bart's yard

Read the story again if the question seems too hard.

67

Read the Page

Explain to children that you will be reading this story as a group. You will read the story, and they will follow in their books.

Request that children put pens, pencils, and markers away, since they will not be writing in their books.

Discuss the Question

Discuss with children the kinds of words that describe places. Then have them read the story, looking for words that describe places. Have children read aloud the word(s) they have found.

Test-Tip

Always look back to the story to find the answer. The answer is always somewhere in the passage.

i **Intervention** Skills

Intervention Guide, for direct instruction and extra practice in vocabulary and comprehension

Leveled Books

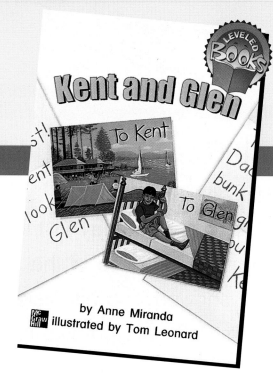

EASY

Kent and Glen

☑ **Blends**

☑ **Setting**

High-Frequency Words:
any, new, old, grow

by Anne Miranda
illustrated by Tom Leonard

Guided Reading

PREVIEW AND PREDICT Take a **picture walk** up to page 5, using the high-frequency words. Have children predict what the story is about and chart their ideas.

SET PURPOSES Children can write or draw why they want to read *Kent and Glen.* For example: *I want to find out who gets to sleep in the top bunk bed.*

READ THE BOOK Ask the following questions as children read or once they have read the story independently.

Pages 2–3: This story is about two brothers writing to each other. Who and where is each brother? (Glen, he's at camp; Kent, he's at home with new bunk beds.) Model: *"To…"* I'm not sure what this word is, but I can blend the letters to read it. The first letter is *K* with the sound /k/. The middle letter is *e*. It stands for /e/. The last letters are *n* and *t*. They make the sounds /n/ and /t/. I can blend the sounds together K e n t Kent. The word is *Kent,* one brother's name. What word on this page ends the same way? *(tent)* Who sees vocabulary words we just learned on page 3? *(new, grow, any)* ***Phonics and Decoding, High-Frequency Words***

Pages 4–5: Where is Glen on pages 4 and 5? (swimming in a pond at camp) ***Story Elements***

Pages 6–7: Why does Kent say, "There is just one top bed!"? (He is reminding Glen that both brothers want the top bunk, but only one can have it.) ***Use Illustrations, Make Inferences***

Page 8: Who sees another vocabulary word we just learned on page 8? *(old)* ***High-Frequency Words***

RETURN TO PREDICTIONS AND PURPOSES Ask children if their predictions were close to the story and why.

LITERARY RESPONSE Use these questions to focus the responses:

• Why does Glen feel he should get the top bunk?

• Have you ever wanted something that somebody else wanted? Tell about it.

Also see the story questions and writing activity in *Kent and Glen.*

See the **Phonics** CD-ROM for practice with blends.

Answers to Story Questions
1. at camp
2. the top bunk
3. when they are away on vacation
4. answers will vary.
5. both stories are about families.

The Story Questions and Activity below appear in the Easy Book.

Story Questions and Activity
1. Where is Glen?
2. What do both boys want?
3. When do people send postcards?
4. Tell about three pictures in the story.
5. How is this story like *Greg's Mask?*

Make a Postcard for Someone
On one side, draw a picture.
On the other side, write a note.
Write the address and add a stamp.
Then send your card.

from *Kent and Glen*

Leveled Books

INDEPENDENT

Dig for Clams

☑ **Blends**
☑ **Setting**
High-Frequency Words: *any, new, old, grow*

by Della Cohen
illustrated by Diane Blasius

Guided Reading

PREVIEW AND PREDICT Have the children take a **picture walk** up to page 5. Have them predict what the story will be about and chart their ideas.

SET PURPOSES Children can write or draw why they want to read *Dig for Clams*. For example: *I want to find out what they do with the clams they find.*

READ THE BOOK Guide children's reading with the following questions or ask them once they have read the story independently.

Pages 2–3: Where are the sisters and what are they doing? (at the beach digging for clams) Model: "*We feel the …* " Let's blend the letters together to read this word. The first letters are *cr*. The sounds are /c/ and /r/. The middle letter is *i*. It stands for /i/. The last letters are *sp*, making the sounds /s/ and /p/. I can blend the sounds c r i s p crisp. The word is *crisp*. How do the girls look? (happy) *Setting, Phonics and Decoding*

Page 5: Who sees a vocabulary word we learned on page 5? *(old)* **High-Frequency Words**

Pages 6–7: Why do the girls put back the little clams? (They still need to grow.) Where do the girls put the bigger clams? (in the pickup truck) *Use Illustrations*

Page 8: Where are the girls now? (at home) What happens to the clams? (Dad cooks them.) *Setting*

RETURN TO PREDICTIONS AND PURPOSES Have children go back and look at their prediction charts and purposes for reading. Were their predictions correct?

LITERARY RESPONSE Focus the responses by asking:

• Have you been to the beach? What did you like about it?

• Do you ever help prepare meals?

Also see the story questions and activity in *Dig for Clams*.

See the **Phonics** **CD-ROM** for practice with blends.

Answers to Story Questions
1. at the beach
2. When the clams grow, they will be good to eat.
3. Yes; they look happy.
4. Clams are picked, cleaned, and then cooked.
5. Answers will vary.

The Story Questions and Activity below appear in the Independent Book.

Story Questions and Activity
1. Where are the girls in the beginning of the story?
2. Why do the girls want the small clams to grow?
3. Do you think the girls like each other? Why?
4. Tell how clams get from the mud to the supper table.
5. What other story have you read where children work together?

Make a Shell Picture
Make a picture with shells.
If you can't find real shells, then use macaroni shells.

from Dig for Clams

Leveled Books

CHALLENGE

Big Brother Little Brother

☑ **Blends**
☑ **Setting**

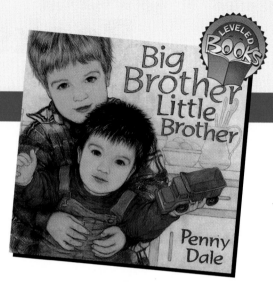

Guided Reading

PREVIEW AND PREDICT Have children discuss each illustration up to page 13. As they take the **picture walk**, have children predict what the story will be about and chart their ideas.

SET PURPOSES Have children write or draw why they want to read *Big Brother Little Brother*. For example: *I want to find out what else Big Brother knows.*

READ THE BOOK Ask the following questions to guide children's reading or to discuss once they have read the story independently.

Pages 2–13: Where are the brothers? (at home) How does Little Brother look on page 4? (unhappy) How does he look on page 8? (scared) Why? (The dog is big.) What word on this page begins with the /br/ sound? *(brother)* **Setting, Phonics and Decoding**

Pages 14–23: What happens when Little Brother wants Big Brother's truck? (He won't give it to him.) So what does Little Brother do? (He takes the truck and hides it.) How do you know he hides it? (On page 23, he takes it out of his crib.) **Make Inferences**

Pages 24–25: What happens on these pages? (Little Brother knows why Big Brother is crying. He brings the truck back to him.) What can you say about both brothers? (They know why the other one is crying or sad.) Why do you think that happens? (because they're brothers) *Use Illustrations*

RETURN TO PREDICTIONS AND PURPOSES Have children discuss their predictions. Ask which ones were close to the story and why. Did they find out what else Big Brother knew?

LITERARY RESPONSE Focus responses by asking:

- Have you ever known how someone close to you feels? Tell about it.

- Have you ever done something nice to make someone else happy? Tell about it.

Also see the story questions and writing activity in *Big Brother Little Brother*.

See the **Phonics CD-ROM** for practice with blends.

Answers to Story Questions

1. Big Brother
2. because Big Brother wouldn't let him have it
3. Answers will vary. They are friends.
4. The story is about how two brothers know each other.
5. Answers will vary.

The Story Questions and Activity below appear in the Challenge Book.

Story Questions and Activity

1. Who knows what Little Brother wants?
2. Why does Little Brother take the truck?
3. What does the story tell you about brothers?
4. What is this story about?
5. What other stories have you read about brothers?

What Can You Do?

What can you do with a brother, a sister or a good friend?

Draw a picture.

Write about your picture.

from Big Brother Little Brother

Bringing Groups Together

Anthology and Leveled Books

Connecting Texts

CHARACTER WEB
Write the story titles on a chart. Discuss with children sibling relationships used in each book. Call on volunteers from each reading level and write their suggestions on the chart.

Use the chart to talk about brothers and sisters.

Greg's Mask
Greg is hurt by his sister's harsh words about his mask.

Kent and Glen
Two brothers argue over who gets the top bunk of new bunk beds.

SIBLINGS

Dig for Clams
Two sisters play well together.

Big Brother Little Brother
Little brother steals big brother's toy truck but gives it back.

Viewing/Representing

GROUP PRESENTATIONS Divide the class into groups, one for each of the four books. (For *Greg's Mask,* combine children of different reading levels.) Have each group do cut-outs of the characters and role-play how they see the characters interacting. Have each group present its roleplay using the cut-outs.

AUDIENCE RESPONSE
Ask children to pay attention to each group's presentations. Ask them to compare and contrast the sibling relationships in the different books.

Research and Inquiry

MORE ABOUT SIBLINGS Have children ask themselves: What else would I like to know about how brothers and sisters get along? Then invite them to do the following:

• Bring in pictures of their siblings and tell about them.

• Invite an older sibling to come speak to the class about what he or she does (high school or college student, soldier, and so on).

*inter*NET
CONNECTION Have children vist **www.mhschool.com/reading** for links to Web pages about brothers and sisters.

JOURNAL Children can draw pictures representing what they learned in their journals.

OBJECTIVES

Children will:

- review stop/continuant blends: *tr, dr, tw, pl, cr, cl.*
- blend letters and read words with blends.

MATERIALS
- index cards
- Teaching Chart 71
- chart paper

Skills Finder

Blends	
Introduce	B2: 96I-J; B3: 8I-J, 38I-J
Review	B2: 123G-H; B3: 37E-F, 37G-H, 67E-F, 97G-H
Test	Book 2, Book 3
Maintain	B3: 23; B4: 13

ALTERNATE TEACHING STRATEGY

STOP/CONTINUANT BLENDS

For a different approach to teaching this skill, see pages T64, T65, T69, and T70.

Review **Blends**

PREPARE

Listen for Stop/Continuant Blends

Give each child an index card with one of the following blends written on it: *tr, pl, cr, tw.*

- Read the following words aloud and have children hold up the cards that match the beginning blend in each one: *trash, crash, twist, plant, crab.*

TEACH

BLENDING Model and Guide Practice with Blends

- Write the following blends on the chalkboard: *tr, pl, cr, tw.* Blend the sounds together aloud.

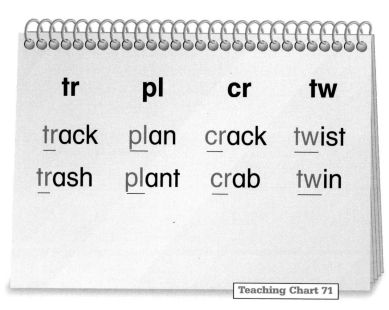

Teaching Chart 71

- Display **Teaching Chart 71**. Run your hand under the letters *t* and *r* and blend the sounds. t r t r
- Repeat, having children blend with you.
- Write the letters *t* and *r* in the first blank space. Run your hand under the letters again, blending the sounds to read the word.
  t r a ck track
- Repeat, having children read the word with you.

Use the Word in Context

Have children use the word in a sentence to reinforce its meaning. Example: *The train runs on the track.*

Repeat the Procedure

- Have children write *tr* in the next blank. Blend sounds to read the word *trash.*

- Continue the activity. Ask volunteers to write blends for each blank space and blend the sounds to read the words.

PRACTICE

BLENDING
Build Words with Blends and Sort

PARTNERS

Write the following letter banks on chart paper:

| tr dr tw |
| pl cr cl |

| a e i o u |

| m p b n |

Have one child choose a blend from the first bank and one or two letters from each of the other banks. Ask another child to write the word. Have the first child say the word. Ask pairs to decide if the words are real. Have children keep a list of the real words. Then have children sort their list of words into groups according to the initial or final blend. ▶ **Linguistic/Visual**

ASSESS/CLOSE

Build and Read Words with Blends

Observe as children build words during the Practice activity. Ask children to read two words aloud from their list.

ADDITIONAL PHONICS RESOURCES

Phonics/Phonemic Awareness Practice Book,
pages 121–124

PHONICS KIT
Hands-on Activities and Practice

McGraw-Hill School
TECHNOLOGY
Phonics **CD-ROM**

activities for practice with Blending and Building Words

DAY 4 **Letter Substitution**
Have children substitute blends to make a new word. For example: *drip/flip, clap/snap,* and *drop/plop.*

Phonics **CD-ROM**

SPELLING/PHONICS CONNECTIONS
Words with blends: See the 5-Day Spelling Plan, pages 67Q–67R.

i Intervention ▶ **Skills Intervention Guide,** for direct instruction and extra practice in Blends

Meeting Individual Needs for Phonics

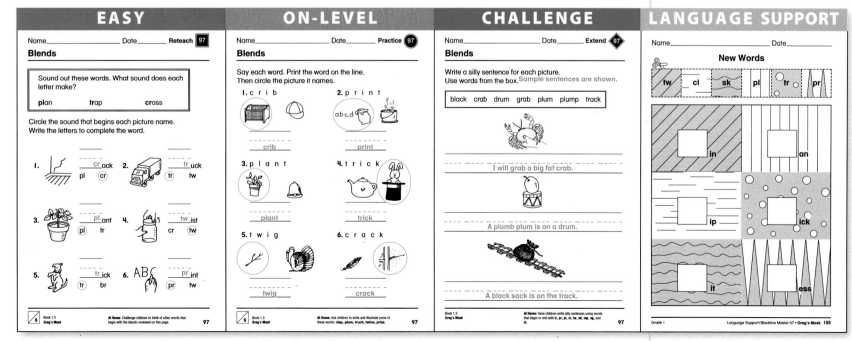

Reteach, 97   **Practice, 97**   **Extend, 97**   Language Support, 105

67F

OBJECTIVES

Children will:

- review stop/continuant blends.
- review continuant/stop blends.
- review continuant/continuant blends.
- cumulative review: **double consonants.**

MATERIALS

- letter cards from the **Word Building Manipulative Cards**
- **Teaching Chart 72**
- **Phonics Practice Reader, Volume 1**

Skills Finder

Blends

Introduce	B2: 96I-J; B3: 8I-J, 38I-J
Review	B2: 123G-H; B3: 37E-F, 37G-H, 67G-H, 97G-H
Test	Book 2, Book 3
Maintain	B3: 23; B4: 13

ALTERNATE TEACHING STRATEGY

BLENDS

For a different approach to teaching this skill, see pages T64, T65, T69, and 70.

Review Blends

PREPARE

Identify Blends Remind children that they have learned to read many words that have consonant letters that blend together. Write the blends *tr*, *st*, and *sl* on the chalkboard, saying them aloud. Ask children to repeat the sounds after you.

Discriminate Among Words with Blends Place word cards for the three types of blends on the chalkboard ledge, for example, *truck*, *stop*, and *sled*. Ask children to find the word that has the sound /st/ and read it aloud. Repeat for the other blends.

TEACH

BLENDING Model and Guide Practice with Blends

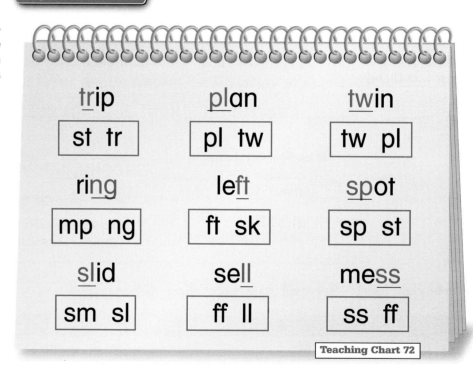

Teaching Chart 72

- Display **Teaching Chart 72**. Explain to children that they can make words by writing one of the two letter blends in the blank space. Tell children that the other letter blend will not make a real word.
- Blend the first example on the chart with children.

  s t i p stip   t r i p trip

- Ask children which word is the real word. (*trip*)
- Have a volunteer write the letter blend *tr* in the space and read the word *trip*.

Use the Word in Context Ask a volunteer to use the word *trip* in a sentence to reinforce its meaning. Example: *We went on a trip to the lake.*

Repeat the Procedure Continue with **Teaching Chart 72**. Have children blend the sounds aloud and tell which letter combinations make real words.

PRACTICE

BLENDING
Build and Sort
Words with
Blends

GROUP

Have children work in small groups. Have each group build as many words with *sp* as possible. Repeat with *ng* and *tr*. Have groups choose two words for each blend to put on a class bulletin board under *sp, ng,* or *tr.* Children should read the words they choose to check their sorting. ▶ **Linguistic/Kinesthetic**

ASSESS/CLOSE

Draw and Label a
Picture

Use your observations from the Practice activity to determine if children need more reinforcement with blends. Have children choose a *sp, ng,* or *tr* word and draw and label a picture.

Read a Decodable
Story

For additional practice reading words with stop/continuant blends and to develop fluency, direct children to read the story *Jill and Cliff's Pumpkins* from the **Phonics Practice Reader, Volume 1.**

ADDITIONAL PHONICS RESOURCES

Phonics/Phonemic Awareness
Practice Book,
pages 121–124

McGraw-Hill School
TECHNOLOGY

Phonics **CD-ROM**

activities for practice with
Blending and Building Words

PHONICS KIT
Hands-on Activities and Practice

DAILY Phonics ROUTINES

DAY 5 **Fluency** Write the words *trick, plum, blot, crash* on the chalkboard. Point to each word and ask children to blend the sounds silently. Then have children read each word aloud.

Phonics **CD-ROM**

 **Intervention** **Skills Intervention Guide,** for direct instruction and extra practice in Blends

Meeting Individual Needs for Phonics

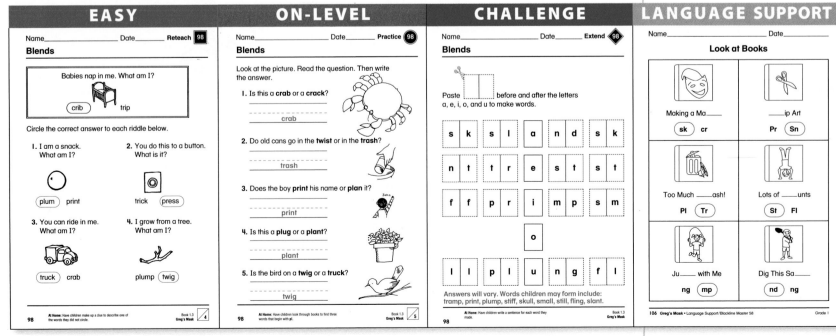

EASY	ON-LEVEL	CHALLENGE	LANGUAGE SUPPORT

Reteach, 98   Practice, 98   Extend, 98   Language Support, 106

Children will compare and contrast animals.

MATERIALS
• Teaching Chart 73

TEACHING TIP

COMPARE AND CONTRAST Ask children to think of other animals that fly besides a duck (robin, bat, crow) and other animals that swim besides a frog (whale, shark, fish). Have children compare and contrast the animals.

Skills Finder

Compare/Contrast

Introduce	B3: 67I-J
Review	B3: 97I-J, 139E-F
Test	Book 3
Maintain	B5: 67

SELF-SELECTED Reading

....

Children may choose from the following titles.

ANTHOLOGY

• *Greg's Mask*

LEVELED BOOKS

• *Kent and Glen*

• *Dig for Clams*

• *Big Brother Little Brother*

Bibliography, pages T98–T99

Introduce Compare and Contrast

PREPARE

Introduce the Concept of Compare and Contrast

Tell children that they can decide how two things are alike and how they are different by reading about them and by looking at pictures. Explain that this is a skill that they can use to better understand the characters and the events in a story.

TEACH

Compare/Contrast

Display **Teaching Chart 73**. Allow children to comment on the pictures of the duck and the frog. Then read the chart aloud.

The duck swims.
The duck flies.

The frog swims.
The frog hops.

_____   _____

Teaching Chart 73

MODEL I can look at the pictures and the sentences to find out about ducks and frogs. The sentences tell me that both animals swim; from the pictures, I can see other ways that they are alike. They both have two eyes. They both live near water. But I see that they are also different. The duck has two legs. The frog has four legs. The duck has wings and feathers; the frog does not.

Ask volunteers to add another fact about ducks and frogs to the **Teaching Chart**. Help children make a list of ways that the duck and frog are alike and different. Ask them to help you create a Venn diagram that will show how the duck and frog differ and how they are alike.

PRACTICE

Compare and Contrast Other Animals

PARTNERS

Have children look at the animal masks in *Greg's Mask* and choose two animals. Have pairs of children draw or write about ways they are alike and different. Encourage children to read their sentences aloud.

▶ **Visual/Linguistic**

ASSESS/CLOSE

More Compare and Contrast

Have children compare and contrast apples and oranges. They can write, draw, and tell about the similarities and differences.

ALTERNATE TEACHING **STRATEGY**

COMPARE AND CONTRAST

For a different approach to teaching this skill, see page T71.

Intervention ▶ **Skills Intervention Guide,** for direct instruction and extra practice in **Comparing and Contrasting**

Meeting Individual Needs for Comprehension

EASY	ON-LEVEL	CHALLENGE	LANGUAGE SUPPORT

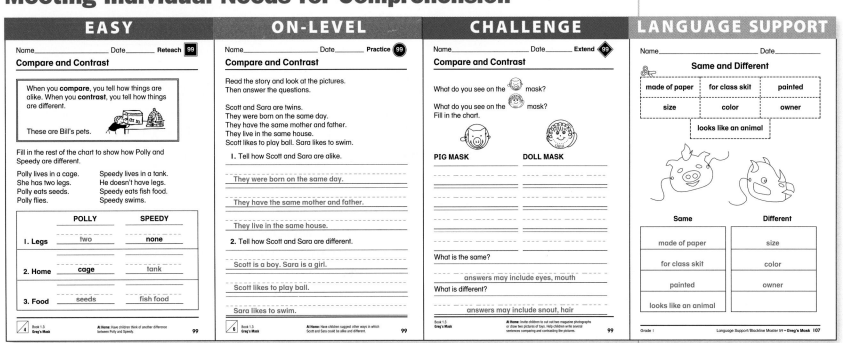

Reteach, 99   **Practice, 99**   **Extend, 99**   **Language Support, 107**

67J

Children will review posses-sives and singular possessive pronouns.

MATERIALS
- **Teaching Chart 74**
- index cards
- hat
- self-stick notes

Skills Finder

Possessives

Introduce	B3: 37K–L
Review	B3: 67K–L, 139I–J
Test	Book 3

LANGUAGE SUPPORT

ESL Note that the Spanish lan-guage does not use apostrophes to signal possessives. It is shown by saying, for example: El gato de Meg. (The cat of Meg.) This may be a source of difficulty for some children whose native lan-guage is not English.

Review **Possessives**

PREPARE

Review the Concept of Singular Possessive Pronouns
Write the words *Juan's bike* on the chalkboard. Then write *his bike.* Have children read the words aloud with you. Remind children that *his* takes the place of *Juan's.*

TEACH

Identify Apostrophes
Read the first phrase on **Teaching Chart 74** together. Point to *Meg's* and ask children what it means. Elicit that it means, in this example, that the bike belongs to Meg.

Meg's bike   Jake's ball

Sal's book   Jan's dog

Teaching Chart 74

MODEL   I can use what I know to help me read words I don't recog-nize. I know the name *Meg.* I can see that the last letter of the word is -*s,* and before that there is an apostrophe. I know that the apos-trophe means that something belongs to someone. The word is *Meg's.*

Ask volunteers to suggest a word that can take the place of *Meg* (her). Have a volunteer read the next phrase and then tell the class what the object is and who it belongs to. Invite a second volunteer to circle the apostrophe. Continue having children suggest a word to replace the possessive in each phrase. Continue until the chart is complete.

PRACTICE

Add Apostrophes

GROUP

On blank index cards, have children write their names with an apostrophe *s* and put the cards in a hat. Invite volunteers to pull a name from the hat, point out the child named on the card, and name an object in the classroom that belongs to the child.

▶ **Kinesthetic/ Linguistic**

ASSESS/CLOSE

Use Possessives in Context

Observe children as they complete the Practice activity. To assess children's understanding, have each child choose an object in the room that belongs to them and write, for example, "Tosha's book" on a self-stick note. Children can place the note on the object.

ALTERNATE TEACHING STRATEGY

POSSESSIVES

For a different approach to teaching this skill, see page T68.

ℹ️ **Intervention** ▶ **Skills Intervention Guide,** for direct instruction and extra practice in Possessives

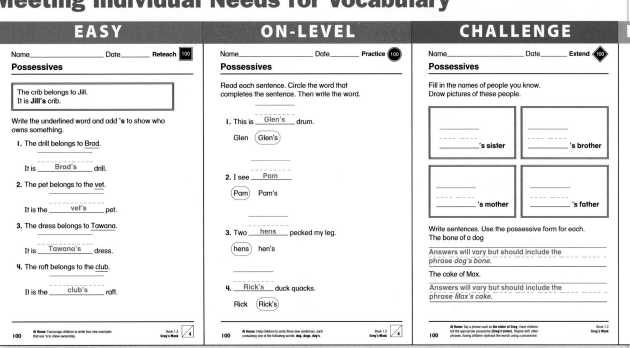

Meeting Individual Needs for Vocabulary

EASY	ON-LEVEL	CHALLENGE	LANGUAGE SUPPORT

EASY — Reteach, 100
ON-LEVEL — Practice, 100
CHALLENGE — Extend, 100
LANGUAGE SUPPORT — Language Support, 108

67L

**Handwriting
CD-ROM**

GRAMMAR/SPELLING
CONNECTIONS

Present Tense: See the 5-Day Grammar and Usage Plan, pages 67O–67P.

Words with Stop/Continuant Blends (initial/final) *tr, pr, pl, cr, tw:* See the 5-Day Plan, Spelling, pages 67Q–67R.

TEACHING TIP

Technology
A spell-checker will not catch a word that has been used incorrectly, such as *their* in place of *there.* Children may use the spell-checker, but remind them to proofread what they write, too.

Handwriting
Remind children to hold the paper with the hand they do not write with so that their paper does not slide. See page T78 for illustrations of this.

Interactive Writing
Make a Chart

Prewrite

LOOK AT THE STORY Have children revisit *Greg's Mask,* noticing again the details of the story and the accompanying pictures. Then tell them that the class will invent two masks that are different from the ones in the story. Children will create a chart comparing what the masks look like, what size they are, what colors they are, what shapes they are, what they're made of, and how they're made. The chart will have pictures and sentences. What animals would they like to make masks of? List their suggestions. Then allow children to vote, and select the two winning masks.

Draft

MAKE COMPARISONS On the chalkboard, make a chart with two columns, one for each mask. Each line of the chart will talk about another part of the mask, and the class will write sentences comparing the two. Help children compose their sentences.

- Begin by saying, for example: *Let's look at the noses. We decided that our elephant mask should have a long trunk and our mouse mask should have a small nose with whiskers on the sides. How could we put that into sentences? The elephant has a long trunk. The mouse has. . . what?* As you say a word with familiar sounds and patterns, challenge children to come up and write it. Write all unfamiliar words yourself. Then work with children to put the words together in a sentence.

- Write sentences about other features of the masks. Encourage children to use their imaginations, rather than striving for com-

plete realism. For example, they may decide that they would like their elephant to be red, not gray.

Revise

PRESENT TENSE VERBS Reread the sentences on the chart aloud. Tell children that all the verbs in the sentences should be written in the present tense, as if the events are happening right now. Have children point out each verb. Then help children determine if all the verbs are written in the present tense.

Publish

CREATE THE CHART Reread the sentences together. Then ask children what they would like to draw on the chart. Perhaps they would like to illustrate each line to show the differences between the features. Discuss different ways of illustrating it, and have them create charts and illustrations. Then copy the sentences onto the appropriate lines.

The elephant's leg is big and fat.

The mouse's leg is small and thin.

Presentation Ideas

MAKE THE MASKS Have children use the information on the chart they created to make a mask. After the masks are completed, have children tell how they used the chart to help them make their masks.

▶ **Representing/Speaking**

PERFORM AN ANIMAL PANTOMIME Invite pairs of children to put on their masks, one for each animal. Have the class give ideas for a pantomime, while the pairs act out what they hear. Encourage the class to watch the actors. Have them make suggestions about how the actors can follow the ideas given. ▶ **Listening/Viewing**

Meeting Individual Needs for Writing

EASY	ON-LEVEL	CHALLENGE
Give Instructions Children can draw pictures showing the steps they would use in making a mask of the animal of their choice. Ask them to look again at *Greg's Mask* and use it as a model. Have them label each step: Step 1, Step 2, and so on. They can then tell the steps to a classmate.	**New Story** Children can work in pairs to write a story about a girl named Kim who makes one of the masks they created on their chart. Have them follow language patterns from *Greg's Mask* as they write the story.	**Write an Invitation** Children can imagine that they're giving a costume party, and write an invitation that gives suggestions for costumes. Remind children to include their name, address, and telephone number in their invitation.

Listening and Speaking

LISTENING STRATEGIES
Remind actors to face the class and to listen carefully to their classmates' ideas before they start pantomiming. Then, after they have performed, encourage them to listen again to the class's suggestions so they can make their pantomime even better.

SPEAKING STRATEGIES
Encourage children to speak in complete sentences. Remind them to stay focused on the topic of their idea for a pantomime.

LANGUAGE SUPPORT

ESL Children can actively participate in the Make a Chart lesson with some support. Use gestures, quick sketches, and multiple examples to provide more context for your ESL learners. For example, use your hand to show a trunk from your nose and make whiskers come out of your cheeks.

PORTFOLIO Invite children to include their charts or another writing project in their portfolio.

5 Day Grammar and Usage Plan

Oral Warm-Up Say the following sentence aloud: *Dad helps me.* Ask children which word shows action now. (*helps*)

Introduce Present Tense Remind children that a verb is a word that shows action. Discuss with children:

> ### Present Tense
>
> - The **tense** of a verb tells when the action takes place.
> - Some verbs tell about actions that happen now.
> - These verbs are in the **present tense.**
> - Add -*s* to most verbs to tell what one person or thing does now.

Daily Language Activity Write the following on the chalkboard: *The hen runs.* Ask children which word shows an action that happens now. (*runs*)

 WRITING Assign daily Writing Prompt on page 38E.

Review Present Tense Remind children that some words show actions that happen now. Write the following sentences on the board: *Greg makes a mask. Tam clips the mask.* Read the sentences aloud, asking children to read with you. Ask children to find the verbs. (*makes, clips*) What do we add to the verb to show that action is happening now? (-*s*)

Daily Language Activity Write the following: *Duck swims.* Ask children to find the verb that shows action happening now. (*swims*) How do you form a verb that shows action now? (add -*s*)

 WRITING Assign the daily Writing Prompt on page 38E.

ESL Without the natural ear for what just "sounds right," many children whose native language is not English may have difficulty with present-tense verbs. For those children, write the following sentences on the chalkboard. Have children read with you as you read the sentences aloud. Emphasize the final *s* sound in each verb. Ask volunteers to circle the final *s* in each verb.

- Pup rides.
- Pup jumps.
- Pig plays.

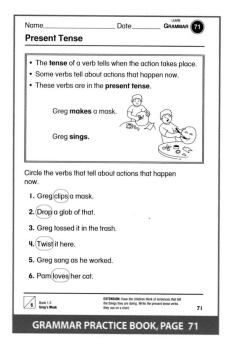

GRAMMAR PRACTICE BOOK, PAGE 71

GRAMMAR PRACTICE BOOK, PAGE 72

Present Tense

DAY 3 — Review and Practice

Learn from the Literature Review with children what present-tense verbs are. Write the following verbs from *Greg's Mask* on the chalkboard: *snip, drop, rip, twist, tape.*

Have children say their own present-tense sentences using *Greg* as the subject and one of those verbs from *Greg's Mask.* Example: *Greg drops the mask.* Write some of the children's sentences on the board and circle the final *s* in each verb. Elicit why each action word ends in *-s.* (The action is happening now.)

Daily Language Activity Have children use the list of verbs from *Greg's Mask* to write a new sentence containing one of the verbs in the present tense and the subject of their choice.

 Assign the daily Writing Prompt on page 38F.

 GRAMMAR PRACTICE BOOK, PAGE 73

DAY 4 — Review and Practice

Review Present Tense Write the following sentence on the board: *Tam find the mask.* Ask: What is wrong with the action word in this sentence? (The *-s* is missing.) How can we make the sentence say that Tam's action is happening now? (Add *-s* to the word *find.*)

Daily Language Activity Ask children to identify the present-tense verbs in the following sentences:

1. *Mack packs his hat.* packs
2. *Nan helps Dad.* helps

Mechanics and Usage Before children begin the daily Writing Prompt on page 38F, you may wish to discuss how book titles are usually written:

Book Titles

- The important words in a book title begin with a capital letter.
- Draw a line under the title of a book.

 Assign the daily Writing Prompt on page 38F.

GRAMMAR PRACTICE BOOK, PAGE 74

DAY 5 — Assess and Reteach

Daily Language Activity Write these sentences on the chalkboard. Read them with children. Have children identify the present-tense verb in each sentence.

1. Meg sits by me. *sits*
2. Stan wags his tail. *wags*

Assess Use page 75 of the **Grammar Practice Book** for assessment.

Reteach Prepare word cards for each sentence presented on Days 1 through 5. Give each group one set. Have them identify the present-tense verbs.

Assign the daily Writing Prompt on page 38F.

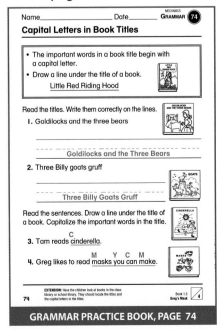

GRAMMAR PRACTICE BOOK, PAGE 75

GRAMMAR PRACTICE BOOK, PAGE 76

5 Day Spelling Plan

DAY 1 — Introduce Spelling Words

Assess Prior Knowledge Write the word *class* on the chalkboard. Circle the *c* and the *l* and ask children what sound each letter makes. Point out that the two sounds come together at the beginning of the word. Pronounce the word slowly and have children repeat it. Then repeat the exercise with the other Spelling Words, focusing on the initial /kl/, /dr/, or /tr/ sound.

	Spelling Words		Challenge Words
1.	**class**	5. trip	7. **any**
2.	**drop**	6. dress	8. **new**
3.	clap		9. **old**
4.	track		10. **grow**

*Note: Words in **dark type** are from the story.*

Write the words *any, new, old, grow* on the chalkboard. Ask children which two words mean the opposite of each other.

Word Study On page 72 of the **Spelling Practice Book** are word study steps and an at-home activity.

Words with Blends

Complete each word by writing **cl**, **tr**, or **dr** on the line.

1. __cl__ ass   2. __dr__ op

3. __tr__ ip   4. __cl__ ap

5. __tr__ ack   6. __dr__ ess

Directions (to teacher)

Write the word class on the chalkboard or form the word with letter cards. Say the word aloud and have children repeat it. Have them listen for the sounds /k/ and /l/ together at the beginning of the word. Then point out the first example with cl filled in.

Display the word drop. Say the word and have children repeat it. Ask them to listen for the two sounds at the beginning of the word (/d/ and /r/). Have them complete the second example.

Display the word trip and repeat the process above, having students listen for /t/ and /r/. Have them complete the third example.

Then display the words clap, track, and dress. Say the words and have children repeat them. Have children listen for /cl/, /tr/, or /dr/ in each word. Then have them complete the page.

Book 1.3
Greg's Mask
71

SPELLING PRACTICE BOOK, PAGE 71

WORD STUDY STEPS AND ACTIVITY, PAGE 72

DAY 2 — Teach the Pattern

Use the Pattern List the words *class, drop, track, clap, dress, trip* on the chalkboard and ask children to repeat them. Write *cl, dr, tr* next to the word list and point to the *cl*. Ask children to read the words that start with this pattern. Repeat the question for *dr* and *tr*.

To extend the activity, write the patterns *cl, dr, tr* in a column on the chalkboard. To their right, write ___*ip*. Write *cl* in the blank space. Point to the letters and blend the sounds together to read *clip*. Erase the *cl* and write in *dr*. Ask children to blend these sounds with you to read *drip*. Repeat with *tr* to have the children build and read *trip*.

Words with Blends

Look at the spelling words in the box.

track dress class drop clap trip

Write the words that begin with **cl**.

1. class   2. clap

Write the words that begin with **tr**.

3. track   4. trip

Write the words that begin with **dr**.

5. drop   6. dress

Book 1.3
Greg's Mask
73

SPELLING PRACTICE BOOK, PAGE 73

LANGUAGE SUPPORT

LANGUAGE SUPPORT

ESL Some non-native speakers may add a vowel sound between consonants. Explain that the /kl/, /dr/, and /tr/ sounds are so close together they cannot be pronounced correctly unless said together. Have children repeat the sounds aloud and ask them to notice how their mouths and tongues move when they say /kl/, /dr/, and /tr/.

Words with Blends

DAY 3 Practice and Extend

Word Meaning: Endings Write the word *class* on the chalkboard and ask children to read it aloud. Say: *This class is doing a good job of listening.* Ask children to repeat the sentence. Then ask volunteers to suggest how they think the sentence would change if it were about more than one class. Emphasize the correct answer: *These classes are doing a good job of listening.* Add *-es* to *class* on the chalkboard and have children repeat the sentence after you. Repeat with the word *dress.*

Identify Spelling Patterns Write this story on the chalkboard: *She took one new dress and one old dress on her trip. But if she grows any bigger, the dresses will not fit.* Have children read it aloud with you. Ask them which words have the spelling patterns *dr* and *tr* and which are Challenge Words.

DAY 4 Practice and Write

Complete Sentences Write on the chalkboard: *This is [your name]'s _____.* Read the sentence aloud and ask children to complete it with a *cl-* word. Continue saying incomplete sentences and asking children to use spelling words to complete them. For example: *Did you _____ your book? How was your _____? Let's _____ hands and sing!*

 Have children use as many spelling words as possible in the daily Writing Prompt on page 38F. Remind them to check their writing for errors in spelling, grammar, and punctuation.

DAY 5 Assess and Reteach

Optional Spelling Test You may wish to give children a spelling test. You may administer it in the following manner: (1) Read the word. (2) Give a simple sentence containing the word. (3) Say the word again. Or you may use page 76 of the **Spelling Practice Book** for the posttest. If you wish, you may create additional sentences for the Challenge Words.

Personal Word List Have children add the words they still find difficult to their personal troublesome words lists in their journals. Have children write a context sentence or draw and label an illustration for each word. Children should refer to these word lists during later writing activities.

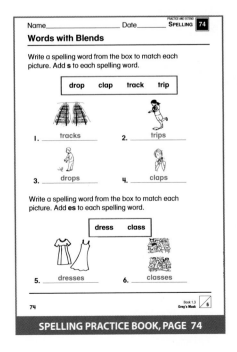

SPELLING PRACTICE BOOK, PAGE 74

SPELLING PRACTICE BOOK, PAGE 75

SPELLING PRACTICE BOOK, PAGE 76

67R

Concept
• Learn Something New

Comprehension
• Compare and Contrast

Phonics
• ch, wh, nk

Vocabulary
• together
• now
• eat
• too

Anthology

Sam's Song

Selection Summary A baby owl is ashamed of her small song, until she learns to accept it as her own. As Sam discovers her song, children may find that they, too, have their own stories to tell.

by Alyssa Satin Capucilli
illustrated by Melissa Iwai

Listening Library

INSTRUCTIONAL pages 70–97

Rhyme applies to Phonics

About the Author Alyssa Satin Capucilli has always loved writing. "I get ideas from the wonderful memories of my own family and from things that I care about," she says. Ms. Capucilli is also a dancer and dance teacher. When she is not writing or dancing, she enjoys taking long walks with her dog Huckleberry.

About the Illustrator Melissa Iwai has been drawing since she was a little girl. By the time she was nine, she was making books for herself. She says, "I always wanted to illustrate children's books." And now she does.

Same Concept, Skills and Vocabulary!

Leveled Books

EASY
Lesson on pages 97A and 97D
`DECODABLE`

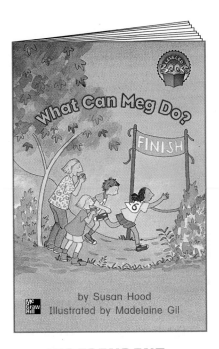

INDEPENDENT
Lesson on pages 97B and 97D

🏠 *Take-Home version available*

`DECODABLE`

CHALLENGE
Lesson on pages 97C and 97D

Leveled Practice

EASY

Reteach, 101-108 Blackline masters with reteaching opportunities for each assessed skill

INDEPENDENT/ON-LEVEL

Practice, 101-108 Workbook with Take-Home Stories and practice opportunities for each assessed skill and story comprehension

CHALLENGE

Extend, 101-108 Blackline masters that offer challenge activities for each assessed skill

Quizzes Prepared by ◆ Accelerated Reader®

Center Activities

Social Studies ... What's in a Name?, *78*

Science .... Owls, *86*

Math .... Story Problems, *82*

Music .... Starry Song, *84*

Language Arts .. Read Aloud, *68G*, Owls and Crickets, *88*

Cultural Perspectives ..... Family Names, *74*

Research and Inquiry ...... Find Out More, *95*

Internet Activities .... www.mhschool.com/reading

Center Activities

Each of these activities takes 15-20 minutes.

Phonics

Picture This!

 Objective: Read words with **PARTNERS** initial and final digraphs.

◆ Display words with *ch*, *wh*, and *nk*.

◆ Have children choose five words and write each on a card.

◆ On the back, children draw a picture for the word. Then partners can practice with their flashcards.

drink

MATERIALS

- Large index cards
- Crayons

Writing

I Can!

 Objective: Write sentences **ONE** that describe things children can do.

◆ Display these sentence frames: "My name is _____. I can _____!"

◆ Have children complete each sentence.

◆ Children draw pictures to illustrate their sentence.

MATERIALS

- Construction paper
- Crayons

Reading and Listening

Independent/Self-Selected Reading

 Objective: Listen and use illustrations to **ONE** understand a story.

Fill the Center with books and corresponding audiocassettes or CD-ROMs children have read or listened to this week. You can also include books from the Theme Bibliography on pages T98 and T99.

Leveled Readers

◆ *What's New at the Zoo?* by Judy Nayer
◆ *What Can Meg Do?* by Susan Hood
◆ *The Cow That Went OINK* by Bernard Most

◆ Theme Big Book *I Go with My Family to Grandma's* by Riki Levinson

◆ *Sam's Song* by Alyssa Satin Capucilli

◆ "Something About Me"—Anonymous

◆ Phonics Practice Reader, Vol. 1

Working with Words

Write Sentences

 Objective: Reinforce vocabulary words: *together, now, eat, too.*

◆ Have children look at pages 84, 89, and 93 and find the vocabulary words *together, now, eat,* and *too.*

◆ Have children work together to write a new sentence for each word.

MATERIALS
- *Sam's Song* in the Student Anthology
- Paper
- Pencil

Science

Animal Homes

Objective: Research and write sentences about animals.

◆ Make available books about animal homes. Children choose an animal and draw a picture of it in its home.

◆ Have children write about their picture: "A _____ lives in a(n) _____."

MATERIALS
- Books about animals
- Drawing paper
- Crayons

An owl lives in a nest.

Social Studies

My Family

Objective: Draw and label a picture of one's family.

◆ Have children cut the top of the construction paper in the shape of a roof to make a house.

◆ Children can write their family's name across the roof as shown.

◆ Then children draw their family and label each person.

MATERIALS
- Construction paper
- Scissors
- Crayons

Jim's Family

Mom Dad Jim

Sam's Song

by Alyssa Satin Capucilli
Illustrated by Melissa Iwai

Suggested Lesson Planner

READING AND LANGUAGE ARTS	**DAY 1** Focus on Reading and Skills	**DAY 2** Read the Literature
● **Phonics Daily Routines**	Daily **Phonics** Routine: **Letter/Sound Relationship,** 68J **Phonics** CD-ROM	Daily **Phonics** Routine: **Build Words,** 70A **Phonics** CD-ROM
● **Phonological Awareness** ● **Phonics** *ch, wh, nk* ● **Comprehension** ● **Vocabulary** ● **Study Skills** ● **Listening, Speaking, Viewing, Representing**	**Read** **Read Aloud,** 68G "The Plumage of the Owl" ☑ **Develop Phonological Awareness,** 68H ☑ **Introduce** *ch, wh, nk,* 68I–68J **Reteach, Practice, Extend,** 101 **Phonics/Phonemic Awareness Practice Book,** 125–128 **Read** **Apply** *ch, wh, nk* "Lunch Munch," 68/69 ⓘ Intervention Program	**Build Background,** 70A Develop Oral Language **Vocabulary,** 70B–70C *together* now eat too **Word Building Manipulative Cards Teaching Chart 75** **Reteach, Practice, Extend,** 102 **Read** **Read the Selection,** 70–93 **Guided Instruction** ☑ *wh, nk, ch* ☑ **Compare and Contrast** **Genre: Story,** 71 **Cultural Perspectives,** 74 ⓘ Intervention Program
● **Curriculum Connections**	**Link** Language Arts, 68G	**Link** Science, 70A
● **Writing**	**Writing Prompt:** Write about how you felt when you learned something new.	**Writing Prompt:** Write about an activity that your family enjoys doing together. 📔 **Journal Writing** Quick-Write, 93
● **Grammar**	**Introduce the Concept: Past Tense,** 97O Daily Language Activity: Identify the word that shows past action. **Grammar Practice Book,** 77	**Teach the Concept: Past Tense,** 97O Daily Language Activity: Identify past-tense verbs in sentences. **Grammar Practice Book,** 78
● **Spelling** *ch, wh, nk*	**Introduce Spelling Words: Words with** *ch, wh, nk,* 97Q **Spelling Practice Book,** 77–78	**Teach the Patterns: Words with** *ch, wh, nk,* 97Q **Spelling Practice Book,** 79

 ✓ = **Skill Assessed in Unit Test**

ⓘ **Intervention Program Available**

Read EVERY DAY

DAY 3 Read the Literature	**DAY 4** Build Skills	**DAY 5** Build Skills
Daily **Phonics** Routine: **Blending,** 95 **Phonics** CD-ROM	Daily **Phonics** Routine: **Fluency,** 97F **Phonics** CD-ROM	Daily **Phonics** Routine: **Writing,** 97H **Phonics** CD-ROM

DAY 3

Rereading for Fluency, 92

Story Questions, 94
　Reteach, Practice, Extend, 103

Story Activities, 95

Study Skill, 96
　☑ **Diagrams**
　　Teaching Chart 76
　　Reteach, Practice, Extend, 104

Test Power, 97

 **Read the Leveled Books, Guided Reading**
　☑ Read Words with *ch, wh, nk*
　☑ Compare and Contrast
　☑ High-Frequency Words

ⓘ Intervention Program

DAY 4

 Read the Leveled Books and the Self-Selected Books

☑ **Review *ch, wh, nk,*** 97E–97F
　Teaching Chart 77
　Reteach, Practice, Extend, 105
　Language Support, 114
　Phonics/Phonemic Awareness Practice Book, 125–128

☑ **Review *ch, wh, nk;* Blends,** 97G–97H
　Teaching Chart 78
　Reteach, Practice, Extend, 106
　Language Support, 115
　Phonics/Phonemic Awareness Practice Book, 125–128

Minilessons, 77, 79, 81, 89, 91

ⓘ Intervention Program

DAY 5

 Read Self-Selected Books

☑ **Review Compare and Contrast,** 97I–97J
　Teaching Chart 79
　Reteach, Practice, Extend, 107
　Language Support, 116

☑ **Introduce Contractions,** 97K–97L
　Teaching Chart 80
　Reteach, Practice, Extend, 108
　Language Support, 117

Listening, Speaking, Viewing, Representing, 97N
　Sing a Song
　Draw a Scene from a Music Video

Minilessons, 77, 79, 81, 89, 91

ⓘ Intervention Program

Activity Social Studies, 68D, 78; Math, 82 | **Activity** Music, 84 | **Activity** Science, 68D, 86

 Writing Prompt: Describe a song you like. Tell why you enjoy singing it.

 Journal Writing, 97D

 Writing Prompt: Write a story about an animal and how it spends a day or night with its family.

Interactive Writing: Make a Song Book, 97M
　Prewrite, Draft

Meeting Individual Needs for Writing, 97N

 Writing Prompt: What if you were an owl? Write about what you like to do, and why it's fun to be an owl.

Interactive Writing, 97M
　Revise and Publish a Song Book

Practice and Write: Past Tense, 97P
　Daily Language Activity: Use past-tense verbs in sentences.

Grammar Practice Book, 79

Practice and Write: Past Tense, 97P
　Daily Language Activity: Identify past-tense sentences.

Grammar Practice Book, 80

Assess and Reteach: Past Tense, 97P
　Daily Language Activity: Identify and form past-tense verbs.

Grammar Practice Book, 81, 82

Practice and Extend: Words with *ch, wh, nk,* 97R

Spelling Practice Book, 80

Practice and Write: Words with *ch, wh, nk,* 97R

Spelling Practice Book, 81

Assess and Reteach: Words with *ch, wh, nk,* 97R

Spelling Practice Book, 82

Read Aloud

The Plumage of the Owl
a folktale retold by Ricardo E. Alegria

A long time ago, the animals used to give parties and balls and have good times together. At this time the birds decided to give a ball, and they invited all the bird family to come. The hawk was in charge of issuing the invitations, and he called upon each bird to invite him personally.

When he came to the owl's house, he found him naked. The owl told him that he could not come to the ball as he had no clothes to wear. The hawk told the other birds about this, and they decided that each one of them would lend the owl a feather so that he could make a dress suit and come to the ball.

The hawk collected feathers of different colors from each and took them to the owl but told him that, after the ball was over, each feather was to be returned to its owner. The owl was delighted with the feathers. He made himself a fine dress suit and appeared at the ball.

Continued on pages T2–T5

Oral Comprehension

LISTENING AND SPEAKING Encourage children to think about comparing and contrasting by reading this folktale. Have children think about the animals in the folktale, and how they are alike and different, as you read. When you are done, ask, "How is the owl like the other animals in the story? How is the owl different from the other animals in the story?"

 **Activity** Ask children to draw the owl's coat. Remind children that the coat contains feathers of many colors from different birds. Help children by providing pictures of various birds and ask children to describe different birds they have seen or read about. When children have finished, have them compare their drawings.

▶ **Visual**

GENRE STUDY: FOLKTALE Tell children that a folktale is a story created by a certain group of people in one place at one time. Folktales are generally passed down from one generation to the next. This folktale comes from Puerto Rico. Point out Puerto Rico on a map. Also explain that folktales often try to explain something. This folktale gives a reason for why owls only come out at night.

Develop Phonological Awareness

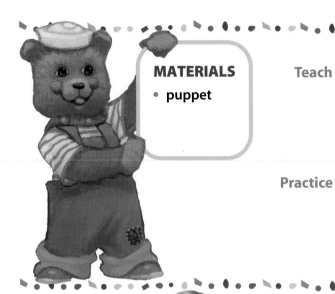

Blend Sounds

Phonemic
Awareness

MATERIALS
* puppet

Teach Have the puppet point to your chin and ask: *What is the word for this part of your face?* (chin) Have the puppet ask children to say the beginning sound they hear in *chin.* (/ch/) Then blend the three sounds in *chin:* /ch/-/i/-/n/ and say the word. Have children repeat after you. Continue with the words *chat* and *when.*

Practice Use the following words to have children practice their blending: *chip, chill, check, inch, munch, bench, what, whisk, sink, thank, bunk.* For each word, say the sounds, for example: /ch/-/i/-/p/. Then have them blend the sounds together to form the word.

Segment Sounds

Phonemic
Awareness

MATERIALS
* Word Building Boxes

Teach Explain that the Word Building Boxes represent the beginning, middle, and ending sounds in a word. Say the word *check,* and identify its three sounds: /ch/-/e/-/k/ as you point to each box. Next, say the sound /ch/. Ask children to identify the box that represents that sound. Repeat for the medial and final sounds.

Practice Have children use the following words for practice with segmenting: *chest, chop, when, lunch, pink, chess, ranch, such.* Have children say the word and segment its sounds. Finally, have children identify the number of sounds in the word.

Substitute Sounds

Phonemic
Awareness

/b/-/u/-/nk/

Teach Have children identify the three sounds in *bank:* /b/-/a/-/nk/. Then explain that you are going to remove the middle sound from *bank,* /a/, and replace it with /u/. Ask children to blend and identify the new word. *(bunk)*

Practice Using the following word sets, have children make new words by changing the medial sound. Say the first word in each set, and give children another medial sound. Then have children say the new word: *bunch, bench; check, chick; sank, sink; chimp, champ; thank, think.*

ASSESSMENT Observe children as they blend sounds, segment sounds, and substitute medial sounds. If children have difficulty, see Alternate Teaching Strategies on page T72.

OBJECTIVES

Children will:

- identify /ch/*ch*, /hw/*wh*, /ngk/*nk*.
- blend and read words with digraphs *ch, wh, nk*.
- blend and read words with *nk*.
- review short vowels; blends *cr, pl, sk*; digraph *ck*.

MATERIALS

- letter and digraph cards from the **Word Building Manipulative Cards**

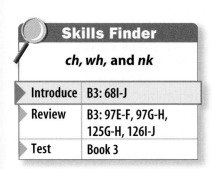

Skills Finder

ch, wh, and nk

Introduce	B3: 68I-J
Review	B3: 97E-F, 97G-H, 125G-H, 126I-J
Test	Book 3

SPELLING/PHONICS CONNECTIONS

Words with *ch, wh,* and *nk*: See the 5-Day Spelling Plan, pages 97Q–97R.

Introduce *ch, wh, and nk*

TEACH

Identify the Letters *ch* as a Symbol for the Sound /ch/

Explain to children that sometimes two letters put together make their own special sound.

- Display the *ch* letter card.
- Point to the card and make the /ch/ sound. Have children repeat after you.

BLENDING
Model and Guide Practice with *ch, wh,* and *nk* Words

- Add the *i* letter card. Help children blend the sounds.

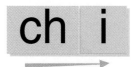

- Place the *n* letter card after the *i* and repeat.

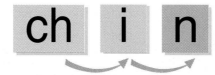

Use the Word in Context

- Use the word in context to reinforce its meaning. Example: *My chin is below my mouth.*

Repeat the Procedure

- Use the following words to continue modeling and guided practice with *ch, wh,* and *nk*.

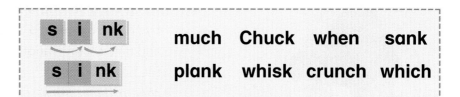

much	Chuck	when	sank
plank	whisk	crunch	which

PRACTICE

LETTER SUBSTITUTION
Build *ch*, *wh*, and *nk* Words with Letter Cards

GROUP

Build the word *chip*, asking children to repeat the sounds after you. Then ask them to substitute the *o* letter card for *i* and have them blend and say *chop*. Continue the activity, building words with /nk/ and /wh/. Have children substitute letters and build new words.

▶ **Visual/Kinesthetic**

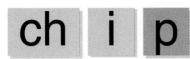

ch i p o

ASSESS/CLOSE

Read and Sort *ch*, *wh*, and *nk* Words

To assess children's ability to blend and read *ch*, *wh*, and *nk* words, observe children as they use the letter cards to build words in the Practice activity. Ask them to organize and write the words on paper according to three groups: *ch*, *wh*, and *nk*.

ADDITIONAL PHONICS RESOURCES

Phonics/Phonemic Awareness Practice Book,
pages 125–128

PHONICS KIT
Hands-on Activities and Practice

McGraw-Hill School
TECHNOLOGY

Phonics CD-ROM
activities for practice with
Blending and Segmenting

Meeting Individual Needs for Phonics

EASY	ON-LEVEL	CHALLENGE

EASY

Name_____ Date_____ **Reteach** 101

ch, wh, nk

Name each picture. Say the sound of the letters.
Notice the new sounds that **ch**, **wh**, and **nk** make.
whale   **ch**ick   li**nk**

Circle the word that completes each sentence. Then write the word.

1. Is my vest in that ___chest___ ?
   (chest) check   chin

2. ___When___ can I feed the hen?
   (When) Whale   While

3. Put that drink in the ___sink___
   think (sink) pink

4. I munch on my ___lunch___
   (lunch) pinch   ranch

Book 1.3
Sam's Song
At Home: Ask children to circle the blend in each of the answers above and to say its sound.   101

ON-LEVEL

Name_____ Date_____ **Practice** 101

ch, wh, nk

Read the words. Then read the riddles. Choose a word to answer each riddle.

| chick | when | branch | wink |

1. I am a small bird.
   What am I?
   ___chick___

2. I am one eye, closed and opened.
   What am I?
   ___wink___

3. I am the arm of a tree.
   What am I?
   ___branch___

4. Ask me what time it happened.
   What are you asking?
   ___when___

Book 1.3
Sam's Song
At Home: Ask children to circle the consonant blends in each word and recite the word.   101

CHALLENGE

Name_____ Date_____ **Extend** 101

ch, wh, nk

Words with **ch**, **wh**, or **nk** are everywhere.
Look on the walls. Look in books. Look in newspapers.
Write the words you find.
Answers will vary. Samples are shown.

ch   ch
___chip___   ___lunch___
___chop___   ___munch___
wh   nk
___whip___   ___chunk___
___whisk___   ___drank___

Book 1.3
Sam's Song
At Home: Have children use some of the words they found to make a poster.   101

Reteach, 101   **Practice, 101**   **Extend, 101**

Daily Routines

DAY 1 **Letter/Sound Relationships** Write *ch* on the chalkboard. Then read a section from *Sam's Song* and ask children to raise their hands when they hear a word with that sound. Repeat with *wh* and *nk*.

DAY 2 **Build Words** Write the spelling of each sound in *ink* and *ank* as you say it. Invite children to write beginning letters to form words. Have children read the words they build.

DAY 3 **Blending** Write *nk*, *ch*, and *wh* on the chalkboard. Write words omitting these initial and final letters and have children complete the words: *crunch, blank, chip, chop, much, when, whisk.*

DAY 4 **Fluency** Write the following words on the chalkboard: *clank, bank, drank, prank, thank.* Read the words with children. Then ask individuals to read the words.

DAY 5 **Writing** Write a list of *nk*, *wh*, and *ch* words on the chalkboard. Ask children to write riddles using one or more of these words.

TESTED OBJECTIVES

Children will read a poem with words containing digraphs *ch*, *wh*, and *nk*.

Apply *ch, wh,* and *nk*

Lunch Munch

Hank sits up on top
When we have lunch.
Mom gives him lots
To chomp and crunch.

He spills his drink.
Chomp, chomp, crunch, munch.
Hank learns to chew
Each bit and bunch.

68

69

Anthology pages 68–69

Read and Build Fluency

READ THE POEM Tell children they will read a poem called *Lunch Munch*. Model reading with expression. Have children chime in on the words *chomp, chomp, crunch, munch*. Children can then read with you.

REREAD FOR FLUENCY Have small groups reread the poem. Have them alternate reading each line of the poem, creating sound effects.

GROUP

READ A DECODABLE STORY For additional practice reading and to develop fluency, have children read *Chet Chick* from **Phonics Practice Reader, Vol. 1.**

Dictate and Spell

DICTATE WORDS Segment the word *drink* into its four individual sounds. Emphasize the digraph *nk* as one sound. Repeat the word aloud and use it in a sentence: *Hank likes to drink milk.* Then have children say the word and write the letter or letters that represent each sound until they make the entire word. Repeat with *lunch, munch, when, chomp, crunch, Hank,* and *bunch* from the poem. Then repeat with other words such as *bank, bench, check, chill, sink, think, yank, whisk,* and *wink.*

JOURNAL

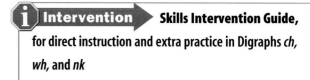

i **Intervention** ▶ **Skills Intervention Guide,** for direct instruction and extra practice in Digraphs *ch, wh,* and *nk*

Build Background

Science

Concept: Learn Something New

Evaluate Prior Knowledge

CONCEPT: LEARN SOMETHING NEW

Ask children to share with the class something new they recently learned to do, such as playing ball, learning a new game, or playing the guitar or piano.

MAKE A CHART ABOUT LEARNING NEW THINGS
Have children brainstorm about how they learned to do something new. Make a chart to record children's suggestions. ▶ **Linguistic**

PROBLEM: LEARN TO PLAY BALL	
ATTEMPTS	**OUTCOMES**
I kept throwing the ball at a wall.	I learned to hold and throw a ball.
I played catch with Mom.	I learned to catch a ball.
I played in the schoolyard with other kids.	I learned to play ball.

DRAW AND LABEL A LEARNING PICTURE

ONE **WRITING** Invite children to draw themselves learning something new. Children can use the chart to help them.

Develop Oral Language

CONNECT WORDS AND ACTIONS

ESL Explain to children that in the story they are going to read, a young bird learns something new. Invite children to pretend to be birds. Ask them to show some things that birds do, such as:

* fly
* hop
* eat

Then have other children ask what they are doing. Model questions such as:

* What are you doing?
* How are you moving?
* Why are you flying?

▶ **Kinesthetic/Linguistic**

DAILY Phonics ROUTINES

DAY 2 **Build Words** Write the spelling of each sound in *ink* and *ank* as you say it. Invite children to write beginning letters to form words. Have children read the words they build.

Phonics CD-ROM

LANGUAGE SUPPORT

To build more background, see pages 109–112 in the **Language Support Book**.

together

eat

too

now

Vocabulary
High-Frequency Words

OBJECTIVES

Children will:

• identify high-frequency words *together*, *too*, *eat*, and *now*.

MATERIALS

• Teaching Chart 75

• Word Building Manipulative Cards *together*, *too*, *eat*, *now*

TEACHING TIP

The following chart indicates words from the upcoming story that children have learned to decode and high-frequency words that have been taught in this lesson.

Decodable		High-Frequency
branch	plink	eat
chest	plunk	now
chick	sank	together
chin	sink	too
chuck	think	
crunch	when	
drink	whish	
much	wink	

SPELLING/VOCABULARY CONNECTIONS

The words *together*, *now*, *eat*, and *too* are Challenge Words. See page 97Q for Day 1 of the 5-Day Spelling Plan.

Tom's Lunch

Mom and Dad and the rest of the bunch
Sat together to eat their lunch.
"Yum," said Sis. "Yum," said Mom.
"I want that, too," said Baby Tom.
Dad said, "Tom, you are just very small.
Now you have no teeth at all."
Tom said, "Look!" and had a grin.
And there was a new tooth that was in.
Then together they had their lunch.
And Big Kid Tom could munch and crunch.

Teaching Chart 75

Auditory

LISTEN TO WORDS Read aloud "Tom's Lunch" on **Teaching Chart 75**. Ask children if they'd ever been told that they were too little to do something. Were they able to do it later?

PLAY A QUESTION-AND-ANSWER GAME Tell children that you will play a game with the high-frequency words. Say the words aloud and read a line from the poem for each one.

• Ask: Which vocabulary word has three syllables? *(together)*

• Ask: Which vocabulary word means the same as "today" and "at this time"? It rhymes with *how* and *cow*. *(now)*

• Ask: Which vocabulary word sounds like other words we know? *(too)* What are they? *(two* and *to)*

• Ask: Which vocabulary word tells you to do something? *(eat)*

Visual

TEACH WORDS Display "Tom's Lunch" on **Teaching Chart 75**. Read the poem, tracking the print with your finger. Next, point to the word *together*. Tell children that this is the word *together*. Have them say the word with you. Ask them to hold up the vocabulary card for *together* and say the word. Repeat this procedure for *too*, *eat*, and *now*.

Hold up vocabulary cards for *together*, *too*, *eat*, and *now* one at a time. Have volunteers read the words and then circle them on the chart.

Word Building Manipulative Cards

GUESS WORDS Pair children. One child displays a vocabulary card without looking at it. The other child gives clues about the word. The first child can guess the word.

Word Wall

This Is What I Mean Tell children that you will tell them the meaning of a word wall word. Have them point to the word that matches the meaning.

right away *(now)*
to put food in your mouth, chew, and swallow *(eat)*
with others *(together)*
also *(too)*

Pick a Letter Choose a word wall word. Draw lines for each letter of the word on the chalkboard. As children suggest letters, write those letters in the word on the appropriate line. Write incorrect letters in a "used letter box". Have children guess all the letters before saying the word.

LANGUAGE SUPPORT

To help children develop understanding and recognition of high-frequency words, see page 109 in the **Language Support Book.**

Assess

Words in Context Ask children to use each of the word wall words in a sentence. Children should then spell the word out loud.

Meeting Individual Needs for Vocabulary

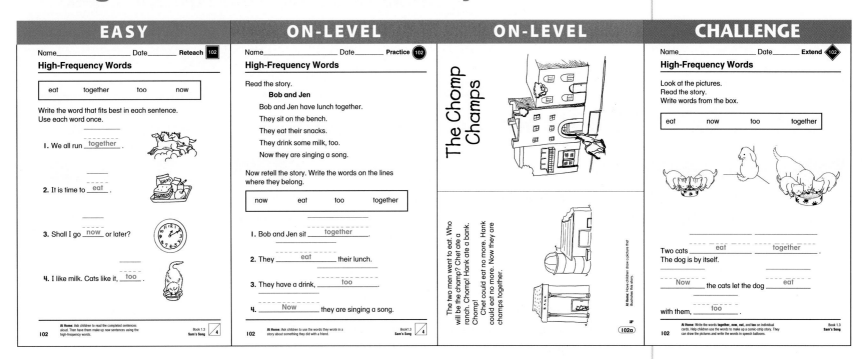

EASY	ON-LEVEL	ON-LEVEL	CHALLENGE
Reteach, 102	Practice, 102	Practice, 102a Take-Home Story	Extend, 102

Comprehension

Prereading Strategies

PREVIEW AND PREDICT Point to the name of the author, Alyssa Satin Capucilli, and read it aloud. Then ask children to point to the name of the illustrator, Melissa Iwai, as you read it aloud. Ask what each person does. Then take a **picture walk** through the story, talking about the illustrations of the owl family and the baby owl in particular. After discussing the illustrations, ask children to say what the story might be about.

Ask children to make predictions about the plot and the characters. Record the predictions and read them aloud.

PREDICTIONS	WHAT HAPPENED
Sam is sad.	
Sam sees a star.	

SET PURPOSES Ask children what they want to find out as they read the story. For example:

- What animals live in the forest?
- How does Sam learn to sing?

READ TOGETHER

(1)

Meet Alyssa Satin Capucilli

Alyssa Satin Capucilli began writing stories when she was just a little girl. When Capucilli grew up and had children, she knew that she wanted a career writing for children. "I get ideas from the wonderful memories of my own family and from things that I care about," she says.

Meet Melissa Iwai

Melissa Iwai has been drawing since she was little. By the time she was nine, she was making books for herself. She says, "I always wanted to illustrate children's books." And now she does.

70

Meeting Individual Needs • Grouping Suggestions for Strategic Reading

EASY

Shared Reading Read the story aloud as you model directionality and track print. Pay particular attention to pages where the print follows a different format, such as page 72. Help children focus on how Sam changes during the story.

ON-LEVEL

Guided Instruction Read the selection with children, using the Comprehension questions. Monitor any difficulties in reading that children may have to determine which parts of the Comprehension section to emphasize. After reading the story with children, have children reread it, using the rereading suggestions on page 92.

CHALLENGE

Independent Reading Have children set purposes before they read. Ask them to read the story independently. Then ask children to retell the story from Sam's point of view. Ask them to compare how Sam felt at the beginning of the story and how she felt at the end of the story.

Sam's Song

by Alyssa Satin Capucilli

illustrated by Melissa Iwai

71

Comprehension

☑ **Phonics** *ch, wh, nk*

☑ **Apply Compare and Contrast**

STRATEGIC READING Explain to children that to understand the story, they can think about how a character changes. Explain that they will use puppets to act out the story and think about how the characters change.

① We are going to read *Sam's Song.* Let's look at the picture at the top of page 70. This is a picture of the author, Alyssa Satin Capucilli. Let's read about her. Now look at the bottom picture. This is Melissa Iwai. She drew the pictures for this story. *Concept of a Book: Author/Illustrator*

② Let's look at the picture on page 71. What do you see? (an owl) Can we tell if it is day or night? How? (It is night. The moon in the dark sky tells us it is nighttime.) *Use Illustrations*

Genre

Story

Remind children that a story is a fictional piece that contains characters, plot (a series of events), and setting.

Activity Have children compare the activities of the owl family with their own. Encourage children to find similarities between the owl family's activities and the activities of their own family.

71

Comprehension

3 **Phonics** *ch*, *wh*, and *nk* Point to where we should begin reading. Listen as I read the first sentence: *"The owls sat on their . . ."* I need to blend the sounds together to read the word. b r a n ch branch
Graphophonic Cues

TRACKING PRINT Let's read the second sentence together. Point to the words *down, down, down*. What is different about these words? (They are printed in a slanted line, down instead of across the page.) Why do you think the words are printed this way? (It shows the meaning of the words.)
Syntactic Cues

4 Look at the pictures on pages 72–73. How is the sky different in the two pictures? (It is still daytime in the picture on page 72. It is nighttime in the picture on page 73.) What does this tell us about the sun on page 72? (The sun is setting.)
Compare and Contrast/Use Illustrations

Fluency

GROUP READING

Model tracking print and rereading to achieve fluency.

• Point to and read aloud the first word in the sentence.

• Run your finger under each word as you read the rest of the sentence without pausing.

• Then have children repeat this process, pointing to each word as they read.

3 The owls sat on their branch. They watched the sun sink down,

down,

down.

72

PREVENTION/INTERVENTION

TRACKING PRINT Point to the word *down*, and ask children to identify the comma that follows the word. Remind them to pause when they see the comma. Then, have children read the sentence with you. You may wish to experiment with deepening your voice as you read *down, down, down*. Give children the opportunity to experiment and read the sentence with expression, as well. Then write *up, up, up* on the chalkboard so the words are written in an upward slanted direction. Encourage children to read these words and raise their voices up as they do so. *Syntactic Cues*

It was pitch black out.
Now they would sing.

73

Comprehension

MULTIPLE-MEANING WORDS Read the sentence that contains the word *pitch*. What do you think the word means in this sentence? (completely) Point out that the word *pitch* also refers to "the throw of the baseball from the pitcher to the batter," as well as "the highness or lowness of a musical sound." Give children examples of these meanings, such as: The batter swung at the first *pitch*. The chorus sang at a high *pitch*. *Semantic Cues*

5 How has the setting changed in the story? (The owls are still in the forest, but it is nighttime.) *Analyze Setting*

TEACHING TIP

SETTING You might want to have children chart the changes in setting through the story. A chart such as the following can be used:

Page	Time of Day	What Happens
73	night	singing

PREVENTION/INTERVENTION

MULTIPLE-MEANING WORDS
Remind children that some words have more than one meaning. Ask children what they think of when they read the word *pitch*. (baseball, music) Then have children read the first sentence on this page again, and review what the word *pitch* means in this sentence. (very, or completely) (Some children may know that pitch is a black material like tar.) Make a list of other phrases that describe colors: *beet red, baby blue, hot pink*. Ask children to talk about other meanings for the words *beet*, *baby*, and *hot*. *Semantic Cues*

Comprehension

6 Point to each name on this page. What type of letters do the names begin with? (capital letters) Why does each name begin with a capital letter? (The name of a person, place, or thing begins with a capital letter.) Let's read the names together. (Mom, Pop, Chuck) *Concepts of Print*

Hold up your puppets of Mom, Pop, and Chuck as you read pages 74–75. *Story Props*

6 "Whooooo!" sang Mom.
"Whooooo!" sang Pop.
Chuck could sing, too.
"Whooooo!" he sang out.

74

FAMILY NAMES Explain that families often have different names and nicknames for family members. Ask if any children know the words for *mother* and *father* in other languages.

▶ **Linguistic/Visual**

Activity Have children draw pictures of family members. Write foreign words for *mother* or *father* on the pictures and make a display.

interNET CONNECTION For links to sites about the family, help children log onto **www.mhschool.com/reading**

Then they sang together.

What a nice song it was!

75

Comprehension

7 **MULTISYLLABIC WORDS** Look at the first sentence. How many parts, or syllables, does the word *together* have? (three) Now read the word aloud. What does it mean? (with one another)

8 What mark do you see at the end of the second sentence? (exclamation mark) What does this mark tell you? (to read with excitement and emotion) Let's read that sentence with emotion. *Concepts of Print/Fluency*

Comprehension

9 Which sentence on this page asks a question? (*What is it?*) Which sentence should be read with an excited voice? (*It's a new chick!*) How do you know? (It ends with an exclamation mark.) *Concepts of Print*

10 How do you think Mom and Chuck feel? (excited) How can you tell? *Use Illustrations/Make Inferences*

TAPING AND LISTENING

 Model tracking print and fluency by reading the text on pages 76–77.

- Run your finger under each word as you read.
- Change your tone of voice for Chuck's question and Mom and Pop's responses.

Then ask a child to read the pages aloud into a tape recorder. Rewind and play the tape and have the child listen. Repeat the taping one or two more times to improve fluency.

One day there was a big fuss.

9 "What is it?" asked Chuck.

"It's a new chick!" said Mom.

76

"Let's call her Sam!" said Pop.

77

Comprehension

11 Who is talking? (Pop) How do you know? (There are quotation marks around the words.) *Concepts of Print*

12 **COMPARE AND CONTRAST** How does Sam look different from Mom, Pop, and Chuck? (She's smaller, her head is white.)

Let's use our puppets to show what's going on. *Story Props*

Minilesson

REVIEW/MAINTAIN

Use Context Clues

Point out that children can use words and pictures to understand new words.

- Have children point to the word *chick* on page 76. Discuss how the picture can help them understand the word. Ask them to describe the baby owl.

- What other baby animal is called a chick?

Activity Invite children to make a list of other words that describe baby animals: dog/puppy, cat/kitten, horse/foal, sheep/lamb. Provide picture books to help.

Comprehension

13 **COMPARE AND CONTRAST** Look at the picture on page 73. Now look at the picture on pages 78–79. How are the pictures alike? How are they different? (alike: owls on branch; different: there are four owls on these pages instead of three. The owls here are singing, not just sitting on a branch. It is not pitch black here as it is on page 73.)

14 **Phonics** *ch, wh,* and *nk* Let's read the first sentence together. Which word has the sound of /ch/? *(branch)* Let's blend the sounds in this word together. b r a n ch branch Where is this sound in the word? (at the end) *Graphophonic Cues*

Let's use our puppets to dramatize this scene. *Story Props*

14 The owls sat on their branch again.
They watched the sun sink
down,

    down,

        down.

78

Activity

Cross Curricular: Social Studies

WHAT'S IN A NAME? Explain that sometimes babies are named after family members or friends. Sometimes babies are given names with a special meaning.

RESEARCH AND INQUIRY Invite children to find out the meaning of

their names. Ask children to create a self-portrait and make a display.

▶ **Visual/Kinesthetic**

Lily. I am named after my Mom's favorite flower.

I am named after my Uncle Jim.

"Whooooo!" sang Mom.

"Whooooo!" sang Pop.

"Whooooo!" sang Chuck.

They looked at Sam.

79

Comprehension

15 How can we tell that Mom, Pop, and Chuck are singing? (Their mouths are open, and Mom and Chuck are waving their wings.) *Use Picture Clues/Make Inferences*

16 **COMPARE AND CONTRAST** How is Sam different from her family? (She's smaller. She doesn't sing.)

Minilesson
REVIEW/MAINTAIN

High-Frequency Words

• Write each of the following high-frequency words from kindergarten on index cards: *the, and, to, a, of, he, I, was.*

Have pairs of children practice by showing each other the words and reading them.

Activity Ask children to use the words in sentences. Tell them to write their sentences and underline the word. Suggest that they draw a picture to illustrate their sentences.

LANGUAGE SUPPORT

ESL Have five children (one child plays the sun) act out these two pages. Ask: Mr. Sun, what are you doing? (*I am sinking down, down, down.*) Mom, what are you doing? (*I am singing "Whooooo!"*) Continue in the same way with Pop and Chuck. What is everyone doing? (*looking at Sam*) Have other groups act out the same skit.

Comprehension

17 Let's read the first sentence together. Why do you think Sam didn't sing? (She was still too young.) *Make Inferences*

18 **Phonics** *ch*, *wh*, and *nk* "She just put her…" Hmm, I think I need to blend the sounds to read this word.
ch i n   chin *Graphophonic Cues*

19 Read the second sentence aloud, emphasizing the words *her mom's wing*. What does the word *mom's* mean? (belongs to her mom) Who does the wing belong to? (Sam's mom) What does this mark (') and *s* after a person's name usually mean? (belongs to the person who is named) *Possessives/Semantic Cues*

P/I **PHONOLOGICAL AWARENESS**
Listen as I read the sentences on this page. Clap when you hear a word that rhymes with *sing*.

TEACHING TIP

MANAGEMENT To keep the entire class engaged, you might have children cut out stars and suns. When the group acting out the story is in a daytime setting, children can hold up their suns. For nighttime settings, children can hold up their stars.

17 But Sam didn't sing.
18 She just put her chin down
19 in her mom's wing.

80

P/I **PREVENTION/INTERVENTION**

PHONOLOGICAL AWARENESS Say the words *sing* and *wing*. Then say each sound in the words /s/-/i/-/ng/. Help children who are having difficulty blend the sounds to say the words. Elicit from them that these words share their two last sounds in common, /i/ and /ng/. Ask children to name other words that rhyme with *sing*, such as *ring*, *bring*, *sting*, and *king*.

"Why can't Sam sing?" asked Chuck.

"Now then," said Mom.

"Sam will sing when she wants to." ㉑

81

Comprehension

⑳ Point to the second word in the sentence. *(can't)* What two words make up this contraction? *(can* and *not)* Let's read the word together. What do you think this word means? *(not able to do something)*

㉑ **COMPARE AND CONTRAST** How did the story begin? *(There were three owls. They sang at night.)* Now what is different? *(Now there are four owls. Sam doesn't sing.)* Let's use our story puppets to act out the story so far. *Story Props*

Minilesson

REVIEW/MAINTAIN

Make Inferences

Remind children that they can use clues in words and pictures to understand how characters are feeling and what might happen next.

• Ask children to talk about how Chuck might be feeling and how Mom might be feeling.

Activity Invite children to compare and contrast how Chuck and Sam are feeling. Have them use their story puppets to act out behavior, dialogue, and feelings.

Comprehension

22 How many sentences are on this page? (four) What mark do all the sentences end with? (period) *Concepts of Print*

23 Why do you think Sam can't sing? *Make Inferences*

SELF-MONITORING STRATEGY

SEARCH FOR CLUES Using pictures can help a reader understand characters and the story.

MODEL I don't understand why Sam can't sing. I can look at the pictures and the words. I see that Sam is just a baby owl. Mom also said she'll sing when she wants to. Maybe she doesn't want to, or maybe she doesn't know how to sing yet.

The owls sat on their branch again.

It was pitch black out.

Mom, Pop, and Chuck sang.

But Sam still couldn't sing.

82

Activity

Cross Curricular: Math

STORY PROBLEMS Use owl cutouts and a drawing of a tree branch to model addition and subtraction problems. Ask a child to put six owls on the tree. Then have two owls fly away. Ask how many are left and write the subtraction sentence.

Activity Have partners draw owls or use owl cutouts to tell stories and write number sentences.
▶ **Visual/Analytical**

Sam's chest sank.   (24)

"Why can't I sing?" she asked.   (25)

Pop put his wing around Sam.   (26)

"Let's go back to the nest," he said.

83

Comprehension

(24) **Phonics** *ch, wh,* and *nk* Let's make the sound that the letters *ch* stand for. Point to the second word in the first sentence. Read the word with me, using your finger to help you blend the sounds of the letters together. ch e s t   chest
Graphophonic Cues

(25) How do you think Sam feels? (sad) How does the author let you know this? (by writing *Sam's chest sank*) *Make Inferences*

(26) Why do you think Pop put his wing around Sam? (to make her feel better) *Draw Conclusions*

LANGUAGE SUPPORT

ESL Role-play pages 82 and 83 by inviting four children to act out the story as you reread the text. Invite children to share times when they needed comfort or share examples from classroom experience. Talk about how saying encouraging words can help everyone.

Comprehension

27 **Phonics** *ch, wh,* and *nk* Let's read the first sentence together. "Sam wouldn't eat or . . ." Let's blend the sounds to read this word. d r i nk drink *Graphophonic Cues*

28 Did the star really wink at Sam? (no) What does the author mean? (The star twinkled.) *Make Inferences*

29 What do you think Sam will wish for? *Make Predictions*

Sam wouldn't eat or drink.   **27**
She just went to bed.
Then she saw a small star wink at her.
"I can wish on it," Sam said.

84

Activity

Cross Curricular: Music

STARRY SONG Sing "Twinkle, Twinkle, Little Star" with children. Move your hand to show the pattern of the melody as you sing. Used gummed stars on chart paper to show the direction of the melody.

Activity Invite children to draw dots or stars and copy the melody line. ▶ **Auditory/Visual**

 inter NET Help children log on to **www.mhschool.com/ reading** for links to sites about music.

"Whoo!" (30)

"What was that?" asked Mom. (31)

85

Comprehension

(30) Let's read the first sentence. Is it a question? (no) How do you know? (It ends with an exclamation mark.) *Concepts of Print*

(31) Who do you think is talking in the first sentence? (Sam) How do you know? (Mom asks *"What was that?"* because she never heard Sam sing. Also, the *whoo* is shorter than the others; it has only 2 *oo's* in it.) Have children compare with the *whooooo* on page 79. *Make Inferences*

Comprehension

32 How many exclamation marks do you see on this page? (three) How do you think we should read these sentences? (in an excited voice) *Concepts of Print*

33 How do you think Mom, Pop, and Chuck feel? (happy, excited) What makes you think so? (The picture shows them smiling, looking happy.) *Use Illustrations/ Make Inferences*

34 **COMPARE AND CONTRAST** How is Sam like Mom, Pop, and Chuck now? (She can sing.)

"Whoo!"

It was Sam!

"You can sing, Sam!" they said.

86

Activity

Cross Curricular: Science

OWLS Display a picture of an owl and identify its features: beak, wings, talons, eyes. Describe some special characteristics of owls: They hunt after dark. They have excellent hearing and eyesight. They have special wing feathers that make their flight silent.

RESEARCH AND INQUIRY Have children make a chart that compares and contrasts owls with other familiar birds. Provide field guides and other nonfiction books to help them. ▶ **Analytical/Linguistic**

OWLS/OTHER BIRDS	
Same:	different:
1. Have wings.	
2. Fly.	
3. Lay eggs.	

"But I can't sing like you," said Sam. **35**

"My song is much too small."

"We'll see about that," said Pop. **36**

"Let's go out together."

87

Comprehension

35 **COMPARE AND CONTRAST** Who is Sam comparing herself to? (her family) How does Sam want to sing? (She wants to make a big sound.)

Let's use our puppets to dramatize what is happening. *Story Props*

36 What do you think Pop means when he says, "We'll see about that"? *Make Inferences*

LANGUAGE SUPPORT

ESL Reread pages 86 and 87 emphasizing intonation used for dialogue and exclamations. Encourage children to read with you to practice the intonation for exclamations and dialogue. You may wish to have some children read pages 86–87. Children can take turns reading Sam's and Pop's lines.

Comprehension

37 Let's blend the sounds together for the first word. wh i sh whish
Graphophonic Cues

38 Show me how a firefly moves.
Pantomime

Whish! Whish!

"What was that?" asked Sam.

"That was a firefly," said Pop.

"That was small," said Sam.

88

Cross Curricular: Language Arts

OWLS AND CRICKETS Read *"The Very Quiet Cricket"* by Eric Carle to the class. Help children compare and contrast Sam and the cricket. Discuss the reasons that both animals are quiet.

Activity Invite children to ask a family member to describe something

that was difficult to learn to do.

Have them ask questions such as:

• What is something that took you a long time to learn?

• How did you learn?

▶ **Auditory/Linguistic**

Plink! Plunk!

"What was that?" asked Sam.

"That was a nut," said Mom.

"That was small, too," said Sam.

39

40

41

89

Comprehension

39 **Phonics** *ch*, *wh*, and *nk* Let's blend the sounds and read the first word. p l i nk plink

Now let's blend the sounds for the second word. p l u nk plunk
Graphophonic Cues

40 What other things in the forest could make the *Plink! Plunk!* sound? *Make Inferences*

41 **COMPARE AND CONTRAST** What does Sam think is also like her? (nut) How do you think this makes Sam feel? (happy) *Make Inferences*

Comprehension

42 **COMPARE AND CONTRAST** Who else does Sam compare herself to? (the mouse)

p/i **PUNCTUATION** How many different ways to end a sentence do you see on this page? (3) What are they? (exclamation mark, question mark, period) *Syntactic Cues*

Crunch! Crunch!

"What was that?" asked Sam.

"I think it's a mouse," said Chuck. **42**

"A mouse is small, too," said Sam.

90

Fluency

SHARED READING

GROUP Have children read along with you. For the first reading, speak louder than the children so that they can hear your intonation and pronunciation. On the second reading, allow children to lead. Read again to help children achieve fluency.

p/i **PREVENTION/INTERVENTION**

PUNCTUATION Remind children that every sentence ends with a special mark. Ask a volunteer to ask a question aloud. Then write the question on the chalkboard without the punctuation. Have a volunteer add punctuation to the sentence. Repeat with an exclamation and a statement. *Syntactic Cues*

The owls sat on their branch.

Mom, Pop, and Chuck sang together.

Sam began to sing.

She saw her star wink at her.

91

Comprehension

PHONOLOGICAL AWARENESS
Listen as I say this sentence: *Sam began to sing.* How many words begin with the /s/ sound? (two)

PREVENTION/INTERVENTION

PHONOLOGICAL AWARENESS Say the following sentences. Ask children to identify the words in each sentence that begin with the /s/ sound:

Sally and Sid sat in the sun.
"Don't be so sad," said Sara.

Ask children to invent their own sentences with /s/ sounds and say them aloud.

Minilesson

REVIEW/MAINTAIN

Main Idea

Explain to children that the main idea tells what the story is about.

Work together to write two sentences that tell the main idea of *Sam's Song.* Ask:

- How did the story begin?
- What did Sam learn to do?
- How did the story end?

Activity Have children summarize the story orally. Focus on the main idea. Then record the sentences that give the main idea.

Comprehension

43 **COMPARE AND CONTRAST** How does Sam feel now compared with how she felt at the beginning of the story? (happy) How do you know? (She is singing.) *Make Connections*

Have groups of four children retell the story, each taking a part of one of the owls. Have them use their puppets to act out parts of the story. Encourage them to talk about how Sam changed during the story. *Summarize/ Story Props*

44 Why do you think this was the owls' best song? *Make Inferences*

SELF-ASSESSMENT

Have children ask themselves the following questions to assess how they are reading:

• How did I use what I know about owls and growing up to help me understand the story?

• How did I use pictures and words to help me understand how Sam changed?

• How did I use the pictures and the letters to help me read the words?

TRANSFERRING THE STRATEGIES

• How can I use these strategies to help me read other stories?

"Whoo!" sang Sam.

It was not big. It was small. **43**

But it was hers!

92

REREADING FOR *Fluency*

 ONE Children who need additional practice can read aloud as they listen to the story on the **Listening Library** recording.

READING RATE When you evaluate reading rate, have children read aloud from the story for one minute. Place a stick-on note after the last word read. Count words read. To

evaluate children's performance, see the Running Record in the **Fluency Assessment** book.

i **Intervention** ▶ For leveled fluency lessons, passages, and norms charts, see **Skills Intervention Guide**, Part 5, Fluency.

The owls sang one last song together. Now Sam sang with them. It was their best song yet!

93

Comprehension

Return to Predictions and Purposes

Reread children's predictions about the story. Ask if the story answered all their questions.

PREDICTIONS	WHAT HAPPENED
Sam is sad.	Sam could not sing like the other owls at first. She then starts to sing.
Sam sees a star.	Sam thinks the small star is winking at her. Sam begins to sing.

Have children discuss their use of story puppets. Did the puppets help children remember the plot of the story?

INFORMAL ASSESSMENT

HOW TO ASSESS

Phonics *ch, wh,* and *nk* Write *nk, ch,* and *wh* on the board. Turn to page 83. Have children read words with these letters.

UNDERSTAND COMPARE AND CONTRAST Have children take a **picture walk** through the book and talk about how Sam changed during the story.

FOLLOW UP

Phonics *ch, wh,* and *nk* Continue to provide practice with these letters by using word cards.

UNDERSTAND COMPARE AND CONTRAST Help children compare and contrast Sam and Chuck. Ask questions that focus on how the owls are alike and different.

LITERARY RESPONSE

QUICK-WRITE Have children draw a picture of Sam in their journals and write what they liked or didn't like about her.

ORAL RESPONSE Have children use their journal entries to discuss these questions:

• If you were a character in the story, what would you say to Sam?

• How did you feel about Sam when she couldn't sing?

SENTENCE STRIPS Children can use strips 1–72 to retell *Sam's Song*.

> **1**
> The owls sat on their branch.

> **2**
> They watched the sun sink down, down, down.

Story Questions

Tell children that now they will read some questions about the story. Help children read the questions. Discuss possible answers.

Answers:

1. It is small. *Literal*

2. Chuck is Sam's older brother. *Inferential/ Characters*

3. Sam's song will be big, like the songs of the other owls. *Inferential/ Make Inferences*

4. Answers will vary. Accept appropriate summaries. *Critical/Summarize*

5. Answers will vary. Accept appropriate examples. *Critical/ Reading Across Texts*

Draw a Picture Help children read the directions in their anthologies. Have children take turns saying the words aloud. Discuss what they associate with these sounds. You might want to offer other examples of sound words: *pow, crackle, boom.*

Story Questions & Activities

READ TOGETHER

❶ How is Sam's song different from the others?

❷ Who is Chuck?

❸ How will Sam's song sound when she is bigger?

❹ What is this story mostly about?

❺ What might Stan say to Sam?

Draw a Picture

Whish, crunch, plunk are sound words. What do you think of when you hear them? Draw pictures of what you hear.

Meeting Individual Needs

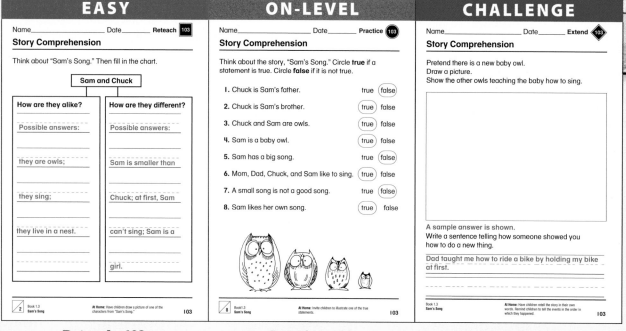

EASY	ON-LEVEL	CHALLENGE
Reteach, 103	Practice, 103	Extend, 103

Put on a Skit

Pick parts to play from "Sam's Song."

Who will be Sam?

Who will be the mouse?

Use sound words in your skit.

Make your voices soft and loud.

Whoo!

Crunch! Crunch!

Find Out More

What songs do you like?

Go to the school library.

Find words to songs you like.

If you can, find tapes of the songs.

Share them with your class.

Play your tape.

Or, sing your song.

95

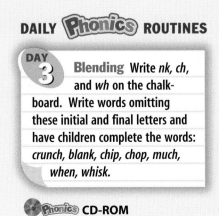

DAILY **Phonics** ROUTINES

DAY 3 **Blending** Write *nk*, *ch*, and *wh* on the chalkboard. Write words omitting these initial and final letters and have children complete the words: *crunch, blank, chip, chop, much, when, whisk.*

Phonics CD-ROM

Story Activities

Put on a Skit

Materials: Use the chalkboard to write down sound words.

Read the directions aloud. Help children who have questions. Encourage the children to be imaginative in their skit; they don't have to stick completely to the story.

GROUP You may want to put on more than one version of the skit, with different groups of children taking the same parts.

Find Out More

RESEARCH AND INQUIRY Again, read the directions aloud, and help children who have questions.

Have children bring in their favorite songs from home, or bring cassettes from the library. If children are too shy to sing alone, perhaps they can sing with a partner. Have children discuss who the composer/band is and what kind of music the song is (e.g., religious, folk, rock, pop).

interNET CONNECTION Have children log on to *www.mhschool.com/reading* to access sites on music.

FORMAL ASSESSMENT

See the Progress Assessment Test for Book 1.3.

Study Skills

DIAGRAMS

OBJECTIVES

Students will learn to gather information from photos.

Remind children that they have just read a story about owls. Tell them that now they will look at photos to learn about different types of owls.

Display **Teaching Chart 76.** Have children look at the photos. Then invite them to describe what they notice about the size of the owls. Together, read the names of the owls. Then help children read the questions below the photos, encouraging them to identify the names that answer each question.

STUDY SKILLS

Owls

Owls are different sizes.

screech owl

elf owl

barn owl

great horned owl

Look at the Owls

❶ Which owl is the biggest?

❷ Which owl is smaller than the screech owl?

Meeting Individual Needs

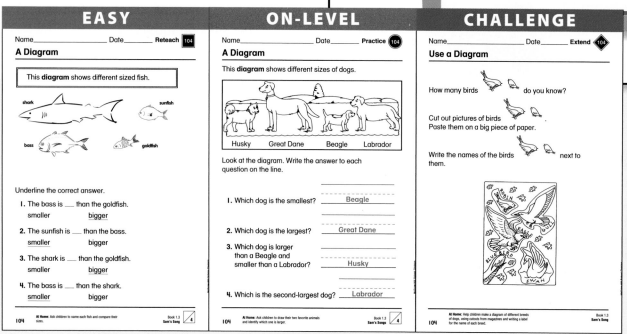

Reteach, 104

Practice, 104

Extend, 104

TEST POWER

Big Ball, Small Ball

Look at these balls.
The baseball is a small ball.
The golf ball is smaller.
The marble is the smallest.

Look at these large balls.
The basketball is large.
The kickball is larger.
The beach ball is the largest.

What is smaller than a baseball?

- 🔘 A marble
- ⚪ A basketball

For each answer choice, ask yourself if it answers the question.

97

Test Power

THE PRINCETON REVIEW

Read the Page

Explain to children that you will be reading this story as a group. You will read the story, and they will follow in their books.

Request that children put pens, pencils, and markers away, since they will not be writing in their books.

Discuss the Question

Talk with children about how to compare things in terms of bigger and smaller. Have them find the line where a ball smaller than a baseball is discussed. Ask them to name the two balls that are said in the story to be smaller than a baseball.

Test-Tip

Sometimes you can use the answer choices to help you locate the answer in the passage. Look at each choice and see which one is better.

Leveled Books

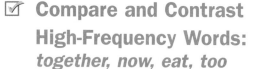

> **i Intervention → Skills**
> **Intervention Guide,** for direct instruction and extra practice in vocabulary and comprehension

EASY

What's New at the Zoo?

☑ **Phonics** Digraphs: *ch, wh, nk*

☑ Compare and Contrast

High-Frequency Words: *together, now, eat, too*

Guided Reading

PREVIEW AND PREDICT As you take the **picture walk** up to page 5, have children predict what the story will be about. Chart their ideas.

SET PURPOSES Have children write or draw why they want to read *What's New at the Zoo*? For example: *I want to find out what they learn at the zoo.*

READ THE BOOK Use questions like the following to guide children's reading or to ask after they have read the story independently.

Pages 2–3: Who sees a word on this page that begins with the sound /ch/? Model: I can blend the sounds of the letters together to read it. The first letters are *ch*. They stand for the sound /ch/. The middle letter is *u*. It stands for the sound /u/. The last letters are *ck*. They stand for the sound /k/. I can blend the sounds together: Ch u ck Chuck. The word is *Chuck*. *Phonics and Decoding*

Pages 4–5: Who sees a vocabulary word we just learned? *(eat) High-Frequency Words*

Pages 7–8: What can Chuck do that big cats also do? (run fast) *Compare and Contrast*

Page 8: Who sees a word on this page that ends in *nk* with the sound /nk/? *(Hank) Phonics and Decoding*

RETURN TO PREDICTIONS AND PURPOSES Discuss children's predictions. Ask which were close to the story and why. Have children review their purposes for reading. Did they find out what the boys learned at the zoo?

LITERARY RESPONSE The following questions will help focus children's responses:

• How are the zoo animals the same? How are they different?

• How are the boys the same as the animals? How are they different?

Also see the story questions and activity in *What's New at the Zoo?*

See the **Phonics CD-ROM** for practice with blends.

Answers to Story Questions

1. to the zoo
2. Answers will vary: monkeys, seals, cats.
3. Monkeys swing, seals swim and eat fish, big cats run fast.
4. Answers will vary.
5. Answers will vary.

The Story Questions and Activity below appear in the Easy Book.

Story Questions and Activity

1. Where do Hank and Chuck go?
2. What do they see at the zoo?
3. What do Hank and Chuck learn at the zoo?
4. Tell three things that happen at the zoo.
5. How is the zoo different from other animal homes you've read about?

What Can You Do?

How fast can you run? Work with a partner. Run across the playground. Your partner can time you. Then your partner can take a turn.

from *What's New at the Zoo?*

Leveled Books

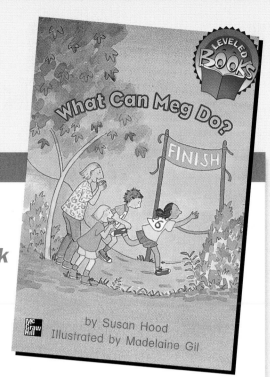

by Susan Hood
Illustrated by Madelaine Gil

INDEPENDENT

What Can Meg Do?

☑ **Phonics** Digraphs: *ch, wh, nk*

☑ **Compare and Contrast**
High-Frequency Words:
together, now, eat, too

Guided Reading

PREVIEW AND PREDICT As you take a **picture walk** up to page 5, have children predict what the story will be about. Chart their ideas.

SET PURPOSES Have children write or draw why they want to read *What Can Meg Do?* For example: *I want to find out what Meg can do.*

READ THE BOOK Use questions like the following to guide children's reading or after they have read the story independently.

Page 3: Which word on page 3 has the /ch/ sound? *(such)* Model: I'm not sure what this word is, but I can blend the letters together to read it. The first letter is *s*, which stands for the sound /s/. The middle letter is *u*. It stands for /u/. The last letters are *ch*. They stand for the sound /ch/. I can blend the sounds of the letters together. s u ch → such. *Phonics and Decoding*

Pages 4-5: What does Frank like to do? (bake cakes) *Analyze Character and Plot*

Pages 6–7: Can you see vocabulary words we just learned? *(together, now)* **High-Frequency Words**

Page 8: Look at the picture and read the page. What is Meg doing now? (playing the drums) What other friend did something musical? (Deb) *Analyze Character and Plot*

RETURN TO PREDICTIONS AND PURPOSES Discuss children's predictions. Ask which were close to the story and why. Have children review their purposes for reading. Did they find out what Meg can do?

LITERARY RESPONSE The following questions will help focus children's responses:

• What do you like to do?

• Is there something you wish you could do? Tell about it.

Also see the story questions and activity in *What Can Meg Do?*

See the **Phonics** CD-ROM for practice with blends.

Answers to Story Questions
1. Ann can run fast.
2. She wants to do something.
3. Answers will vary.
4. Meg plays the drums.
5. In both stories something new is learned.

The Story Questions and Activity below appear in the Independent Book.

Story Questions and Activity
1. What can Ann do?
2. What does Meg want?
3. Why is it good to have something that you do well?
4. Tell what Meg does in this story.
5. How is this like *Sam's Song?*

Talent Show Act
Show the class something that you can do well. Then give a lesson to the class.

from What Can Meg Do?

Leveled Books

The Cow That Went OINK

written and illustrated by
Bernard Most

CHALLENGE

The Cow That Went OINK

- ☑  **Digraphs:** *ch, wh, nk*

- ☑ **Compare and Contrast**

Guided Reading

PREVIEW AND PREDICT Discuss each illustration up to page 15. Take a **picture walk**, and have children predict what the story will be about. Chart their ideas.

SET PURPOSES Have children write or draw why they want to read *The Cow That Went OINK*.

READ THE BOOK Use questions like the following to guide children's reading or after they have read the story independently.

Pages 2–13: How is the cow that went oink different from the other cows? (He can't say moo.) *Compare and Contrast*

Pages 14–27: What did the cow teach the pig? (how to say oink) What did the pig teach the cow? (how to say moo) Were the cow and the pig patient teachers? (yes) Why? (They knew how the other felt about making the wrong sound.) How is the pig like the cow? (The pig also makes the wrong sound.) *Analyze Character and Plot*

Pages 28–31: What happens on these pages? (The cow learns to say moo; the pig learns to say oink.) What makes the cow and the pig special now? (They are the only animals on the farm that can make two sounds.) *Compare and Contrast*

RETURN TO PREDICTIONS AND PURPOSES Discuss children's predictions. Ask which were close to the story and why. Have children review their purposes for reading. Did they find out if the pig learned to say oink?

LITERARY RESPONSE The following questions will help focus children's responses:

- Have you ever felt bad because you couldn't do something? Tell about it.

- Have you ever helped someone learn to do something new? Tell about it.

Also see the story questions and writing activity in *The Cow That Went OINK*.

See the **Phonics** **CD-ROM** for practice with blends.

Answers to Story Questions

1. Moo
2. They were laughed at by other animals.
3. Answers may vary.
4. A cow went oink. A pig went moo. They were laughed at by the other animals. The cow taught the pig to oink. The pig taught the cow to moo.
5. *Picnic Farm*

The Story Questions and Activity below appear in the Challenge Book.

Story Questions and Activity

1. What sound did the pig make?
2. Why were the cow and pig sad?
3. Will the cow and pig make friends with the other animals?
4. Tell the story in your own words.
5. Name another story you read that happens on a farm.

Animal Sounds

Pick an animal.

Think of a new sound it might make. Draw a picture to show what the other animals think.

Write a sentence about your picture.

from *The Cow That Went OINK*

Bringing Groups Together

Anthology and Leveled Books

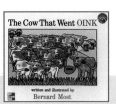

Connecting Texts

CLASS DISCUSSION Lead a discussion of how the unit theme Learning Something New applies to each of the stories:

- What did the characters learn in each story?

- Would you like to learn what one of the characters has learned? Explain why.

CHARACTER WEB Have children create a web to compare what the main characters from the stories learned.

Sam's Song
Sam learns that she has a good song.

What's New at the Zoo?
The brothers learn about zoo animals.

Learning Something New

What Can Meg Do?
Meg learns to play the drums.

The Cow That Went OINK
The cow and the pig learn new words.

Viewing/Representing

GROUP PRESENTATIONS Divide the class into groups, one for each of the four books. (For *Sam's Song*, combine children of different reading levels.) Have each group draw pictures of the main events and orally summarize the book. Have each group present its pictures and summary.

AUDIENCE RESPONSE Ask children to pay attention to each group's presentation. Allow time for questions after each group presents.

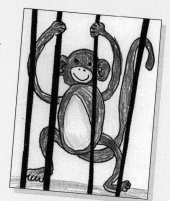

Research and Inquiry

MORE ABOUT LEARNING SOMETHING NEW Have children ask themselves: What else would I like to know about learning something new? Then invite them to do the following:

- Demonstrate to the class a special skill they may have.

- Ask a grown-up to demonstrate or tell about a special skill.

interNET CONNECTION Have children log on to **www.mhschool.com/reading** for links to web pages about learning something new.

 Children can draw pictures representing what they learned in their journals.

Children will:

- blend and read words with *nk* and the digraphs *ch* and *wh*.

MATERIALS

- **Teaching Chart 77**
- letter and digraph cards from the **Word Building Manipulative Cards**

Skills Finder

ch, wh, and nk

Introduce	B3: 68I-J
Review	B3: 97E-F, 97G-H, 125G-H, 126I-J
Test	Book 3

ALTERNATE TEACHING STRATEGY

REVIEW *ch, wh, nk*
For a different approach to teaching this skill, see pages T72 and T73.

Review ch, wh, and nk

PREPARE

Listen for *ch, wh*, and *nk*   Have children make the sound /hw/ with you. Have children touch their noses when they hear a word with the /hw/ sound: *chair, plunk, when, where, chick, whale, skunk, which, pink*. Repeat with *nk* and *ch*.

TEACH

Review Symbols for *ch, wh, nk*   Remind children of the sound/symbol relationships of /ch/*ch*, /hw/*wh*, /nk/*nk*. Write the following on the chalkboard and have children repeat the sounds after you: *ch, wh, nk*.

BLENDING Model and Guide Practice with *ch, wh, nk*   Display **Teaching Chart 77**. Run your hand under the letters *ch* and make the sound /ch/. Have children make the sound with you. Write *ch* in the blank. Blend the sounds to read the word.   ch i n   chin

ch	wh	nk
<u>ch</u>in	<u>wh</u>en	ba<u>nk</u>
<u>ch</u>op	<u>wh</u>isk	tha<u>nk</u>
crun<u>ch</u>	<u>wh</u>ich	sa<u>nk</u>
mu<u>ch</u>	<u>wh</u>at	cra<u>nk</u>

Teaching Chart 77

Use the Word in Context   Invite volunteers to use the word in a sentence to reinforce its meaning. Example: *His hand is on his chin.*

Repeat the Procedure   Have children write the missing letters in each blank space and blend the sounds of the letters together to read the word.

PRACTICE

SEGMENTING
Identify and Sort Words with *ch*, *wh*, and *nk*

GROUP

Give three children one of the letter cards for *ch*, *wh*, and *nk*. Then write words with these letters on the chalkboard. Have volunteers point to a word, read it, and then point to the child holding that letter combination. Then have children sort the words into three columns: *ch*, *wh*, *nk*. Tell them to identify the column which has the greatest number of words. ▶ **Linguistic/Spatial**

ASSESS/CLOSE

Read Words with *ch*, *wh*, and *nk*

To see if children have mastered blending and reading *ch*, *wh*, and *nk* words, observe them as they read words during the Practice activity.

ADDITIONAL PHONICS RESOURCES

Phonics/Phonemic Awareness Practice Book, pages 125–128

PHONICS KIT
Hands-on Activities and Practice

McGraw-Hill School
TECHNOLOGY
Phonics CD-ROM

activities for practice with **Blending and Building Words**

DAILY Phonics ROUTINES

DAY 4

Fluency Write the following words on the chalkboard: *clank, bank, drank, prank, thank.* Read the words with children. Then ask individuals to read the words.

Phonics CD-ROM

SPELLING/PHONICS CONNECTIONS

Words with *ch*, *wh*, and *nk*: See the 5-Day Spelling Plan, pages 97Q–97R.

ℹ️ **Intervention** ▶ Skills
Intervention Guide, for direct instruction and extra practice in *ch*, *wh*, and *nk*

Meeting Individual Needs for Phonics

EASY	ON-LEVEL	CHALLENGE	LANGUAGE SUPPORT

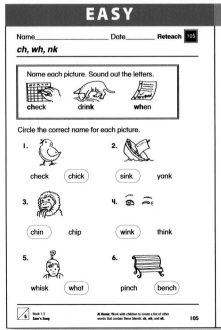

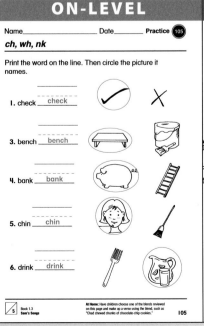

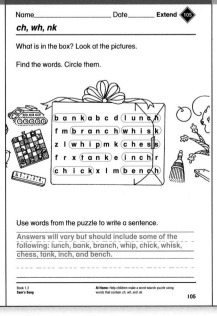

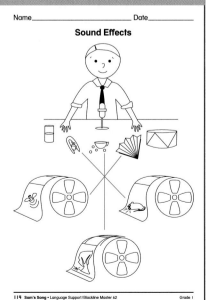

Reteach, 105   **Practice, 105**   **Extend, 105**   Language Support, 114

97F

OBJECTIVES

Children will:

- review *ch, wh, nk.*
- review blends.
- cumulative review: **short *a, e, i, o, u.***

. . . .

MATERIALS

- **Teaching Chart 78**
- letter and digraph cards from the **Word Building Manipulative Cards**
- **Phonics Practice Reader, Volume 1**

Skills Finder

_ch, wh,_ and _nk_

Introduce	B3: 68I-J
Review	B3: 97E-F, 97G-H, 125G-H, 126I-J
Test	Book 3

TEACHING TIP

MANAGEMENT Keep the Teaching Chart activity running smoothly and without frustration by encouraging children to try out several letter possibilities in the blank space. Let them know that it's okay if they do not create a real word immediately.

ALTERNATE TEACHING
STRATEGY

. . . .

REVIEW *ch, wh, nk;* **BLENDS**

For a different approach to teaching this skill, see pages T64, T65, T69, T70, T72, and T73.

Review ch, wh, nk; Blends

PREPARE

Identify _ch, wh, nk_   Remind children that the letters *ch* stand for the sound /ch/. Review sounds for the letters *wh* and *nk.*

TEACH

BLENDING Model and Guide Practice with _ch, wh, nk,_ and Blends   Write *ch, wh, nk* and blends on the chalkboard. Ask children to repeat the sounds for each symbol after you.

wh	ch	tr	sk	nk

lun**ch**	ma**sk**	**tr**ust
when	mu**ch**	**tr**ack
chin	si**nk**	**wh**ich

Teaching Chart 78

Display **Teaching Chart 78**. Explain to children that two letters can be written in each blank space to complete words. Children can choose one of the letter pairs from the box at the top of the chart. Model the first example: l u n ch lunch

Use Word in Context   Use the word in context to reinforce its meaning. Example: *I ate a delicious lunch today.*

Repeat the Procedure   Have children write the missing letters in each blank space and blend the sounds of the letters together to read the word.

PRACTICE

**BLENDING
Build and Read
Words with *ch, wh,
nk,* and Blends**

GROUP

Give each child a letter card with a consonant, *ch, wh, nk,* or a vowel. Have children mingle and try to find others with letters that will help them build words with *ch, wh, nk,* and blends. Have them read and write the words. Then have children exchange and read one another's words.

▶ **Linguistic/Kinesthetic**

ASSESS/CLOSE

**Read Words with
ch, *wh*, *nk*, and
Blends and Use in
Context**

Assess children's mastery of blending and reading words with *ch, wh, nk,* and blends by observing them in the Practice activity. Have children choose two words they made in the activity and write a sentence for each.

**Read a
Decodable Story**

For additional practice reading words with *ch, wh, nk* and blends, and to develop fluency, direct children to read the story *Lunch Kit* from the **Phonics Practice Reader, Volume, 1.**

ADDITIONAL PHONICS RESOURCES

**Phonics/Phonemic Awareness
Practice Book,
pages 125–128**

PHONICS KIT
Hands-on Activities and Practice

McGraw-Hill School
TECHNOLOGY

Phonics CD-ROM

**activities for practice with
Blending and Building Words**

DAILY **Phonics** ROUTINES

DAY 5 **Writing** Write a list of *nk, wh,* and *ch* words on the chalkboard. Ask children to write riddles using one or more of these words.

Phonics CD-ROM

i **Intervention** **Skills
Intervention Guide,** for direct instruction and extra practice in *ch, wh,* and *nk* and blends

Meeting Individual Needs for Phonics

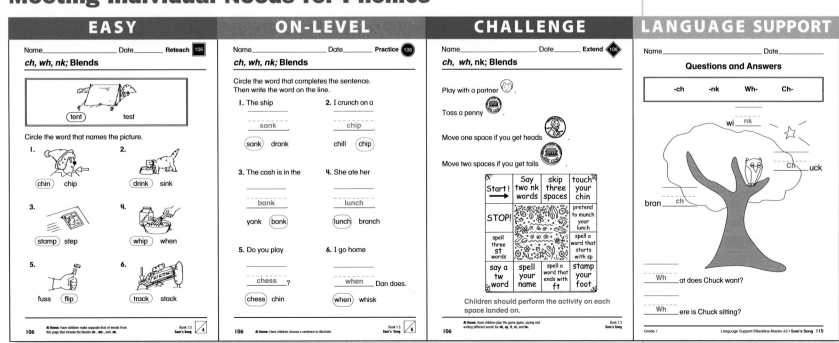

EASY	ON-LEVEL	CHALLENGE	LANGUAGE SUPPORT
Reteach, 106	Practice, 106	Extend, 106	Language Support, 115

97H

OBJECTIVES

Children will compare and contrast people and animals of different ages.

....

MATERIALS
- **Teaching Chart 79**

Skills Finder	
Compare/Contrast	
Introduce	B3: 67I-J
Review	B3: 97I-J, 139E-F
Test	Book 3
Maintain	B5: 67

TEACHING TIP

COMPARE AND CONTRAST Have children think about how they were different when they were babies. Ask: *Could you talk? Could you read? Could you draw?*

SELF-SELECTED
Reading

....

Children may choose the following titles.

ANTHOLOGY

- *Sam's Song*

LEVELED BOOKS

- *What's New at the Zoo?*
- *What Can Meg Do?*
- *The Cow That Went OINK*

Bibliography, pages T98–T99

Review Compare and Contrast

> **PREPARE**

Review the Concept of Compare and Contrast

Remind children that they can learn how people, animals, and objects are alike and different by reading, observing, looking at pictures, and using their day-to-day experiences.

> **TEACH**

Compare and Contrast

Display **Teaching Chart 79**. Discuss the pictures and read the chart together.

She sleeps. She drives a car. She reads.
She sleeps. She eats. She plays.

Teaching Chart 79

MODEL I can look at the pictures and the sentences to compare the woman and the little girl. The woman and the little girl do one thing that is the same and other things that are different. They both sleep. The woman drives a car. The little girl plays with toys.

Ask volunteers to draw a circle around the thing the woman and child do that is the same. Then, have children use the sentences and pictures from the **Teaching Chart** to create a Venn diagram to compare and contrast the woman and the child. Point out that the middle area of the diagram should list a characteristic that the woman and child share.

Continue the Diagram

Help children use the pictures and sentences, as well as what they know about small children and grown-ups, to continue comparing and contrasting the woman and the child. Ask children to indicate the correct section on the Venn diagram for their suggestions.

▶ **Visual/Linguistic**

ASSESS/CLOSE

Compare Animals

Invite children to compare animal babies and mothers, such as a puppy and a dog. Encourage them to be as detailed as possible in their descriptions. Have children create a new Venn diagram for their ideas. Ask children to write one sentence telling how the animals are alike and one sentence telling how they are different.

ALTERNATE TEACHING STRATEGY

COMPARE AND CONTRAST

For a different approach to teaching this skill, see page T71.

ⓘ **Intervention** ▶ **Skills**

Intervention Guide, for direct instruction and extra practice in Comparing and Contrasting

Meeting Individual Needs for Comprehension

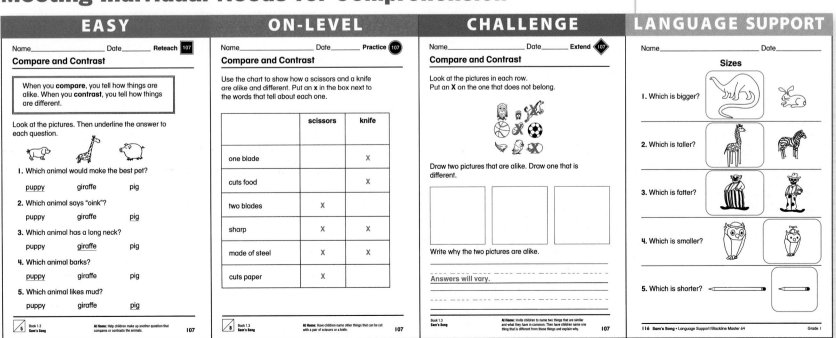

EASY	ON-LEVEL	CHALLENGE	LANGUAGE SUPPORT
Reteach, 107	Practice, 107	Extend, 107	Language Support, 116

 **OBJECTIVES**

Children will read words with contractions.

MATERIALS

- **Teaching Chart 80**
- letter cards from the **Word Building Manipulative Cards.**

Skills Finder

Contractions

Introduce	B3: 97K-L
Review	B3: 125K-L, 139K-L
Test	Book 3

TEACHING TIP

APOSTROPHES Some children may think the apostrophe should be located between the two words being contracted, for example: *was'nt*. Be sure they understand that it takes the place of the missing letter(s): *wasn't*.

Introduce Contractions

PREPARE

Introduce Contractions Use letter cards to make the words *I am*. Read the words together. Then take away the letter *a* and insert an apostrophe. Read the new word. Explain that a *contraction* is a shorter way to write and say two words.

TEACH

Identify Contractions Display **Teaching Chart 80**. Point to the word *I'm* and read it together with children. Then model for children how understanding contractions can help them read.

Teaching Chart 80

MODEL I can use what I know to help me read words I don't recognize. I know the word *I*. I know that an apostrophe in a word sometimes takes the place of a letter or letters from another word. I also know that *m* makes the sound /m/, so I think the word is *I'm*.

Ask a volunteer to circle the word in the contraction (I) and then write the words that make up the contraction *I'm* below it on the chart. (I am) Have children continue this process until the chart is complete.

PRACTICE

Read, Write, and Use Contractions in Sentences

 GROUP

Write the following contractions on index cards: *can't, it's, let's, I'm, he's,* and *she's.* Give a child one of the cards and ask him or her to read the contraction and say the two words it stands for. Help children write the words on the cards. Ask another child to use the contraction in a sentence. Continue with the other contractions.

▶**Visual/Linguistic**

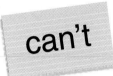  

can't   she's   I'm

ASSESS/CLOSE

Identifying Contractions

Invite children to use the contraction cards from the Practice activity. Say the following sentences aloud, repeating the pronoun and/or verb(s) after the sentence is read. Tell children to hold up the card with the contraction those words form, and say the contraction.

- She is my best friend. (She's)
- I cannot stand on my head. (can't)
- Let us go to the store. (Let's)

ALTERNATE TEACHING STRATEGY
....

CONTRACTIONS

For a different approach to teaching this skill, see page T74.

i **Intervention** ▶ **Skills**

Intervention Guide, for direct instruction and extra practice in Contractions

Meeting Individual Needs for Vocabulary

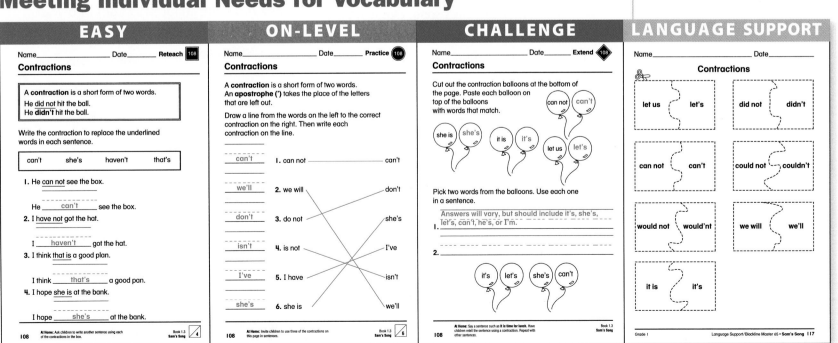

EASY	ON-LEVEL	CHALLENGE	LANGUAGE SUPPORT
Reteach, 108	Practice, 108	Extend, 108	Language Support, 117

Handwriting
CD-ROM

Interactive Writing
Make a Song Book

GRAMMAR/SPELLING CONNECTIONS

See the 5-Day Grammar and Usage Plan on past-tense verbs, pages 97O–97P.

Words with Digraphs *ch, wh, nk:* See the 5-Day Spelling Plan, pages 97Q–97R.

TEACHING TIP

Technology Most word-processing programs have a function that allows you to indent. Show children how to use the "File" option on the drop-down menu at the top of the screen to set different margins.

Prewrite

LOOK AT THE STORY PATTERN Have children revisit *Sam's Song,* reading carefully and trying to imagine what the family's song and Sam's song sound like. Then tell them that the class will create a book telling about the family's song and Sam's song. The book will have pictures and sentences that compare the songs. Who sings high notes or low notes? Who sings loud notes or soft notes? What kind of tune do they sing? Is it happy or sad, fast or slow? What words do they use in their song? List children's ideas.

Draft

WRITE ABOUT THE SONGS Tell children that on each page of the book they will tell about the songs. Guide them to suggest sentences using words they know.

• Begin by saying, for example, *Let's start by telling about the family's song. Was it long or short? The owls sang a long song. How about Sam? Sam sang a short song.* As you say a word with familiar sounds and patterns, challenge children to come up and write it. Write all unfamiliar words yourself. Then work with children to put the words together into a sentence.

• Encourage children to come up with new ideas. Have children decide when they've come up with enough sentences to describe and compare the songs.

Revise

PROPER NOUNS Remind children that a proper noun tells someone's name, such as Sam, and always begins with a capital letter. As you reread the sentences, have children raise their hands every time you read a proper noun. Then draw two lines under the capital letter found at the beginning of each proper noun.

Publish

CREATE THE SONG BOOK Reread the sentences together. Then ask each child to create two pages for the book, one page for the family's song and one for Sam's song. Discuss different ways of illustrating the pages: music notes, pictures of the singers, pictures of the words in the song. Have children create the illustrations, then copy the appropriate text onto each page. Then assemble the children's pages into your class's "Song Book for Sam."

Presentation Ideas

SING A SONG Invite volunteers to sing a song they are familiar with, perhaps in pairs. Ask the other children to listen carefully, and then describe it.

▶ **Listening/Speaking**

DRAW A SCENE FROM A MUSIC VIDEO Encourage children to imagine a video of the family's or Sam's song. Have them draw a scene from that video.

▶ **Representing/Viewing**

Meeting Individual Needs for Writing

EASY	ON-LEVEL	CHALLENGE
Draw Pictures Children can draw pictures showing scenes from a favorite song. Then have them imagine a song that a cat named Pat might sing and draw pictures showing scenes from that song. Have them label each picture either "My song" or "Pat's song."	**New Story** Children can work in groups to write a new story about a family of dogs that sings a song. Have them follow the language pattern of *Sam's Song* as they write their story.	**Journal Entry** Children can write a journal entry telling about a time when they sang a special song. What was the song about? What were some of the words? What did the song sound like? How did they feel when they sang it?

5Day Grammar and Usage Plan

Oral Warm-Up Perform actions such as erasing the chalkboard and closing a window. Ask children to describe what you did.

Introduce Past Tense Review that the tense of a verb tells when the action takes place. Discuss with children:

> **Past Tense**
>
> • Some verbs tell about actions that have already happened.
>
> • These verbs are in the **past tense**.
>
> • Most verbs in the past tense end with -*ed*.

Daily Language Activity Write the following sentence on the chalkboard: *Sam kicked the ball.* Ask children to find the word that shows action that has already happened. (*kicked*)

 Assign the daily Writing Prompt on page 68E.

Review Past Tense Remind children that yesterday they learned about words that show action that has already happened. Write the following sentence on the chalkboard: *Sam picked a song.* Ask children which word tells about something that has already happened. (*picked*) Remind children that most words in the past tense end with -*ed*.

Daily Language Activity Write the following sentences on the chalkboard: *Chuck helped Sam. Sam fixed the song.* Ask children to find the word that shows an action has happened already in each sentence. Ask children what letters are at the end of each word. (-*ed*)

 Assign the daily Writing Prompt on page 68E.

Name_____ Date_____ LEARN GRAMMAR 77

Past Tense

• Some verbs tell about actions that already happened.
• These verbs are in the **past tense**.
• Most verbs in the past tense end in -*ed*.
  The owls **watched** the sun.

Read the sentences. Circle the verbs that tell about actions that already happened.

1. The owls watched the sun.
2. The owls looked at Sam.
3. Sam talked to Mom and Pop.
4. Chuck asked the owls about the sun.
5. A star winked at Sam.

Book 1.3 Sam's Song   EXTENSION: Have the children think of actions they took earlier today. Then have them tell sentences about those actions.   77

GRAMMAR PRACTICE BOOK, PAGE 77

Name_____ Date_____ LEARN AND PRACTICE GRAMMAR 78

Past Tense

• Some verbs tell about actions in the past.
• Most verbs in the past end with -*ed*.
  Mom **talked** to Sam.

Read the sentences. Circle the verb that tells about past actions.

1. We ___ watch, (watched) the owls.
2. Sam ___ want, (wanted) to sing.
3. The star ___ wink, (winked) at Sam.
4. The mouse ___ crunch, (crunched).
5. Mom and Pop ___ look, (looked) at Sam.

78   EXTENSION: The children can draw pictures to illustrate one of the sentences they completed above.   Book 1.3 Sam's Song

GRAMMAR PRACTICE BOOK, PAGE 78

Same Concept, Skills and Vocabulary!

Leveled Books

In the Lake

by Gary Apple
illustrated by Sarah Snow

EASY
Lesson on pages 125A and 125D

`DECODABLE`

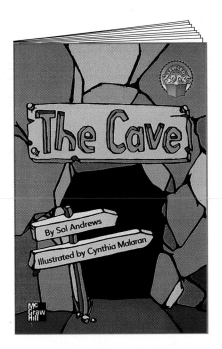

The Cave

By Sol Andrews

Illustrated by Cynthia Malaran

INDEPENDENT
Lesson on pages 125B and 125D

🏠 *Take-Home version available*

`DECODABLE`

Great Snakes!

by Fay Robinson
Illustrated by Jean Day Zallinger

CHALLENGE
Lesson on pages 125C and 125D

Leveled Practice

EASY
Reteach, 109-116 Blackline masters with reteaching opportunities for each assessed skill

INDEPENDENT/ON-LEVEL
Practice, 109-116 Workbook with Take-Home Stories and practice opportunities for each assessed skill and story comprehension

CHALLENGE
Extend, 109-116 Blackline masters that offer challenge activities for each assessed skill

Quizzes Prepared by Accelerated Reader®

Center Activities

Social Studies ...	Child vs. Pet Care, *118*
Science	Snake Facts, *98D*
	Hot Snakes, *110*
Math	Make a Snake, *98D*
	Snake Facts, *104*
Language Arts ..	Read Aloud, *98G*
Cultural Perspectives	Snake Tales, *114*
Writing	About a Snake, *122*
Research and Inquiry	Find Out More, *123*
Internet Activities	www.mhschool.com/reading

98B

CENTER Activities

Each of these activities takes 15-20 minutes.

Phonics

Make Long *a* Words

Objective: Substitute consonants to build long *a: a-e* words.

(PARTNERS)

◆ Have children write this spelling pattern: ___ *a* ___ *e*.

◆ Partners take turns adding consonants or consonant blends to make long *a* words.

MATERIALS
- Phonics Letter Cards from the Word Building Manipulative Cards (consonants)
- Construction paper
- Pencil

Writing

Snake Sentences

Objective: Write sentences about a snake.

(GROUP)

◆ Display the last question of the story.

◆ Have children write why they would or would not like to have a snake as a pet. Use the sentence frame: *I would/ would not like a pet snake because* _____.

◆ Children can draw a picture for their sentence.

MATERIALS
- Paper
- Crayons

Reading and Listening

Independent/Self-Selected Reading

Objective: Listen and use illustrations to understand a story.

(ONE)

Fill the Center with books and corresponding audiocassettes or CD-ROMs children have read or listened to this week. You can also include books from the Theme Bibliography on pages T98 and T99.

Leveled Readers

◆ *In the Lake* by Gary Apple
◆ *The Cave* by Sol Andrews
◆ *Great Snakes!* by Fay Robinson

◆ Theme Big Book *I Go with My Family to Grandma's* by Riki Levinson

◆ *Snakes* by Frances Minters

◆ "Something About Me"—Anonymous

◆ Phonics Practice Reader, Vol. 1

Working with Words

Slithery Search

Objective: Reinforce vocabulary words: *know, where, under, why.*

PARTNERS

MATERIALS
- **Paper**
- **Pencil**

◆ Have children write each word.

◆ Partners look through *Snakes* and find the sentences that contain each word.

◆ Together, children write each sentence and draw a snake around the vocabulary word.

Science

Snake Facts

Objective: Compare and contrast snakes.

GROUP

MATERIALS
- **Snake picture books**
- **Paper**
- **Crayons**

◆ Make available books with photos of snakes.

◆ Have children name five snakes. Encourage children to describe them.

◆ Have children draw and label their favorite snake.

Math 3+2

Make a Snake

Objective: Counting up to 5, 6, 7, or 8.

ONE

MATERIALS
- **Construction paper**
- **Paper strips 1 inch wide and 4 inches long**
- **Scissors**
- **Glue**
- **Crayons**

◆ Provide children with paper snake heads and strips. Each head should have a number from 5 to 8 written on it.

◆ The number on the snake head should match the number of loops the child makes from the strips.

◆ Children glue their strips into loops and connect them to make a chain.

◆ Children can add details to their snake heads, such as eyes and a tongue.

Suggested
Lesson Planner

READING AND LANGUAGE ARTS	DAY 1 — Focus on Reading and Skills	DAY 2 — Read the Literature
Phonics Daily Routines	Daily **Phonics** Routine: Discriminating, 98J **Phonics** CD-ROM	Daily **Phonics** Routine: Letter Substitution, 100A **Phonics** CD-ROM
Phonological Awareness **Phonics** *Long a: a-e* **Comprehension** **Vocabulary** **Study Skills** **Listening, Speaking, Viewing, Representing**	**Read** **Read Aloud,** 98G "The Snake" ☑ **Develop Phonological Awareness,** 98H ☑ **Introduce Long *a: a-e*,** 98I–98J **Reteach, Practice, Extend,** 109 **Phonics/Phonemic Awareness Practice Book,** 129–132 **Read** **Apply Long *a: a–e*** "Snake's Trip," 98/99 **Intervention Program**	**Build Background,** 100A Develop Oral Language **Vocabulary,** 100B–100C know where under why **Word Building Manipulative Cards** **Teaching Chart 81** **Reteach, Practice, Extend,** 110 **Read** **Read the Selection,** 100–121 **Guided Instruction** ☑ Long *a: a-e* ☑ Compare and Contrast **Genre: Narrative Nonfiction,** 101 **Cultural Perspectives,** 114 **Intervention Program**
Curriculum Connections	**Link** Language Arts, 98G	**Link** Science, 100A
Writing	**Writing Prompt:** Imagine that you look down and see a snake. Write about what it looks like and what it is doing.	**Writing Prompt:** What if you were a snake? What would you look like? What would you like to do? **Journal Writing** Quick-Write, 121
Grammar	**Introduce the Concept: *Is* and *Are*,** 125O Daily Language Activity: Understand when to use *is*. **Grammar Practice Book,** 83	**Teach the Concept: *Is* and *Are*,** 125O Daily Language Activity: Complete sentences with *is* or *are*. **Grammar Practice Book,** 84
Spelling *Long a: a-e*	**Introduce Spelling Words: Words with Long *a: a-e*,** 125Q **Spelling Practice Book,** 83–84	**Teach the Patterns: Words with Long *a: a-e*,** 125Q **Spelling Practice Book,** 85

    Intervention Program Available

DAY 3 — Read the Literature

Daily Phonics Routine:
Blending, 123

Phonics **CD-ROM**

Reread for Fluency, 120

Story Questions, 122
Reteach, Practice, Extend, 111

Story Activities, 123

Study Skill, 124
☑ Diagrams
Teaching Chart 82
Reteach, Practice, Extend, 112

Read **Read the Leveled Books,** 125A–125D
Guided Reading
☑ Long *a: a-e*
☑ Compare and Contrast
☑ High-Frequency Words

 Intervention Program

 **Math,** 98D, 104

 Writing Prompt: What if you had a pet snake? What is its name? Where does it live?

 Journal Writing, 125D

Practice and Write: *Is and Are,* 125P
Daily Language Activity: Use *is* or *are* in sentences.

Grammar Practice Book, 85

Practice and Extend: Words with Long *a: a-e,* 125R

Spelling Practice Book, 86

DAY 4 — Build Skills

Daily Phonics Routine:
Fluency, 125F

Phonics **CD-ROM**

Read **Read the Leveled Books and the Self-Selected Books**

☑ **Review Long *a: a-e,*** 125E–125F
Teaching Chart 83
Reteach, Practice, Extend, 113
Language Support, 123
Phonics/Phonemic Awareness
Practice Book, 129–132

☑ **Review *a-e; ch, wh, nk,*** 125G–125H
Teaching Chart 84
Reteach, Practice, Extend, 114
Language Support, 124
Phonics/Phonemic Awareness
Practice Book, 129–132

Minilessons, 105, 109, 111, 113, 115, 119

 Intervention Program

 Science, 98D, 110

 Writing Prompt: Imagine you and your pet snake are going on a trip. Where would you go? What would you do?

Interactive Writing, 125M
Prewrite, Draft

Meeting Individual Needs for Writing, 125N

Practice and Write: *Is and Are,* 125P
Daily Language Activity: Write sentences with *is* or *are.*

Grammar Practice Book, 86

Practice and Write: Words with Long *a: a-e,* 125R

Spelling Practice Book, 87

DAY 5 — Build Skills

Daily Phonics Routine:
Writing, 125H

Phonics **CD-ROM**

Read **Read Self-Selected Books**

☑ **Review Story Elements,** 125I–125J
Teaching Chart 85
Reteach, 115, Practice, 91,
Extend, 115
Language Support, 125

☑ **Review Contractions,** 125K–125L
Teaching Chart 86
Reteach, Practice, Extend, 116
Language Support, 126

Listening, Speaking, Viewing, Representing, 125N
Give a Speech
Act Out a Story

Minilessons, 105, 109, 111, 113, 115, 119

 Intervention Program

Social Studies, 118

Writing Prompt: Write about your favorite kind of snake. Tell why you like this kind of snake.

Interactive Writing, 125M
Revise, Publish

Assess and Reteach: *Is and Are,* 125P
Daily Language Activity: Complete sentences with *is* or *are.*

Grammar Practice Book, 87–88

Assess and Reteach: Words with Long *a: a-e,* 125R

Spelling Practice Book, 88

Read Aloud

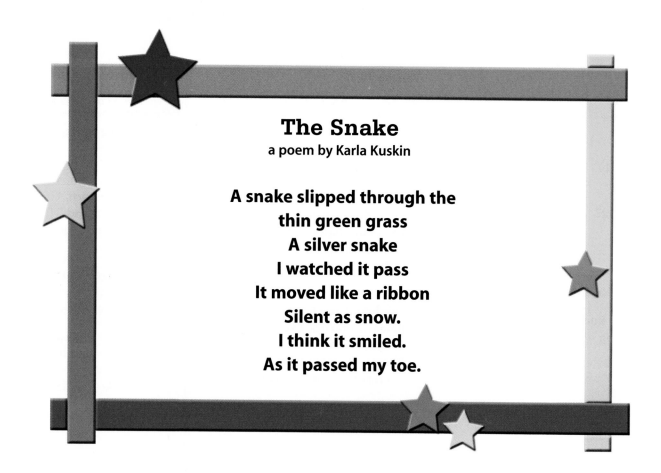

The Snake

a poem by Karla Kuskin

A snake slipped through the
thin green grass
A silver snake
I watched it pass
It moved like a ribbon
Silent as snow.
I think it smiled.
As it passed my toe.

Oral Comprehension

LISTENING AND SPEAKING Motivate children to think about how sounds in a poem can reflect its topic by reading this poem about a snake passing through the grass. With children, make the hissing /s/ sound of a snake. Then ask children to listen for this sound as you read the poem, and to raise their hands each time they hear the /s/ sound. When you are done, ask, "Why do you think the poet put so many words with the /s/ sound in the poem?"

Activity Ask children to paint a picture of the scene described in "The Snake." Have children review the poem for ideas on details and colors to include.

▶ **Visual**

GENRE: POEM Poems use descriptive words and phrases to create a picture in the reader's mind. Ask volunteers to find examples of descriptive phrases such as "moved like a ribbon" or "silent as snow." Discuss with children how this descriptive imagery helps them picture the snake.

Poems may also use the literary technique of *alliteration*. Explain that when two or more words in a row start with the same consonant sound, this is called alliteration. Point out "green grass" and "silver snake" as examples of alliteration.

Develop Phonological Awareness

Blend Sounds
Phonemic Awareness

MATERIALS
• puppet

Teach Have the puppet say: *Listen as I blend these sounds together—/f/-/ā/-/d/. What word did I say? (fade)* Have the puppet continue by saying the sounds in *bake.* Have the puppet say: *What word did I say? (bake)* Have children then identify the sound they hear in the middle of *fade* and *bake.* (/ā/)

Practice Have the puppet say the sounds for the words below, having children blend the sounds together to form the words *make, came, date, daze, gave, lane, late, safe, shake.*

Segment Sounds
Phonemic Awareness

MATERIALS
• pictures of long *a* words, such as *cake, cave, gate, grape, lake, plane, plate, snake, vase, game, rake, skate, tape, wave*

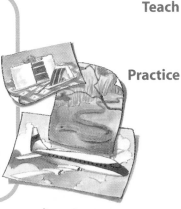

Teach Hold up one of the pictures, such as the picture of the *lake.* Say the word *lake.* Then segment the sounds in the word, identifying its three sounds: /l/-/ā/-/k/. Have children repeat after you.

Practice Continue the activity with the remaining pictures. First have children say each word. Then have them segment the sounds in each word. Last, have the children identify the number of sounds in the word.

Delete Sounds
Phonemic Awareness

MATERIALS
• Phonics Picture Card: *game*

Teach Hold up the Phonics Picture Card for *game.* Say the word and identify the three sounds in the word: /g/-/ā/-/m/. Then explain that if you remove the beginning sound, /g/, from *game,* what is left is *–ame.* Continue by explaining that if you remove the final sound, /m/, from *game,* what is left is *ga-.*

Practice Have children repeat each of the following words after you, leaving off first the initial sound and then the final sound: *chase, date, fake, late, name, sale, shame, shape, take, tame, wade.*

INFORMAL ASSESSMENT Observe children as they blend sounds, segment sounds, and delete initial and final sounds. If children have difficulty, see Alternate Teaching Strategies on page T75.

OBJECTIVES

Children will:

- identify long *a* in *a-e* words.
- blend and read long *a-e* words.
- review *wh* and *sh*; blends *sn, sc, fl*; consonants.

MATERIALS

- long *a* and letter cards from the **Word Building Manipulative Cards**

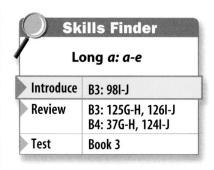

Skills Finder

Long *a: a-e*	
Introduce	B3: 98I-J
Review	B3: 125G-H, 126I-J B4: 37G-H, 124I-J
Test	Book 3

SPELLING/PHONICS CONNECTIONS

Words with long *a*: See the 5-Day Spelling Plan, pages 125Q–125R.

TEACHING TIP

RHYMING WORDS Have children work in pairs. Say *make* and *lake* aloud. Ask children if the words rhyme and why. Then ask them to think of other words that rhyme with *make*. (*cake, take, rake, snake, bake*)

Introduce Long *a: a-e*

TEACH

Identify the Letters *a-e* as a Symbol for /ā/

Let children know they will learn to read words with the letters *a-e* that have the long *a* sound.

- Display the *a-e* letter card and say /ā/.

BLENDING Model and Guide Practice with Long *a: a-e* Words

- Have children repeat the long *a* sound as you point to the *a-e* card.
- Tell children that the line between the *a* and the *e* is a space for a consonant and that the *e* will be silent.
- Place the *d* letter card over the blank between *a* and *e*.
- Blend the sounds together to say *ade*. Have children repeat.

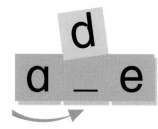 

- Place an *m* letter card at the beginning of *ade*. Run your hand under the letters and say *made*. Have children repeat after you.

 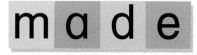

Use the Word in Context

- Use the word in a sentence to reinforce its meaning. Example: *I made a snake out of clay.*

Repeat the Procedure

- Use the following words to continue modeling and guided practice with long *a: a-e.*

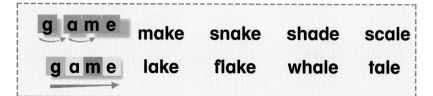

	make	snake	shade	scale
	lake	flake	whale	tale

PRACTICE

**LETTER SUBSTITUTION
Building Long *a*
Words with
Letter Cards**

Build the word *safe* and ask children to repeat each sound after you. Replace the *f* with an *l*. Have children repeat the word *sale*. Continue by having children change one letter each time to build and read the following words: *safe, same, tame, take, make.* ▶ **Linguistic/Kinesthetic**

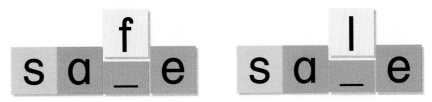

ASSESS/CLOSE

**Read and Write
Words with
Long *a***

To assess children's ability to blend and read long *a* words, observe them as they build and read words in the Practice activity. Have them choose two words and write a sentence using each one.

ADDITIONAL PHONICS RESOURCES

Phonics/Phonemic Awareness Practice Book,
pages 129–132

PHONICS KIT
Hands-on Activities and Practice

McGraw-Hill School
TECHNOLOGY

Phonics CD-ROM
activities for practice with Blending and Segmenting

Meeting Individual Needs for Phonics

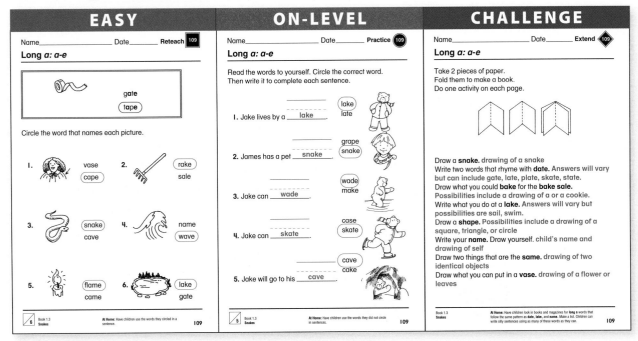

EASY

ON-LEVEL

CHALLENGE

Reteach, 109   Practice, 109   Extend, 109

Daily Routines

DAY 1 **Discriminating** Say some similar long *a-e* and short *a* words and ask children to raise hands when they hear the long *a* sound. Examples: *snake/snack, back/bake, rake/rack.*

DAY 2 **Letter Substitution** Using the letter cards, have pairs of children build the word *cake.* One child changes a consonant and the partner reads the new word.

DAY 3 **Blending** Write the spelling of each sound in *scale* as you say it. Have children repeat after you. Ask children to blend the sounds to read the word. Repeat with *plate* and *whale.*

DAY 4 **Fluency** Write some sentences on the chalkboard and have children identify and read the long *a-e* word(s). Examples: *Jane is in grade 1. She has a cake in the shape of a grape.*

DAY 5 **Writing** Have children write a long *a: a-e* word to complete the sentence: *I have a _____ .* (Examples: *name, cake, game, cape, gate, grape, plate*)

TESTED
OBJECTIVES

Children will read a poem
with words containing
long *a: a-e.*

Apply **Long *a: a-e***

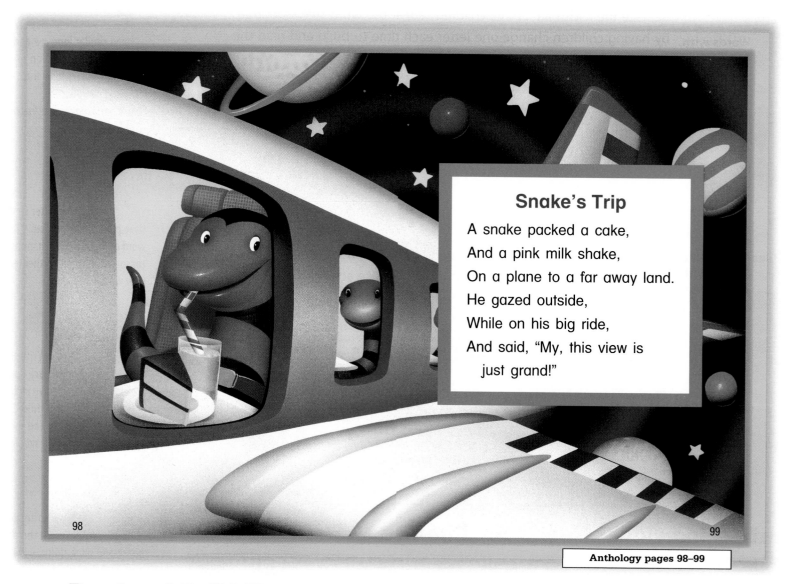

Snake's Trip

A snake packed a cake,
And a pink milk shake,
On a plane to a far away land.
He gazed outside,
While on his big ride,
And said, "My, this view is
just grand!"

98

99

Anthology pages 98–99

Read and Build Fluency

READ THE POEM Tell children they will read a poem
called *Snake's Trip.* Provide auditory modeling, pausing
at commas and reading the exclamatory sentence with
excitement. Then have children read with you.

REREAD FOR FLUENCY Have pairs of children do
repeated readings of the poem until they
achieve fluency.

PARTNERS

READ A DECODABLE STORY For
additional practice reading and to
develop fluency, have children read
Jake's Rake from **Phonics Practice
Reader, Vol. 1.**

Dictate and Spell

DICTATE WORDS Segment the word *cake* into its
three individual sounds. Repeat the word aloud
and use it in a sentence: *The snake ate his cake.*
JOURNAL
Point out the silent *e* in *snake, ate,* and *cake.* Then have
children say the word and write the letter or letters that
represent each sound until they make the entire word.
Repeat with *snake, shake, plane,* and *gazed* from the
poem. Then repeat with long *a* words not from the
poem, such as *brave, came, fake, gave, safe, scale, shape,
trade,* and *wake.*

i **Intervention** ➤ **Skills Intervention Guide,** for
direct instruction and extra practice in Long *a*

Build Background

Science

Concept: Reptiles

Evaluate Prior Knowledge

CONCEPT: REPTILES Ask children to share what they know about reptiles, naming different kinds of reptiles and their characteristics. Use the following activity to give children more information about reptiles.

MAKE A WORD WEB FOR REPTILES
Work with children to create a word web to record some characteristics about reptiles.

▶ **Linguistic**

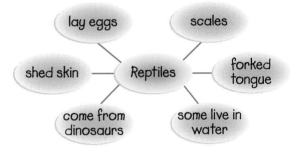

Reptiles
- lay eggs
- scales
- shed skin
- forked tongue
- come from dinosaurs
- some live in water

> Graphic Organizer 29

MAKE A REPTILE PICTURE Create
  a list of various kinds of reptiles. Encourage children to
ONE   WRITING
draw a picture of a reptile. Suggest that children refer to the reptile web for ideas. Have children write a sentence describing their picture.

Develop Oral Language

CONNECT WORDS AND ACTIONS

ESL Invite children to pretend to be snakes. Ask them to show some things that snakes do.

Examples:
- Wriggle like a snake.
- Make a hissing sound.
- Flick your tongue out.

Prompt children to say what they are doing. Model questions such as:
- What are you doing?
- What does a hiss sound like?

▶ **Kinesthetic/Linguistic**

DAILY Phonics ROUTINES

DAY 2 **Letter Substitution**
Using the letter cards, have pairs of children build the word *cake*. One child changes a consonant and the partner reads the new word.

Phonics CD-ROM

LANGUAGE SUPPORT

To build more background, see pages 118–121 in the **Language Support Book**.

OBJECTIVES

Children will:

• identify high-frequency words *where, know, why,* and *under*.

MATERIALS

• Teaching Chart 81

• Word Building Manipulative Cards *where, know, why, under*

TEACHING **TIP**

The following chart indicates words from the story that children have learned to decode in this lesson and high-frequency words that have been taught. As children read, observe any difficulties they may have in reading these words.

Decodable		High-Frequency
safe	made	know
make	snake(s)	under
lake	scales	where
		why

SPELLING/VOCABULARY CONNECTIONS

The words *know, under, where,* and *why* are Challenge Words. See page 125Q for Day 1 of the 5-Day Spelling Plan.

---

where

why

know

under

Vocabulary
High-Frequency Words

Where Are There Snakes?

(Where) are there snakes?
In ponds and in lakes.
In the sun and the shade.
On a hill. In a glade.
Do you know (why) they nest?
Do you (know) how they rest?
In caves and in bogs.
On branches and logs.
In the grass. (Under) rocks.

Teaching Chart 81

Auditory

LISTEN TO WORDS Without displaying it, read aloud, "Where Are There Snakes?" on **Teaching Chart 81**. Ask children what they know about snakes. Do any of them have a snake for a pet?

RHYME HIGH-FREQUENCY WORDS Have children aurally identify each high-frequency word using the following activity:

• Read aloud the first line of "Where Are There Snakes?" Ask children which words rhyme.

• Say aloud one of the high-frequency words. Ask children to aurally identify words that rhyme with that word, and use both words in a sentence.

• Repeat this activity with each of the high-frequency words.

Visual

TEACH WORDS Display "Where Are There Snakes?" on **Teaching Chart 81**. Read the poem. Next, point to and say the word *where.* Have children say the word with you. Ask them to hold up the vocabulary card for *where* and say the word. Repeat this procedure for *know, why,* and *under*.

Hold up vocabulary cards for *where, know, why,* and *under* one at a time. Have volunteers read the words and then circle them on the chart.

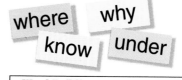

Word Building Manipulative Cards

BE AN ORCHESTRA Divide the class into numbered groups. Write a number next to each line of the poem and have groups copy that line. By lines with high-frequency words, write all the numbers. Then "conduct" the poem.

Word Wall

Rhyming on the Word Wall
Tell children that you will say a sentence that tells about a word wall word. Children who think they know the word wall word should raise their hands. Have volunteers come up and identify the word being described.

This word rhymes with *thunder* and *blunder*. *(under)*

This word starts with *w* and rhymes with *there*. *(where)*

This word rhymes with *go* and *tow*. *(know)*

This word starts with *w* and rhymes with *fly*. *(why)*

Clap Chant Clap
Review the word wall words for this lesson. Make sure children can identify them correctly. Then have children clap the letters, chant the letters, and clap the letters again for each word.

Assess

Clap , Say, Write
Repeat the clap, chant, clap exercise. But, instead of chanting, simply say the word. Then have children write the spelling of the word. Repeat for all of the word wall words.

Meeting Individual Needs for Vocabulary

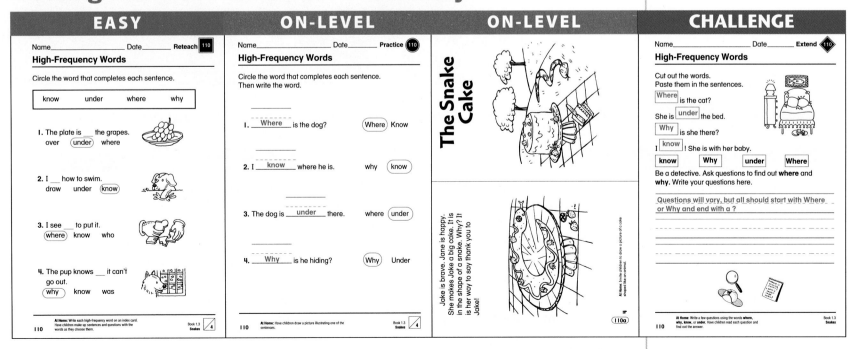

EASY	ON-LEVEL	ON-LEVEL	CHALLENGE

Reteach, 110 | Practice, 110 | Practice, 110a Take-Home Story | Extend, 110

100C

Comprehension

Prereading Strategies

PREVIEW AND PREDICT Ask a volunteer to read the title of the story. Then, point to and read aloud the name of the author. Explain that many people's photographs are in the story, so there is no "illustrator." Take a **picture walk** and discuss what children see. Have children notice similarities and differences between the snakes in the photographs. Point out a few long *a* words and high-frequency words as you go.

- Do you think the story is going to be realistic or a fantasy?
- What is the story most likely about?

Have children make predictions about the story; write their predictions on the chart and read them aloud.

SET PURPOSES Ask children what they want to find out as they read the story. For example:

- What and how do snakes eat?
- Would a snake be a good pet?
- Are snakes dangerous?

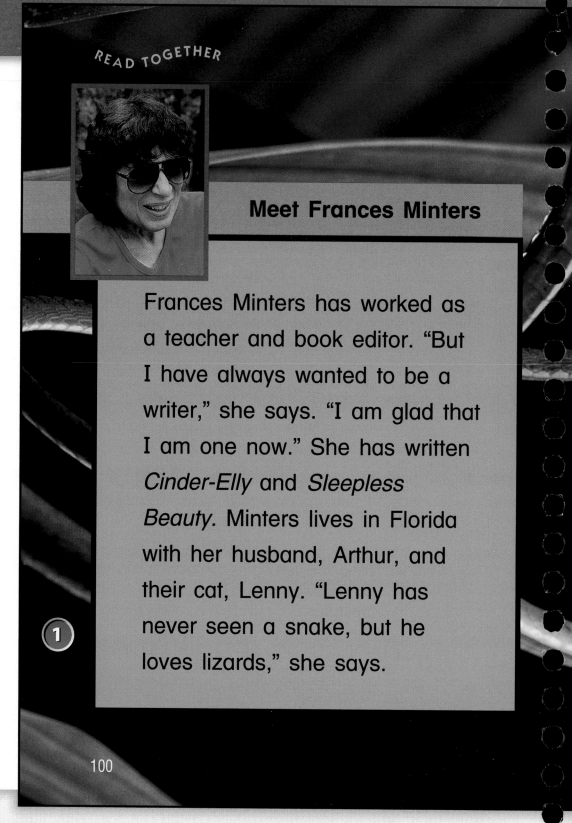

READ TOGETHER

Meet Frances Minters

Frances Minters has worked as a teacher and book editor. "But I have always wanted to be a writer," she says. "I am glad that I am one now." She has written *Cinder-Elly* and *Sleepless Beauty*. Minters lives in Florida with her husband, Arthur, and their cat, Lenny. "Lenny has never seen a snake, but he loves lizards," she says.

① 100

Meeting Individual Needs · Grouping Suggestions for Strategic Reading

EASY	ON-LEVEL	CHALLENGE
Shared Reading Read the story aloud as you track print and model directionality. Invite children to join in on repetitive words and phrases. As you read with children, model the strategy of paying attention to comparing and contrasting the various snakes to help children understand what is happening in the story.	**Guided Instruction** Read the story with children, using the Comprehension questions. Monitor any difficulties in reading that children have to determine which prompts in the Comprehension section to emphasize. After reading the story, have children reread it, using the rereading suggestions on page 120.	**Independent Reading** Have children set purposes before they read. Remind them that as they read, they should focus on how snakes are alike and how they are different. After reading, have children tell what they learned about snakes. Children can use the questions on page 122 for a group discussion.

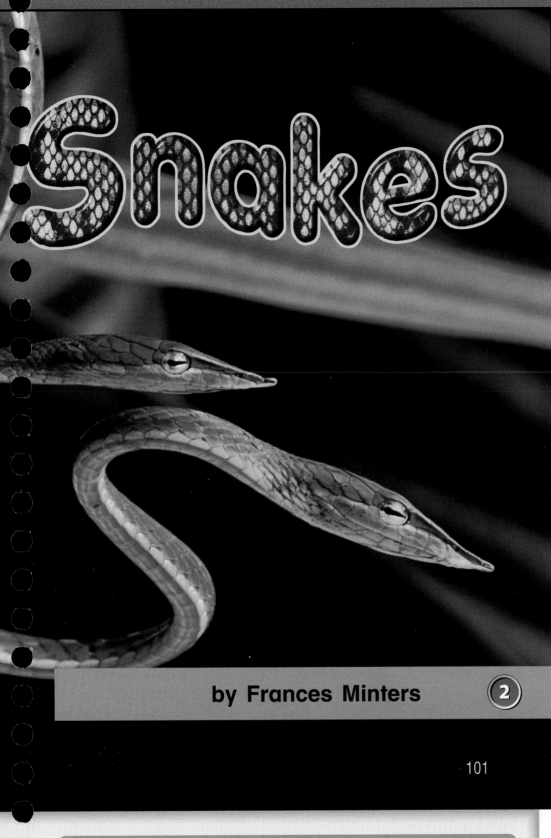

Snakes

by Frances Minters ②

101

Comprehension

 ✓ **Phonics** Long *a: a-e*

 ✓ **Apply Compare and Contrast**

STRATEGIC READING Tell children that paying special attention to how the snakes in the story are the same and different will help them understand what they read. Explain that they will use a Same and Different chart to keep track of the information in the story.

SAME	DIFFERENT

① We are going to read *Snakes* by Frances Minters. Let's read about the author. Why do you think she wanted to write about snakes? *Concept of a Book: Author/Illustrator*

② **COMPARE AND CONTRAST** Look at the snakes in the picture on page 101. Are the snakes the same or different? (same)

Genre

Narrative Nonfiction

Explain to children that a narrative nonfiction piece can:

• relate facts about a specific subject.

• use photographs to illustrate information.

• show a subject in its natural setting.

Activity After reading *Snakes*, ask the children to explain how they knew the story was real. Have them relate facts about snakes that they learned from the story.

LANGUAGE SUPPORT

A blackline master for making a Same and Different chart can be found in the **Language Support Book**. Children can write and draw their comparisons of snakes as they read the story.

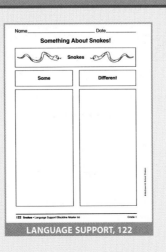

Name_____ Date_____
Something About Snakes!

Snakes

Same	Different

122 **Snakes** • Language Support/Blackline Master A6   Grade 1

LANGUAGE SUPPORT, 122

101

Comprehension

3 Look at the small picture at the top of page 102. Is the snake big or small? (small) Look at the man in the big picture. What is on his shoulder? (a snake) Is the snake big or small? (big) *Use Illustrations*

4 **COMPARE AND CONTRAST** Are the snakes on this page the same or different? (different) How are they different? (One is big, one is small.) Let's write what we know on the chart. *Graphic Organizer*

SAME	DIFFERENT
	Some snakes are small. Others are big.

5 **Phonics** **LONG** *a: a-e* Let's read this page together: "*There are a lot of . . .*" This word is the same as the title of the story. Let's blend the sounds of the letters together to read the word. s n a k(e) s snakes *Graphophonic Cues*

Fluency

REREAD IN PAIRS

PARTNERS Have children read the story aloud with a partner to help achieve fluency.

- Read page 102 aloud.
- Ask one child in each pair to read the first sentence on page 102 aloud.
- Ask the partner to repeat the sentence.
- Ask children to switch roles and read the second sentence.

There are a lot of snakes in the world.
There are big snakes and small snakes.

102

LANGUAGE SUPPORT

ESL Illustrations are key to helping ESL children understand the text. As you finish reading a sentence or a page, point to the illustrations to clarify what you have just read. You may wish to point to a map or globe to make sure that children acquiring English understand the phrase "in the world."

You can find snakes in hot lands ⑥ and in damp lands.

103

Comprehension

TRACKING PRINT Show me with your finger how you would read the sentence on this page. *Syntactic Cues*

⑥ COMPARE AND CONTRAST Let's read this sentence aloud. You can find snakes in hot lands and in damp lands. Can a place be both hot and damp? (yes) What would a place be like that was the opposite of hot and damp? (cold and dry) Look at the pictures. Do you think snakes live in places that are cold and damp? (yes) What about places that are hot and dry? (yes) Let's put this information on our chart. *Graphic Organizer*

SAME	DIFFERENT
	Some snakes are small. Others are big.
	Some snakes live in hot lands. Others live in damp lands.

---

p/i PREVENTION/INTERVENTION

TRACKING PRINT On the chalkboard, write several sentences that turn lines. Have children use chalk in one color to draw arrows underneath each line and chalk in a second color to draw an arrow from one line to the next to show directionality and return sweep. Then have children use the arrows they drew to help them read each sentence aloud. Use the following sentences:

• My pet rabbit likes to eat lettuce and carrots.

• The cat ran under the bed and hid there.

Syntactic Cues

Comprehension

7 Look at the photographs of the people and the snake on this page. Do you think the people looking at the snake in this picture are in danger? Tell why you answered as you did. *Make Inferences*

8 Look at the boy on this page. Does he think the snake will harm him? (no) How can you tell? (This snake is confined in a glass container. The boy doesn't look afraid.) *Use Picture Clues/Make Inferences*

7 Most of the snakes that you see
8 will not harm you.

104

Activity

Cross Curricular: Math

SNAKE FACTS Share these facts about snakes, using the chalkboard to illustrate approximate measurements.

- The "spitting" cobra, a snake that lives in Africa, can spit its poison 6 to 8 feet.
- One of the smallest snakes in the world grows to be only 6 inches.

RESEARCH AND INQUIRY Have partners look through encyclopedias and reptile books to find other snake facts to share. ▶ **Visual**

interNET CONNECTION For information on math activities, have children log on to **www.mhschool.com/reading**.

But some snakes can. (9) (10)
So be safe! (11)

105

ESL The word *harm* on page 104 may be unfamiliar to ESL children. Use the synonym *hurt* to make sure they understand. Extend the sentence "But some snakes can _____ you" with the words *harm* and *hurt* to ensure that children understand.

Comprehension

(9) Read the first sentence with me: *But some snakes can.* What is this sentence about? (Some snakes can harm you.) What words are understood after the word *can*? (*harm you*) **Make Inferences**

(10) Let's read the second line on this page: *So be safe!* If you get too close to a dangerous snake, what might happen? (It might bite you.) **Make Inferences**

(11) **COMPARE AND CONTRAST** What is another thing we know about how snakes are not all the same? (Some are dangerous, some are not.) Let's put that on our chart. **Graphic Organizer**

Minilesson
REVIEW/MAINTAIN
Make Inferences

Remind children that pictures can tell you things about the story that are not in the words.

- Have children imagine what the people on page 104 might be saying to each other.

- Ask children to guess how the people and the snakes are feeling.

- Discuss what has been done to keep both the people and the snake safe.

Activity Have children draw a picture of a snake in a cage with lots of things for the snake to slide under, over, and around. Brainstorm what some of them might be. (rock, log, plant, pond)

Comprehension

 BLENDING WITH SHORT *u* Look at the fifth word in the second sentence. Read this word, using your finger to help you remember to blend the sounds of the letters together. l u m p lump
Graphophonic Cues

12 What do you think that big lump inside the snake is? (a rat, an egg, a mouse) Let's read to find out. *Make Inferences*

13 Let's read the last sentence on the page: *That lump is a big rat!* How could such a big rat get through the snake's small mouth? (Responses may vary: the snake opens its mouth wide, it eats the rat very slowly.) *Critical Thinking*

14 Point to the word *know* in the first sentence. Now read it aloud. What do you know about snakes? *High-Frequency Words*

12 Do you know how a snake eats?
13 Look at that big lump in its body.
14 That big lump is a big rat!

106

PREVENTION/INTERVENTION

BLENDING WITH SHORT *u*
Children can work in pairs. One child uses letter cards *b, h, m,* and *s.* The partner uses letter cards *g, m, n,* and *t.* They share a *u* letter card. The first child chooses a letter to start a short *u* word and the partner chooses a letter to end the word. Children build a word, then blend the letters together to read the word. Check to see that children are blending words that make sense. If the letters make a nonsense word, ask children to choose a different first or last letter.
Graphophonic Cues

A snake can make its mouth very big. (15)
That is how it can eat such big things.

107

Comprehension

(15) **Phonics** **LONG *a: a–e*** Let's read the first sentence. "*A snake can . . .* hmm, what's this word?" It looks a little bit like the word *snake*, doesn't it? We can blend the letter sounds to read it as a long *a*, silent *e* word. m͝ a͝ k(e) → make *Graphophonic Cues*

Comprehension

16 **COMPARE AND CONTRAST** Let's read the first sentence on this page: *Can a snake run?* Why can't snakes really run? (because snakes don't have legs) This is the same for all snakes. Let's add it to our chart. *Graphic Organizer*

SAME	DIFFERENT
Snakes don't have legs.	Some snakes are small. Others are big.
	Some snakes live in hot lands. Others live in damp lands.

17 Let's look at the photograph on this page. Look at the tracks the snake is leaving in the sand. How would your tracks in the sand be different? (Children would leave footprints.) Why don't snakes leave footprints? (because they don't have feet; they slither) *Use Illustrations/Draw Conclusions*

16 Can a snake run?
17 A snake has no legs. It can't run.

108

108 *Snakes*

But a snake can move. **(18)**
It can get where it wants to go.

109

Comprehension

(18) Look at the photograph on this page. Where do you think the snake is going? Why might it be going there? *Make Inferences*

Comprehension

19 **Phonics** **LONG** *a: a-e* The last
word in the first sentence looks like
another long *a*, silent *e* word. Let's blend the
sounds of the letters together to read it.
s a f(e) safe. *Graphophonic Cues*

20 Let's read the next sentence on this
page: *A snake can be safe under a rock
or in a log*. Why do you think the snake is
safe in these places? (Responses may vary: It
is protected from other animals or bad
weather.) *Make Inferences*

Ⓢ ELF-MONITORING STRATEGY

SEARCH FOR CLUES Go back through
the story and look for clues to help you
remember what you have learned.

- How are all snakes alike?
- How are some snakes different from others?

19 Where can a snake be safe?
20 A snake can be safe under a rock
or in a log.

110

Activity

Cross Curricular: Science

HOT SNAKES Explain that snakes lie in
the sun to get warm. Their blood gets
warmer or colder depending on the outside temperature; they are called cold-
blooded animals. Human blood stays
about the same temperature all the time;
we are called warm-blooded animals.

RESEARCH AND INQUIRY If possible, invite a worker from the zoo, a local
science center, or a pet store to class
with a live snake. Ask him/her to explain
to the class how a snake lives, and how
snakes vary from each other.
▶ **Kinesthetic**

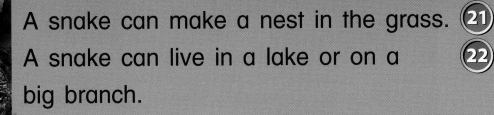

A snake can make a nest in the grass. **21**

A snake can live in a lake or on a **22**

big branch.

111

Comprehension

21 Look at the three snakes on pages 110–111. What places are they in? (rocks, tree, water) What does this tell us about where snakes live? (that snakes can live in different habitats, or places) *Use Illustrations/Draw Conclusions*

22 **COMPARE AND CONTRAST** What does this page tell us about things snakes can and can't do? If they can live in a tree, they must be able to do what? (climb) If they live in a lake, what must they be able to do? (swim) Let's put this on the chart. *Graphic Organizer*

SAME	DIFFERENT
Snakes don't have legs.	Some snakes are small. Others are big.
	Some snakes live in hot lands. Others live in damp lands.
	Some snakes can climb. Others can swim.

Minilesson

REVIEW/MAINTAIN

Digraph *ch*

Emphasize the final sound of the word *branch* as you read page 111. Write *ch* on the chalkboard. Ask children to:

- find the word that ends with the letters *ch*.
- repeat the sound these letters make.
- identify the same sound in these words and write the words on a piece of paper:

  crunch   champ   pinch

Activity Ask children to suggest words that begin or end in the /ch/ sound.

Phonics CD-ROM Have children use the interactive phonics activities for more reinforcement.

Comprehension

POSSESSIVES Listen as I read the sentences on this page. Point to the word that shows whose skin the sentence is talking about. Whose skin is it? (the snake's) What part of the word lets you know the skin belongs to the snake? (the apostrophe and the s) *Syntactic/Semantic Cues*

23 **Phonics** LONG *a: a-e* Now let's read the sentence together. Can you point to all the words on this page with the long *a: a-e* sound? We can read these words: *snake's, scales, made. Graphophonic Cues*

23 Do you know that a snake's skin is made of small scales?

112

PREVENTION/INTERVENTION

POSSESSIVES Play a "Belongs To" game with children to reinforce possessives. Write and draw several phrases on the chalkboard using names of children in the classroom and the name or a picture of something that belongs to them, for example: *Jack's hat*. Have volunteers read the phrase and then point out the child and the article belonging to that child. Children may wish to draw and label a favorite possession. Remind children to include the apostrophe and *s* on each label. *Syntactic/Semantic Cues*

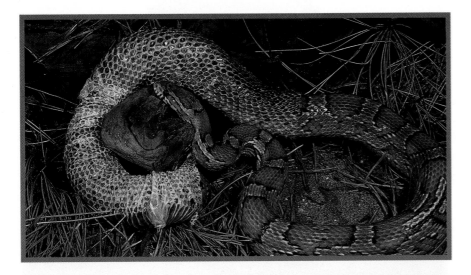

A snake can grow a new skin under its old skin. Then the old skin falls off.

113

Comprehension

24 Look at the two photographs on this page. How do you think the snake gets its old skin off? Let's add "skin falls off" to our chart about how snakes are the same. *Use Illustrations/Graphic Organizer*

TEACHING TIP

MAKE CONNECTIONS You might want to bring in an article or nonfiction story about a snake that is common to the area in which the children live. Read the article aloud to children, or summarize the main ideas, and pass the material around the classroom. This activity will expand *Snakes* further into the "real" world.

Minilesson

REVIEW/MAINTAIN

Cause and Effect

Remind children that sometimes one thing happens that leads to another thing happening.

- Have children look at page 113 and identify what is happening. (The snake is shedding its skin.)
- Ask them what happened first, and what happened second. (The snake grows a new skin; the old skin falls off.)
- Then ask children how the first event might have caused the second event. (The new skin pushes the old skin off; the snake crawls out of the old skin.)

Activity Invite children to perform a simple act, such as rolling a pencil off their desks. Then ask them to explain what happened because of that first event.

Comprehension

(25) Let's read this page together: *A snake has eyes, but it does not have lids. A snake has ears, but you cannot see them.* Now, let's pretend we're snakes. Cover your ears with your hands, as if they're hidden.
Pantomime

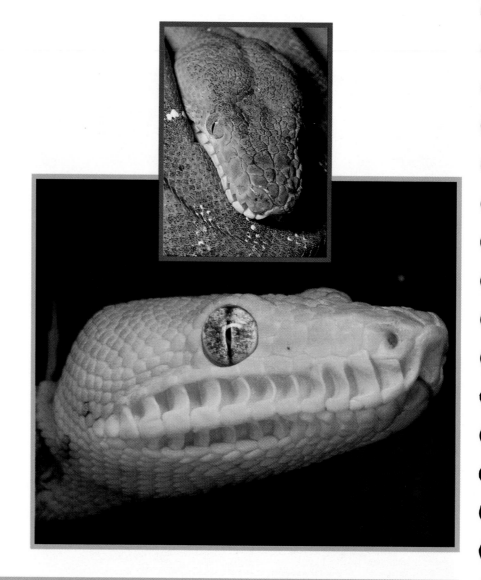

(25) A snake has eyes, but it does not have lids. A snake has ears, but you cannot see them.

114

CULTURAL PERSPECTIVES

SNAKE TALES Tell children that in the country of Ireland a holiday is celebrated in remembrance of a man who, so the story goes, rid the country of snakes. He is called Saint Patrick and the holiday is St. Patrick's Day. In other countries, however, snakes are considered very lucky and are greatly admired.

Activity Help children look for folk tales and cultural myths that use snakes as symbols. For example, the Hopi Indians do a sacred snake dance for rain and good crops. Make a bulletin board display of pictures, drawings, and folktales.
▶ **Visual**

A snake can hiss. A snake's hiss **26**
is like this: Sssss. **27**

115

Comprehension

26 Count how many times you see the letter *s* on this page. (fourteen) Do you think there are more or fewer *s*'s on the page right before this one? Count to check your guess. (Possible answer: There are nine *s*'s, five fewer than on this page.) ***Make and Confirm Predictions***

27 Let's make the sound of that snake's hiss: *Sssss!* What letter does it sound like? (*s*) What other animal sounds can we make? How about these? *Purrrr, meowww!* ***Pantomime***

Minilesson

REVIEW/MAINTAIN

Final Consonants

Emphasize the final sound of words that end in *s* as you read the page. Ask children to:

- find the words on the page that end in *s* and point to them.
- say the sound the *s* makes at the end of each word.
- read the words that end in *s*.

Activity Invite volunteers to frame the final *s* in each word while saying the sound it makes.

Phonics CD-ROM Have children use the interactive phonics activities for more reinforcement with initial and final consonants.

ESL Children who have trouble with final *s* consonants can listen as you reread pages 114–115. Emphasize the hard *s* sound (/z/s) at the end of *eyes, ears, does, lids,* and *sounds.* Emphasize the soft *s* sound at the end of *hiss* and *this.* Other decodable words include: *is, has* (hard *s*) and *bus, fuss, kiss* (soft *s*).

Comprehension

28 Look at the picture on this page. What do you see? (eggs) Listen to me read the sentence: *Do you know about baby snakes?* What do you think we will learn about? *Make and Confirm Predictions*

29 **COMPARE AND CONTRAST** What other animals do you know about that lay eggs? (Possible responses include all kinds of birds, other reptiles, amphibians, fish, and insects.) What animals don't lay eggs? (Answers will vary.)

28
29 Do you know about baby snakes?

116

A baby snake has an egg tooth. **30**

The snake uses it to get out of its shell. **31**

When the snake is out of the shell,

its egg tooth falls out.

117

Comprehension

30 How many sentences are there on this page? (three) How can you tell? (three initial capital letters, three periods) *Concepts of Print*

31 Let's look at the small picture on this page. What do you notice? (a baby snake with a tooth) Why do you think the baby snake needs a tooth? (to help it open the shell) Now let's read this page together. *Make Predictions*

BLEND WITH SHORT *e* Let's read the first two sentences together. Which words have a short *e* sound? *(egg, get, shell)* *Graphophonic Cues*

PREVENTION/INTERVENTION

BLEND WITH SHORT *e* Write the word *shell* on the chalkboard. Underline the *sh* and ask children what sound the letters make. Then extend the line under the *e* and ask what sound the short *e* makes. Extend the line under the *ll* and ask what sound these letters make. Have children blend the sounds to repeat the word with you as you move your hand smoothly beneath the word. Repeat this activity with other short *e* words from the story: *legs, get, nest.* *Graphophonic Cues*

Comprehension

32 Let's read the sentence on this page: *Baby snakes can get their own food.* How do you think the baby snakes will change as they get older? (They will grow bigger and longer.) *Make Predictions*

33 Look at the photograph on this page. What is the snake eating? (a worm) Why is the baby snake eating a worm instead of big rats like the big snake on page 106? (It is too small to eat a rat.) *Draw Conclusions*

32 Baby snakes can get
33 their own food.

118

Activity

Cross Curricular: Social Studies

CHILD VS. PET CARE Explain that many animals live with their young for only a short time. Humans live with their young until they are grown. Ask children to share their ideas about taking care of babies as opposed to caring for a pet. Make a chart listing their ideas.

RESEARCH AND INQUIRY Invite children to look through books and magazines for ideas on child and pet care.
▶ **Linguistic/Logical**

interNET **CONNECTION** For more information about animal and child care, go to **www.mhschool.com/reading**.

babies need

bottles

someone to change their diapers

baths

cuddles

The small snakes will get big very fast. **34**
They will get as big as their mom
and dad.

119

Comprehension

SHORT *a, e, i, o* Read the second sentence. Pick out a word that has a short *a* sound. (*dad*) What is the short *a* sound? (/a/) Can you find two other words in the sentence with the short *a* sound? (*as, and*) Can you find three other words in the sentence that have a short *i*, short *e*, or short *o* sound? (*will, big; get; mom*)

34 Let's look at the photograph on this page. Which snake in the picture do you think is the youngest? (smallest) Which is the oldest? (largest) Why do you think this? (Snakes grow bigger as they get older.) *Draw Conclusions*

Minilesson

REVIEW/MAINTAIN

Summarize

Remind children that when they summarize a story, they should tell only the main parts:

• the main idea.

• the most important events or facts.

• how the story ends.

Ask children the following about their summaries of *Snakes*:

• Would you tell what the snakes look like?

• Would you tell what the snakes are doing?

Activity Have children orally summarize the story. Guide their responses to focus on the main points. Instead of retelling each page, have children summarize the main idea: Snakes are alike in some ways and different in others.

PREVENTION/INTERVENTION

SHORT *a, e, i, o* Reinforce the different short vowel sounds for *a, e, i,* and *o*. Children work in pairs. Give each pair several word cards for each of the short vowels *a, e, i,* and *o*.

Children shuffle the cards together. One child shows a word card and reads the word. The partner identifies the short vowel sound and points to the letter. *Graphophonic Cues*

Comprehension

35 **COMPARE AND CONTRAST** Do you think any kind of snake could be a good pet for a human? (not dangerous ones) Let's add this to our chart. *Graphic Organizer*

SAME	DIFFERENT
Snakes don't have legs.	Some snakes are small. Others are big.
Snakes have scales.	Some snakes live in hot lands. Others live in damp lands.
Snakes grow new skin and let the old skin fall off.	Some snakes can climb. Others can swim.
	Some snakes make good pets. Others don't.

RETELL THE STORY Have children go in a circle to retell the story. *Summarize*

STUDENT SELF-ASSESSMENT

Have children ask themselves the following questions to assess how they are reading.

- How did I use the pictures in the story to help me compare ways snakes are alike and different?

- How did I use what I know about snakes to help me compare how they are alike and different?

- How did I use the letters and sounds I know to help me read the words in the story?

TRANSFERRING THE STRATEGIES

- How can I use these strategies to help me read other stories?

120

REREADING FOR *Fluency*

PARTNERS Children can work in pairs to practice fluency. Have them take turns reading a page to their partners.

READING RATE When you evaluate reading rate, have children read aloud from the story for one minute. Place a stick-on note after the last word read. Count words read. To

evaluate children's performance, see the Running Record in the **Fluency Assessment** book.

Intervention For leveled fluency lessons, passages, and norms charts, see **Skills Intervention Guide**, Part 5, Fluency.

Would you like to have a snake as a pet? Tell why or why not!

121

Comprehension

Return to Predictions and Purposes

Reread children's predictions about the story and discuss them. Ask if their questions were answered. Discuss which predictions need revision.

PREDICTIONS	WHAT HAPPENED
This story is about something real.	I learned about what snakes are like.
There are many kinds of snakes.	Snakes are different sizes. Some live in dry lands. Others live near the water.

Have children talk about using the Same and Different chart. How did it help them understand comparisons?

INFORMAL ASSESSMENT

HOW TO ASSESS

Phonics LONG *a: a-e* Have children turn to page 111 and read all the long *a-e* words in the sentences. *(snake, make, lake)*

COMPARE AND CONTRAST Ask children to tell how snakes are alike and different.

FOLLOW UP

Phonics LONG *a: a-e* Make a list of long *a: a-e* words and model blending the sounds as children read the words aloud.

COMPARE AND CONTRAST Children having trouble using the chart to make comparisons can use self-stick notes labeled *same* and *different* where they find good examples.

LITERARY RESPONSE

QUICK-WRITE Have children draw and label a picture in their journals of one way snakes are alike or not alike. Ask them to write a question about something they might like to know about snakes.

ORAL RESPONSE Have children use their journal entries to discuss these questions:

• Which snake in the story would you like most as a pet? Give your reasons.

• Which snake would you least want as a pet? Why?

SENTENCE STRIPS Children can use strips 1–43 to retell *Snakes*.

> 1
> There are a lot of snakes in the world.

> 2
> There are big snakes and small snakes.

121

Story Questions

Tell children that now they will read some questions about the story. Help children read the questions. Discuss possible answers.

Answers:

1. The skin is made of small scales. *Literal/Details*

2. Answers will vary. Accept appropriate responses. (These may include: to scare people away, to talk to other snakes.) *Inferential/Make Inferences*

3. No; Some snakes can harm you. *Inferential/Make Inferences*

4. Answers will vary. Accept appropriate responses. *Critical/Summarize*

5. Answers will vary. Accept appropriate examples. *Critical/Reading Across Texts*

Write About a Snake Help children read the directions in their anthologies. You may want to ask the librarian to help children find materials about snakes.

Story Questions & Activities

READ TOGETHER

1. What is a snake's skin made of?

2. Why might a snake hiss?

3. Are all snakes good pets? Why?

4. Name three snake facts.

5. Could a snake be in "Stan's Stunt"?

Write About a Snake

Find out about one snake.

Write two sentences about it.

Tell where it lives.

Tell about the food it eats.

he cobra lives in Asia.
eats frogs and fish.

Meeting Individual Needs

EASY

Name_____ Date_____ Reteach **111**

Story Comprehension

Use the sentences to fill in the chart.

1. Snakes can be pets.   4. Snakes have no legs.
2. Snakes can eat rats.   5. Snakes can hiss.
3. Some snakes have fangs.   6. Snakes can be very long.

What I knew.	What I learned.
Answers will vary, depending upon children's experience.	

Book 1.3
Snakes   **At Home:** Have children draw a picture illustrating one of the things they learned about snakes.   111

Reteach, 111

ON-LEVEL

Name_____ Date_____ Practice **111**

Story Comprehension

Think about what you have learned in "Snakes." Draw a line to the word that completes each sentence.

1. Snakes live in   rat
2. A snake can chomp a   pets
3. Snakes have no   slip
4. A snake can hang from a   legs
5. A snake can twist and   branch
6. Some snakes make good   lakes

Book 1.3
Snakes   **At Home:** Have children name other animals that can live in trees.   111

Practice, 111

CHALLENGE

Name_____ Date_____ Extend **111**

Story Comprehension

Read the question.
Write **yes** or **no**.

Can you find snakes in hot lands?

_____yes_____

Can a snake eat a rat?

_____yes_____

Does a snake have ears?

_____yes_____

Can you see a snake's ears?

_____no_____

Draw a picture of a baby snake. Show the snake getting food.

Book 1.3
Snakes   **At Home:** Fold a piece of construction paper in half. Have children write a title and author and draw a picture on the cover. Encourage children to use facts about snakes they learned from the story as they write a snake book.   111

Extend, 111

A Big Hiss!

Draw a big snake.

Think about snakes.

What words remind you of snakes?

Share the words with your class.

Write the words
in your snake picture.

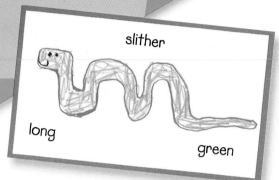

slither

long

green

Find Out More

Choose a kind of snake from the story.

Find out one more fact about it.

Write down that fact.

123

Story Activities

A Big Hiss!

Materials: large sheets of paper, crayons or felt-tipped markers

Read the directions aloud. Help children who have questions. Have them share their thoughts about snakes with one another. Is anyone afraid of snakes? Would anyone like to have a pet snake?

GROUP After the children have drawn their snakes, divide the class into groups that reflect their feelings about snakes: those who like snakes; those who are afraid of snakes; those who wouldn't want a pet snake. Have each group discuss its position, and then have the groups participate in a mock debate.

Find Out More

RESEARCH AND INQUIRY Again, read the directions aloud, and help children who have questions. Then have them work in pairs.

PARTNERS

Have the librarian help pairs of children find books on snakes. Ask each pair to choose one snake to study. Where does the snake live? What does it eat? Have partners share their research with the class.

 *inter*NET **CONNECTION** Have children log on to ***www.mhschool.com/reading***, where they can access sites about reptiles.

FORMAL **ASSESSMENT**

See the Progress Assessment Test for Book 123.

123

Study Skills

DIAGRAMS

**OBJECTIVES**

Students will learn to study illustrations to gather information.

Remind children that they have just read a story about snakes. Tell them that now they will look at pictures to learn about the different lengths of snakes.

Have children read the title and the names of the snakes. Then invite children to describe what they notice about each snake. Help children read the questions below the illustrations, encouraging them to identify the labels that answer each question.

STUDY SKILLS

READ TOGETHER

Snake Lengths

Snakes are different lengths.

boa constrictor

sidewinder

anaconda

rattlesnake

Look at the Snakes

1 Which snakes are longer than the sidewinder? Point to them.

2 Which snakes are shorter than the anaconda? Point to them.

Meeting Individual Needs

EASY	ON-LEVEL	CHALLENGE

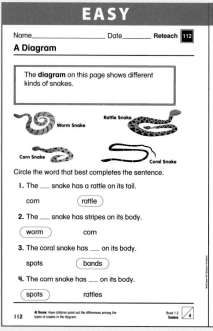

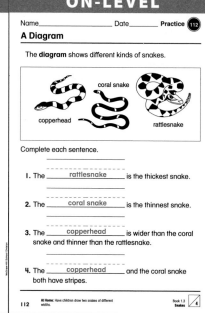

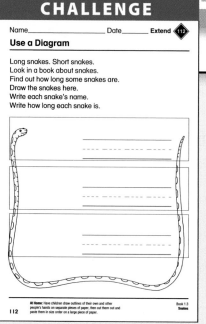

Reteach, 112   **Practice, 112**   **Extend, 112**

TEST POWER

Sam and the Frog

Sam is a brown dog.

Jon is a green frog.

Sam is bigger than Jon.

Jon is just a small frog.

Sam has lots of fur.

Jon has no fur.

Of course not, he is a frog.

Who has more fur?

○ Jon the frog

● Sam the dog

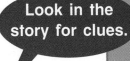

Look in the story for clues.

125

Test Power

THE PRINCETON REVIEW

Read the Page

Explain to children that you will be reading this story as a group. You will read the story, and they will follow in their books.

Request that children put pens, pencils, and markers away, since they will not be writing in their books.

Discuss the Question

Ask children to find the place in the passage where fur is discussed. Have them read those lines, and discuss with them the meaning of "lots of fur" as opposed to "no fur."

Test-Tip

Always look back to the story to find the answer. The answer is always somewhere in the passage.

Leveled Books

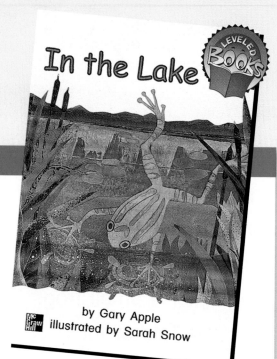

EASY

In the Lake

 Long *a: a-e*

☑ Compare and Contrast
High-Frequency Words:
know, under, where, why

by Gary Apple
illustrated by Sarah Snow

Guided Reading

PREVIEW AND PREDICT Discuss each illustration up to page 5, using the high-frequency words. As you take the **picture walk**, have children predict what the story is about. Chart their ideas.

SET PURPOSES Have children write or draw why they want to read *In the Lake*. For example: *I want to find out what else is in the lake.*

READ THE BOOK Use questions like the following to guide children's reading or after they have read the story independently.

Pages 2–3: Model: "Look at that big . . ." I'm not sure what this word is, but I can blend the letters together to read it. I see that this word ends with a consonant, *k*, and then *e*. That tells me that the *e* is silent, so I know that this *a* has the long *a* sound, /ā/. I can blend the sounds together: l a k(e) lake. The word is *lake*. *Phonics and Decoding*

Pages 4–5: Who sees another word with long *a* and silent *e*? (skate) *Phonics and Decoding*

Pages 6–7: Who sees a vocabulary word we just learned? *(under) High-Frequency Words*

Page 8: Who else enjoys the lake as the animals do? (kids) *Compare and Contrast*

RETURN TO PREDICTIONS AND PURPOSES Discuss children's predictions. Did they find out what is in the lake?

LITERARY RESPONSE The following questions will help focus children's responses:

• Besides being a place to swim and get fish to eat, how else are lakes important to people?

• How can you keep lakes clean and pretty? Tell about it.

Also see the story questions and activity in *In the Lake*.

See the **Phonics** CD-ROM for practice with long *a*.

Answers to Story Questions

1. Possible answers: fish, ducks, bugs, frogs, snakes
2. Then other things can't hurt them.
3. Answers will vary.
4. Answers will vary.
5. *Snakes*

The Story Questions and Activity below appear in the Easy Book.

Story Questions and Activity

1. Name two animals that live in a lake.
2. How does it help small fish to be hard to see?
3. What other animals might live in a lake?
4. Tell about the pictures in this story.
5. In what other story did you read about snakes?

Make a Lake Picture

Use paper and crayons. Cut out fish and other things that live in a lake. Paste them on your paper. Then draw some other things like plants and rocks.

from In the Lake

Leveled Books

INDEPENDENT

The Cave

☑ **Long *a: a-e***

☑ **Compare and Contrast**

High-Frequency Words:
know, under, where, why

Guided Reading

PREVIEW AND PREDICT Discuss each illustration up to page 5, using the high-frequency words. As you take the **picture walk**, have children predict what the story is about. Chart their ideas.

SET PURPOSES Have children write or draw why they want to read *The Cave*. For example: *I want to find out what's in that cave.*

READ THE BOOK Use questions like the following to guide children's reading or after they have read the story independently.

Pages 2–3: Let's look at the pictures and read these pages. Model: "Chad and . . ." I'm not sure what this word is, but I can blend the letters together to read it. The first letter is *D*. It stands for the sound /d/. The middle letter is *a*, but I see that this word ends with a consonant, *v*, and then *e*. That tells me that the *e* is silent, so I know that this *a* has the long *a* sound, /ā/. I can blend the sounds together: D a v(e) Dave. The word is *Dave*, one of the squirrel's names. *Phonics and Decoding*

Pages 5: Who sees more words with long *a* and silent *e* on page 5? *(came, cake)* *Phonics and Decoding*

Pages 6–7: What do the other guests have that Chad and Dave don't have? (gifts for the party) *Compare and Contrast*

Page 8: Who sees a vocabulary word we just learned? *(know)* *High-Frequency Words*

RETURN TO PREDICTIONS AND PURPOSES Discuss children's predictions. Did they find out what's in the cave?

LITERARY RESPONSE The following questions will help focus children's responses:

• Why do you bring gifts to a party?

• Was it right for the snake to invite the squirrels? Why or why not?

Also see the story questions and writing activity in *The Cave*.

See the **CD-ROM** for practice with long *a*.

Answers to Story Questions
1. a big frog
2. for a party
3. Answers will vary.
4. A big snake brought grapes and plums. A big frog brought a drum. Two small frogs brought gifts.
5. Answers will vary.

The Story Questions and Activity below appear in the Independent Book.

Story Questions and Activity
1. Who brought the drum?
2. Why did the animals bring things to the cave?
3. Whose birthday is it?
4. Tell about what the animals brought.
5. Tell about another birthday story you have read.

Write a Story
Write about a birthday. Draw a picture. Share your story with the class.

from The Cave

Leveled Books

Great Snakes!

by Fay Robinson
Illustrated by Jean Day Zallinger

CHALLENGE

Great Snakes!

☑ Long *a: a-e*
☑ Compare and Contrast

Guided Reading

PREVIEW AND PREDICT Discuss each illustration up to page 15. As you take the **picture walk**, have children predict what the story is about. Chart their ideas.

Discuss with children that the book is a poem. Read a few pages with children so they get the rhythm of the story.

SET PURPOSES Have children write or draw why they want to read *Great Snakes!* For example: *I want to find out all about these snakes.*

READ THE BOOK Use questions like the following to guide children's reading or after they have read the story independently.

Pages 4–13: Let's read these pages together and look at the pictures. What is this book about? (all different kinds of snakes) How are they different? (Snakes look different and live in different places.) *Use Illustrations/Compare and Contrast*

Pages 14–25: Are all snakes dangerous? (no) What page shows one kind of danger-ous snake? (page 15) How are snakes like chickens? (They hatch from eggs.) *Compare and Contrast/Details/Use Illustrations*

Pages 22: What are the rhyming words on this page? (rattles, battles). *Phonics and Decoding*

RETURN TO PREDICTIONS AND PURPOSES Discuss children's predictions. Ask which were close to the story and why. Have children review their purposes for reading. Did they find out about a lot of snakes?

LITERARY RESPONSE The following questions will help focus children's responses:

- Have you ever felt a snake? Tell about it.
- Is it right to be afraid of snakes?

Also see the story questions and writing activity in *Great Snakes!*

See the **Phonics** CD-ROM for practice with long *a*.

Answers to Story Questions

1. Possible answers: climb, slide. hang, glide
2. Deserts, trees, mountains, seas
3. Answers will vary.
4. Different types of snakes, what they do, where they live.
5. *Snakes*

The Story Questions and Activity below appear in the Challenge Book.

Story Questions and Activity

1. Name three things a snake can do.
2. Where might a snake live?
3. Would a snake make a good pet?
4. Tell what this story is about.
5. What is another story you read with snakes in it?

Where Do Snakes Live?

Find out where snakes live. Use books from the library. Draw a picture of a snake in its home. Color your picture.

from Great Snakes!

Bringing Groups Together

Anthology and Leveled Books

Connecting Texts

CLASS DISCUSSION
Lead a discussion of how the theme of reptiles applies to each of the stories. Call on volunteers from each reading level to discuss what they read. Some questions might be:

- Which reptiles go to the party in *The Cave?* (frogs, small snakes, a big snake)

- What can the snakes in *In the Lake* do? (They can swim on top of and under the water.)

SNAKE WEB Have children create a web to compare the snakes from the stories.

Snakes
Some snakes are dangerous, others are not.

In the Lake
Snakes can swim on top of and under water.

SNAKES

The Cave
Many animals have a birthday party for a snake.

Great Snakes!
Snakes live in different places and do different things.

Viewing/Representing

GROUP PRESENTATIONS Divide the class into groups, one for each of the four books. (For *Snakes*, combine children of different reading levels.) Have each group draw pictures of the main events and orally summarize the book. Have each group present its pictures and summary.

AUDIENCE RESPONSE
Ask children to pay attention to each group's presentation. Allow time for questions after each group presents.

Research and Inquiry

MORE ABOUT SNAKES Have children ask themselves: What else would I like to know about snakes? Then invite them to do the following:

- Look at classroom picture books to find out more about snakes.

- Ask a local veterinarian to come and speak about snakes.

inter**NET** **CONNECTION** Have children log on to **www.mhschool.com/reading** for links to Web pages about snakes.

JOURNAL

Children can draw pictures representing what they learned in their journals.

OBJECTIVES

Children will:

- review long *a: a-e*.
- blend and read long *a: a-e* words.

MATERIALS

- long *a* cards and letter cards from the **Word Building Manipulative Cards**
- **Teaching Chart 83**

Skills Finder

Long *a: a-e*

Introduce	B3: 98I-J,
Review	B3: 125E-F, 126I-J; B4: 37G-H, 65G-H, 95G-H
Test	Book 3

ALTERNATE TEACHING STRATEGY

REVIEW LONG *a*

For a different approach to teaching this skill, see pages T75 and T76.

Review Long *a: a-e*

PREPARE

Listen for Long *a: a-e* — Read the following sentences aloud and ask children to clap when they hear a word with a long *a* sound:

- The <u>snake</u> can't <u>rake</u> or <u>make</u> a <u>cake</u>. It can swim in a <u>lake</u>.
- Write *snake* on the chalkboard. Remind children that the letters *a-e* in *snake* stand for the long *a* sound. The *e* is silent.

Discriminate Between Long and Short *a*

- Write the following short and long *a* words on the chalkboard: *map, cape, cat, cake, lake.*
- As you point to each word, have children pronounce it.

TEACH

BLENDING Model and Guide Practice with Long *a* Words

- Display **Teaching Chart 83**. Run your hand under the letters in the first example as you blend the sounds together to say *cave*. Have children blend and read the word with you: c a_ve cave.

Teaching Chart 83

Use the Word in Context

- Invite volunteers to use the word in a sentence to reinforce its meaning. Example: *Bats sometimes live in a cave.*

Repeat the Procedure

- In the second example, model blending with *m* to form *came*.
- Continue, asking volunteers to create new words using the other two letters. Help them blend the sounds together.

PRACTICE

Build and Sort Long *a*: *a-e* Words with Letter Cards

GROUP

Have children work in groups of four or five with a long vowel card. Give each child in the group two consonant letter cards. Ask them to make long *a*: *a-e* words with the cards. Have them blend and read the words they made. Then encourage children to see how many word families they can create. For example: how many *-ake* words can they make as opposed to *-ate* words? (*make, bake, cake,* or *late, mate, date*)

▶**Linguistic/Kinesthetic**

ASSESS/CLOSE

Build and Read Long *a*: *a-e* Words

To assess children's mastery of blending and reading long *a-e* words, check the words they built in the Practice activity. Ask them to read some of the words from their lists aloud.

ADDITIONAL PHONICS RESOURCES

Phonics/Phonemic Awareness Practice Book, pages 129–132

PHONICS KIT
Hands-on Activities and Practice

McGraw-Hill School
TECHNOLOGY
 **CD-ROM**

activities for practice with **Blending and Building Words**

DAY **4** **Fluency** Write some sentences on the chalkboard and have children identify and read the long *a-e* word(s). Examples: *Jane is in grade 1. She has a cake in the shape of a grape.*

CD-ROM

SPELLING/PHONICS CONNECTIONS

Words with long *a*: *a-e*; see the 5-Day Spelling Plan, pages 125Q–125R.

i Intervention ▶ **Skills** Intervention Guide, for direct instruction and extra practice in Long *a*: *a-e*

Meeting Individual Needs for Phonics

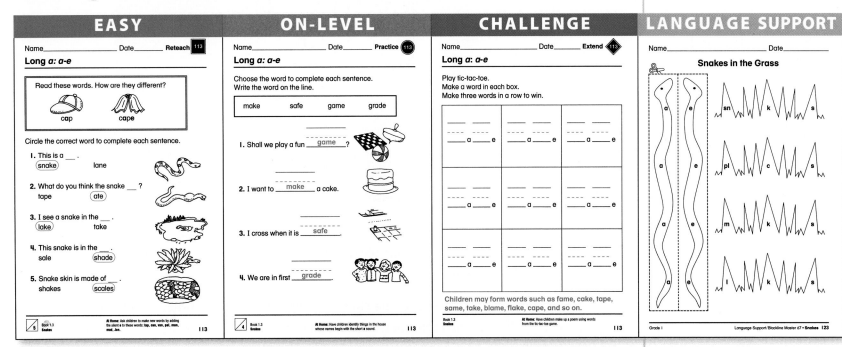

Reteach, 113   Practice, 113   Extend, 113   Language Support, 123

OBJECTIVES

Children will:

- review long *a*: *a-e*.
- review: *ch, wh, nk*.
- cumulative review: consonants; short vowels.

······································

MATERIALS
- **Teaching Chart 84**
- **Phonics Practice Reader, Volume 1**

Skills Finder	
Long *a*: *a-e*	
Introduce	B3: 98I-J
Review	B3: 125G-H, 126I-J; B4: 37G-H, 65G-H, 124I-J
Test	Book 3

ALTERNATE TEACHING STRATEGY
····································

LONG *a*: *a-e*

For a different approach to teaching this skill, see pages T75 and T76.

Review *a-e; ch, wh, nk*

PREPARE

Identify Letters *a-e* as the Symbol for /ā/

Remind children that the letters *a-e* stand for the sound /ā/. Write the letters *a-e* on the chalkboard and say the sound aloud. Tell children to repeat the sound after you. Repeat with the letters *ch, wh,* and *nk*.

Discriminate Between Long *a* and Short *a* and *ch, wh,* and *nk* Words

Write the following short and long *a* words on the chalkboard: *cap/cape, pan/pane,* and *plan/plane*. Ask volunteers to identify and read the words that have a long *a* sound. *(cape, pane, plane)* Repeat with the letters *ch, wh,* and *nk*, using the following words: *chimp, when, sink, why, much, bank*.

TEACH

BLENDING Model and Guide Practice with Long *a, e, i, o, u* Words

- Display **Teaching Chart 84**. Explain to children that you are going to choose letters from the boxes to write a word.

- Model building the first word. Write the letters *ch a s e* on the lines. Have children blend the sounds: c h a s e chase.

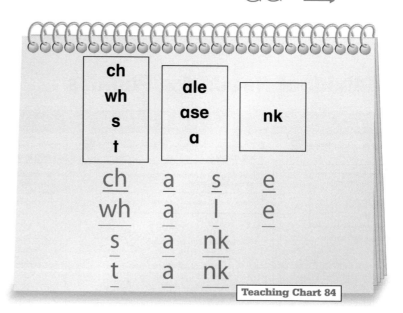

Teaching Chart 84

Use the Word in Context

Invite volunteers to use the word in a sentence. Example: *The dog wants to chase the ball.*

Repeat the Procedure

Continue until the chart is complete, asking volunteers to blend sounds together. If a nonsense word is formed, erase a letter and have children choose a different letter.

PRACTICE

Build Long *a*: *a-e* Words

PARTNERS

Have children brainstorm other long *a*: *a-e* words using the words on **Teaching Chart 84** as a reference. Have children work in pairs. The first child writes a word with long *a*. The partner reads it. Have children take turns. ▶**Linguistic/Visual**

ASSESS/CLOSE

Write a Short Story Using Long *a*: *a-e* Words

To assess children's mastery of blending and reading long *a-e* words, check the words they built in the Practice activity. Then have them write two-sentence stories, using words displayed on the bulletin board that children brainstormed in the Practice activity.

Read a Decodable Story

For additional practice reading words with long *a* and to develop fluency, direct children to read the story *Kate's Cake* from the **Phonics Practice Reader, Volume 1.**

ADDITIONAL PHONICS RESOURCES

Phonics/Phonemic Awareness Practice Book, pages 129–132

PHONICS KIT
Hands-on Activities and Practice

McGraw-Hill School
TECHNOLOGY
Phonics CD-ROM
activities for practice with Blending and Building Words

DAILY Phonics ROUTINES

DAY 5

Writing Have children write a long *a*: *a-e* word to complete the sentence: *I have a _____ .* (Examples: *name, face, cake, game, cape, gate, grape, plate.*)

Phonics CD-ROM

i Intervention ▶ Skills **Intervention Guide**, for direct instruction and extra practice in Long *a*: *a-e*

Meeting Individual Needs for Phonics

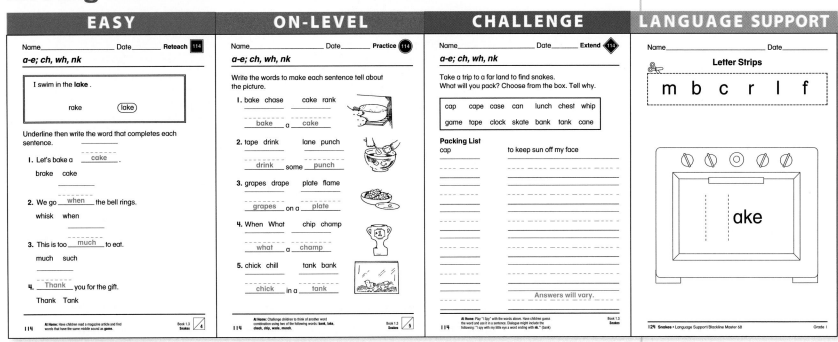

Reteach, 114   **Practice, 114**   **Extend, 114**   **Language Support, 124**

OBJECTIVES

Children will recognize and describe settings.

....

MATERIALS

- **Teaching Chart 85**

- strips of paper

Skills Finder

Story Elements

Introduce	B2: 35I–J
Review	B2: 65I–J, 137E–F; B3: 371I–J, 139G–H
Test	Book 2, Book 3
Maintain	B3: 89; B4: 25, 107, 109

TEACHING TIP

SETTING Divide children into small groups. Pass out magazines with detailed photos or pictures. Have children look at the illustrations and discuss the settings. Ask them to be detailed in their descriptions of the settings

SELF-SELECTED Reading

....

Children may choose from the following titles.

ANTHOLOGY

- *Snakes*

LEVELED BOOKS

- *In the Lake*

- *The Cave*

- *Great Snakes*

Bibliography, pages T98–T99

125I *Snakes*

Review Story Elements

PREPARE

Review the Concept: Setting

Tell children they can learn about where stories take place by looking at the pictures, reading the words, and using what they already know.

TEACH

Identify and Select Settings That Make Sense

Display **Teaching Chart 85**. Encourage children to comment on what they see. Explain that they will make their own paper snakes and they will decide where to put the snakes on the chart by remembering what they learned in the story.

MODEL From looking at these pictures and remembering the story, I think the prickly cactus would not be a good place for the snake, because it might hurt the snake. A house would not be a good place for a snake who was not a pet, either. Maybe my snake could live under a rock or in a log.

Where Would Your Snake Like to Live?

You can find snakes in hot lands.

A snake can live in a lake or on a big branch.

Teaching Chart 85

Give each child a strip of paper to use as a snake. Children may wish to draw faces and patterns on the snakes. Ask volunteers to place their snakes in an appropriate place on the chart. Then have children choose other settings for their snakes and explain how they know it is a good place for the snake.

PRACTICE

Draw a Setting

GROUP

Have children work in groups to brainstorm other appropriate settings for their snakes. Encourage them to draw murals that show this setting or write sentences that describe it. ▶ **Visual**

ALTERNATE TEACHING STRATEGY

SETTING

For a different approach to teaching this skill, see page T67.

ℹ️ **Intervention** ▶ **Skills Intervention Guide**, for direct instruction and extra practice in Setting

ASSESS/CLOSE

Relate to Personal Experience

Ask children to describe the setting where they live. Invite them to draw murals showing their homes, neighborhoods, and communities. Or suggest that they bring in photographs to illustrate their descriptions. Encourage them to be as detailed as possible in their descriptions.

Meeting Individual Needs for Comprehension

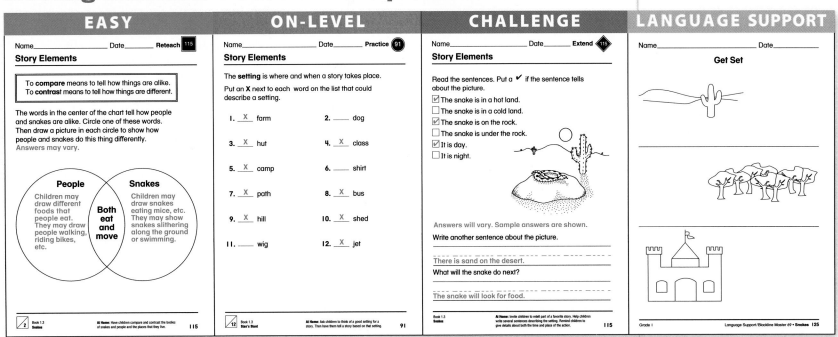

Reteach, 115   **Practice, 91**   **Extend, 115**   **Language Support, 125**

OBJECTIVES

Children will
- review contractions.
- understand the concept of double negatives.

....

MATERIALS
- **Teaching Chart 86**
- index cards

Skills Finder

Contractions

Introduce	B3: 97K-L
Review	B3: 125K-L, 139K-L
Test	Book 3

TEACHING **TIP**

DOUBLE NEGATIVES
You may wish to introduce the concept of double negatives to children, especially if they have grasped the concept of contractions with ease. Explain that two negatives occurring in a row are the same as a single positive For example: *I can't not do that for you* has the same meaning as *I can do that for you.*

Review Contractions

PREPARE

Review the Concept
Write the word *can* on the chalkboard. Ask a volunteer to name something he or she can do. (skate, swim, draw) Then say: *Some people can___, and some people cannot___.* Write the words *cannot* and *can't* next to the word *can.* Help children see the difference in spelling between the two negative words.

TEACH

Identify Root Words
Track the sentence on **Teaching Chart 86** as you read with the children: *The snake can move but it can't run.* Point to the word *can't* and ask children if they recognize the word *can* in this word.

The snake can move
but it can't run.

We do rake but we don't bake.

Are you or aren't you in Grade 1?

Teaching Chart 86

MODEL I can use what I know to help me read difficult words. I know the word *can.* I can see the apostrophe and letter *-t* at the end of the word. I know that the apostrophe stands for a letter or letters that are missing. I know that *not* is often shortened by taking away the letter *-o* and replacing it with an apostrophe. The word is *can't* and it means *cannot.*

Repeat for the other two sentences. Invite volunteers to underline the root words.

PRACTICE

Make Contractions

PARTNERS

Write the words *do, are, could,* and *would* on index cards. Give each pair of children a blank index card and a card with *do, are, could,* and *would*. One child reads the word and says its opposite. The partner writes a contraction of the word's opposite on an index card by using the root word and adding *-n't.* ▶ **Linguistic/Visual**

ASSESS/CLOSE

Use Contractions in Context

Invite pairs of children to make up stories using both of their words. Ask children to tell their stories to the class. They may also wish to act them out. Call on other children to identify which is the root word and which shows its opposite.

ALTERNATE TEACHING STRATEGY

CONTRACTIONS

For a different approach to teaching this skill, see page T74.

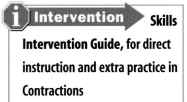

i **Intervention** **Skills**

Intervention Guide, for direct instruction and extra practice in **Contractions**

Meeting Individual Needs for Vocabulary

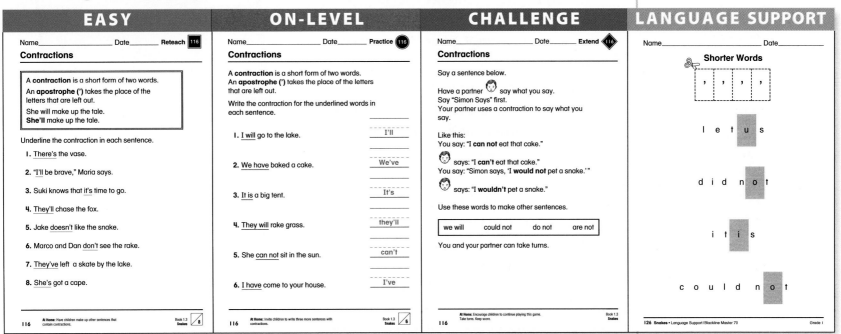

EASY	ON-LEVEL	CHALLENGE	LANGUAGE SUPPORT

Name_____ Date_____ **Reteach** 116

Contractions

A **contraction** is a short form of two words.
An **apostrophe (')** takes the place of the letters that are left out.
She will make up the tale.
She'll make up the tale.

Underline the contraction in each sentence.

1. There's the vase.
2. "I'll be brave," Maria says.
3. Suki knows that it's time to go.
4. They'll chase the fox.
5. Jake doesn't like the snake.
6. Marco and Dan don't see the rake.
7. They've left a skate by the lake.
8. She's got a cape.

116 **At Home:** Have children make up other sentences that contain contractions. Book 1.3 **Snakes** 8

Name_____ Date_____ **Practice** 116

Contractions

A **contraction** is a short form of two words.
An **apostrophe (')** takes the place of the letters that are left out.

Write the contraction for the underlined words in each sentence.

1. I will go to the lake. — I'll
2. We have baked a cake. — We've
3. It is a big tent. — It's
4. They will rake grass. — they'll
5. She can not sit in the sun. — can't
6. I have come to your house. — I've

116 **At Home:** Invite children to write three more sentences with contractions. Book 1.3 **Snakes** 6

Name_____ Date_____ **Extend** 116

Contractions

Say a sentence below.

Have a partner 😊 say what you say.
Say "Simon Says" first.
Your partner uses a contraction to say what you say.

Like this:
You say: "I **can not** eat that cake."

😊 says: "I **can't** eat that cake."
You say: "Simon says, 'I **would not** pet a snake.'"

😊 says: "I **wouldn't** pet a snake."

Use these words to make other sentences.

we will	could not	do not	are not

You and your partner can take turns.

At Home: Encourage children to continue playing this game. Take turns. Keep score.

116 Book 1.3 **Snakes**

Name_____ Date_____

Shorter Words

✂ [, , , ,]

l e t u s

d i d n o t

i t i s

c o u l d n o t

126 **Snakes** • Language Support/Blackline Master 70 Grade 1

Reteach, 116   **Practice, 116**   **Extend, 116**   **Language Support, 126**

125L

Handwriting CD-ROM

GRAMMAR/SPELLING CONNECTIONS

Is and *Are*: See the 5-Day Grammar and Usage Plan, pages 125O–125P.

Words with Long *a: a-e* (silent *e* rule): See 5-Day Spelling plan, pages 125Q–125R.

TEACHING TIP

Technology
It is quite easy to make corrections to documents on the computer. But encourage those children who input their work to aim for accuracy at the keyboard, even if that means typing more slowly.

Handwriting
Remind children of the correct way to position their paper before they begin writing. For specific instructions for left and right-handed children, refer to page T78.

Interactive Writing
Make a Mural

Prewrite

LOOK AT THE STORY PATTERN Have children revisit *Snakes* and guide them to notice again the language pattern of the story. Then tell them that the class will create a mural comparing the life of a snake to the life of a cat. The mural will have pictures and sentences. Have them make lists, comparing snakes and cats. (Examples: *Which animal is born from an egg? Which animal crawls and which animal runs on legs? Which animal has fur and which animal has scales?*)

Draft

MAKE COMPARISONS Have each child choose one comparison from their list. Guide them to write a sentence for the comparison, using the language pattern of *Snakes*.

- Begin by saying, for example, *A snake has no legs. It can't run. What about a cat?* As you say a word or sentence with familiar sounds and patterns, challenge children to come up and write it. Write all unfamiliar words yourself.

- Continue this process for the rest of the comparisons on the list. (Example: *A snake can live in a tree. A cat lives on the ground.*)

Revise

IS AND ARE Invite children to reread the sentences. They should look for the words *is* and *are*. Then have children locate the nouns in these sentences and tell if the nouns are plural or singular. Once children have determined the type of noun in the sentence, have them check and see if the verb appears in its correct tense (*is* or *are*).

Publish

CREATE THE MURAL Reread children's comparisons together. Then ask children to make a mural using the sentences as a visual guide. Discuss different ways of organizing it and illustrating the mural. Have children create the mural together. Then have children copy the appropriate text onto the mural.

A snake can live in a tree. A cat lives on the ground.

Presentation Ideas

GIVE A SPEECH Invite children to make believe they're either a cat or a snake. Then have them give a speech about their life. Encourage them by asking: *Where do you live? What do you do all day? How big do you expect to grow?* ▶ Speaking/Listening

ACT OUT A STORY Guide pairs of children to act out different scenes from the lives of a snake and a cat, without speaking. Each child should choose the role of the snake or the cat. Have the other children guess the animal that the child is role-playing.

▶ Representing/Viewing

Listening and Viewing

LISTENING STRATEGIES
Remind children how a good audience behaves when listening to a speaker. They should keep their eyes on the speaker and their hands in their laps.

VIEWING STRATEGIES
Ask children to watch the actors carefully so they can figure out what's being depicted. Ask them to describe how different children depict the same animal.

LANGUAGE SUPPORT

ESL If children need help writing, have them refer to *Snakes* and follow the language pattern of the story. Have them work with a fluent partner to illustrate and write a comparison between a cat and a snake.

Invite children to include PORTFOLIO their murals or another writing project in their portfolio.

Meeting Individual Needs for Writing

EASY	ON-LEVEL	CHALLENGE
Draw Pictures Children can draw pictures showing how two animals of their choice are different. Have them label their pictures with simple sentences, following the language pattern from *Snakes*.	**New Story** Children can work in groups to write a new story, comparing snakes and dogs. Have children follow the format of the sentences in the mural that the class created.	**Journal Entry** Children can make believe they're a snake, and write a journal entry comparing themselves to another animal of their choice.

5 Day Grammar and Usage Plan

DAY 1 Introduce the Concept

Oral Warm-up Read aloud the following: *The cat is fat. The cats are fat.* Ask children to tell which words changed in the sentences. (*cat, is; cats, are*)

Introduce *Is* and *Are* Discuss with children:

Is and *Are*

- The words *is* and *are* are verbs that tell about the present.

- The word *is* tells about one person, place, or thing.

- The word *are* tells about more than one person, place, or thing.

Daily Language Activity Write the following on the chalkboard: *The girl is sad.* Ask how many people the first sentence tells about. (one) Tell children to use *is* to tell about one person or thing.

 WRITING Assign daily Writing Prompt on page 98E.

Name_____ Date_____ **LEARN GRAMMAR 83**

Is and Are

- The words *is* and *are* are verbs that tell about the present.
  - The snake <u>is</u> on the log.
  - The big snakes <u>are</u> on the log.

Read the sentences. Draw a circle around the verbs *is* and *are*.

1. The big snakes (are) together.

2. The baby snakes (are) in shells.

3. That baby snake (is) out of the shell.

4. The snakes (are) safe.

5. A snake (is) safe in a log.

Book 1.3 Snakes **EXTENSION:** Have the children tell sentences that have *is* or *are* as verbs. 83

GRAMMAR PRACTICE BOOK, PAGE 83

DAY 2 Teach the Concept

Review *Is* and *Are* Remind children that yesterday they learned about using *is.* Write the following on the chalkboard: *The bag is red. The bags are red.* Read the sentences aloud with children. Ask children which sentence tells about one thing (*The bag is red.*) and which tells about more than one thing. (*The bags are red.*) Tell children to use *are* to tell about more than one person or thing.

Daily Language Activity Write the following on the chalkboard: *The snake _____ fast. The snakes_____ fast.* Ask children which sentence tells about one thing (the first sentence) and which tells about more than one thing (the second sentence). Have children complete the sentences using *is* or *are*.

 WRITING Assign the daily Writing Prompt on page 98E.

Name_____ Date_____ **LEARN AND PRACTICE GRAMMAR 84**

Is and Are

- The words *is* and *are* are verbs that tell about the present.
- The word *is* tells about one person, place, or thing.
- The word *are* tells about more than one person, place, or thing.
  - The snake **is** hungry.   The snakes **are** hungry.
  - One snake   More than one snake

Read these sentences. Find *is* in a sentence and draw one snake. Find *are* in a sentence and draw more than one snake.

1. That snake is on the rock.   one

2. The snakes are big.   more than one

3. The snakes are safe under the rocks.   more than one

4. That snake is not my pet.   one

5. The baby snake is out of the shell.   one

84 **EXTENSION:** Have the children find the word in each sentence that tells them to write *is* or *are*. Book 1.3 Snakes 5

GRAMMAR PRACTICE BOOK, PAGE 84

Is and Are

DAY 3 — Review and Practice

Learn from the Literature Discuss with children how to use the verbs *is* and *are*. Write the following sentence from *Snakes* on the chalkboard:

> **That big lump is a big rat!**

Ask children how many things the sentence is talking about? (one) Write this sentence: *Those big lumps _____ big rats!* here. What verb would you use in this sentence? (*are*) Why? (The sentence tells about two things.)

 Daily Language Activity
Have children brainstorm a list of things from *Snakes*. Then have them write two sentences, one using *is* and one using *are*. Example: *The snake is in the grass. Two snakes are in the grass.*

 Assign the daily Writing Prompt on page 98F.

DAY 4 — Review and Practice

Review *Is and Are* Write these sentences on the board: *The ducks are tame. Mack is glad. The rugs are damp.* Have children tell if the sentence tells about one or more than one person, animal, or thing.

Daily Language Activity Write the following sentence on the chalkboard: *The ship is big.* Ask children to rewrite the sentence, using *ships.* (*The ships are big.*)

Mechanics and Usage Before assigning the daily Writing Prompt for Day 4, review:

> ### Sentence Punctuation
> - Begin every sentence with a capital letter.
> - End a statement with a period.
> - End an exclamation with an exclamation point.

 Assign the daily Writing Prompt on page 98F.

DAY 5 — Assess and Reteach

Daily Language Activity Write the following sentences on the board. Have children complete the sentences using *is* or *are* correctly.

1. The sack _____ tan. is
2. The packs _____ wet. are
3. The bugs _____ pests. are
4. The lamp _____ lit. is

Assess Use page 87 of the **Grammar Practice Book** for assessment.

Reteach Prepare word cards for each sentence presented on Days 1 through 5. Give each group one set. Have them tell why *is* or *are* is used in each sentence.

Use page 88 of the **Grammar Practice Book** for additional reteaching.

 Assign the daily Writing Prompt on page 98F.

Name_____ Date_____ **GRAMMAR 85** PRACTICE AND WRITE

Is and Are

- The words *is* and *are* are verbs that tell about the present.
- The word *is* tells about one person, place, or thing.
- The word *are* tells about more than one person, place, or thing.
  - This **is** a safe snake.
  - These snakes **are** not safe.

Read the sentences.
Write *is* in the sentences that tell about one person, place, or thing.
Write *are* in the sentences that tell about more than one person, place, or thing.

1. There __are__ a lot of snakes in the world.
2. The snakes __are__ moving.
3. A snake's skin __is__ made of scales.
4. The snake __is__ safe in a log.
5. This snake __is__ not safe.

Book 1.3 *Snakes* EXTENSION: Have the children draw pictures and is on the pictures of one and are on those that are more than one. 85

GRAMMAR PRACTICE BOOK, PAGE 85

Name_____ Date_____ **GRAMMAR 86** MECHANICS

Correcting Sentences with *Is and Are*

- Begin every sentence with a capital letter.
- End a statement with a period.
- End an exclamation with an exclamation point.

Read the sentences. Circle the words that need to be capitalized. Write the correct end mark.

1. (the) snake is in a log .
2. (is) a snake in the tree ?
3. (look) at all those snakes !
4. (are) they safe snakes ?
5. (that) snake is in a hot land .
6. (where) are all the snakes ?
7. (look) out for the big snake !
8. (that) snake is not my pet .

86 EXTENSION: Have the children make the incorrect sentences correct. Book 1.3 *Snakes*

GRAMMAR PRACTICE BOOK, PAGE 86

Name_____ Date_____ **GRAMMAR 87** TEST

Test

Read each sentence. Circle the correct verb.

1. There _____ a lot of snakes.
   (are)   is
2. There _____ big snakes and small snakes.
   (are)   is
3. One snake _____ in the log.
   are   (is)
4. One snake _____ in the damp land.
   are   (is)
5. That _____ a big rat!
   are   (is)

Book 1.3 *Snakes* 87

GRAMMAR PRACTICE BOOK, PAGE 87

5 Day Spelling Plan

ESL Spanish speakers pronounce *e* like the English long *a*. To help children link long *a* with the letter *a*, write the following words on the chalkboard: *shake, gave, bake, shave*. Pronounce the words and point to the vowels in each word. Have children say the long *a* sound when you point to the letter *a*.

TEACHING TIP

The spelling words in this lesson contain the long *a* sound and follow the pattern CVCe (consonant-vowel-consonant-*e*) or CCVCe (consonant-consonant-vowel-consonant-*e*). The silent *e* at the end of each word helps make the *a* long. Compare the vowel sounds in *made* and *snake* with those in *mad* and *snack*. Remind children to remember the silent *e* in these spelling words.

DAY 1 — Introduce Spelling Words

Assess Prior Knowledge Write the words *snake, made, lake, came, shade, name* on the chalkboard. Read the words aloud. Ask children what vowel sound they hear in each word. (long *a*) Explain that only the long *a* sound is heard in these words. The letter *e* is silent.

Write the words *know, under, where, why* on the chalkboard. Read them aloud as you point to each one. Make up gestures for each word.

Spelling Words		Challenge Words
1. **snake**	4. came	7. **know**
2. **made**	5. shade	8. **where**
3. **lake**	6. name	9. **under**
		10. **why**

*Note: Words in **dark type** are from the story.*

DAY 2 — Teach the Pattern

Sort and Build Words Write the Spelling Words in random order on the chalkboard. Draw three columns and label them with the spelling patterns *-ade, -ake, -ame*. Have children read each Spelling Word and suggest its appropriate column.

Encourage children to build new words using the spelling patterns and the following letters: *c, f, m, s, t, w*. Write these new words on the chalkboard. Have children read the new words aloud, stressing the long *a* in each word. Contrast the sound of the long *a* with the sound of the short *a* by holding your hand over the silent *e* in the words *fade, made*, and *same*.

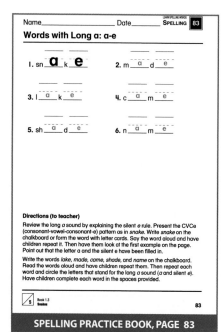

SPELLING PRACTICE BOOK, PAGE 83

WORD STUDY STEPS AND ACTIVITY, PAGE 84

SPELLING PRACTICE BOOK, PAGE 85

Words with Long *a: a-e*

DAY 3 Practice and Extend

Word Meaning: Answer Riddles
Write the Spelling Words on the chalkboard. Ask children to use the words to answer these riddles:

> This is the place you go to get away from the sun.
>
> This is the place where fish live.
>
> This animal moves fast.
>
> It does not have legs.
>
> This word rhymes with *came*.

Identify Spelling Patterns Write this sentence on the chalkboard: *Do you know the name of this snake?* Have a volunteer read it aloud. Ask children to tell which words have the spelling patterns *-ade*, *-ake*, or *-ame*, and which are Challenge Words. Repeat the question for these sentences: *I do not know why we came to this lake. Where is the shade to sit in?*

DAY 4 Practice and Write

Complete Sentences Write the following sentence on the chalkboard: *The snake _____ a nest in the tall grass.* Read it aloud and invite children to complete it with an *-ade* word. Read the completed sentence and have children repeat it after you. Then write *The snake made a nest in the _____.* Ask children to complete the sentence with an *-ade* word, and read it together. Then ask them to complete the same sentence with an *-ake* word. Continue writing sentences and giving children patterns to use in completing them.

 WRITING Have children use as many Spelling Words as possible in the daily Writing Prompt on page 98F. Remind them to check their writing for errors in spelling, grammar, and punctuation.

DAY 5 Assess and Reteach

Optional Spelling Test You may wish to give children a spelling test. You may administer it in the following manner: (1) Read the word. (2) Give a simple sentence containing the word. (3) Say the word again. Or you may use page 88 of the **Spelling Practice Book** for the posttest. If you wish, you may create additional sentences for the Bonus Words.

Personal Word List Have children add **JOURNAL** the words they still find difficult to their lists of troublesome words in their journals. Ask them to write a sentence or draw a picture and label it for each word. Children should refer to these word lists during later writing activities.

Name_____ Date_____ **SPELLING 86**
PRACTICE AND EXTEND

Words with Long *a : a-e*

Read the sentences. Complete each spelling word with **ade, ame,** or **ake.**

1. You can swim in a l_____ake_____ .

2. My n_____ame_____ is Jake.

3. When it is hot, I sit in the sh_____ade_____ .

4. A sn_____ake_____ is an animal that cannot run.

5. The baby snake c_____ame_____ out of its shell.

6. The snake m_____ade_____ a nest in the grass.

86   Book 1.3 Snakes 6

SPELLING PRACTICE BOOK, PAGE 86

Name_____ Date_____ **SPELLING 87**
PRACTICE AND WRITE

Words with Long *a : a-e*

Read the story. Use the spelling words to complete the story.

My _____name_____ is Sam. I am

a baby _____snake_____ . I

_____came_____ out of a shell. I used my egg tooth to get out.

My Mom and Dad swim in a

_____lake_____ with the other snakes.

When it is hot, they rest in

the _____shade_____ of the tree.

They _____made_____ a nest for me in the grass. I like it there!

6   Book 1.3   87

SPELLING PRACTICE BOOK, PAGE 87

Name_____ Date_____ **SPELLING 88**
SPELLING TEST

Words with Long *a : a-e*

Look at the words in each set. One word in each set is spelled correctly. Use a pencil to color in the circle in front of that word. Before you begin, look at the sample sets of words. Sample A has been done for you. Do Sample B by yourself. When you are sure you know what to do, you may go on with the rest of the page.

Sample A
- (A) make
- (B) mak
- (C) maek

Sample B
- (D) sikn
- (E) singk
- (F) sink

1.
- (A) nam
- (B) naem
- (C) name

2.
- (D) lak
- (E) lake
- (F) laek

3.
- (A) sanke
- (B) snak
- (C) snake

4.
- (D) made
- (E) maed
- (F) madde

5.
- (A) caem
- (B) came
- (C) camme

6.
- (D) shade
- (E) shede
- (F) shead

88   Book 1.3 Snakes 6

SPELLING PRACTICE BOOK, PAGE 88

Cumulative Review with **Expository Text**

Time to Review

Anthology

Let's Camp Out!

Selection Summary A family gets together and hits the trail, as children learn about setting up camp, making a fire, and cooking food outdoors.

Rhyme applies to Phonics

Listening Library

INSTRUCTIONAL pages 128–139

Reread Leveled Books

EASY
Lesson on pages 139A and 139D

`DECODABLE`

INDEPENDENT
Lesson on pages 139B and 139D

🏠 *Take-Home version available*

`DECODABLE`

CHALLENGE
Lesson on pages 139C and 139D

Leveled Practice

EASY

Reteach, 117-124 Blackline masters with reteaching opportunities for each assessed skill

INDEPENDENT/ON-LEVEL

Practice, 117-124 Workbook with Take-Home Stories and practice opportunities for each assessed skill and story comprehension

CHALLENGE

Extend, 117-124 Blackline masters that offer challenge activities for each assessed skill

Quizzes Prepared by 📖 **Accelerated Reader**

Center Activities

Science	The Night Sky, *126D,* Tell How You Do It, *136*
Social Studies	What Do You See?, *126D* Play Stuck-in-the-Mud, a Camp Game, *137*
Research and Inquiry	Find Out More, *137*
Internet Activities	www.mhschool.com/reading

Center Activities

Each of these activities takes 15-20 minutes.

Phonics

Digraph Sort

Objective: Sort pictures according to their beginning and ending sounds.

GROUP

◆ Make several photocopies of each card.

◆ Label each box with one of the digraphs: *ch-, wh-, -nk*.

◆ Have children place the cards in the appropriate box according to their beginning or ending sounds.

MATERIALS

• Phonics Picture Cards (*cheese, whale, sink*) from the Word Building Manipulative Kit.

• 3 shoe boxes

Writing

Make a List

Objective: Identify and write names of objects in photographs.

PARTNERS

◆ Partners look through the story and make a list of things they would take on a camping trip.

◆ Then they work together to think of more things they would take, and add them to the list.

MATERIALS

• *Let's Camp Out!* in the Student Anthology

• Paper

• Pencil

Reading and Listening

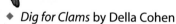

Independent/Self-Selected Reading

Objective: Listen and use illustrations to understand a story.

ONE

Fill the Center with books and audiocassettes or CD-ROMs children have read or listened to this week. You can also include books from the Theme Bibliography on pages T98 and T99.

Leveled Readers

◆ *Bat Helps Out* by Ellen Dreyer
◆ *Two Tests* by Becky Gold
◆ *Cat Tracks* by Shirley Frederick
◆ *Walking Through the Jungle* by Debbie Harter
◆ *Kent and Glen* by Anne Miranda

◆ *Dig for Clams* by Della Cohen
◆ *Big Brother* by Penny Dale
◆ *What's New at the Zoo?* by Judy Nayer
◆ *What Can Meg Do?* by Susan Hood
◆ *The Cow That Went OINK* by Bernard Most
◆ *In the Lake* by Gary Apple
◆ *The Cave* by Sol Andrews
◆ *Great Snakes!* by Fay Robinson

◆ *Let's Camp Out!* by TIME FOR KIDS

◆ "Something About Me"—Anonymous

Working with Words

Flashcard Search

 PARTNERS

Objective: Reinforce vocabulary words: *try, old, eat, under.*

◆ Have partners write each word on an index card.

◆ Partner 1 shows a card. Partner 2 says the word, finds the story sentence that contains it, and creates a new sentence with it.

MATERIALS
- *Let's Camp Out!* in the Student Anthology
- Index cards
- Markers

Social Studies

What Do You See?

PARTNERS

Objective: Make a list of things to see in the woods.

◆ Have partners fold a sheet of paper and label one half *Day* and the other half *Night*.

◆ Children can draw pictures of animals they might see on a hike during the day and while camping at night.

MATERIALS
- Drawing paper
- Crayons
- Pencil

Science

The Night Sky

ONE

Objective: Follow a model to make two constellations.

◆ Have children examine the photo of the Big Dipper and Little Dipper on page 134.

◆ Children use silver foil stars to make their own Big Dipper and Little Dipper and silver or white crayons to connect the stars.

◆ Children can then write a sentence to describe their picture.

MATERIALS
- *Let's Camp Out!* in Student Anthology
- Black paper
- Foil stars
- Silver or white crayons

Suggested Lesson Planner

READING AND LANGUAGE ARTS	**DAY 1** *Focus on Reading and Skills*	**DAY 2** *Read the Literature*
● **Phonics Daily Routines**	Daily **Phonics** Routine: **Segmenting,** 126J **Phonics** CD-ROM	Daily **Phonics** Routine: **Blending,** 128A **Phonics** CD-ROM
● **Phonological Awareness** ● **Phonics** *Review* ● **Comprehension** ● **Vocabulary** ● **Study Skills** ● **Listening, Speaking, Viewing, Representing**	**Read** **Read Aloud,** 126G "The Night We Slept Outside" ☑ **Develop Phonological Awareness,** 126H ☑ **Review** *a-e; ch, wh, nk;* **Blends,** 126I–126J **Teaching Chart 87** **Reteach, Practice, Extend,** 117 **Phonics/Phonemic Awareness Practice Book,** 133–136 **Read** **Review** "Camp Out," 126/127 **Intervention Program**	**Build Background,** 128A Develop Oral Language **Vocabulary,** 128B–128C *try old* *eat under* **Word Building Manipulative Cards** **Teaching Chart 88** **Reteach, Practice, Extend,** 118 **Read** **Read the Selection,** 128–135 **Guided Instruction** ☑ **Cumulative Review** ☑ **Setting** **Genre: Informational Story,** 129 **Intervention Program**
● **Curriculum Connections**	**Link** Language Arts, 126G	**Link** Social Studies, 128A
● **Writing**	**Writing Prompt:** Write about going camping. What do you like about it? What don't you like?	**Writing Prompt:** Write instructions for someone who has never been camping. Tell what you will need, and what you will do. **Journal Writing** Quick-Write, 135
● **Grammar**	**Introduce the Concept: Contractions with** *Not,* 139O Daily Language Activity: Identify the contraction *isn't.* **Grammar Practice Book,** 89	**Teach the Concept: Contractions with** *Not,* 139O Daily Language Activity: Make the contractions *isn't* and *aren't.* **Grammar Practice Book,** 90
● **Spelling** *Words from Science*	**Introduce Spelling Words: Words from Science,** 139Q **Spelling Practice Book,** 89–90	**Teach the Patterns: Words from Science,** 139Q **Spelling Practice Book,** 91

DAY 3 *Read the Literature*	**DAY 4** *Build Skills*	**DAY 5** *Build Skills*
Daily **Phonics** Routine: **Fluency,** 137 **Phonics** CD-ROM	Daily **Phonics** Routine: **Writing,** 139F **Phonics** CD-ROM	Daily **Phonics** Routine: **Letter Substitution,** 139H **Phonics** CD-ROM

Rereading for Fluency, 134
 	
 Story Questions, 136
    Reteach, Practice, Extend, 119
 	
 Story Activities, 137
 	
 Study Skill, 138
    ☑ Diagrams
    Teaching Chart 89
    Reteach, Practice, Extend, 120
 	
 Read **Read the Leveled Books, Guided Reading**
    ☑ Cumulative Review
    ☑ Main Idea
    ☑ High-Frequency Words
 	
 ⓘ Intervention Program
	Read **Read the Leveled Books and Self-Selected Books**
	
	 ☑ **Review Compare and Contrast,** 139E–139F
	    Teaching Chart 90
	    Reteach, Practice, Extend, 121
	    Language Support, 132
	    Phonics/Phonemic Awareness
	    Practice Book, 133–136
	
	 ☑ **Review Story Elements,** 139G–139H
	    Teaching Chart 91
	    Reteach, Practice, Extend, 122
	    Language Support, 133
	    Phonics/Phonemic Awareness
	    Practice Book, 133–136
	
	 Minilessons, 131, 133
	
	 ⓘ Intervention Program
		Read **Read Self-Selected Books**
		
		 ☑ **Review Possessives,** 139I–139J
		    Teaching Chart 92
		    Reteach, Practice, Extend, 123
		    Language Support, 134
		
		 ☑ **Review Contractions,** 139K–139L
		    Teaching Chart 93
		    Reteach, Practice, Extend, 124
		    Language Support, 135
		
		 Listening, Speaking, Viewing, Representing, 139N
		
		 Minilessons, 131, 133
		
		 ⓘ Intervention Program

Activity Social Studies, 126D	**Activity** Science, 126D	

Writing Prompt: Where would you like to go camping? Why? You can choose a real or imaginary place.
 	
 Journal Writing, 139D
	Writing Prompt: Go camping in your house. Write about where you set up camp, what you used for a tent, and what you did that night.
	
	 Interactive Writing, 139M
	    Prewrite, Draft
	
	 Meeting Individual Needs for Writing, 139N
		Writing Prompt: Write a story about a snake, a frog, and a bat that go camping. What kinds of things do they do together?
		
		 Interactive Writing, 139M
		    Revise, Publish

Practice and Write: Contractions with ***Not,*** 139P
    Daily Language Activity: Use contractions in sentences.
 	
 Grammar Practice Book, 91
	Practice and Write: Contractions with ***Not,*** 139P
	    Daily Language Activity: Change words into contractions.
	
	 Grammar Practice Book, 92
		Assess and Reteach: Contractions with ***Not,*** 139P
		    Daily Language Activity: Identify and spell contractions.
		
		 Grammar Practice Book, 93–94

Practice and Extend: Words from Science, 139R **Spelling Practice Book,** 92	**Practice and Write: Words from Science,** 139R **Spelling Practice Book,** 93	**Assess and Reteach: Words from Science,** 139R **Spelling Practice Book,** 94

Language Arts

Read Aloud

The Night We Slept Outside
a story by Anne and Harlow Rockwell

I was right.

On Friday we asked Mom again.

"Well," she said, "you have been very good all week.

"You have put away your things and done your homework."

"And we have our sleeping bags," I said.

"All right," said Mom. "You may sleep outside tonight for a special treat."

"Terrific!" I said.

"Great!" said Robert.

That night, when it was time for bed, Robert and I took our sleeping bags out of the closet.

We put them outside on the deck.

We put on our shorts, and I put on my T-shirt with a picture of a grizzly bear on it.

"Aren't you going to put on your pajamas?" said Mom.

"No," I said. "We are having an adventure. You don't wear pajamas

Continued on pages T2–T5

Oral Comprehension

LISTENING AND SPEAKING Motivate children to think about setting by reading this story about some children who want to sleep outside. Ask children to picture where the children in the story are at the beginning and the end of the story. When you are done, ask, "Where are the children at the end of the story?" Then ask, "What's it like out there? Why do the children in the story enjoy sleeping outside?"

 Have children work in small groups to act out "The Night We Slept Outside." Help children identify the roles that must be played. Remind children that they can use their own words when playing the parts. You

may also wish to have children explain why they want to sleep outside and why it is fun. ▶ **Kinesthetic/ Auditory/Linguistic**

GENRE STUDY: STORY Remind children that a story features characters who do something interesting or must solve a problem. Ask children to name the characters in this story, and to tell what interesting things they do.

Develop Phonological Awareness

Blend Sounds
Phonemic Awareness

MATERIALS
- puppet

Teach Have the puppet say: *Listen carefully as I blend these sounds together: /t/-/e/-/n/-/t/. What word did I say?* (tent) Have the puppet continue by blending together the sounds for *chase:* /ch/-/ā/-/s/. Have the puppet ask: *What word did I say?* (chase)

Practice Have the puppet say the sounds for the words below, asking children to blend the sounds together to form the words: *hint, late, past, stem, lamp, rake, flip, melt,* and *spot.*

Segment Sounds
Phonemic Awareness

MATERIALS
- Word Building Boxes
- red, yellow, and green paper circles

Teach Segment the sounds in the word *chat.* Identify its three sounds: /ch/-/a/-/t/. Have children repeat after you. Then using the Word Building Boxes and the paper circles, ask children to place the red circle in the box that represents the sound /ch/, the yellow circle in the box that represents the sound /a/, and the green circle in the box that represents the sound /t/.

Practice Continue the activity using the following words: *check, gate, chill, shape, when, name,* and *shake.* Have children say each word and segment its sounds. Have them then place the red, yellow, and green circles in the box that represents the initial, medial, or final sound.

Delete Sounds
Phonemic Awareness

MATERIALS
- colored blocks (three per child)

Teach Say the word *shade.* Point to each colored block as you identify its three sounds: /sh/-/ā/-/d/. Then explain that if you remove the beginning sound /sh/ from *shade,* what is left is *-ade.* If you remove the final sound /d/ from *shade,* what is left is *shā-.*

Practice Continue with the following words: *vase, such, went, hand, spell, drink, chase,* and *camp.* Have children repeat each word. Ask them to say the word without its beginning sound and then without its final sound. Tell them to remove the corresponding block.

INFORMAL ASSESSMENT Observe children as they blend sounds, segment sounds, and delete initial and final sounds. If children have difficulty, see Alternate Teaching Strategies on pages T64, T69, T72, T75.

OBJECTIVES

Children will:

- review long *a: a-e; ch, wh, nk;* blends.
- blend and read words with long *a: a-e; ch, wh, nk;* blends.
- review short *a;* consonants.

MATERIALS

- letter, digraph, and long *a* cards from the **Word Building Manipulative Cards**
- Teaching Chart 87

Skills Finder

Long *a: a-e*

Introduce	B3: 98I-J
Review	B3: 125E-F, 125G-H; B4: 37G-H, 65G-H, 95G-H
Test	Book 3

TEACHING TIP

SILENT *e* Help children understand the role of silent *e* by offering a word pair such as *pal* and *pale*. Ask children to repeat after you as you blend the sounds to form each word.

Review *a-e; ch, wh, nk;* Blends

PREPARE

Identify Short *a;* Long *a: a-e; ch, wh, nk;* Blends

Let children know that they will review the sounds they learned in this unit. Write the following letter combinations on the chalkboard: *a–e, ch, wh, nk, st, tr, fl, nd.*

- Point to the letter combinations and have volunteers tell you the sounds they make.

TEACH

BLENDING Model and Guide Practice with Words with Long *a : a-e; ch, wh, nk;* Blends

- Display **Teaching Chart 87**. Tell children that sometimes only one of the letters or letter pairs will form a word.

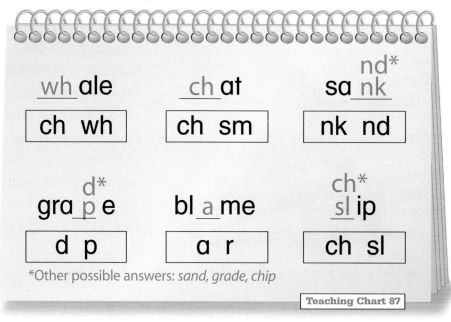

Teaching Chart 87

- Complete the first example with children. Blend the sounds of the letters together.

  ch a l(e) ⟶ chale   wh a l(e) ⟶ whale

- Have children repeat after you.
- Ask which is the real word. (whale)
- Invite a volunteer to write the missing letters in the blank.

Use the Word in Context
- Use each word in context to reinforce its meaning. Example: *A whale lives in water.*

Repeat the Procedure
- Have children write the missing letters in each blank space and blend the sounds of the letters to read the word.

PRACTICE

BLENDING
Unscramble
Words and Blends

PARTNERS

Give pairs of children groups of letter cards to form words. Have children unscramble letters and read the word. Repeat with different words. Use the following examples: *t-ch-a (chat)*, *s-ch-a-e (chase)*, *l-wh-a-e (whale)*, *d-t-r-a-e (trade)*, *k-a-e-f-l (flake)*, *i-nk-s (sink)*. ▶**Visual/Kinesthetic**

          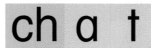

ASSESS/CLOSE

Build and Read
Words with Long
a: a-e, ch, wh, nk,
and Blends

To assess children's ability to blend and read words with long *a*: *a-e*, *ch*, *wh*, *nk*, and blends, observe children as they unscramble and build words in the Practice activity. Have children turn to page 127 in their books and read *Camp Out* aloud.

ADDITIONAL PHONICS RESOURCES

Phonics/Phonemic Awareness
Practice Book,
pages 133–136

PHONICS KIT
Hands-on Activities and Practice

McGraw-Hill School
TECHNOLOGY

Phonics **CD-ROM**
activities for practice with
Blending and Segmenting

Meeting Individual Needs for Phonics

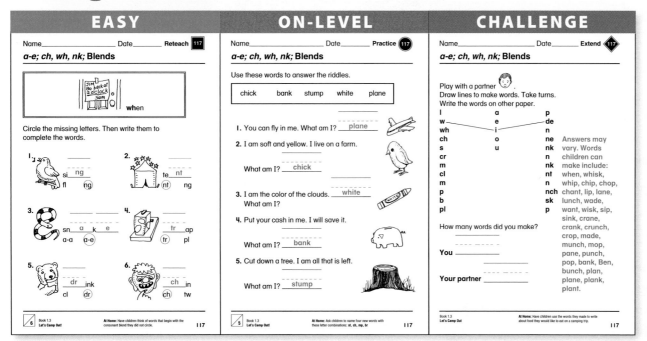

Reteach, 117   Practice, 117   Extend, 117

DAY 1 **Segmenting** Distribute letter boxes. As you say each word, ask children to write the letter or letters for each sound in a separate box. Words to include: *rake, twig, chin, rock, frame, when, ink, tape.*

DAY 2 **Blending** Make three bags of letter cards. Call on a child to pick a card from each. Have children blend the sounds and say if it is a real word. (Bag 1: *ch, wh, tr, s*; Bag 2: *a-e, a, u*; Bag 3: *nk, l, d*)

DAY 3 **Fluency** Write a list of words sorted by spelling pattern. Ask children to blend and read them silently. Then ask pairs of children to read each set.

DAY 4 **Writing** Give children the words you used on Day 1. Ask them to pick a word and make a rhyme for it. Children may write and illustrate their rhymes.

DAY 5 **Letter Substitution** Give small groups sets of letter cards. Children work together to build words. Then taking turns, each child changes a letter in one of the words to make a new word.

TESTED **OBJECTIVES**

Children will read a poem containing consonant blends, digraph *ch,* and long *a: a-e.*

Apply # *a-e; ch, wh, nk;* Blends

Camp Out

Tramp, tramp, tramp down the track,
See our caps and big backpacks.
I am Chet and that is Jake,
We set up camp next to a lake.
Look at Jake fish in the lake!
He will get us a bass to bake.
Put up the tent and we are in.
It is night—when dreams begin.

126   127

Anthology pages 126–127

Read and Build Fluency

READ THE POEM Tell children they will read a poem called *Camp Out.* Model reading by pausing every two lines at the rhyming words. Track print by sliding your finger under the words. Have children read with you.

REREAD FOR FLUENCY Have pairs of children reread the poem. Have one child pretend to be Chet and read the poem while Jake dramatizes the actions.

PARTNERS

READ A DECODABLE STORY For additional practice reading and to develop fluency, direct children to read one of this week's **Phonics Practice Reader, Vol. 1** stories.

Dictate and Spell

DICTATE WORDS Segment the word *camp* into its four individual sounds. Repeat the word aloud and use it in a sentence: *The camp is next to the lake.* Then have children say the word and write the letter or letters that represent each sound until they make the entire word. Repeat with *tramp, track, Chet, Jake, next, bake, tent,* and *when* from the poem. Then repeat with other words not in the poem: *jump, spell, name, plant, twist, branch, chick,* and *came.*

JOURNAL

i **Intervention** **Skills Intervention Guide,** for direct instruction and extra practice in Consonant Blends; Digraphs *ch, wh,* and *nk;* Long *a:a-e*

Build Background

Concept: Camping

Anthology and Leveled Books

Evaluate Prior Knowledge

CONCEPT: CAMPING Ask children if they have ever gone camping or if they have ever seen pictures, books, or movies about camping. Ask them where people usually camp. Use the following activities to organize and spark their thinking about camping.

MAKE A CHART ABOUT CAMPING

Create a chart about camping with three columns: ACTIVITIES (things you do); SETTING (things you see); EQUIPMENT (things you need). Record children's suggestions.

▶ **Linguistic/Visual**

ACTIVITIES (things you do)	CAMPING SETTING (things you see)	EQUIPMENT (things you need)
looking at stars, sleeping	woods country stream	tent sleeping bag pack

> Graphic Organizer 30

MAKE A CAMPING SCENE Ask children
to draw a picture of a camping scene. They may draw on their own experience or look at pictures to help them. Have children label as much of the drawing as they can.

Develop Oral Language

UNDERSTAND USE OF OBJECTS You

ESL may help children build background information by displaying photographs, drawings, and realia (for example, a real day pack, sleeping bag, tent, mess kit). Have children use the realia to role-play camping out. Ask simple questions as you show each object:

- What do you do in a tent? (sleep)
- What do you put in a backpack? (clothes, food, sleeping bag)
- How do you cook? (at a campfire)
- What do you sleep in? (sleeping bag)

DAILY **Phonics** ROUTINES

DAY 2 **Blending** Make three bags of letter cards. Call on a child to pick a card from each. Have children blend the sounds and say if it is a real word. (Bag 1: *ch, wh, tr, s;* Bag 2: *a-e, a, u;* Bag 3: *nk, l, d*)

Phonics CD-ROM

LANGUAGE SUPPORT

For additional material on building background, see the **Language Support Book**, pages 127–130.

OBJECTIVES

Children will:

- identify high-frequency words *under, eat, old,* and *try.*

MATERIALS

- Teaching Chart 88
- Word Building Manipulative Cards *under, eat, old, try*

TEACHING **TIP**

The following chart indicates words from the upcoming story that children have learned to decode and high-frequency words that have been taught in previous lessons.

Decodable		High-Frequency
when	make	try
camp	sticks	old
help	tent	eat
nest	things	under
sing	trip	
songs	twigs	
spot		

SPELLING/VOCABULARY CONNECTIONS

The words *under, eat, try,* and *old* are Challenge Words. See page 139Q for Day 1 of the 5-Day Spelling Plan.

---

under

old

eat

try

Vocabulary

High-Frequency Words

We Like to Camp Out

We like to camp out.
We have lots of fun
Under a tent
And out in the sun.
With old sticks and twigs,
We make a hot flame.
We eat and we sing
And we try a new game.

Teaching Chart 88

Auditory

LISTEN TO WORDS Without displaying it, read aloud "We Like to Camp Out" on **Teaching Chart 88**. Ask children if any of them have ever camped out. Ask them to share their experiences with the class.

PEEK OUT FOR HIGH-FREQUENCY WORDS Have children aurally identify each high-frequency word using the following activity:

- Say aloud one of the high-frequency words. Read a line of the poem where the word appears.

- Tell children to make believe they're in a tent while you read the line again. When they hear the high-frequency word, they should pantomime lifting the flap on their tent and looking outside while repeating the word.

- Repeat this activity with each of the high-frequency words.

Visual

TEACH WORDS Display "We Like to Camp Out" on **Teaching Chart 88**. Read the poem, tracking the print with your finger. Next, point to the word *under.* Tell children that this is the word *under.* Have them say the word with you. Ask them to hold up the vocabulary card for *under* and say the word. Repeat this procedure for *eat, old,* and *try.*

Hold up vocabulary cards for *under, eat, old,* and *try* one at a time. Have volunteers read the words and then circle them on the chart.

Word Building Manipulative Cards

BUILD A WORD TENT Tell partners they are going to set up a "word tent." One **PARTNERS** child displays a vocabulary card while the other writes a sentence using that word. Then they switch. Every time they build a sentence, give them a "pole" (use pencils).

Word Wall

Order Up Ask children to look at the letters in the word wall words very carefully. Tell them if the words were listed in a dictionary, they would be listed in ABC order. Then ask children to point to and name the word wall words in ABC order. *(eat, old, try, under)* List the words in ABC order on the chalkboard.

Look it Up Give each child a dictionary. Ask each child to look up the word wall words in order. Read each definition with children. Then ask children to copy the spelling of the words from the dictionary. Have them use each word in a new sentence.

LANGUAGE SUPPORT

To help children develop understanding and recognition of high-frequency words, see page 135 in the **Language Support Book**.

Assess

Tell Me!
Spell Me! Use the dictionary definitions that the children found to practice spelling the word wall words. Read each definition aloud to the class. Then have them tell the name of the word that you just defined. Have them spell the word out loud.

Meeting Individual Needs for Vocabulary

EASY	ON-LEVEL	ON-LEVEL	CHALLENGE
Reteach, 118	Practice, 118	Practice, 118a Take-Home Story	Extend, 118

128C

Comprehension

Prereading Strategies

PREVIEW AND PREDICT Have children read the title and preview the story, looking for strong clues about setting.

- Where might this story take place? How can you tell?
- What do you think the story will be about?

Have children make predictions about story and setting. Chart children's predictions and read them aloud.

PREDICTIONS	WHAT HAPPENED
The story takes place in the country.	
The family is going camping.	

SET PURPOSES Ask children what they want to find out as they read the story. For example:

- Where will the family go?
- What will they do at the campsite?

Let's Camp Out!

128

Meeting Individual Needs · Grouping Suggestions for Strategic Reading

EASY	ON-LEVEL	CHALLENGE
Shared Reading Read the story aloud as you track print and model directionality. As you read, focus on pointing out the setting (where people are) and the activities (what people are doing). Point out high-frequency words. Let children chime in as you read them.	**Guided Instruction** Ask children to read the story with you. Monitor any difficulties that children may have to determine which of the Comprehension questions to emphasize. After rereading the story with the class, have children reread it, using the rereading suggestions on page 134.	**Independent Reading** Have children set purposes before they read. Remind children that visualizing the setting can help them understand what is happening and what the characters are doing. After they read, have volunteers retell the story. Children can also use the questions on page 136 for a group discussion.

You can go on a trip.
1 Get your pack and let's go!

129

LANGUAGE SUPPORT

A blackline master of the camping-out web can be found in the **Language Support Book.**

Camping may be an unfamiliar activity for second-language learners. Preview the photographs in the selection to build background knowledge for those children unfamiliar with camping.

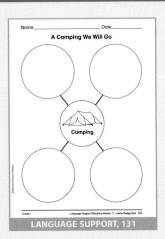

Name_____ Date_____
A Camping We Will Go

Camping

Grade 1   Language Support/Blackline Master 71 • Let's Camp Out 131

LANGUAGE SUPPORT, 131

Comprehension

☑ **Phonics** Long *a: a-e; wh;* and Blends

☑ **Apply Setting**

STRATEGIC READING Tell children that paying attention to things they see in the setting will help them understand the story and the characters. Let children know that they will draw quick sketches inside the bubbles around their camping-out web to remember what the characters saw within the setting.

1 **ANALYZE SETTING** We are going to read *Let's Camp Out!* Make sure you have your setting web and crayons so you can learn about the setting as you read. Look at the illustration. In the first circle on your web, draw a picture of what the family is doing. *Graphic Organizer*

129

Comprehension

② **Phonics** **DIGRAPH** *wh* Let's look at the first word on this page. Remember that the letters *wh* make one sound together. Let's say the *wh* sound together. Now let's blend the rest of the word: wh e n when. *Graphophonic Cues*

③ **ANALYZE SETTING** Take out your web. Draw the place where the family puts up the tent. What makes it a "good spot"? (It is in a clearing sheltered by trees.) *Visual Literacy/Draw Conclusions/Graphic Organizer*

(p/i) **DIGRAPH** *ck* Find the third word in the second line and read it aloud. *Graphophonic Cues*

TEACHING TIP

MODEL AND RETELL THE STORY Use clay, sticks, and rocks to make a model campsite with the class. Make the surface of the ground full of sticks and rocks with both bumps and smooth places. Ask children to find a good place to put a tent. Help children see that you would most likely look for a smooth place to sleep more comfortably. Then have children retell the story using their model.

② When you camp, you sleep in a tent.
③ Try to pick a good spot to put up your tent.

130

(p/i) **PREVENTION/INTERVENTION**

DIGRAPH *ck* Model blending *pick* for children. Have children say the word aloud with you. Then write ___ *ick* on the chalkboard. Have volunteers take turns picking individual letter cards out of a hat. Each child can go to the chalkboard and try the letter in the blank space to see if it forms a word they know. *Graphophonic Cues*

You can go on a hike.

Look around you for things like a nest. ⑤

131

Comprehension

④ **ANALYZE SETTING** What does the family see on the hike? (nest) Draw a picture in the next circle on your web.
Graphic Organizer

⑤ **Phonics** **BLENDS** What is the last word on the page?

MODEL I'll blend the *s-t* first: *st*. Now I can go back to the beginning of the word:
n e s t nest.

Let's reread the whole sentence together.
Graphophonic Cues

LANGUAGE SUPPORT

ESL Point to the illustrations on page 130 and 131 as you read the text. If your children have had no experience with camping, you will need to be resourceful in making this book understandable. You may wish to do the following: Bring in a tent and set it up; take a nature walk; have a barbecue to taste foods cooked outdoors.

Comprehension

6 Look at the picture and the words. On your web, draw the fire. *Graphic Organizer*

7 Why are twigs and sticks used? (They burn easily.) What else could be used? (paper) *Critical Thinking*

8 **Phonics** **BLENDING WITH LONG** *a: a-e* Find the word that begins with *m* in the first sentence. Let's blend it together. Remember that the final *e* is silent. m a k(e), make *Graphophonic Cues*

p/i **TRACKING PRINT** Point to the first word in the first sentence. *(you)* Point to the last word in the same sentence. *(fire)* *Syntactic Cues*

---

7 You can use old sticks and twigs to
8 make a fire. It can help you warm up.

132

Fluency

GROUP READING

GROUP Have children read each sentence two times. The first time, have them point to each word. The second time, let them sweep their fingers along the sentence in a smooth line. Then let them read the whole page once more, running their fingers across each sentence.

---

p/i **PREVENTION/INTERVENTION**

TRACKING PRINT Tell children that some sentences are longer than one line. Ask children to run their fingers under the sentence as you read it aloud. Ask them to point to the period at the end of the sentence. Do the same with the sentence on page 133. *Syntactic Cues*

Food tastes good when you (10)
eat it outside. (9)

133

Comprehension

(9) ANALYZE SETTING Where does the family eat? (outdoors) How do they keep their food fresh? (They keep it on ice; they use food that doesn't need refrigeration.) How do they cook their food? (over a fire) *Critical Thinking*

(10) Phonics DIGRAPH *wh* *Food tastes good w . . . .* Who remembers the sound that *wh* makes? (/hw/) Let's say *wh* together. Now let's blend the word: wh e n *when.* *Graphophonic Cues*

Minilesson

REVIEW/MAINTAIN

Main Idea

Remind the class that the main idea tells what a story is about. Work with children to find a concept that sums up the main idea of this story. Have them:

- reread the title of the story.
- review the pages they have read so far.
- think about how all the events are alike. (All are camping activities.)

Activity Write the main idea on a picture of a tent: *A family goes camping.* Include supporting details on the ropes that hold up the tent: *They take a hike. They build a fire.* Leave some ropes blank to fill in after children have read the last two pages of the story.

LANGUAGE SUPPORT

ESL Review the events that have taken place in the story thus far. Make a list of "camping words" with the class: *pack, tent, hike, campfire,* and so on. Reinforce understanding by inviting children to pantomime the actions appropriate to each camping word.

133

Comprehension

⑪ ANALYZE SETTING What can the family see in the night sky? (stars) Draw some in your web. *Graphic Organizer*

ORGANIZE INFORMATION Ask children to work in groups of four to tell the major events of the story. Let them use their web drawings as a guide. One student narrates the events. The other three pretend to be characters and act out the story.

STUDENT SELF-ASSESSMENT

Have children ask themselves the following questions to assess how they are reading:

- How did drawing pictures in the setting web help me to understand where the story took place?

- How did I use the pictures and letters and sounds I know to help me read the words in the story?

  TRANSFERRING THE STRATEGIES

- How can I use these strategies to help me read other stories?

⑪ You can sing songs together under the stars. Look for the Big Dipper!

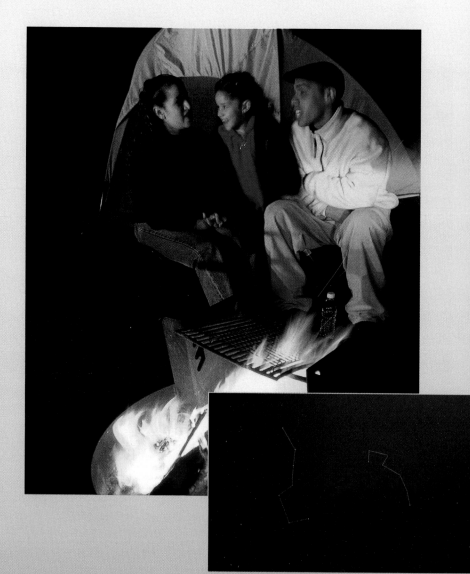

134

REREADING FOR *Fluency*

PARTNERS Children who need fluency practice can take turns reading with a partner, with or without listening to the story on the recording.

READING RATE When you evaluate reading rate, have children read aloud from the story for one minute. Place a stick-on note after the last word read. Count words read. To evaluate children's performance, see the Running Record in the **Fluency Assessment** book.

ℹ Intervention For leveled fluency lessons, passages, and norms charts, see **Skills Intervention Guide**, Part 5, Fluency.

Sleep well in your tent.

See you when the sun is up!

A story from the editors of *TIME FOR KIDS*.

135

Comprehension

Return to Predictions and Purposes

Reread children's predictions about the story. Discuss the predictions, noting which ones need to be revised. Then ask children if the story answered the questions they had before they read.

PREDICTIONS	WHAT HAPPENED
The story takes place in the country.	The story takes place in a wooded area surrounded by animals, hills, and rocks.
The family is going camping.	The family camps out together, eats over a fire, goes on a hike, and sleeps under the stars.

HOW TO ASSESS

 **BLENDING DIGRAPHS**
Have children point to and read the third word in the second sentence on page 135. (*when*)

SETTING Have children describe the setting of the camping trip.

FOLLOW UP

 BLENDING DIGRAPHS
Continue to model the blending of digraphs for children who are having trouble.

SETTING If children are having trouble recognizing the setting of the story, ask them to look at the pictures in the story again. Ask: What does the place the family went camping look like?

LITERARY RESPONSE

QUICK-WRITE Invite children to reflect on the various aspects of camping out as depicted in the story. Have them draw and write about the best part.

ORAL RESPONSE Encourage children to use their journal entries to discuss these questions:

• What is fun about going camping?

• How is sleeping in a tent different from sleeping in a bedroom?

SENTENCE STRIPS Children can use strips 1–14 to retell *Let's Camp Out!*

> 1
> You can go on a trip.

> 2
> Get your pack and let's go!

Story Questions

Tell children that they will now read some questions about the story. Help them read the questions. Discuss possible answers.

Answers:

1. You can use old sticks and twigs. *Literal/Details*

2. People camp outside. They may camp out in the woods, the mountains, or at the beach. *Inferential/Make Inferences*

3. Possible answer: You may hear animal sounds (hooting, buzzing, growling, howling), the wind, or branches breaking. *Inferential/Make Inferences*

4. Possible answer: You hike, you make a campfire, you sleep in a tent. *Critical/Summarize*

5. You may see an owl. *Critical/Reading Across Texts*

Tell How to Do It Help children read the directions in their anthologies.

Story Questions & Activities

READ TOGETHER

① What do you need for a campfire?

② Where do people camp out?

③ What sounds do you hear camping?

④ Name three things you can do camping.

⑤ Which animals from "Stan's Stunt" might you see when you camp out?

Tell How to Do It

How do you roast marshmallows? Tell what you need. Tell how to roast them. Then draw a picture of yourself roasting them.

Meeting Individual Needs

EASY	ON-LEVEL	CHALLENGE
Name_____ Date_____ **Reteach** 119	Name_____ Date_____ **Practice** 119	Name_____ Date_____ **Extend** 119
Story Comprehension	**Story Comprehension**	**Story Comprehension**
Here is a picture of the camp in "Let's Camp Out!" Draw a new picture in each circle. Show other things that were described in the story.	Read the statements. Underline the things you might do on a camping trip.	What would you do on a camping trip? Make a postcard. Write what you did. Draw a picture. Write who you will send your card to.

EASY column:

Possible drawing: tents

Possible drawing: hiking, seeing a nest

Possible drawing: the stars at night

Possible drawing: campfires

Book 1.3 Let's Camp Out! · **At Home:** Have children write a few sentences about what it might be like to go camping. · 119

ON-LEVEL column:

1. sleep in a tent
2. wade in a lake
3. shop for gifts
4. sit by a fire
5. look at the stars
6. put on a pack
7. chat on the phone
8. find a nest
9. sing songs
10. see a movie
11. see a frog
12. take a hike

Book 1.3 Let's Camp Out! · **At Home:** Have children draw a picture of something they might see on a camping trip. · 119

CHALLENGE column:

To: _____

Book 1.3 Let's Camp Out! · **At Home:** Have children plan a camping trip they would like to take. They should decide where they would like to go and when, how long they would stay, what they would take with them, and what they would do once they were there. · 119

Reteach, 119   **Practice, 119**   **Extend, 119**

Play Stuck-in-the-Mud, a Camp Game

One person is IT. IT tags someone.

The person tagged stands still.

That person is stuck in the mud.

The game is over when IT tags everyone.

Then someone else can be IT.

Find Out More

Learn a camp song.

Share it with the class.

137

Story Activities

Play *Stuck-in-the-Mud*: a Camp Game

GROUP Prepare children by briefly discussing group games that they like to play outside (for example, tag, dodgeball).

- Show a chart with rules for the game. Act out or demonstrate the rules to help children understand.
- Ask volunteers to demonstrate the game.
- Play the game outside.

Find Out More

RESEARCH AND INQUIRY Have children seek out older siblings, parents, or teachers as references. Ask children to have their resource people record the song for them on audiocassette or transcribe the song on paper.

Activity Once all children have learned their song, stage a sing-along around a pretend campfire (with or without resource people as invited guests). You can bring real popcorn to the event.

 *inter***NET** **CONNECTION** Help children log on to **www.mhschool.com/reading**, where they can learn more about camping.

FORMAL ASSESSMENT

After page 137, see Selection and Unit Assessments.

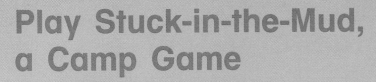
DAILY Phonics ROUTINES

DAY 3 **Fluency** Write a list of words sorted by spelling pattern. Ask children to blend and read them silently. Then ask pairs of children to read each set.

Phonics **CD-ROM**

Study Skills

DIAGRAMS

✓OBJECTIVES

Children will:

• read a diagram identifying parts of a tent.

• learn how a tent stays up.

Display **Teaching Chart 89**. Look at the tent diagram with the class. Have volunteers identify the labeled parts on the chart. Read the labels with the class and discuss the function of each part. (Poles hold up the tent. Ropes keep the tent tight. Stakes secure the tent to the ground.) Then have children answer each question.

Answers:

1. the poles and the stakes

2. There are two poles.

Ask children to draw their own diagram of a tent and label the parts.

Meeting Individual Needs

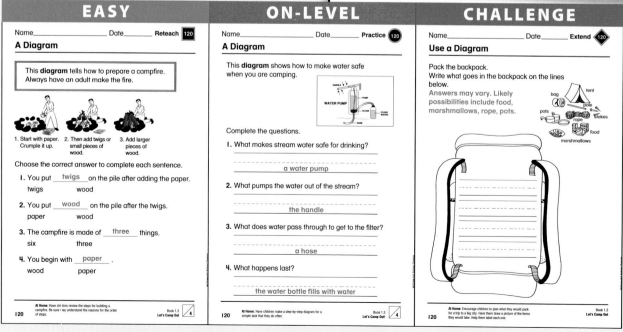

Reteach, 120   Practice, 120   Extend, 120

STUDY SKILLS

READ TOGETHER

Diagram of a Tent

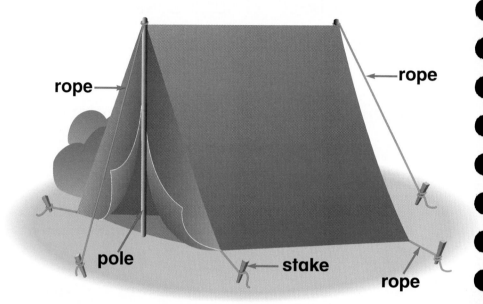

rope

rope

pole   stake

rope

Look at the Diagram

❶ What holds the ropes in place?

❷ How many poles are there?

TEST POWER

Let's Camp Out

Let's camp here.

There are lots of trees.

And the woods are nice and quiet.

Let's put up the tent.

Make sure the door is closed.

We don't want to sleep with the bugs.

Now let's cook dinner.

After dinner, we can tell stories.

Where does this story take place?

⬤ In the woods

○ In a parking lot

Think about the story as you read it.

139

Test Power
THE PRINCETON REVIEW

Read the Page

Explain to children that you will be reading this story as a group. You will read the story, and they will follow in their books.

Request that children put pens, pencils, and markers away, since they will not be writing in their books.

Discuss the Question

Discuss with children the kinds of words that describe places. Then have them read the story, looking for words that describe places. Have children read aloud the word(s) they have found.

Test-Tip

While you read the story, ask yourself: Where is this story taking place?

 **Intervention** ▶ **Skills**
Intervention Guide, for direct instruction and extra practice in vocabulary and comprehension

 **Phonics**

- review long *a: a-e*
- review *ch*, *wh*, and *nk* digraphs

☑ **Comprehension**

- review, compare, and contrast
- review setting

Answers will vary. Have children cite examples from the story to support their answers.

EASY

Story Questions for Selected Reading

1. Who is the main character in the story?
2. Which illustrations did you like best? Why?
3. How was the story problem solved?
4. If you could be a character in the story, who would you be? Why?
5. Did you like the story? Why or why not?

Draw a Picture

Draw a picture for the selected story.

Self-Selected Reading
Leveled Books

EASY

 UNIT SKILLS REVIEW

☑ **Phonics**

☑ **Comprehension**

Help children self-select an Easy Book to read and apply phonics and comprehension skills.

Guided Reading

PREVIEW AND PREDICT Discuss the illustrations in the beginning of the book. As you take the **picture walk**, have children predict what the story will be about. List their ideas.

SET PURPOSES Have children write or draw why they want to read the book. Have them share their purposes.

READ THE BOOK Use the following items to guide children's reading, or to discuss after they have read the story independently. Model blending and other phonics and decoding strategies for children who need help.

- Let's retell the story in our own words. *Summarize*

- Can you find any story words that are spelled with the long *a: a-e* sound? *Phonics and Decoding*

- Do you think this story is real or make-believe? *Distinguish Between Fantasy and Reality*

RETURN TO PREDICTIONS AND PURPOSES Discuss children's predictions. Ask which were close to the book contents and why. Have children review their purposes for reading. Did they find out what they wanted to know?

LITERARY RESPONSE Have children discuss questions such as:

- What parts of the book were most interesting?

- What might be another good title for the book?

 **CD-ROM**

Self-Selected Reading
Leveled Books

INDEPENDENT

UNIT SKILLS REVIEW

☑

☑ **Comprehension**

Help children self-select an Independent Book to read and apply phonics and comprehension skills.

Guided Reading

PREVIEW AND PREDICT Discuss the illustrations in the beginning of the book. As you take the **picture walk**, have children predict what the story will be about. List their ideas.

SET PURPOSES Have children write or draw why they want to read the book. Have them share their purposes.

READ THE BOOK Use the following items to guide children's reading, or to discuss after they have read the story independently. Model blending and other phonics and decoding strategies for children who need help.

- Can you find any words from the story that have the *ch*, *wh*, or *nk* digraphs? *Phonics and Decoding*

- Let's look at the pictures. Can you tell me where the story takes place? *Use Illustrations*

- Was the ending of the story a surprise? Did it end as you thought it would? *Make Predictions*

RETURN TO PREDICTIONS AND PURPOSES Discuss children's predictions. Ask which were close to the book contents and why. Have children review their purposes for reading. Did they find out what they wanted to know?

LITERARY RESPONSE Have children discuss questions such as:

- What parts of the book were most interesting?

- What might be another good title for the book?

 **CD-ROM**

☑

- review long a: a-e

- review *ch, wh,* and *nk* digraphs

☑ **Comprehension**

- review, compare, and contrast

- review setting

Answers will vary. Have children cite examples from the story to support their answers.

INDEPENDENT

Story Questions for Selected Reading

1. Where does this story take place?

2. Did the story teach you anything new? What?

3. Did you like the ending? Why or why not?

4. What caused the main event to happen?

5. How is the main character like you? How is he or she different?

Draw a Picture

Draw a picture for the selected story.

 **Phonics**

- review long *a: a-e*
- review *ch*, *wh*, and *nk* digraphs

☑ **Comprehension**

- review compare and contrast
- review setting

Answers will vary. Have children cite examples from the story to support their answers.

Self-Selected Reading
Leveled Books

CHALLENGE

 **UNIT SKILLS REVIEW**

☑ **Phonics**

☑ **Comprehension**

Help children self-select a Challenge Book to read and apply phonics and comprehension skills.

Guided Reading

PREVIEW AND PREDICT Discuss the illustrations in the beginning of the book. As you take the **picture walk**, have children predict what the story will be about. List their ideas.

SET PURPOSES Have children write or draw why they want to read the book. Have them share their purposes.

READ THE BOOK Use the following items to guide children's reading, or to discuss after they have read the story independently. Model blending and other phonics and decoding strategies for children who need help.

- Who is your favorite character in the story? Why? *Analyze Character and Plot*

- Can you list the important events in the story as they happened? *Summarize*

- What parts of the story did you find most interesting? Why? Has anything similar happened to you? *Analyze Character and Plot*

RETURN TO PREDICTIONS AND PURPOSES Discuss children's predictions. Ask which were close to the book contents and why. Have children review their purposes for reading. Did they find out what they wanted to know?

LITERARY RESPONSE Have children discuss questions such as:

- What parts of the book were most interesting?

- What might be another good title for the book?

 **CD-ROM**

CHALLENGE

Story Questions for Selected Reading

1. If you could change something about the story, what would it be?

2. Did you learn anything new from the story?

3. If you could talk to the author, what questions would you ask?

4. Did anything surprise you about the story? What was it?

5. Could this story be made into a TV show? Why or why not?

Draw a Picture

Draw a picture for the selected story.

Activities

Bringing Groups Together

Anthology and Leveled Books

Connecting Texts

CLASS DISCUSSION
Have children choose their favorites from the Leveled Books and Anthology selections in this unit. Lead a discussion of how the unit theme *Stories to Tell* applies to each of the stories:

- Did anything interesting happen to the characters in the story that you think would be exciting to share with others?

- Can you think of an interesting experience you had recently?

CHARACTER WEB
Have children create a web to compare main characters from the stories. Who are they? What did they experience? A sample web is shown at right.

The Cow that Went OINK
A cow says "oink" instead of "moo."

The Cave
Two squirrels accidentally stumble into a birthday party for a snake.

Stories to Tell

Walking Through the Jungle
A girl goes exploring through various environments.

Kent and Glen
Two brothers write letters to each other, relating their experiences at home and at a summer camp.

Viewing/Representing

GROUP PRESENTATIONS Ask children to choose their favorite book and then divide them into groups. Have children create art murals for a scene in their stories by drawing together on large sheets of paper.

AUDIENCE RESPONSE Have children display their murals on the wall and explain what happened in the story. Tell what they found interesting about each performance. Suggest that children ask questions about any parts of the story they would like to know about.

Research and Inquiry

STORIES OF PEOPLE Divide children into partners. Have them choose a well-known person and research the events of that person's life. Invite children to list reasons why the person is well-known, and present a short report of the person's accomplishments to the class.

interNET
CONNECTION Have children log on to **www.mhschool.com/reading** to access links to various biographical sites about people.

JOURNAL Children can write and draw what they learned in their journals.

Children will compare and contrast different settings.

MATERIALS
• Teaching Chart 90

Skills Finder

Compare/Contrast

Introduce	B3: 67I-J
Review	B3: 97I-J, 139E-F
Test	Book 3
Maintain	B5: 67

TEACHING TIP

MANAGEMENT When you create a Venn diagram, be sure that you've made the circles large enough to fit all the children's suggestions.

House	Both	Tent
bed		sleeping bag
many rooms	places to sleep	one room
can't be moved	keep you dry	can be moved

Review Compare and Contrast

PREPARE

Reinforce Alike and Different Remind children that they can understand how two things are alike and different by reading about them and by looking at pictures of them. They can also learn by using their own experience, or comparing a familiar object with an unfamiliar one.

TEACH

Compare and Contrast Display **Teaching Chart 90**. Allow children to comment on the pictures of the house and the tent. Then read the chart aloud.

MODEL From these sentences I see that when you go camping, you sleep in a sleeping bag. When you stay at home, you sleep in a bed. Some things are the same, though. The tent and the house both are places to sleep. They also keep people dry.

Ask volunteers to add a sentence under each picture showing how people cook when at home and when camping.

He sleeps in a bag under the stars.

He sleeps in a bed under a roof.

Teaching Chart 90

Have children refer to the sentences and pictures from the chart to help create a Venn diagram comparing and contrasting a tent and a house.

PRACTICE

Compare Drawings

PARTNERS

Have partners pick one activity that families do, such as eating, sleeping, and playing together. One partner illustrates the activity when it is done camping out. The other partner illustrates the activity when it is done at home. Children can compare their pictures and discuss how the activity is similar and different. ▶ **Visual**

ASSESS/CLOSE

Compare Events

Let children pick one event from *Let's Camp Out!* to compare with something they do around their home, for example, taking a hike vs. taking a walk. Have them draw and write one reason why these two events are alike and one reason why they are different.

DAILY Phonics ROUTINES

DAY 4
Writing Give children the words you used on Day 1. Ask them to pick a word and make a rhyme for it. Children may write and illustrate their rhymes.

Phonics CD-ROM

ALTERNATE TEACHING STRATEGY

COMPARE AND CONTRAST

For a different approach to teaching this skill, see page T71.

 **Intervention ▶ Skills Intervention Guide,** for direct instruction and extra practice in Comparing and Contrasting

---

Meeting Individual Needs for Comprehension

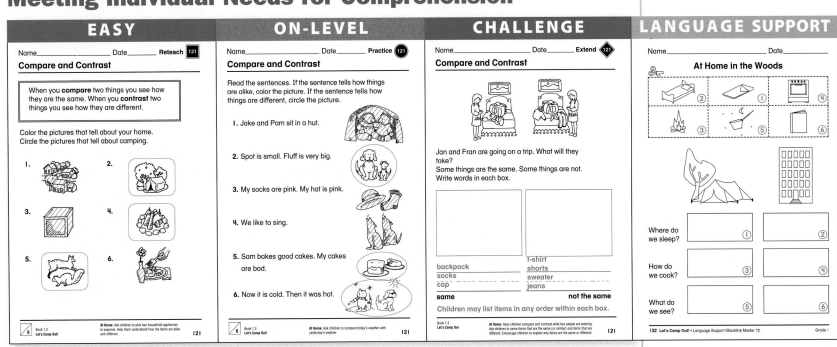

EASY	ON-LEVEL	CHALLENGE	LANGUAGE SUPPORT
Reteach, 121	Practice, 121	Extend, 121	Language Support, 132

TESTED

Children will review how to analyze setting.

....

MATERIALS
• **Teaching Chart 91**

Skills Finder	
Story Elements	
Introduce	B2: 35I–J
Review	B2: 65I–J, 137E–F; B3: 37I–J, 125I–J, 139G–H
Test	Book 2, Book 3
Maintain	B3: 89; B4: 25, 107, 109

TEACHING TIP

SETTING To help children brainstorm words for their setting, show pictures of different settings from nature calendars, books, and magazines.

Review Story Elements

PREPARE

Review the Concept of Setting

Remind children that setting includes the place where the story happens, the time when the story happens, and the conditions in the story, such as the weather.

TEACH

Review Setting

Display **Teaching Chart 91**. Allow children to comment on the picture of the camping scene. Then read the chart aloud.

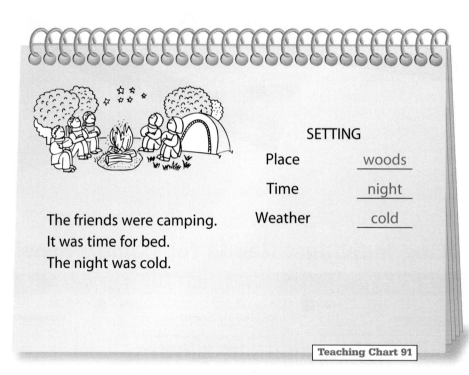

The friends were camping.
It was time for bed.
The night was cold.

SETTING

Place — woods
Time — night
Weather — cold

Teaching Chart 91

MODEL Looking at the picture, I see people sitting around a fire. I also see trees and tents. The first sentence says that they are camping. So I can figure out where the story takes place—in the woods. I also notice that it's dark outside and read that it's time for bed. So when the story is happening must be late at night. I know that it's cold outside based on what I read.

Have children refer to the sentences and pictures from the **Teaching Chart**. Elicit as many words as you can to describe place, time, weather. Ask volunteers to add words in the appropriate spot on **Teaching Chart 91**.

DAILY  ROUTINES

DAY 5   Letter Substitution
Give small groups sets of letter cards. Children work together to build words. Then taking turns, each child changes a letter in one of the words to make a new word.

PRACTICE

Locate the Setting of a Story

PARTNERS

Ask partners to choose another selection they have read. Have children review the story. Invite them to complete a three-column chart about the setting, including Place, Time, and Weather. Ask them to label the chart with the story title. ▶ **Linguistic/Logical**

SETTING OF SNAKES		
PLACE	TIME	WEATHER
Desert	noon	Very hot

 CD-ROM

ALTERNATE TEACHING STRATEGY

SETTING

For a different approach to teaching this skill, see page T67.

ASSESS/CLOSE

Create a Setting

Invite children to create a setting for an original story. Have them draw the setting using as much detail as possible. Ask them to add the following labels to the bottom of their drawing and fill in the information: Place, Time, Weather.

Intervention ▶ **Skills Intervention Guide,** for direct instruction and extra practice in Setting

Meeting Individual Needs for Comprehension

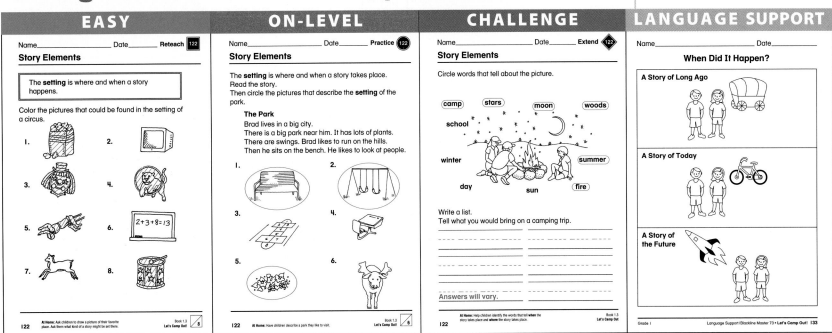

EASY	ON-LEVEL	CHALLENGE	LANGUAGE SUPPORT

Reteach, 122   Practice, 122   Extend, 122   Language Support, 133

TESTED OBJECTIVES

Children will review possessives.

MATERIALS
• **Teaching Chart 92**

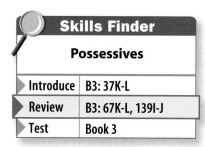

Skills Finder	
Possessives	
Introduce	B3: 37K–L
Review	B3: 67K–L, 139I–J
Test	Book 3

<u>Review</u> Possessives

PREPARE

Act It Out Have a volunteer stand up to give you his or her pencil. Write the child's name on the chalkboard, then ask the class whose pencil it is. Add -'s to the child's name as the class responds. Explain that adding -'s shows that something belongs to someone.

TEACH

Identify Possessives Track the first sentence on **Teaching Chart 92** as you read it with children: *This is Tom's cat.* Then point to the cat. Ask the class who owns the cat. (Tom)

1. This is Tom's cat.　　2. We are going to Pat's house.

3. I see the bird's nest.

Teaching Chart 92

MODEL As I read the first sentence, I see the name *Tom* with an -'s at the end. The -'s tells me that something belongs to Tom. The next word is *cat*. So the cat must be the thing that belongs to Tom. It's *Tom's* cat.

Ask a volunteer to circle the part of the word that shows the cat belongs to Tom. ('s) Repeat the procedure with the other sentences.

PRACTICE

Add 's 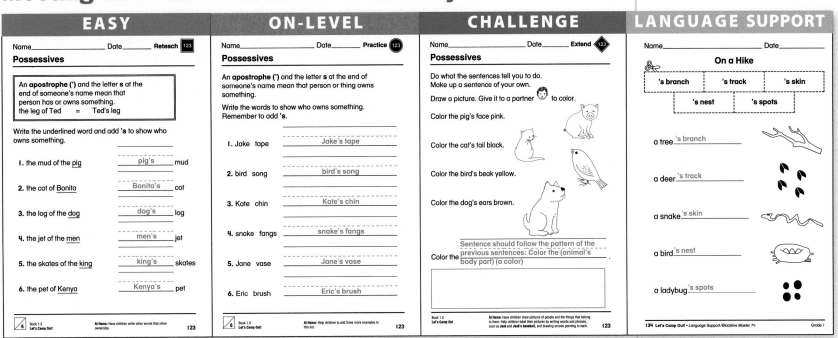 Write a list on the board showing an object and a person, place, or thing belonging to that object. For example:

OBJECT	BELONGS TO
bat	Sam
bed	Ted
fish	Mom
tent	boy

Ask children to work in small groups to label and illustrate the items on the list. Make sure they use -'s to show possession. ▶ **Visual/Linguistic**

ASSESS/CLOSE

Show Possession Invite children to tell you how to change the following into -'s phrases:

- a car that belongs to Dad (Dad's car)
- a hat that belongs to a lady (lady's hat)
- a dog that belongs to a boy (boy's dog)

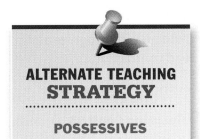

ALTERNATE TEACHING STRATEGY

POSSESSIVES

For a different approach to teaching this skill, see page T68.

ℹ **Intervention** ▶ **Skills Intervention Guide,** for direct instruction and extra practice in Possessives

Meeting Individual Needs for Vocabulary

EASY — Reteach, 123

Name_____ Date_____ **Reteach** 123

Possessives

An **apostrophe (')** and the letter **s** at the end of someone's name mean that person has or owns something.
the leg of Ted   =   Ted's leg

Write the underlined word and add **'s** to show who owns something.

1. the mud of the <u>pig</u> — pig's mud
2. the cot of <u>Bonita</u> — Bonita's cot
3. the log of the <u>dog</u> — dog's log
4. the jet of the <u>men</u> — men's jet
5. the skates of the <u>king</u> — king's skates
6. the pet of <u>Kenya</u> — Kenya's pet

Book 1.3 Let's Camp Out! **At Home:** Have children write other words that show ownership. 123

ON-LEVEL — Practice, 123

Name_____ Date_____ **Practice** 123

Possessives

An **apostrophe (')** and the letter **s** at the end of someone's name mean that person or thing owns something.

Write the words to show who owns something. Remember to add **'s**.

1. Jake tape — Jake's tape
2. bird song — bird's song
3. Kate chin — Kate's chin
4. snake fangs — snake's fangs
5. Jane vase — Jane's vase
6. Eric brush — Eric's brush

Book 1.3 Let's Camp Out **At Home:** Help children to add three more examples to this list. 123

CHALLENGE — Extend, 123

Name_____ Date_____ **Extend** 123

Possessives

Do what the sentences tell you to do. Make up a sentence of your own.

Draw a picture. Give it to a partner to color.

Color the pig's face pink.

Color the cat's tail black.

Color the bird's beak yellow.

Color the dog's ears brown.

Color the _Sentence should follow the pattern of the previous sentences: Color the (animal's body part) (a color)_

Book 1.3 Let's Camp Out **At Home:** Have children draw pictures of people and the things that belong to them. Help children label their pictures by writing words and phrases, such as **Jack** and **Jack's baseball**, and drawing arrows pointing to each. 123

LANGUAGE SUPPORT — Language Support, 134

Name_____ Date_____

On a Hike

's branch	's track	's skin
's nest		's spots

a tree 's branch

a deer 's track

a snake 's skin

a bird 's nest

a ladybug 's spots

134 **Let's Camp Out!** • Language Support/Blackline Master 74 Grade 1

Reteach, 123   **Practice, 123**   **Extend, 123**   Language Support, 134

139J

OBJECTIVES

Children will recognize and read contractions.

....

MATERIALS

• **Teaching Chart 93**

• index cards

🔍	**Skills Finder**
	Contractions
Introduce	B3: 97K-L
Review	B3: 125K-L, 139K-L
Test	Book 3

Review **Contractions**

PREPARE

Form Contractions

Write *Let us play* on the chalkboard. Read the sentence aloud. Ask children if they can think of a shorter way of saying *Let us*. Then have a volunteer come to the board, cross out the *-u*, and add an apostrophe. Read the new sentence: *Let's play*. Remind children that a contraction is made up of two words, and that an apostrophe takes the place of the missing letter or letters.

TEACH

Identify Word Parts

Track the first sentence on **Teaching Chart 93** as you read it with children. Point to the word *she's*. Find out if children recognize part of this word. (*she*) Explain that the *-'s* is a short way of saying *is*. So *she's* is a short way of saying *she is*. Have a volunteer underline the root word and write *is* under *-'s*. Write the following equation: *She + is = She's*.

She's not happy.
— is

He couldn't hit the ball.
— not

She'll sit down.
— will

Teaching Chart 93

MODEL I can use what I already know to help me read new words. I know the word *she*. I can see the last letter of the word is *s*. I remember that *'s* is a short way of saying *is*. The word is *she's* and it means *she is*.

Follow the same procedure with the other sentences on the chart.

Form Contractions

PARTNERS

Distribute blank index cards to children. Write *I, Let, He, are, n't, 's,* and *'m* on the chalkboard. Have children copy each on a separate index card. Partners can use the cards to form contractions. Have them keep a list of the contractions. ▶ **Linguistic**

are	n't

ALTERNATE TEACHING STRATEGY

CONTRACTIONS

For a different approach to teaching this skill, see page T74.

ASSESS/CLOSE

Identify Contractions in Sentences

Invite children to use words from the previous activity. Say some sentences aloud, repeating the verb after the sentence is read. Tell children to hold up the cards for that word. Encourage them to tell what two words can take the place of the contraction and still make sense in the sentence. Use the following sentences:

* He's not here today.   (He's = He + is)
* I'm going to the zoo.   (I'm = I + am)
* They aren't playing.   (aren't = are + not)

ⓘ Intervention ▶ **Skills Intervention Guide,** for direct instruction and extra practice in Contractions

Meeting Individual Needs for Vocabulary

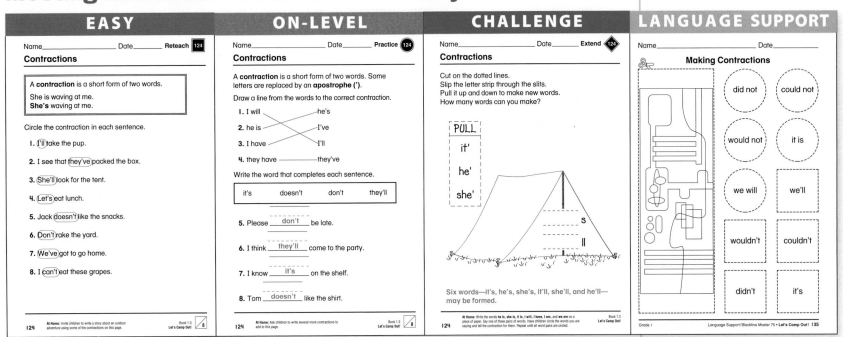

Reteach, 124   Practice, 124   Extend, 124   Language Support, 135

Handwriting CD-ROM

GRAMMAR/SPELLING CONNECTIONS

See the 5-Day Grammar and Usage Plan on contractions with *not,* pages 139O–139P.

See the 5–Day Spelling Plan on Words from Science, pages 139Q–139R.

TEACHING TIP

Technology Word processing programs include a function for setting automatic page breaks. Children who want to leave room for illustrations may choose to break their work into a few pages. Help them figure out how to put in page breaks.

Timeline Tell children that a timeline or flowchart can help them organize their thoughts. Create a simple timeline of the events that occur in the course of a school day to demonstrate.

Interactive Writing

Write a Story

Prewrite

TALK ABOUT CAMPING Have children revisit *Let's Camp Out!,* noticing again the words and pictures. Tell them that the class will write a story about a day camping out. Say that they'll compare that day with a day they might have at home. Begin by making a list of places where children might like to camp out. Then have them suggest things that they might do. Also list what they would do on a typical day at home. How are the activities similar or different?

Draft

WRITE A CLASS STORY Tell children that the class will write a story about a day camping out. They will tell how that day compares to a day at home. Help children compose the sentences that they would like to include. Guide them to suggest sentences using familiar words, sounds, and language patterns.

- Begin by saying, for example: *Where do we wake up when we're camping out?* (in a tent) *Can anybody give me a sentence about that? Where do we wake up at home?* (in a bed) *Can anybody give me a sentence about that?* As children say a word with familiar sounds and patterns, challenge them to come up and write it. Write all unfamiliar words yourself.

- Encourage them to write about meals, play, resting, chores, the presence or absence of TV, how they keep warm and dry, how they have light at night, and so on.

Revise

CONTRACTIONS Model for children how to crook their index finger to look like an apostrophe. Reread the class story and invite children to put their index finger apostrophes in the air every time you read a contraction. Encourage children to check these contractions to see if they are spelled correctly.

Publish

CREATE THE STORY Reread the story together with children. Discuss different ways of illustrating it. What part of the story should go on each page? Have children create illustrations. Then tell them to copy the appropriate story text onto each page.

Presentation Ideas

MAKE A MAP Ask children to imagine a spot for camping out. Invite them to make a map of their spot. Where are the trees? Is there a hiking trail? Is there a lake, a pond, or a beach? Where do they pitch the tent? Where do they build the fire?

▶ **Representing/Viewing**

TELL A CAMPFIRE STORY Encourage volunteers to tell a story or sing a song as if the class were sitting around a campfire. (If possible, arrange the chairs in a circle.)

▶ **Speaking/Listening**

Where we saw the raccoon

Meeting Individual Needs for Writing

EASY	ON-LEVEL	CHALLENGE
Draw Pictures Children can draw pictures, illustrating what kinds of things they would pack to go camping. Have them write labels for their pictures.	**New Story** Children can work in pairs to write a new story about a boy and girl named Sid and Kit, and their experiences camping with their cat.	**Journal Entry** Children can write a journal entry, telling a story about a brother and sister who decide to camp in their backyard. What did they do and see? What was going on in the house while they were camping? What did they do differently from the people in the house?

5 Day Grammar and Usage Plan

Oral Warm-Up Write: *The cans _____ on the shelf.* Ask children whether they would use *is* or *are*. *(are)* Why? (There is more than one can.)

Introduce Contractions Tell children that in a contraction two words are joined and a letter is left out. Present:

> **Contractions**
>
> - A **contraction** is a short form of two words.
> - An **apostrophe (')** takes the place of the letters that are left out.

Daily Language Activity Write: *The cat is not old. The cat isn't old.* Point out the contraction *isn't*. Ask children what two words from the first sentence form the contraction in the second. *(is not)*

 WRITING Assign the daily Writing Prompt on page 126E.

Review Contractions Remind children that a contraction is two words combined into one. Write these sentences on the chalkboard: *The girls are not home. The girls aren't home.* Point out the contraction *aren't*. Ask children what two words from the first sentence form the contraction in the second. *(are not)*

Daily Language Activity Write *is not* and *are not*. Erase the *o* in each and add an apostrophe to form contractions. Then ask children which letter is missing from the contractions. *(o)*

 WRITING Assign the daily Writing Prompt on page 126E.

LANGUAGE SUPPORT

ESL Contractions will be difficult for your ESL children. Work with them to complete the **Grammar Practice Book** pages orally. The more they hear contractions properly used, the more they will be able to incorporate them into their own speech and writing.

TEACHING TIP

DOUBLE NEGATIVES If you find that children are ready to grasp the concept of double negatives, it may be useful to introduce them in conjunction with contractions. If this is the case, explain to children that two negatives that appear in a row have the same effect as one positive. For example, *He can't not go to the store* has the same meaning as *He can go to the store.*

Grammar Practice Book Page 89

Name_____ Date_____ **GRAMMAR** 89

Contractions with *Not*

- A **contraction** is a short form of two words.
  You <u>are not</u> going on a hike. — Long form
  You <u>aren't</u> going on a hike. — Short form

Read the sentences. Draw a circle around the short form of two words.

1. Greg (isn't) packing for a trip.
2. They (aren't) packing for a trip.
3. You (aren't) a singer.
4. You are not a singer.
5. Pam is not getting her pack.
6. Pam (isn't) getting her pack.

Book 1.3
Let's Camp Out!   EXTENSION: Have the children think of sentences with contractions. Write the contractions on a chart.   89

GRAMMAR PRACTICE BOOK, PAGE 89

Grammar Practice Book Page 90

Name_____ Date_____ LEARN AND PRACTICE **GRAMMAR** 90

Contractions with *Not*

- A **contraction** is a short form of two words.
- An **apostrophe (')** takes the place of the letters that are left out.
  She is not picking up sticks. — is not
  She isn't picking up sticks. — isn't

Read the sentences. Draw a circle around the two words that were joined in the contractions.

1. Pam isn't looking at the Big Dipper.
   (is not)   not at   Pam is
2. Max isn't a singer.
   (is not)   Max is   not a
3. They aren't packing.
   (are not)   They are   not packing
4. Greg isn't picking up sticks.
   Greg is   (is not)   not picking
5. They aren't warmed up.
   (are not)   They are   not warmed

EXTENSION: Have the children look for contractions in trade books that have been read to them. Write the contractions they find on a chart.   Book 1.3
Let's Camp Out!   5   90

GRAMMAR PRACTICE BOOK, PAGE 90

Contractions with *Not*

DAY 3 — Review and Practice

Learn from Literature Review the contractions *isn't* and *aren't* with children. Write the following sentence from page 129 of *Let's Camp Out!* on the chalkboard:

> **Get your pack and let's go!**

Point out the contraction *let's*. Tell children that *let's* combines *let* and *us*. The apostrophe replaces the *u* in *us*. Then write *isn't* and *aren't* on the chalkboard. Ask children what letter the apostrophe replaces in each contraction. *(o)*

Daily Language Activity Write the following sentences on the chalkboard: *This spot is not good. The children are not warm. The sun is not up. The sticks are not dry.* Ask children to say the sentences aloud, using contractions for *is not* and *are not*.

 WRITING Assign the daily Writing Prompt on page 126F.

DAY 4 — Review and Practice

Review Contractions Write the following sentence on the chalkboard and ask children what the contraction means: *He isn't on the bus. (is not)*

Daily Language Activity Write the following sentences on the chalkboard: *She is not sad. The bikes are not red. The ducks are not big. Pat is not slow.* Ask volunteers to change the underlined words into contractions.

Mechanics and Usage Review the use of apostrophes in contractions:

> ### Apostrophes
> Use an apostrophe in place of the letters left out of a contraction.

 WRITING Assign the daily Writing Prompt on page 126F.

DAY 5 — Assess and Reteach

Daily Language Activity Write the following sentences on the chalkboard: *The stars are not bright. The moon is not out.* Ask children to identify the words in each which can be joined to form a contraction. *(are not, is not)* Have children spell the contractions, including the apostrophes.

Assess Use page 93 of the **Grammar Practice Book** for assessment.

Reteach Make sets of cards. Each set should include *is, are, n, o, t*, and apostrophes. Have children use cards to spell *is not* and *are not*. Then help them remove *o*'s, insert apostrophes, and move letters together to form contractions.

 WRITING Assign the daily Writing Prompt on page 126F.

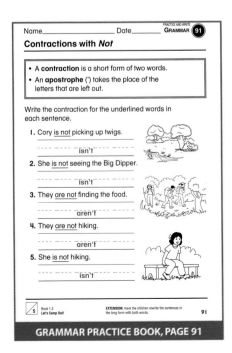

Name_____ Date_____ PRACTICE AND WRITE **GRAMMAR 91**

Contractions with *Not*

- A **contraction** is a short form of two words.
- An **apostrophe** (') takes the place of the letters that are left out.

Write the contraction for the underlined words in each sentence.

1. Cory <u>is not</u> picking up twigs.
   _____ isn't

2. She <u>is not</u> seeing the Big Dipper.
   _____ isn't

3. They <u>are not</u> finding the food.
   _____ aren't

4. They <u>are not</u> hiking.
   _____ aren't

5. She <u>is not</u> hiking.
   _____ isn't

Book 1.3 *Let's Camp Out!*   EXTENSION: Have the children rewrite the sentences in the long form with both words.   **91**

GRAMMAR PRACTICE BOOK, PAGE 91

Name_____ Date_____ MECHANICS **GRAMMAR 92**

Contractions with *Not*

- A **contraction** is a short form of two words.
- A **contraction** is a way of saying two words as one.
- Two words are joined and a letter is left out.
- An **apostrophe** (') takes the place of the letters that are left out.
   You **are not** going on a hike.
   You **aren't** going on a hike.

Correct the contractions. Put in the apostrophe ('). Write the contraction.

1. That isnt our food. _____ isn't

2. They arent making a fire. _____ aren't

3. Greg isnt finding our tent. _____ isn't

4. Isnt that a big tent? _____ isn't

5. They arent sleeping. _____ aren't

92   EXTENSION: Have the children tell the two words that were joined to make the contractions in this exercise.   Book 1.3 *Let's Camp Out!*

GRAMMAR PRACTICE BOOK, PAGE 92

Name_____ Date_____ TEST **GRAMMAR 93**

Contractions with *Not*

Circle the two words that make the contraction.

1. Greg isn't going on a trip.
   Greg (is not) going on a trip.

2. Greg isn't going to get a pack.
   Greg (is not) going to get a pack.

3. They aren't making a fire.
   They (are not) making a fire.

4. They aren't sleeping in a tent.
   They (are not) sleeping in a tent.

5. Greg isn't looking for the Big Dipper.
   Greg (is not) looking for the Big Dipper.

6. They aren't sleeping in a tent.
   They (are not) sleeping in a tent.

Book 1.3 *Let's Camp Out!*   93

GRAMMAR PRACTICE BOOK, PAGE 93

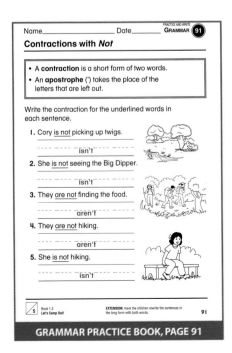

GRAMMAR PRACTICE BOOK, PAGE 94
139P

5 Day Spelling Plan

ESL Be sure to introduce spelling words by using each in a sentence. Use gestures, visuals, or realia to make sure ESL children understand what the word means. Monitor how children are pronouncing vowel sounds and give additional help as needed.

DAY 1 — Introduce Spelling Words

Assess Prior Knowledge Write the Spelling Words on the chalkboard and read them aloud with children. Ask children to match the words with these clues: gives us light and keeps us warm *(sun)*; tiny branches of a tree *(twigs)*; long pieces of wood *(sticks)*; rain that freezes in the sky *(snow)*; made of dirt and water *(mud)*; heat made by burning *(fire)*.

	Spelling Words		Challenge Words
1. **sticks**	4. **fire**	7. **try**	9. **eat**
2. **sun**	5. snow	8. **old**	10. **under**
3. **twigs**	6. mud		

*Note: Words in **dark type** are from the story.*

Write the Challenge Words on the chalkboard and read them aloud. Have volunteers use each word in a sentence.

Word Study On page 89 of the **Spelling Practice Book** are word study steps and an at-home activity.

DAY 2 — Teach the Pattern

Sort the Words Write the Spelling Words on the board in random order. Draw four columns and label them: Three Letters, Four Letters, Five Letters, and Six Letters. Encourage children to read each word aloud and suggest its appropriate column.

To extend the activity, give children cards with the following letters and word parts: *f, g, ire, sn, ow, m, d, st, i, ck, s, u, n,* and *tw.* Say *sticks.* Have children choose the cards that spell the word. Repeat for the remaining Spelling Words.

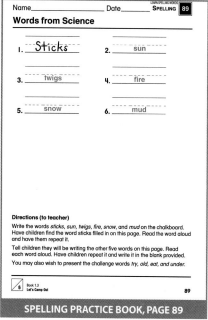

SPELLING PRACTICE BOOK, PAGE 89

WORD STUDY STEPS AND ACTIVITY, PAGE 90

SPELLING PRACTICE BOOK, PAGE 91

Words from Science

Word Meaning: Answer Riddles
Write the Spelling Words on the chalkboard. Have volunteers use the words to answer riddles. As a clue, tell how many letters the word has. For example:

- **It shines in the sky. (3)** sun
- **It burns. (4)** fire
- **You can ski on it. (4)** snow
- **It rhymes with *figs*. (5)** twigs

Identify the Words
Write the following sentences on the chalkboard and invite children to read them aloud with you: *We can use the sticks to make a fire. Then we can eat under the stars.* Ask volunteers to underline the Spelling and Challenge Words.

Complete Sentences
Write the following sentences on the chalkboard: *You can use _____ and _____ to make fire.* (sticks, twigs) *It feels hot when the _____ is out.* (sun) *The pig plays in the _____.* (mud) Invite children to use Spelling Words to complete each sentence. Have volunteers create sentences for remaining words.

WRITING Have children use as many spelling words as possible in the daily Writing Prompt on page 126F. Remind them to check their writing for errors in spelling, grammar, and punctuation.

Optional Spelling Test
You may wish to give children a spelling test. You may administer the test in the following manner: (1) Read the word. (2) Give a simple sentence containing the word. (3) Say the word again. Or you may use page 94 of the **Spelling Practice Book** for the posttest. If you wish, you may create additional sentences for the Challenge Words.

Personal Word List
If children are still having trouble with any words in the lesson, have them add to their "troublesome words" list in their journal. Have children illustrate each word. Children should refer to their word lists in future writing activities.

Name_____ Date_____ SPELLING 92

Words from Science

Look at each picture. Complete each sentence with a spelling word.

1. When the ___sun___ is out, it can be hot.
2. They make cakes out of _____ ___mud___ just for fun.
3. We can make a man out of ___snow___ .
4. A ___fire___ can make us warm.

Each spelling word below tells about more than one. Rewrite each word so that it tells about only one.

5. sticks ___stick___
6. twigs ___twig___

92

SPELLING PRACTICE BOOK, PAGE 92

Name_____ Date_____ SPELLING 93

Words from Science

Read the story. Use the spelling words to complete the story.

We like to hike when the ___sun___ is hot.

When it is wet, we sink into the ___mud___ . We carry big ___sticks___ so we will not fall.

We even hike when there is ___snow___ on the ground. We get lots of ___twigs___ from trees to make a ___fire___ . Then it is hot!

93

SPELLING PRACTICE BOOK, PAGE 93

Name_____ Date_____ SPELLING 94

Words from Science

Look at the words in each set. One word in each set is spelled correctly. Use a pencil to color in the circle in front of that word. Before you begin, look at the sample sets of words. Sample A has been done for you. Do Sample B by yourself. When you are sure you know what to do, you may go on with the rest of the page.

Sample A
- (A) think
- (B) tink
- (C) thingk

Sample B
- (D) came
- (E) cam
- (F) camme

1. (A) stics
   (B) stiks
   (C) sticks

2. (D) muhd
   (E) mudd
   (F) mud

3. (A) snow
   (B) sno
   (C) snoe

4. (D) fier
   (E) fire
   (F) frire

5. (A) tigs
   (B) twigs
   (C) twigz

6. (D) sun
   (E) sunn
   (F) sunne

94

SPELLING PRACTICE BOOK, PAGE 94

139R

Wrap Up the Theme

Stories to Tell

Each one of us has a different story to tell.

REVIEW THE THEME Remind children that all the selections in this unit relate to the theme Stories to Tell. Which story did children like best? Why? How were the stories different? How were they alike? Ask children to name other stories or movies they know that also fit the theme Stories to Tell.

READ THE POEM Read "You're an Author Now" by Kalli Dakos aloud to children. As they listen, ask children to think about how the child and the teacher in the poem feel about the child's writing. After reading, discuss how the poem connects to the theme Stories to Tell. Lead children to see that writing is one way that a person can tell his or her own story.

Reread the poem, having children echo the last word in each of the longer lines. Encourage children to listen to the rhymes.

LISTENING LIBRARY The poem is available on **audiocassette** and on **compact disc.**

MAKE CONNECTIONS Have children work in small groups to brainstorm a list of ways that the stories, poems, and the *Time for Kids* magazine article relate to the theme Stories to Tell.

Groups can then compare their lists as they share them with the class.

140

LOOKING AT GENRE

Have children review *Sam's Song* and *Snakes*. What makes *Sam's Song* fantasy? What makes *Snakes* nonfiction?

Help children list the key characteristics of each literary form or genre. Encourage children to give other examples of fiction and nonfiction.

FANTASY STORY *Sam's Song*	NONFICTION ARTICLE *Snakes*
• Characters are made up.	• Gives facts and information about a real subject.
• Animals could not talk or act this way in real life.	• Has no made-up characters.

You're an Author Now

I'm writing,
I'm writing,
I'm writing in my book.
I'm writing,
I'm writing,
Oh, Teacher, come and look.

You're writing,
You're writing,
I'm glad you've learned how.
You're writing,
You're writing,
You're an author now.

by Kalli Dakos

141

LEARNING ABOUT POETRY

Literary Devices: Repetition Read the poem aloud with children. Ask children what words are repeated in the poem. Discuss with children why the poet might have repeated these words. Point out that repeating the word *writing* expresses the child's excitement at having learned to write.

 Response Activity. As you read the poem, have children act out what the poem describes. Children can mime writing to the rhythm of the poem.

Research *and Inquiry*

Complete the Theme Project
GROUP Have children work in teams to complete their group project. Remind children that the information that they have gathered on their person or place can be presented in any creative way. Encourage children to share tasks so that each member of the team can contribute to the project.

Make a Classroom Presentation
Have teams take turns presenting their projects. Be sure to include time for questions from the audience.

Draw Conclusions Have children draw conclusions about what they learned from researching, preparing, and sharing their projects. Was the resource chart they made helpful? What other resources did they use? What conclusions have children reached about their topic? Finally, ask children if doing the project has changed their opinion of people or places in their neighborhood in any way.

Ask More Questions Would children like to learn the story of another person or place in their neighborhood? You might encourage the teams to continue their research and prepare another presentation.

Reading Media

OBJECTIVES Children will:

- recognize and read various types of media.
- compare one type of media to another.
- be aware that some messages try to influence the way they think and act.

BUILD BACKGROUND Ask children to think about the ways they get information. Encourage children to share their own experiences with billboards or television programs. Is there one particular billboard in their community or along a nearby highway that they especially like? What is their favorite television commercial? Why do they like that particular television commercial?

INTRODUCE Ask children to **preview** pages 142–143 by looking carefully at the pictures. Then **set puposes**. **Say:**

- One of these two pictures shows a billboard. The other shows a newspaper. Which is which?
- How are the billboard and the newspaper the same? How are they different? Explain that billboards and newspapers are both types of *media*. Tell children that the job of these and other kinds of media is to inform and entertain people.

Explain that there are basically two kinds of media. *Print media*—like billboards, newspapers, and magazines—use words and pictures to tell us things. *Nonprint media*—like television, movies, radio, and music CDs—use moving pictures and/or sound to tell us things. Both print and nonprint media can entertain us and give us information. **Say:**

- Some parts of the media, like movies, videos, and cartoons on television, are there to entertain us.
- Other parts of the media, like television news programs and the articles we see in the newspaper, are there to give us information.
- Still other parts of the media, like the advertisements we see on television, on billboards, and in magazines, are there to get us to do something, like buy a toy or be a good citizen.

PRACTICE/APPLY Read pages 142–143 aloud with children. **Say:**

- What topic are these two kinds of media telling us about?
- Which of the two kinds of media do you like better? Why?
- In the newspaper story, why do you think the children are spending their time picking up litter? (to make the park clean and beautiful again)
- How is the newspaper message different from the billboard message? (The newspaper uses small pictures and small print to tell a specific story. The billboard uses large pictures and large print to give a general message.)
- How are these messages the same? (They both encourage us not to litter.)
- Why do you think the topic of litter is written about in two different media? (There are different ways of pointing out the importance of something.)

LANGUAGE SUPPORT

ESL Help children with the terms *television, newspaper, magazine, billboard,* and *advertisement* by holding up pictures of these items while using the words orally in context. Invite children to choose one of the following and draw a picture of it: a television, a radio, a magazine cover, and a roadside billboard. Encourage them to label their picture according to the kind of media shown.

Reading for Information

Reading Media

READ TOGETHER

A billboard and a newspaper are both examples of media. Each tells us things in different ways.

A billboard tells us something with large pictures and large print.

A newspaper tells us things with small pictures and small print.

Town News
Fall Edition

Town Kids Show the Way

Children spent their Saturday picking up litter. Our town park looks beautiful again.

Questions

❶ Name two kinds of media.

❷ Which kind of media do you see more often?

142   Reading for Information

Reading Media   143

ANSWERS TO QUESTIONS

1. A billboard and a newspaper are two kinds of media.
2. We probably see billboards more than newpapers, because we pass them so often on buildings, streets, and highways.

TRANSFER THE STRATEGY Point out to children that we can use different media to do the same thing. For instance, if children wanted to find out what the weather would be like tomorrow, they might listen to the radio, watch the weather report on television, look for the weather report in today's newspaper, or find a weather website on the Internet. Or, if children wanted to be entertained, they could read a book or magazine, watch a television program or video, play a computer game, go to the movies, or listen to the radio or music CDs. Ask children to think about ways the media can influence them. Ask: What does a television commercial about a new toy make you want to do?

Make a Billboard

Help children come up with ideas for a billboard that persuades people to do something the children believe in, such as recycling or being kind to animals. (One example might be a billboard that encourages people to keep their dogs safe from traffic by keeping them on a leash when walking them.) Children could create individual versions of the billboard by making posters using crayons, colored paper, and other art materials.

VOCABULARY

GROUP Have a volunteer select a vocabulary word from the unit selections. Then have the other children ask *yes* or *no* questions in order to determine what the word is. Encourage them to ask definition-related questions, as opposed to spelling questions.

Unit Review

Stan's Stunt

try	their
fall	would

Greg's Mask

any	old
new	grow

Sam's Song

together	eat
now	too

Snakes

know	where
under	why

Let's Camp Out!

try	eat
old	under

Name_____ Date_____ Practice **125**

High-Frequency Words Review

Underline the word that tells about each picture.

1. The apple will _____.

   fall   rang

2. Let it _____.

   grow   jump

3. They _____ grapes.

   snag   **eat**

4. The _____ shack is red.

   old   new

5. He is _____ the tent.

   on   **under**

6. This is _____ pet pig.

   bad   **their**

PRACTICE BOOK, 125–126

GRAMMAR

Have partners write three sentences **PARTNERS** each about what they did before coming to school this morning. Then have them rewrite their own sentences, this time taking out all the verbs. Have them exchange papers with each other, and fill in the missing verbs.

Unit Review

Stan's Stunt
Verbs

Greg's Mask
Present Tense

Sam's Song
Past Tense

Snakes
Is and *Are*

Let's Camp Out!
Contractions with *Not*

Name_____ Date_____ GRAMMAR **95**

Verbs

Read the sentences in the box. Look at the part with the line under it. What is the best way to say this part? Mark the letter for your answer.

> Frog jumps. Jumping Stan. The others jump.
> (1)

1. Ⓐ Stan jumps.
   Ⓑ Stan jumping.
   Ⓒ Stan jump.

> Mom, Pop, and Chuck sing. Sam with them.
> (2)

2. Ⓐ Sam with Chuck sing.
   Ⓑ Pop and Sam sings.
   Ⓒ Sam sings with them.

> Owl blink. Stan watches Owl. Stan blinks like Owl.
> (3)

3. Ⓐ Owl blinks.
   Ⓑ Blink Owl.
   Ⓒ Owl blinking.

> Last night, I wanted to eat. I look for pizza.
> (4)

4. Ⓐ I looks for Pizza.
   Ⓑ I looked for pizza.
   Ⓒ Pizza for I look.

GRAMMAR PRACTICE BOOK, 95–96

SPELLING

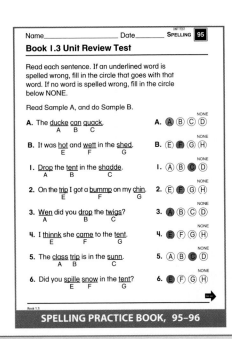

GROUP Give each of five groups the spelling words for one selection. Have one member of each group write a sentence that contains a spelling word on a sheet of paper. Then pass the paper to another group member who will do the same for a different spelling word. Continue until all the words are used.

Unit Review

Blends
bump
spill
tent

Long *a: a-e*
snake
came
shade

Blends
class
drop
trip

Science Words
sun
snow
twigs

ch, wh, nk
chin
when
think

SPELLING PRACTICE BOOK, 95–96

✓ SKILLS & STRATEGIES

Phonics and Decoding
☑ Blends
☑ Blends
☑ *ch, wh, nk*
☑ Long *a: a-e*

Comprehension
☑ Story Elements
☑ Compare and Contrast

Vocabulary Strategies
☑ Possessives
☑ Contractions

Study Skills
☑ Diagrams

Writing
Interactive Writing

MCGRAW-HILL READING

Unit Test

Student Name: _____

Date: _____

Grade 1 • Book 3

McGraw Hill

BOOK 3 ASSESSMENT

Assessment
Follow-Up

Use the results of the informal and formal assessment opportunities in the unit to help you make decisions about future instruction.

SKILLS AND STRATEGIES	Reteaching Blackline Masters	Alternate Teaching Strategies	Skills Intervention Guide
Phonics and Decoding			ⓘ
Blends: Continuant/Stop	85, 89, 90, 98, 106, 117	T64, T65	✓
Blends: Stop/Continuant	93, 97, 98, 106, 117	T69, T70	✓
ch, wh, nk	101, 105, 106, 114, 117	T72, T73	✓
Long *a: a-e*	109, 113, 114, 117	T75, T76	✓
Comprehension			
Story Elements	91, 115, 122	T67	✓
Compare and Contrast	99, 107	T71	✓
Vocabulary Strategies			
Possessives	92, 100, 123	T68	✓
Contractions	108, 116, 124	T74	✓
Study Skills			
Diagrams	88, 96, 104, 112, 120	T66	✓

Writing	Alternate Writing Project–Easy	
Interactive Writing	37N, 67N, 97N, 125N, 139N	

McGraw-Hill School
TECHNOLOGY

CD-ROM provides extra phonics support.

inter **NET**
CONNECTION
Research & Inquiry ideas. Visit **www.mhschool.com/reading.**

Glossary

Introduce children to the Glossary by inviting them to look through the pages, describing and discussing what they see there.

Explain that the Glossary will help them find out the meanings of words. Explain that the **Glossary** is a special kind of dictionary just for words from the selections in this book. You will probably want to give a simple definition of *dictionary*, such as: "a book that shows how words are spelled and what they mean."

Point out that words in a glossary, like words in a dictionary, are listed in **alphabetical order.** Explain that in this glossary, not all the letters of the alphabet are represented.

Point out the **entry words.** Ask children to note that each entry word is printed in heavy black type and that it appears on a line by itself. Also point out that each entry word is used in a sentence and is illustrated in a picture. Mention that there are two sentences for some of the words; in such cases, the second sentence includes a word that has the same meaning as the entry word. Also mention that each picture helps to make the meaning of the accompanying word clearer.

Give children time to study the Glossary and discover what information it includes.

Glossary

This glossary can help you to find out the meanings of words in this book that you may not know.

The words are listed in alphabetical order. There is a picture and a simple sentence for each word. You can use the picture and sentence to help you understand the meaning of each word.

Sample Entry

Main Entry   Sample Sentence

Branch

A bird is sitting on the **branch.**

Another word for **branch** is *limb.*

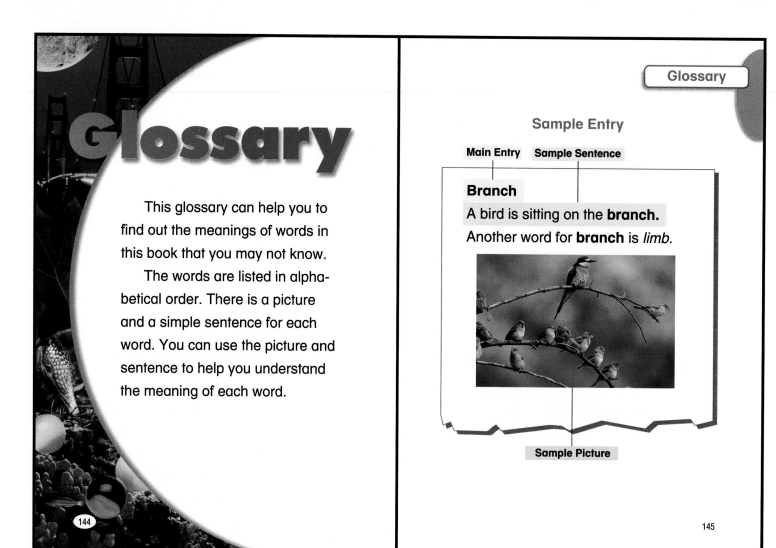

Sample Picture

Baby

The **baby** drinks from a bottle.

Branch

A bird is sitting on the **branch.**

Another word for **branch** is *limb.*

Eyes

Len sees with his **eyes.**

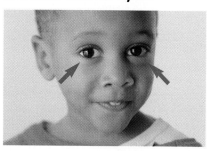

Fire

Be careful around the **fire.**

Glossary

Frog

The **frog** can hop.

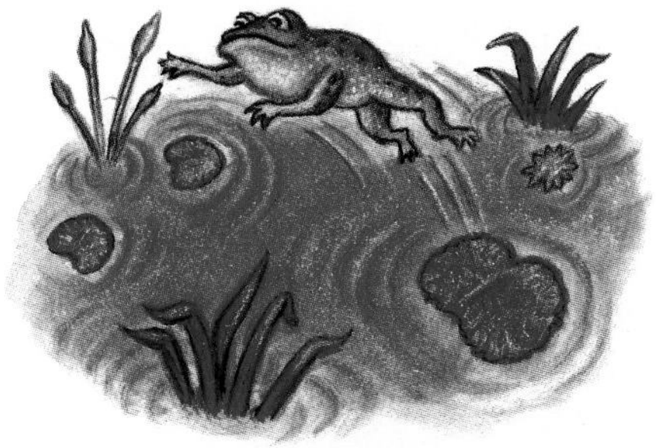

Mask

The **mask** covers Mark's face.

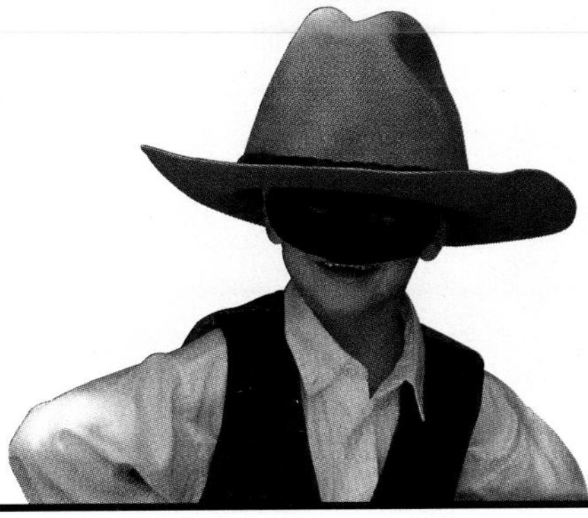

Glossary

Nest

The **nest** is the bird's home.

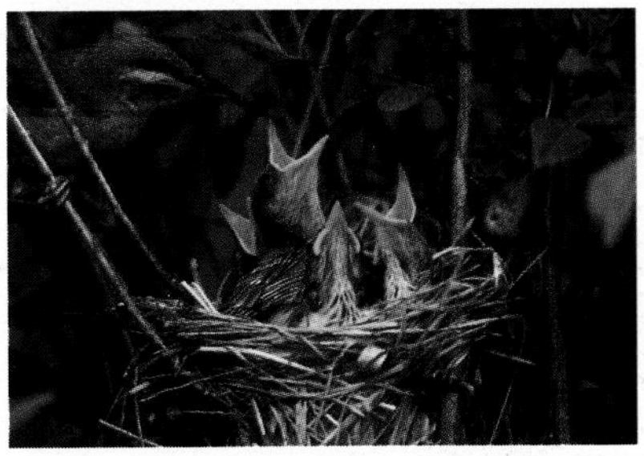

Nut

The squirrel cracks the **nut** to eat it.

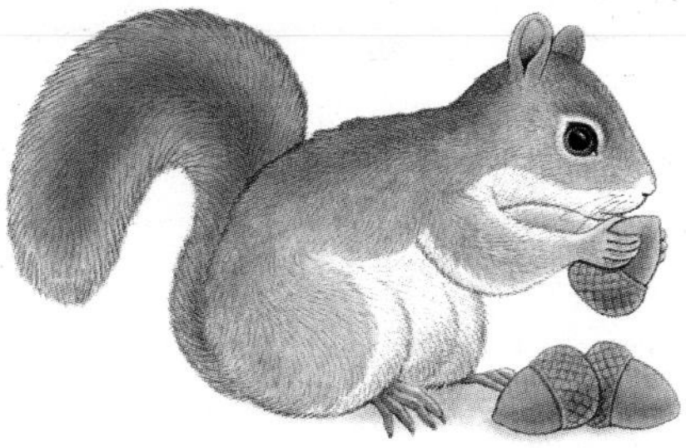

Glossary

Star

Wish upon a **star.**

Sun

The **sun** is shining brightly.

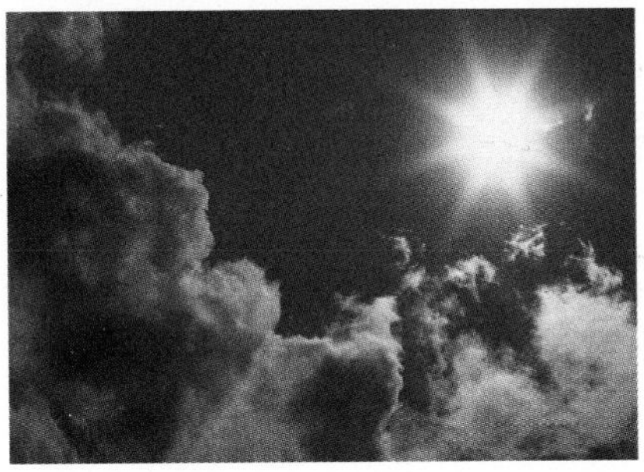

Glossary

Tail

This cat has a long **tail.**

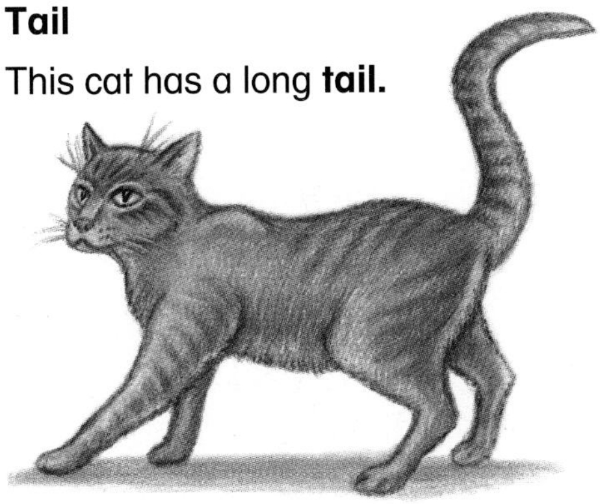

Tape

Tape holds things in place.

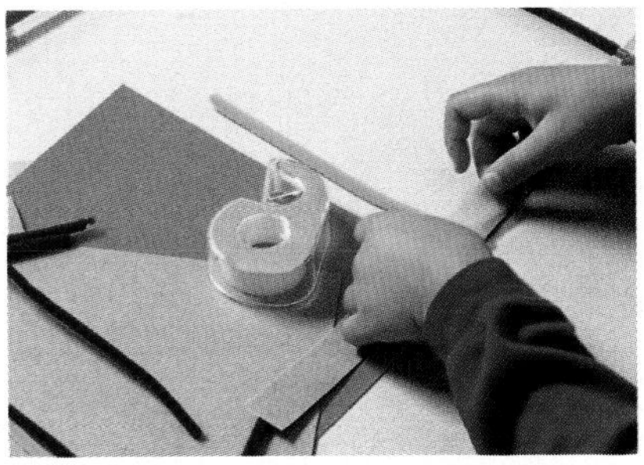

Tent

It can be fun to sleep in a **tent.**

Tooth

When your **tooth** gets loose,
it falls out.

152

Trash

Throw your **trash** out.

Another word for **trash** is *garbage.*

Wink

You use your eye when you **wink.**

153

Cover Illustration: Mary GrandPré

The publisher gratefully acknowledges permission to reprint the following copyrighted material:

"The Lion and the Mouse" by Aesop from THE BOOK OF VIRTUES by William J. Bennett. Copyright © 1993 by William J. Bennett. Used by permission of Simon and Schuster.

Making Faces" from TICKLE DAY by Charles Ghigna. Text copyright © 1994 by Charles Ghigna. Illustrations copyright © 1994 by Cyd Moore. Used by permission of Hyperion Books for Children.

"The Night We Slept Outside" by Anne Rockwell and Harlow Rockwell. Copyright © 1983 by Anne Rockwell and Harlow Rockwell. Used by permission of Aladdin Books, Macmillan Publishing Company.

"On Our Way" from CATCH A LITTLE RHYME by Eve Merriam. Copyright © 1966 by Eve Merriam. Reprinted by permission of Marian Reiner for the author.

"The Plumage of the Owl" from THE THREE WISHES by Ricardo E. Alegría. Copyright © 1969 by Ricardo E. Alegría. Used by permission of the author.

"The Snake" from DOGS & DRAGONS, TREES & DREAMS by Karla Kuskin. Copyright © 1980 by Karla Kuskin. Used by permission of HarperCollins Publishers.

ZB Font Method Copyright © 1996 Zaner-Bloser. Manuscript handwriting models. Used by permission.

Art/Illustrations
Linda Weller, 8D, 38C, 38H, 98D, 98H, 126H

Photography
All photographs are by Macmillan/McGraw-Hill (MMH); Clara Aich for MMH; Ken Karp for MMH; Dave Mager for MMH; Mike Provost for MMH; and John Serafin for MMH.

The publisher gratefully acknowledges permission to reprint the following copyrighted material:

"Something About Me," anonymous from READ-ALOUD RHYMES FOR THE VERY YOUNG. Copyright © 1986 by Alfred A. Knopf, Inc. Illustrations copyright © 1986 by Marc Brown. Reprinted by permission of Alfred A. Knopf.

"You're an Author Now" by Kalli Dakos from MRS. COLE ON AN ONION ROLL AND OTHER SCHOOL POEMS. Text copyright © 1995 Kalli Dakos. Reprinted with the permission of Simon & Schuster Books for Young Readers, an imprint of Simon & Schuster Children's Publishing Division.

Illustration
Helen Ward, 6–7; Randall Enos, 8–9; Pam Levy, 10–33, 35cl; Daniel Del Valle, 34br, 35cr, 64b, 94b, 122br, 123cr; Bernard Adnet, 37, 125; Jean Hirashima, 38–39; Winky Adam, 40–63; 64tl, 64cr, 65c; Eldon Doty, 67–69, 139; Melissa Iwai, 70–93, 94cr, 95br; John Chinn, 96; Ken Bowser, 97br; Mas Miyamoto, 97tr; Bill Mayer, 98–99; Angela Adams, 124, 126–7; Nancy Tobin, 137; Menny Borovski, 138; John Hovell, 140–1; Felipe Galindo, 146, 152, 153; Peter Fasolino, 148, 151; John Carozza, 149.

Photography
5: c.r. Corbis/David Northcolt. 10 b. Photo courtesy of the artist. 10: t. Seth Knowles. 36: PhotoDisc, Inc./Photodisc. 40: t. Kirchoff/Wohlberg 212-644-2020. 40: b. Courtesy of the artist. 70: b. Courtesy Melissa Iwai. t. Photo Credit: Kirchoff/Wohlberg, Inc.; 100: t. Courtesy of Frances Minters. 100–101: Tim Davis/Tony Stone. 102: i. Stephen Collins/Photo Researchers. 102: Michael Habicht/Animals Animals. 103: t. Michael and Patricia Fogden/Corbis. 103: b. PhotoDisc. 104–105: Joseph Bailey/National Geographic. 105 t. Joe McDonald/Animals Animals. 105: b. F. Stuart Westmorland/Photo Researchers. 106: Michael Fogden/Animals Animals. 107: Michael Fogden/Animals Animals. 108: Paul Chesley/Tony Stone. 109: OSF K. Atkinson/Animals Animals. 110: Michael Fogden/Animals Animals. 111: David Northcolt/Corbis. 111: i. Joe McDonald/Animals Animals. 112: Zig Leszczynski/Animals Animals. 113: Zig Leszczynski/Animals Animals. 113: Zig Leszczynski/Animals Animals. 114: t. Michael Fogden/Animals Animals. 114: b. Gregory Dimijian, MD/Photo Researchers. 115: Tom Bean/Tony Stone. 116: Zig Leszczynski/Animals Animals. 116–117: Zig Leszczynski/Animals Animals. 118: Bill Beatty/Animals Animals. 119: Zig Leszczynski/Animals Animals. 120–121: David J. Sams/Tony Stone. 122: b.l. Gregory Dimijian, MD/Photo Researchers. 123: t.r. David Northcolt/Corbis. 131: c.l. Gilbert S. Grant/Photo Researchers. 131: c.r. Spencer Grant/Photo Researchers. 134: b. S. Nielsen/Bruce Coleman. 144: l. PhotoDisc. 145: Zefa Germany/The Stock Market. 146: b. Zefa Germany/The Stock Market. 146: b. The Stock Market/U–AT. 147: V. Jackson/Photo Network. 147: t. Steve Prezant/The Stock Market. 148: b. Bokelberg/GJ Images/The Image Bank. 149: The Stock Market/Zefa Germany. 150: b. Tim Brown/Tony Stone. 150: t.l. Derke/O'Hara/Tony Stone Images. 152: b. David Stoecklein/The Stock Market. 153: PhotoDisc. : Kirchoff/Wohlberg.

READING FOR INFORMATION
All photographs are by Macmillan/McGraw-Hill (MMH); Ken Karp for MMH; Dave Mager for MMH; and Lawrence Migdale for MMH, except as noted below:
Illustration
142–143: Bernand Adnet

Backmatter Contents

Read Aloud Selections T2

Annotated Workbooks T6

Alternate Teaching Strategies T64

Handwriting T78

Teachers' Resources

Awards, Authors
  and Illustrators T94
Theme Bibliography T98
Directory of Resources T100

Word List T102
Scope and Sequence T114
Index T122

Scoring Chart T128

The Lion and the Mouse
from a fable by Aesop

One day a great lion lay asleep in the sunshine. A little mouse ran across his paw and wakened him. The great lion was just going to eat him up when the little mouse cried, "Oh, please, let me go, sir. Some day I may help you."

The lion laughed at the thought that the little mouse could be of any use to him. But he was a good-natured lion, and he set the mouse free.

Not long after, the lion was caught in a net. He tugged and pulled with all his might, but the ropes were too strong. Then he roared loudly. The little mouse heard him, and ran to the spot.

"Be still, dear Lion, and I will set you free. I will gnaw the ropes."

With his sharp little teeth, the mouse cut the ropes, and the lion came out of the net.

"You laughed at me once, " said the mouse. "You thought I was too little to do you a good turn. But see, you owe your life to a poor little mouse."

Making Faces
Charles Ghigna

Draw a big circle,
Put a nose in place,
Add two ears
To your funny face.

Long hair, short hair
On its head?
Black hair, blond hair,
Brown or red?

Blue eyes, brown eyes,
Glasses or not,
Give it a smile
And what have you got?

A lady? A man?
A boy or a girl?
A bald-headed daddy?
A baby with a curl?

Look at the face
That you drew.
Now look in the mirror—
Is it you?

The Plumage of the Owl
El Plumaje del Mucaro
a Puerto Rican folk tale retold by Ricardo E. Alegría

A long time ago, the animals used to give parties and balls and have good times together. At this time the birds decided to give a ball, and they invited all the bird family to come. The hawk was in charge of issuing the invitations, and he called upon each bird to invite him personally.

When he came to the owl's house, he found him naked. The owl told him that he could not come to the ball as he had no clothes to wear. The hawk told the other birds about this, and they decided that each one of them would lend the owl a feather so that he could make a dress suit and come to the ball.

The hawk collected feathers of different colors from each and took them to the owl but told him that, after the ball was over, each feather was to be returned to its owner. The owl was delighted with the feathers. He made himself a fine dress suit and appeared at the ball.

▶ But the owl was very vain, and so pleased was he with the suit of many colors that he could hardly enjoy the ball for thinking of how he would be naked again after it ended, when he had to return all the fine feathers. When no one was looking, he left the ball and hid in the forest.

The other birds are still looking for him; they want their feathers back. And this is why the owl is never seen by day, only at night when the other birds are sleeping.

The Snake
Karla Kuskin

A snake slipped through the thin green grass
A silver snake
I watched it pass
It moved like a ribbon
Silent as snow.
I think it smiled.
As it passed my toe.

▶ Continue reading here.

The Night We Slept Outside

Anne and Harlow Rockwell

I was right.

On Friday we asked Mom again.

"Well," she said, "you have been very good all week."

"You have put away your things and done your homework."

"And we have our sleeping bags," I said.

"All right," said Mom. "You may sleep outside tonight for a special treat."

"Terrific!" I said.

"Great!" said Robert.

That night, when it was time for bed, Robert and I took our sleeping bags out of the closet.

We put them outside on the deck.

We put on our shorts, and I put on my T-shirt with a picture of a grizzly bear on it.

"Aren't you going to put on your pajamas?" said Mom.

"No," I said.

"We are having an adventure.

You don't wear pajamas on an adventure."

"Of course not," said Robert.

"All right," said Mom.

"But don't forget to brush your teeth."

"We will do that outside," said Robert.

And we did. We brushed our teeth at the outside faucet.

We filled a thermos bottle with water.

Mom kissed us good-night and went into the house.

We crawled into our sleeping bags and looked up at the sky.

We could see so many stars!

We tried to find the ones whose names we knew.

Our neighbor's lights went out.

The lights in our house went out.

It was very dark except for the stars.

"This is fun," I said to Robert.

"It sure is," he said to me.

Stan's Stunt • PRACTICE

Name______________ Date________ **Practice 85**

Blends

Sound out and say each word. Print the word on the line. Then circle the picture it names.

1. spin

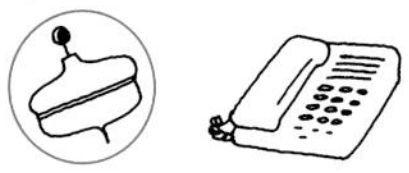

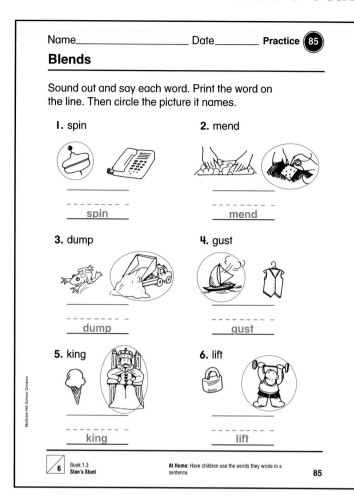

spin

2. mend

mend

3. dump

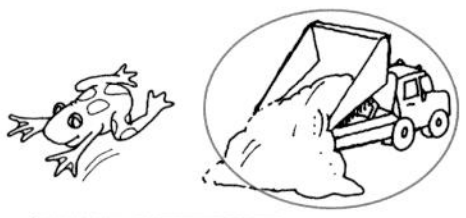

dump

4. gust

gust

5. king

king

6. lift

lift

McGraw-Hill School Division

At Home: Have children use the words they wrote in a sentence.

Name______________ Date________ **Practice 86**

High-Frequency Words

try	fall	their	would

Look at the picture. Choose a word from the box to finish each sentence.

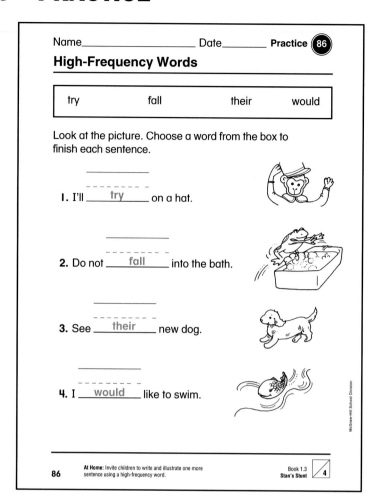

1. I'll try on a hat.

2. Do not fall into the bath.

3. See their new dog.

4. I would like to swim.

McGraw-Hill School Division

At Home: Invite children to write and illustrate one more sentence using a high-frequency word.

The Raft

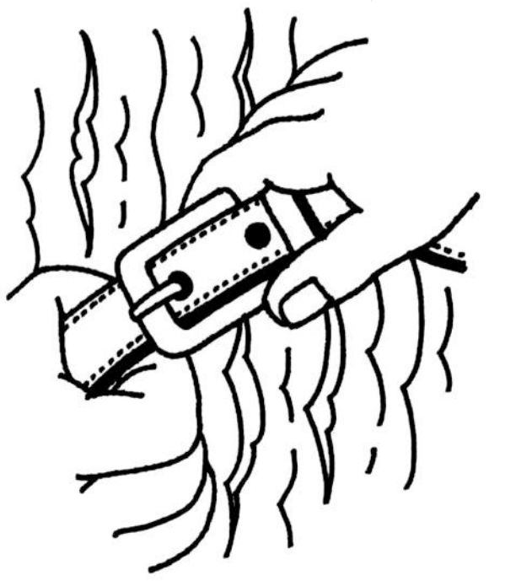

The man held a belt for Jack to grab. Jack got it.
The man got Jack and Pam back to their camp. Pam and Jack had a rest. It was good to be off the raft!

At Home: Have children tell about a trip they took. Was it fun? What was special about it?

Pam and Jack had a raft. They got on. Their raft went fast. Pam and Jack did not see the log. The raft hit the log. It made Jack jump. Pam saw him fall into the water.

Stan's Stunt McGraw-Hill School Division

Pam held out a vest. Jack put it on. He said he would try to get back on the raft. But he saw the raft would tilt if he did.
Then a man by a tent saw them.

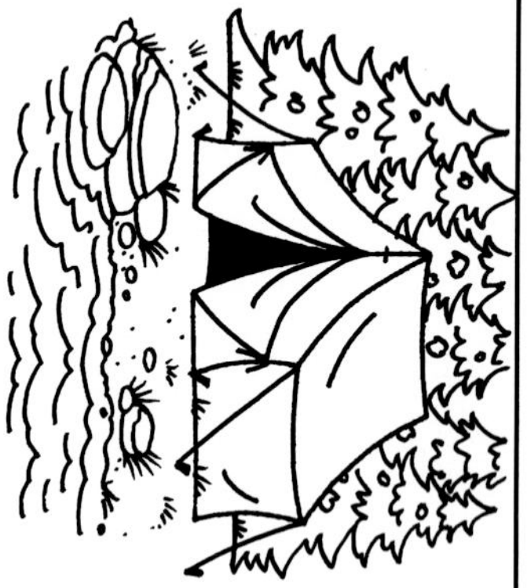

Stan's Stunt • PRACTICE

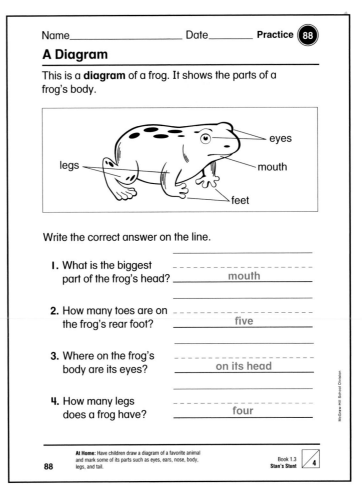
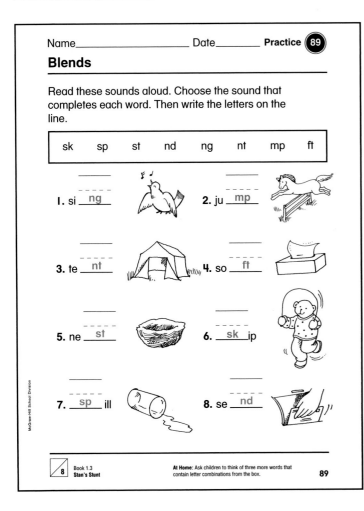
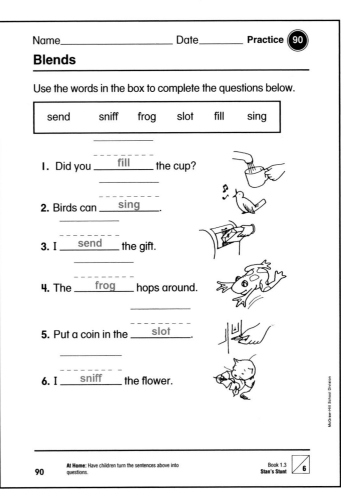

Stan's Stunt • PRACTICE

Possessives

Name_____ Date_____ Practice 92

Apostrophe (') s at the end of a name or thing means that the person or thing owns something.

Write the words to show who owns something. Remember to add **'s**.

1. Jack cat Jack's cat

2. bird nest bird's nest

3. Kim ship Kim's ship

4. king gems king's gems

5. Tom lamp Tom's lamp

6. dog stick dog's stick

92

At Home: Invite children to illustrate a few of the examples above.

Book 1.3 **Stan's Stunt** 6

T8 *Annotated Workbooks*

Stan's Stunt • RETEACH

Blends

Read these words.

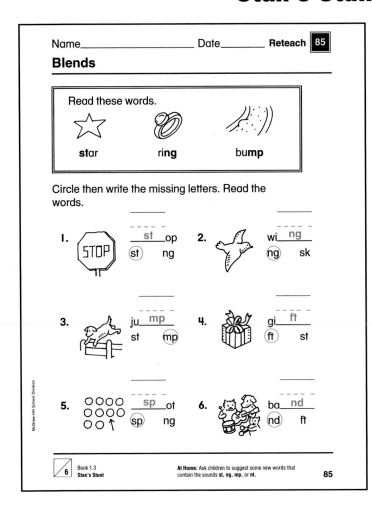

star   ri**ng**   bu**mp**

Circle then write the missing letters. Read the words.

1. _st_op
    (st)   ng

2. wi_ng_
    (ng)   sk

3. ju_mp_
    st   (mp)

4. gi_ft_
    (ft)   st

5. _sp_ot
    (sp)   ng

6. ba_nd_
    (nd)   ft

Book 1.3
6   **Stan's Stunt**
At Home: Ask children to suggest some new words that contain the sounds **st, ng, mp,** or **nt.**
85

High-Frequency Words

try	fall	their	would

Write the word from the box that completes each sentence.

1. She _____would_____ like a glass of milk.

2. I _____try_____ to lift the pot.

3. Jim and Jen look for _____their_____ dog.

4. The apples _____fall_____ from the tree.

86
At Home: Use the underlined words to make flash cards. Take turns with children choosing cards and making up sentences with the words.
Book 1.3
Stan's Stunt   4

Story Comprehension

Think about "Stan's Stunt." Then color the picture that answers the question.

1. What is Frog's stunt?   2. What is Owl's stunt?

3. What is Bat's stunt?   4. What do Owl and Frog do when Stan's tail goes up?

5. What is Stan's stunt?

Book 1.3
5   **Stan's Stunt**
At Home: Have children write a caption for each of the pictures they colored in.
87

A Diagram

A **diagram** is a picture that explains something. This diagram shows the parts of a bat's body.

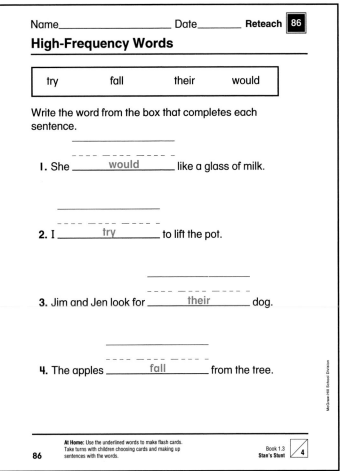

Underline the word that best completes each sentence.

1. The bat has very large ___.
   eyes   ears

2. There are two ___ on the bat.
   mouths   wings

3. The bat has one ___.
   mouth   ear

4. The wings on the bat are like___.
   legs   arms

88
At Home: Have children point to and name the parts of the bat shown in the diagram.
Book 1.3
Stan's Stunt   4

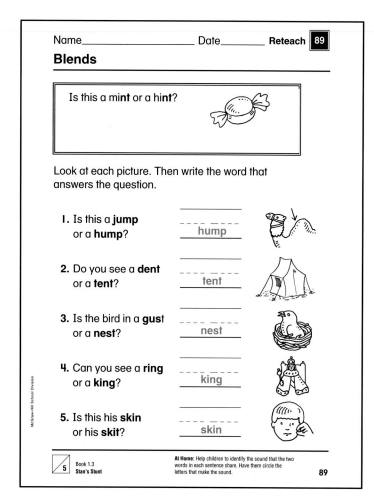

Name_____ Date_____ **Reteach** 89

Blends

Is this a m**int** or a h**int**?

Look at each picture. Then write the word that answers the question.

1. Is this a **jump** or a **hump**? _____ hump
2. Do you see a **dent** or a **tent**? _____ tent
3. Is the bird in a **gust** or a **nest**? _____ nest
4. Can you see a **ring** or a **king**? _____ king
5. Is this his **skin** or his **skit**? _____ skin

Book 1.3
Stan's Stunt
At Home: Help children to identify the sound that the two words in each sentence share. Have them circle the letters that make the sound.
89

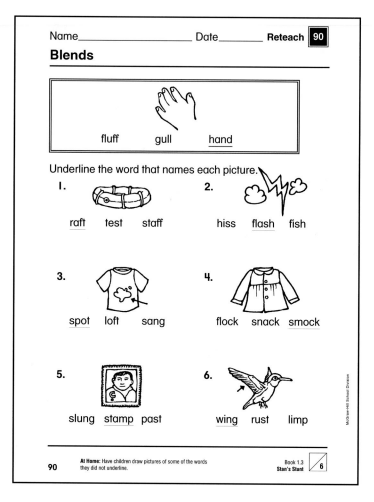

Name_____ Date_____ **Reteach** 90

Blends

fluff   gull   <u>hand</u>

Underline the word that names each picture.

1. <u>raft</u>   test   staff
2. hiss   <u>flash</u>   fish
3. <u>spot</u>   loft   sang
4. flock   snack   <u>smock</u>
5. slung   <u>stamp</u>   past
6. <u>wing</u>   rust   limp

90
At Home: Have children draw pictures of some of the words they did not underline.
Book 1.3
Stan's Stunt

Name_____ Date_____ **Reteach** 91

Story Elements

The time and place of a story is called the **setting.**

Read the story. Look at the pictures. Circle the things you might see at or near Ann's home.

Ann's Home
Let's go to Ann's farm. She has a lot of pets. I see her milk a cow. She gets eggs from the hen. She puts her dog in the bath. Then she sits by the tree to sing.

Book 1.3
Stan's Stunt
At Home: Have children draw a picture of Ann's house. Then have them tell their own story about what goes on there.
91

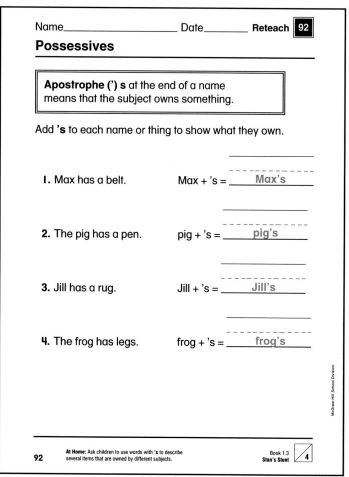

Name_____ Date_____ **Reteach** 92

Possessives

Apostrophe (') s at the end of a name means that the subject owns something.

Add **'s** to each name or thing to show what they own.

1. Max has a belt.   Max + 's = _____ Max's
2. The pig has a pen.   pig + 's = _____ pig's
3. Jill has a rug.   Jill + 's = _____ Jill's
4. The frog has legs.   frog + 's = _____ frog's

92
At Home: Ask children to use words with 's to describe several items that are owned by different subjects.
Book 1.3
Stan's Stunt

Stan's Stunt • EXTEND

Blends

Add 2 letters on each side to make words.
Choose letters from the box.

st	sp	sw	mp	ng	ft	nt

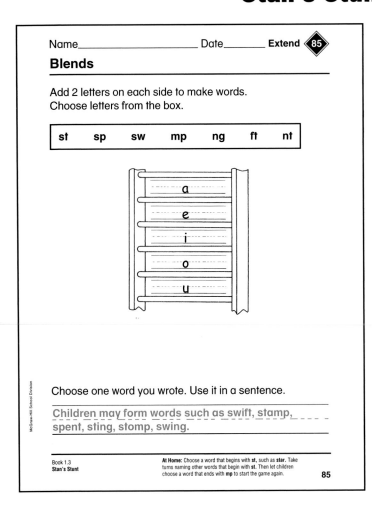

a

e

i

o

u

Choose one word you wrote. Use it in a sentence.

Children may form words such as swift, stamp,
spent, sting, stomp, swing.

Book 1.3
Stan's Stunt

At Home: Choose a word that begins with **st**, such as **star**. Take
turns naming other words that begin with **st**. Then let children
choose a word that ends with **mp** to start the game again.

85

High-Frequency Words

Draw an **X** on the picture that does **not** go with the
sentence.
Two dogs try a stunt.

The cat may fall.

The owls blink their eyes.

What stunt would a duck do?
Write a sentence.

Children should cross out the two dogs eating
from the dish, the cat standing on the ground,
and the owl blinking one eye.

86

At Home: Write the words **try, fall, their,** and **would** on
index cards. Place the cards face down. Take turns choosing
cards and using the word in a sentence.

Book 1.3
Stan's Stunt

Story Comprehension

Put on a play. Work with a group.
Will you be Stan or Owl or Frog or Bat?
Make a mask to show who you are.
You will need:

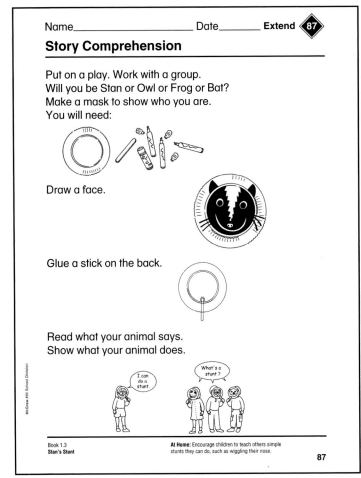

Draw a face.

Glue a stick on the back.

Read what your animal says.
Show what your animal does.

Book 1.3
Stan's Stunt

At Home: Encourage children to teach others simple
stunts they can do, such as wiggling their nose.

87

Use a Diagram

Unscramble each word.
Use the words in the box for help.
Write the words on the lines.

head	tail	claws	body	eyes	nose	paws

DEAH _____head_____   ITAL _____tail_____

SLCAW _____claws_____   DBOY _____body_____

YEES _____eyes_____   SONE _____nose_____

SPAW _____paws_____

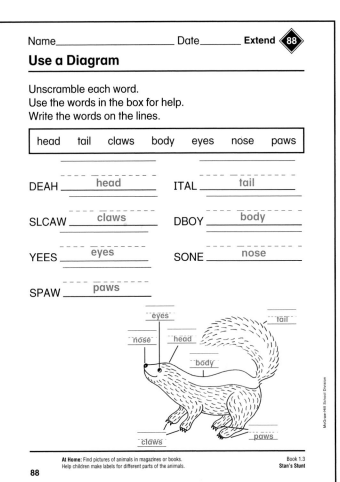

At Home: Find pictures of animals in magazines or books.
Help children make labels for different parts of the animals.

88

Book 1.3
Stan's Stunt

Blends

Name_____ Date_____ Extend 89

| spell | swing | thump | mend | stuck |

Circle the five words

```
A   B   K  (S  P  E  L  L)
X  (M  E  N  D)  B  U  Q
(T  H  U  M  P)  Z  X  V
G   H   L  (S  T  U  C  K)
O   A  (S  W  I  N  G)  U
```

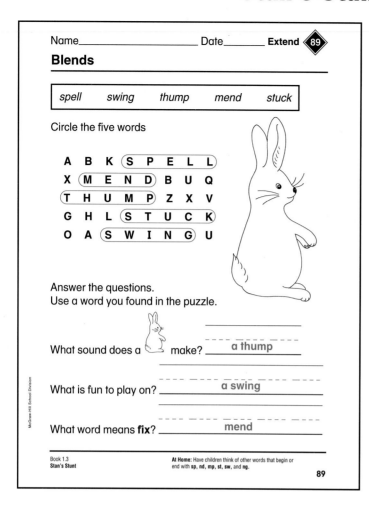

Answer the questions.
Use a word you found in the puzzle.

What sound does a 🐰 make? __a thump__

What is fun to play on? __a swing__

What word means **fix**? __mend__

At Home: Have children think of other words that begin or end with sp, nd, mp, st, sw, and ng.

89

Blends

Name_____ Date_____ Extend 90

Find fish with words that start with **st, sp,** and **sk.** Color the fish red.
Find fish with words that end with **ng, nd,** and **ft.** Color the fish blue.

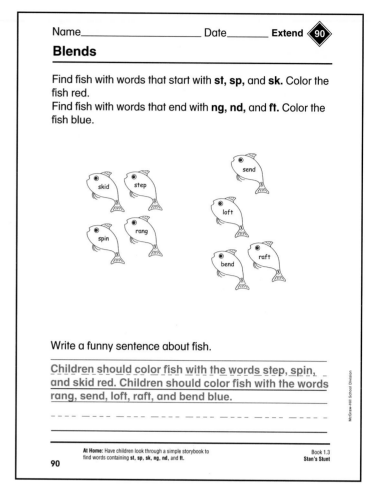

Write a funny sentence about fish.

__Children should color fish with the words step, spin,__
__and skid red. Children should color fish with the words__
__rang, send, loft, raft, and bend blue.__

At Home: Have children look through a simple storybook to find words containing st, sp, sk, ng, nd, and ft.

90

Story Elements

Name_____ Date_____ Extend 91

Read the sentences. Put a ✔ if the sentence tells about the picture.

- ✔ The frog is in the woods.
- ✔ It is night.
- ☐ The owl is in the zoo.
- ☐ It is day.
- ☐ The sun is shining.
- ✔ The moon is in the sky.
- ✔ The trees are tall.

Write another sentence about the picture.

_____

At Home: Have children cut out a magazine photograph or draw a picture of a scene. Help children fill out a chart describing the setting. Use these headings: When Where Details.

91

Possessives

Name_____ Date_____ Extend 92

Read the words. Draw the pictures.

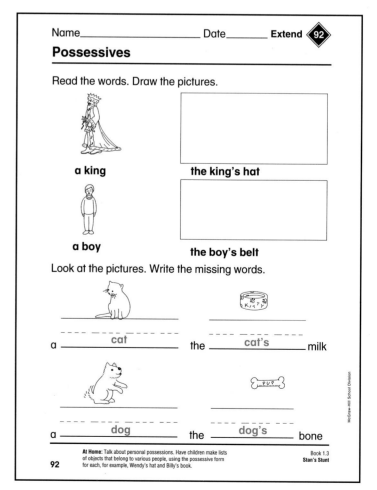

a king   **the king's hat**

a boy   **the boy's belt**

Look at the pictures. Write the missing words.

a __cat__   the __cat's__ milk

a __dog__   the __dog's__ bone

92

At Home: Talk about personal possessions. Have children make lists of objects that belong to various people, using the possessive form for each, for example, Wendy's hat and Billy's book.

Verbs

- A **verb** is a word that shows action.

Frog (**jumps**)
↓
(**verb**)

Owl (**blinks**)
↓
(**verb**)

Read the sentences.
Draw a circle around the verbs.

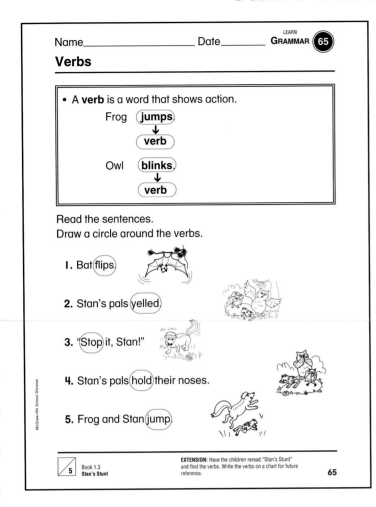

1. Bat (flips)

2. Stan's pals (yelled)

3. "(Stop) it, Stan!"

4. Stan's pals (hold) their noses.

5. Frog and Stan (jump)

McGraw-Hill School Division

| Book 1.3 **Stan's Stunt** | EXTENSION: Have the children reread "Stan's Stunt" and find the verbs. Write the verbs on a chart for future reference. | 65 |

Verbs

- A **verb** is a word that shows action.

I (**draw**) skunks.
↓
(**verb**)

You (**sleep**) in a tent.
↓
(**verb**)

Look at the pictures.
Find the stunts.
Draw a circle around the words that tell about the actions.

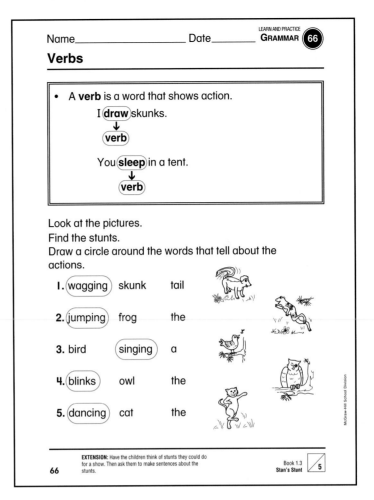

1. (wagging) skunk tail

2. (jumping) frog the

3. bird (singing) a

4. (blinks) owl the

5. (dancing) cat the

McGraw-Hill School Division

| 66 | EXTENSION: Have the children think of stunts they could do for a show. Then ask them to make sentences about the stunts. | Book 1.3 **Stan's Stunt** 5 |

Writing Verbs in Sentences

- A **verb** is a word that shows action.

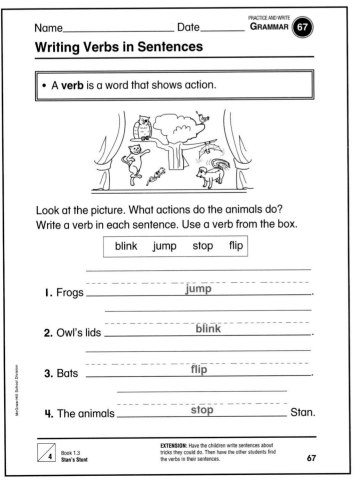

Look at the picture. What actions do the animals do?
Write a verb in each sentence. Use a verb from the box.

| blink | jump | stop | flip |

1. Frogs _____ **jump** _____.

2. Owl's lids _____ **blink** _____.

3. Bats _____ **flip** _____.

4. The animals _____ **stop** _____ Stan.

McGraw-Hill School Division

| Book 1.3 **Stan's Stunt** | EXTENSION: Have the children write sentences about tricks they could do. Then have the other students find the verbs in their sentences. | 67 |

Commas in a Letter

- Use a comma after the greeting in a letter.

Dear Grandmother,

- Use a comma after the closing in a letter.

Love,

Rick

Make a comma after each greeting. Make a comma after each closing.

Dear Kyle,
    I like to read. The bat in our book flips.
                Your friend,
                Catherine

Dear Ann,
    We enjoy our stunts. We jump like frogs.
                Your friend,
                Megan

McGraw-Hill School Division

| 68 | | Book 1.3 **Stan's Stunt** 4 |

Stan's Stunt • GRAMMAR

Name_____ Date_____ **TEST GRAMMAR** 69

Test

Read the sentences. Circle the verbs.

1. I (jump) all day.

2. Owl's lids (blink).

3. I (see) Owl's stunt.

4. (Look) at Stan's tail.

5. The animals (stop) Stan.

6. Stan and frog (bump).

7. (Draw) the animals.

8. I (read) books.

McGraw-Hill School Division

8 / Book 1.3
Stan's Stunt

69

Name_____ Date_____ **MORE PRACTICE GRAMMAR** 70

More Practice with Verbs

> • A **verb** is a word that shows action.

> **Mechanics:**
> • Use a comma after the greeting and the closing in a letter.

Find the verb. Write the verb to make a sentence.

1. Stan _____ **jumps** _____.

   the   jumps   red

2. Owl _____ **blinks** _____.

   blinks   on   frog

   _____

3. Owl _____ **plays** _____ with Frog.

   stunt   plays   the

Put the missing commas in this letter.

Dear Stan,
   Please stop your stunt.
                 Your friend,
                 Frog

McGraw-Hill School Division

70

Book 1.3
Stan's Stunt / 5

Stan's Stunt • SPELLING

Name_____ Date_____

Words with Blends

Complete each word by writing the letters **mp**, **nt**, or **sp** on the line.

1. bu **mp**

2. we ___ nt

3. ___ sp ___ ill

4. ju ___ mp

5. te ___ nt

6. ___ sp ___ ell

Directions (to teacher)

Write the word *bump* on the chalkboard or form the word with letter cards. Say the word aloud and have children repeat it. Have them listen for the sounds /m/ and /p/ together at the end of the word. Then have them look at the first example. Point out that *mp* has been filled in.

Display the word *went*. Say the word and have children repeat it. Ask them to listen for the two sounds at the end of the word (/n/ and /t/). Have them complete the second example.

Display the word *spill* and repeat the process above, having students listen for the sounds at the beginning of the word (/s/ and /p/). Have them complete the third example.

Then display the words *jump, tent,* and *spell*. Say the words and have children repeat them. Have children listen for /mp/, /nt/, or /sp/ in each word. Then have them complete the page.

Name_____ Date_____

Words with Blends

Using the Word Study Steps

1. LOOK at the word.
2. SAY the word aloud.
3. STUDY the letters in the word.
4. WRITE the word.
5. CHECK the word.
   Did you spell the word right? If not, go back to step 1.

> **Spelling Tip**
>
> Rhyming words are often spelled alike. A word you know can help you spell a new word.
>
> w + ent = went
> t + ent = tent

Word Scramble

Unscramble each set of letters to make a spelling word.

1. mbup ___ bump

2. nett ___ tent

3. lpsil ___ spill

4. tenw ___ went

5. pjmu ___ jump

6. lpsel ___ spell

To Parents or Helpers:
Using the Word Study Steps above as your child comes across any new words will help him or her spell well. Review the steps as you both go over this week's spelling words.
Go over the Spelling Tip with your child. Ask if he or she knows other words that rhyme with the spelling words. Help your child write new words that rhyme with the word he or she wants to spell.
Help your child complete the spelling activity.

Name_____ Date_____

Words with Blends

Look at the spelling words in the box.

tent bump spell jump spill went

Write the words that end with **mp**.

1. ___ bump

2. ___ jump

Write the words that end with **nt**.

3. ___ went

4. ___ tent

Write the words that begin with **sp**.

5. ___ spill

6. ___ spell

Name_____ Date_____

Words with Blends

Look at the picture. Write two rhyming spelling words to complete the sentences.

1. Dad and I ___ went camping.

2. We slept in a ___ tent.

Look at the spelling words in the box.

bump   jump   spill   spell

Write a spelling word to complete each sentence. Add s to each word.

3. Pat ___ spills a cup of milk.

4. Sam ___ jumps up and down.

5. He ___ bumps his leg on a rock.

6. Pam ___ spells the words well.

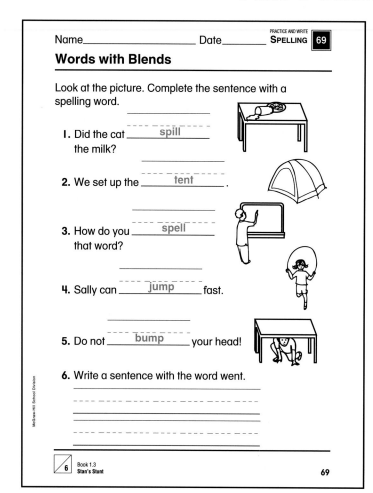

Name_____ Date_____ **PRACTICE AND WRITE** **SPELLING** `69`

Words with Blends

Look at the picture. Complete the sentence with a spelling word.

1. Did the cat _____ spill _____ the milk?

2. We set up the _____ tent _____.

3. How do you _____ spell _____ that word?

4. Sally can _____ jump _____ fast.

5. Do not _____ bump _____ your head!

6. Write a sentence with the word went.

_____

_____

_____

`6` Book 1.3 **Stan's Stunt** 69

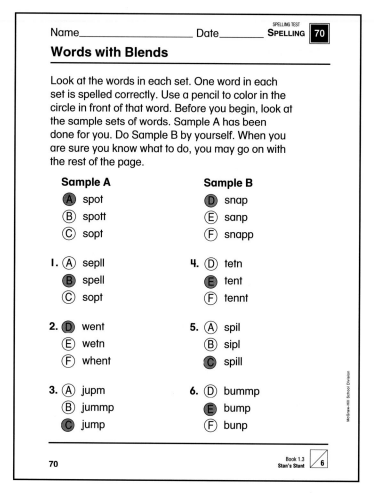

Name_____ Date_____ **SPELLING TEST** **SPELLING** `70`

Words with Blends

Look at the words in each set. One word in each set is spelled correctly. Use a pencil to color in the circle in front of that word. Before you begin, look at the sample sets of words. Sample A has been done for you. Do Sample B by yourself. When you are sure you know what to do, you may go on with the rest of the page.

Sample A
- (A) spot
- (B) spott
- (C) sopt

Sample B
- (D) snap
- (E) sanp
- (F) snapp

1.
- (A) sepll
- (B) spell
- (C) sopt

4.
- (D) tetn
- (E) tent
- (F) tennt

2.
- (D) went
- (E) wetn
- (F) whent

5.
- (A) spil
- (B) sipl
- (C) spill

3.
- (A) jupm
- (B) jummp
- (C) jump

6.
- (D) bummp
- (E) bump
- (F) bunp

70 Book 1.3 **Stan's Stunt** `6`

Practice 93

Name_____ Date_____ Practice **93**

Blends

Read each of the blends. Write one blend to complete the name of each picture.

tw	pl	pr	cr	tr

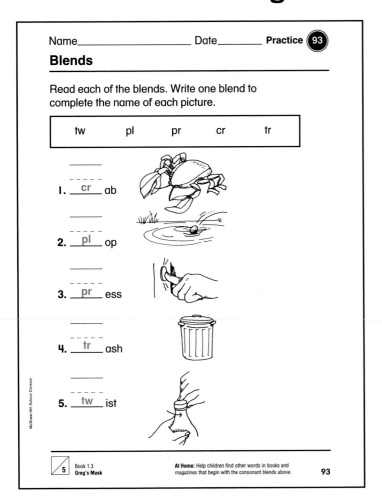

1. __cr__ ab

2. __pl__ op

3. __pr__ ess

4. __tr__ ash

5. __tw__ ist

5 Book 1.3
Greg's Mask

At Home: Help children find other words in books and magazines that begin with the consonant blends above.

93

Practice 94

Name_____ Date_____ Practice **94**

High-Frequency Words

Read each sentence. Circle the word that completes the sentence. Then write the word.

new	old	any	grow

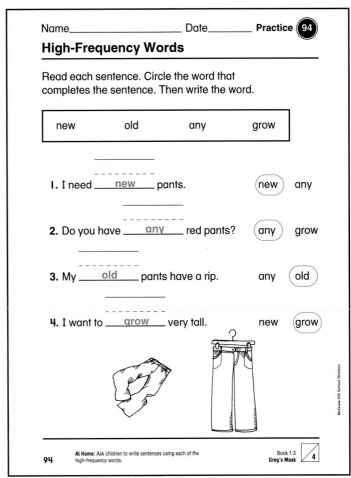

1. I need ___new___ pants.   (new)   any

2. Do you have ___any___ red pants?   (any)   grow

3. My ___old___ pants have a rip.   any   (old)

4. I want to ___grow___ very tall.   new   (grow)

94

At Home: Ask children to write sentences using each of the high-frequency words.

Book 1.3
Greg's Mask   4

The Trash Plant

Bob put a new bat in the plant. "No," said the man. "New things are still good. We can use them again."

"Good idea!" said Bob.

At Home: Have children name other things that might end up in a trash plant.

4

94a

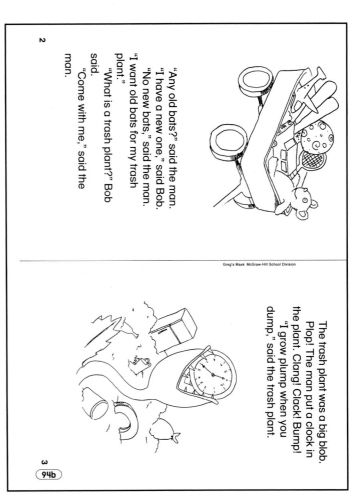

2

"Any old bats?" said the man. "I have a new one," said Bob. "No new bats," said the man. "I want old bats for my trash plant."

"What is a trash plant?" Bob said.

"Come with me," said the man.

The trash plant was a big blob. Plop! The man put a clock in the plant. Clang! Clack! Bump!

"I grow plump when you dump," said the trash plant.

3

94b

Greg's Mask • PRACTICE

Name_____ Date_____ Practice **95**

Story Comprehension

Read each sentence about "Greg's Mask."
Write the name of the person it describes.

Miss Willis	Greg	Tam

1. Her class did a skit. _____ Miss Willis

2. He made a mask. _____ Greg

3. She did not like the mask. _____ Tam

4. He put the mask in the trash. _____ Greg

5. She said, "Where is your mask?" _____ Miss Willis

6. She came to school with the mask. _____ Tam

Name_____ Date_____ Practice **96**

A Diagram

This is a **diagram** of a sports center. The diagram shows what can be played at the center.

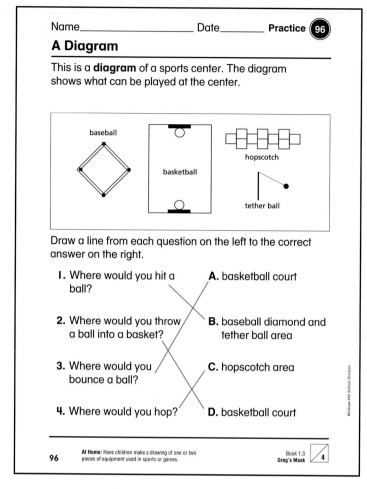

Draw a line from each question on the left to the correct answer on the right.

1. Where would you hit a ball?   **A.** basketball court

2. Where would you throw a ball into a basket?   **B.** baseball diamond and tether ball area

3. Where would you bounce a ball?   **C.** hopscotch area

4. Where would you hop?   **D.** basketball court

Name_____ Date_____ Practice **97**

Blends

Say each word. Print the word on the line.
Then circle the picture it names.

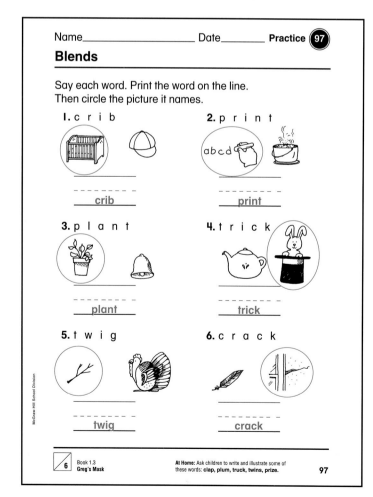

1. c r i b   crib

2. p r i n t   print

3. p l a n t   plant

4. t r i c k   trick

5. t w i g   twig

6. c r a c k   crack

Name_____ Date_____ Practice **98**

Blends

Look at the picture. Read the question. Then write the answer.

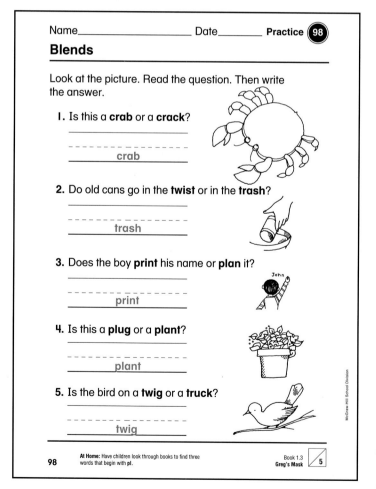

1. Is this a **crab** or a **crack**?

   crab

2. Do old cans go in the **twist** or in the **trash**?

   trash

3. Does the boy **print** his name or **plan** it?

   print

4. Is this a **plug** or a **plant**?

   plant

5. Is the bird on a **twig** or a **truck**?

   twig

Greg's Mask • PRACTICE

Compare and Contrast

Read the story and look at the pictures.
Then answer the questions.

Scott and Sara are twins.
They were born on the same day.
They have the same mother and father.
They live in the same house.
Scott likes to play ball. Sara likes to swim.

1. Tell how Scott and Sara are alike.

They were born on the same day.

They have the same mother and father.

They live in the same house.

2. Tell how Scott and Sara are different.

Scott is a boy. Sara is a girl.

Scott likes to play ball.

Sara likes to swim.

6 Book 1.3
Greg's Mask

At Home: Have children suggest other ways in which
Scott and Sara could be alike and different.

99

Possessives

Read each sentence. Circle the word that
completes the sentence. Then write the word.

I. This is ___Glen's___ drum.

Glen (Glen's)

2. I see ___Pam___.

(Pam) Pam's

3. Two ___hens___ pecked my leg.

(hens) hen's

4. ___Rick's___ duck quacks.

Rick (Rick's)

100

At Home: Help children to write three new sentences, each
containing one of the following words: **dog, dogs, dog's.**

Book 1.3
Greg's Mask 4

T19

Greg's Mask • RETEACH

Name_____ Date_____ **Reteach** `93`

Blends

Read the words. Say the sound spelled by each letter in the word.

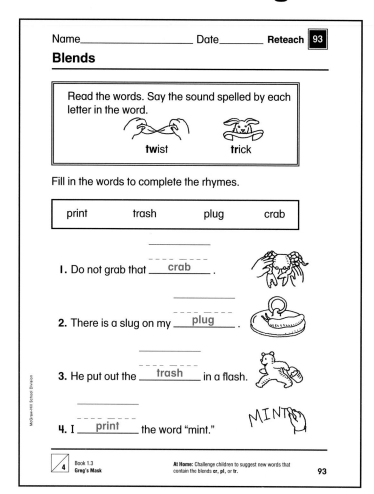

twist   **tr**ick

Fill in the words to complete the rhymes.

print	trash	plug	crab

1. Do not grab that ___crab___ .

2. There is a slug on my ___plug___ .

3. He put out the ___trash___ in a flash.

4. I ___print___ the word "mint."

4 | Book 1.3
Greg's Mask

At Home: Challenge children to suggest new words that contain the blends **cr**, **pl**, or **tr**.

93

Name_____ Date_____ **Reteach** `94`

High-Frequency Words

Read the story. Then circle the word that completes each sentence.

Jan's dog is very old.
He sits in the garden.
Jan just got him a new hat.
He watches the plants grow.
Are there any dog snacks left?
Jan wants to bring him one.

The dog is very ___ .
young   (old)   sick

He just got a ___ hat.
(new)   bad   pink

The dog likes to watch the plants ___ .
lick   run   (grow)

Jan asks if there are ___ snacks.
(any)   old   from

94

At Home: Invite children to write new sentences for each of the words.

Book 1.3
Greg's Mask | 4

Name_____ Date_____ **Reteach** `95`

Story Comprehension

Think about what happened first, next, and last in "Greg's Mask." Then draw the pictures in the right order.

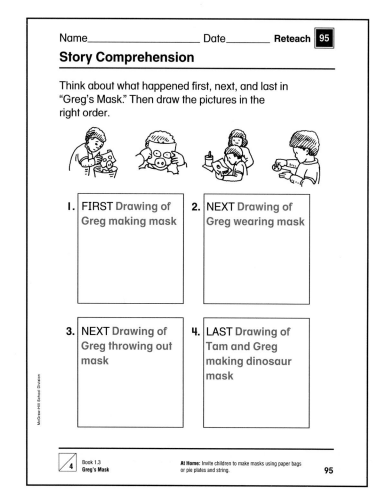

1. FIRST Drawing of Greg making mask

2. NEXT Drawing of Greg wearing mask

3. NEXT Drawing of Greg throwing out mask

4. LAST Drawing of Tam and Greg making dinosaur mask

4 | Book 1.3
Greg's Mask

At Home: Invite children to make masks using paper bags or pie plates and string.

95

Name_____ Date_____ **Reteach** `96`

A Diagram

A **diagram** describes something. This is a diagram of a music room.

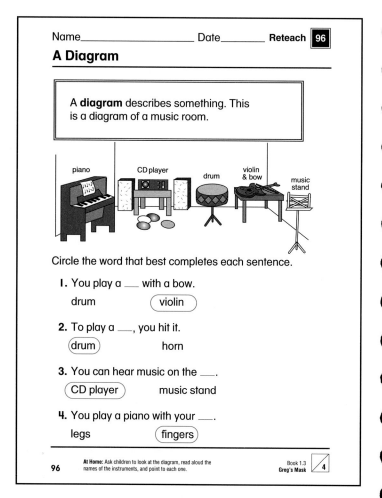

piano   CD player   drum   violin & bow   music stand

Circle the word that best completes each sentence.

1. You play a ___ with a bow.
drum   (violin)

2. To play a ___, you hit it.
(drum)   horn

3. You can hear music on the ___.
(CD player)   music stand

4. You play a piano with your ___.
legs   (fingers)

96

At Home: Ask children to look at the diagram, read aloud the names of the instruments, and point to each one.

Book 1.3
Greg's Mask | 4

Greg's Mask • RETEACH

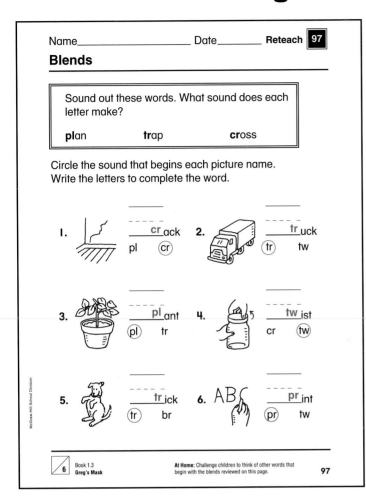

Name_____ Date_____ **Reteach** 97

Blends

> Sound out these words. What sound does each letter make?
>
> **pl**an   **tr**ap   **cr**oss

Circle the sound that begins each picture name.
Write the letters to complete the word.

1. _____**cr**ack   pl   (cr)

2. _____**tr**uck   (tr)   tw

3. _____**pl**ant   (pl)   tr

4. _____**tw**ist   cr   (tw)

5. _____**tr**ick   (tr)   br

6. _____**pr**int   (pr)   tw

6   Book 1.3   **Greg's Mask**   **At Home:** Challenge children to think of other words that begin with the blends reviewed on this page.   97

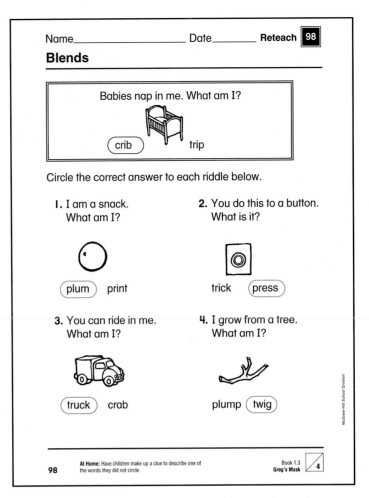

Name_____ Date_____ **Reteach** 98

Blends

> Babies nap in me. What am I?
>
> (crib)   trip

Circle the correct answer to each riddle below.

1. I am a snack. What am I?

   (plum)   print

2. You do this to a button. What is it?

   trick   (press)

3. You can ride in me. What am I?

   (truck)   crab

4. I grow from a tree. What am I?

   plump   (twig)

98   **At Home:** Have children make up a clue to describe one of the words they did not circle.   Book 1.3   **Greg's Mask**   4

Name_____ Date_____ **Reteach** 99

Compare and Contrast

> When you **compare**, you tell how things are alike. When you **contrast**, you tell how things are different.
>
> These are Bill's pets.

Fill in the rest of the chart to show how Polly and Speedy are different.

Polly lives in a cage.   Speedy lives in a tank.
She has two legs.   He doesn't have legs.
Polly eats seeds.   Speedy eats fish food.
Polly flies.   Speedy swims.

	POLLY	SPEEDY
1. Legs	two	none
2. Home	cage	tank
3. Food	seeds	fish food

4   Book 1.3   **Greg's Mask**   **At Home:** Have children think of another difference between Polly and Speedy.   99

Name_____ Date_____ **Reteach** 100

Possessives

> The crib belongs to Jill.
> It is **Jill's** crib.

Write the underlined word and add **'s** to show who owns something.

1. The drill belongs to <u>Brad</u>.

   It is _____**Brad's**_____ drill.

2. The pet belongs to the <u>vet</u>.

   It is the _____**vet's**_____ pet.

3. The dress belongs to <u>Tawana</u>.

   It is _____**Tawana's**_____ dress.

4. The raft belongs to the <u>club</u>.

   It is the _____**club's**_____ raft.

100   **At Home:** Encourage children to write four new examples that use **'s** to show ownership.   Book 1.3   **Greg's Mask**   4

Greg's Mask • EXTEND

Name_____ Date_____ **Extend** 93

Blends

Draw pictures to match the words.

a black truck	a big plant	a baby's crib	a small drum

Pick two pictures. Write a sentence about each picture.
Answers will vary. A sample answer is shown.

_____

I will grow a big plant in class.

- -
_____
_____
_____
_____
_____

Children will draw a black truck, a big plant, a
baby's crib, and a small drum.

Book 1.3
Greg's Mask

At Home: Help children make up tongue twisters or silly
sentences using words from their pictures.

93

Name_____ Date_____ **Extend** 94

High-Frequency Words

Work with a partner.
Open a toy shop.
Make signs for your shop.
Use words from the box.

any	new	old	grow

Signs will vary. Samples are shown.
Write your signs here.

Any toy pig in shop 25¢

New Doll 50¢

Old Truck 10¢

Toy Dog That Grows 60¢

You will need: card ____, glue ____, sticks ____,

markers ____. Write one sign on each card.

Glue a stick ____ to the back of each card.

At Home: Encourage children to make storage labels for
shelves and drawer fronts using the words on this page and
others.

94

Book 1.3
Greg's Mask

Name_____ Date_____ **Extend** 95

Story Comprehension

Write a letter to Greg. Tell him why you like his mask.
Tell him about a mask you would like to make.
Dear Greg,

Letters will vary. They should say something positive
about Greg's mask and describe or name another kind
of mask.

- -
_____
_____
_____
_____
_____
_____
_____
_____

Your friend,

- - - - - - - - - - - - - - - - -

Book 1.3
Greg's Mask

At Home: Have children create simple masks using
materials such as paper plates, paint, tissue paper, yarn,
and pipe cleaners.

95

Name_____ Date_____ **Extend** 96

Use a Diagram

Greg made a mask. You can make a hat.

Step 1

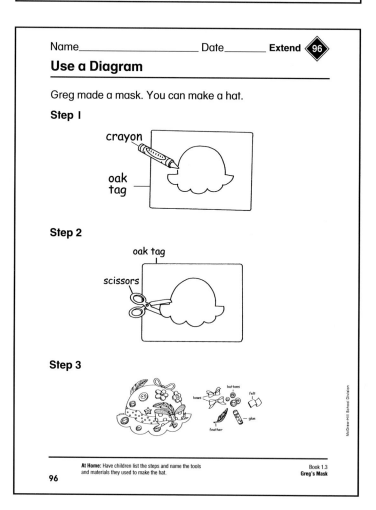

Step 2

Step 3

At Home: Have children list the steps and name the tools
and materials they used to make the hat.

96

Book 1.3
Greg's Mask

Greg's Mask • EXTEND

Blends

Write a silly sentence for each picture.
Use words from the box. Sample sentences are shown.

black crab drum grab plum plump track

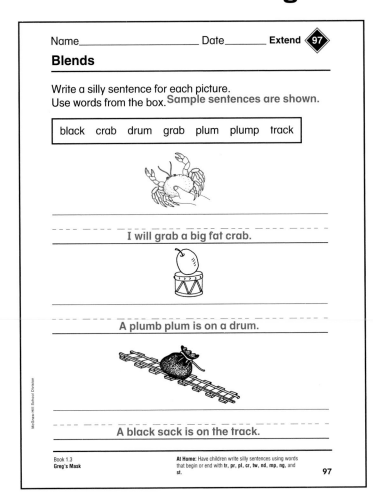

_____
I will grab a big fat crab.

_____
A plumb plum is on a drum.

_____
A black sack is on the track.

Book 1.3
Greg's Mask

At Home: Have children write silly sentences using words that begin or end with **tr, pr, pl, cr, tw, nd, mp, ng,** and **st.**

97

Blends

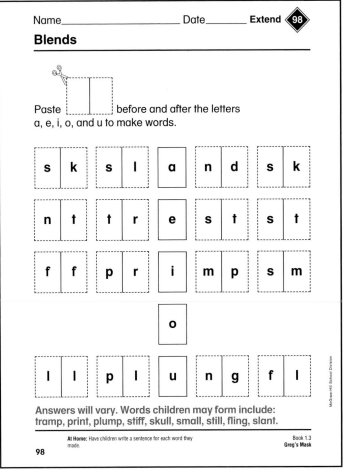

Paste [ ] before and after the letters
a, e, i, o, and u to make words.

s	k		s	l		a		n		d		s	k

n	t		t	r		e		s		t		s	t

f	f		p	r		i		m		p		s	m

o

l	l		p	l		u		n		g		f	l

Answers will vary. Words children may form include:
tramp, print, plump, stiff, skull, small, still, fling, slant.

At Home: Have children write a sentence for each word they made.

98
Book 1.3
Greg's Mask

Compare and Contrast

What do you see on the [image] mask?

What do you see on the [image] mask?
Fill in the chart.

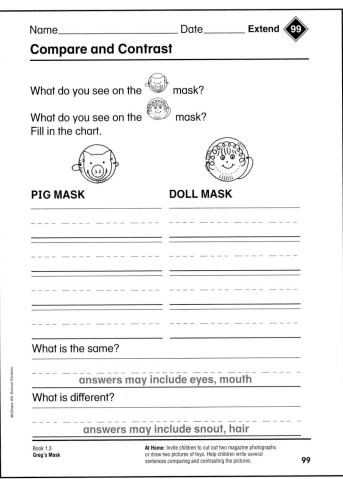

PIG MASK   **DOLL MASK**

_____   _____
_____   _____
_____   _____
_____   _____
_____   _____

What is the same?
_____
answers may include eyes, mouth

What is different?
_____
answers may include snout, hair

Book 1.3
Greg's Mask

At Home: Invite children to cut out two magazine photographs or draw two pictures of toys. Help children write several sentences comparing and contrasting the pictures.

99

Possessives

Fill in the names of people you know.
Draw pictures of these people.

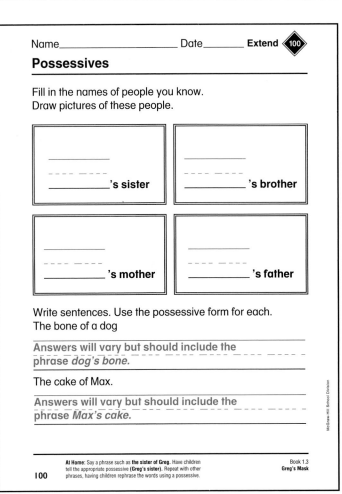

_____'s sister   _____'s brother

_____'s mother   _____'s father

Write sentences. Use the possessive form for each.
The bone of a dog

**Answers will vary but should include the
phrase _dog's bone._**

The cake of Max.

**Answers will vary but should include the
phrase _Max's cake._**

At Home: Say a phrase such as **the sister of Greg.** Have children tell the appropriate possessive (**Greg's sister**). Repeat with other phrases, having children rephrase the words using a possessive.

100
Book 1.3
Greg's Mask

Greg's Mask • GRAMMAR

Present Tense

- The **tense** of a verb tells when the action takes place.
- Some verbs tell about actions that happen now.
- These verbs are in the **present tense**.

Greg **makes** a mask.

Greg **sings.**

Circle the verbs that tell about actions that happen now.

1. Greg (clips) a mask.

2. (Drop) a glob of that.

3. Greg tossed it in the trash.

4. (Twist) it here.

5. Greg sang as he worked.

6. Pam (loves) her cat.

EXTENSION: Have the children think of sentences that tell the things they are doing. Write the present tense verbs they use on a chart.

71

Present Tense

- **Present tense** verbs tell about actions that happen now.
- Add **-s** to most verbs to tell what one person or thing does now.

Greg **sings**.

Look at the picture. Write -s at the end of the verbs that show the actions of one person or thing.

1. Greg make __s__ a mask.

2. Tam clip __s__ the mask.

3. Greg help __s__ Tam.

4. Tam twist __s__ the mask.

5. Greg put __s__ it on.

EXTENSION: Have the children read the sentences after they write -s at the end of the verbs. Then have them draw a circle around the verbs that tell what each person is doing now.

Present Tense

- The **tense** of a verb tells when the action takes place.
- Some verbs tell about action that happens now.
- These verbs are in the **present tense**.
- Add -s to most verbs to tell what one person or thing does now.

Tam **snips** the mask.

Choose a verb from the box. Write the correct verb in the sentence.

| flips | makes | blinks | likes | sings |

1. Bat _____ flips _____.

2. Owl _____ blinks _____.

3. Greg _____ makes _____ a mask.

4. Tam _____ likes _____ Greg's mask.

5. Bird _____ sings _____.

EXTENSION: Have the children think of words that tell their actions when they are making an art project. Make a list of these words on a chart, putting -s at the end of each if appropriate.

73

Capital Letters in Book Titles

- The important words in a book title begin with a capital letter.
- Draw a line under the title of a book.

Little Red Riding Hood

Read the titles. Write them correctly on the lines.

1. Goldilocks and the three bears

_____

Goldilocks and the Three Bears

2. Three Billy goats gruff

_____

Three Billy Goats Gruff

Read the sentences. Draw a line under the title of a book. Capitalize the important words in the title.

3. Tam reads cinderella.
           C

4. Greg likes to read masks you can make.
                      M   Y   C   M

EXTENSION: Have the children look at books in the class library or school library. They should locate the titles and the capital letters in the titles.

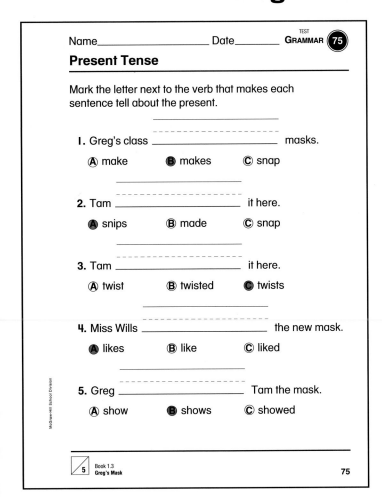

Present Tense

Mark the letter next to the verb that makes each sentence tell about the present.

1. Greg's class _____ masks.

   Ⓐ make   Ⓑ makes   Ⓒ snap

2. Tam _____ it here.

   Ⓐ snips   Ⓑ made   Ⓒ snap

3. Tam _____ it here.

   Ⓐ twist   Ⓑ twisted   Ⓒ twists

4. Miss Wills _____ the new mask.

   Ⓐ likes   Ⓑ like   Ⓒ liked

5. Greg _____ Tam the mask.

   Ⓐ show   Ⓑ shows   Ⓒ showed

Present Tense

- The **tense** of a verb tells when the action takes place.
- Some verbs tell about action that happens now.
- These verbs are in the **present tense**.
- Add **-s** to most verbs to tell what one person or thing does now.

Write the sentences. Add **-s** to the verbs.

1. Greg sing.

   _____ sings _____

2. Tam clip it.

   _____ clips _____

3. Miss Wills like my mask.

   _____ likes _____

4. Greg put on his mask.

   _____ puts _____

5. Tam make a new mask.

   _____ makes _____

Greg's Mask • SPELLING

Name_____ Date_____

Words with Blends

Complete each word by writing **cl**, **tr**, or **dr** on the line.

1. **cl** ass
2. **dr** op
3. **tr** ip
4. **cl** ap
5. **tr** ack
6. **dr** ess

Directions (to teacher)

Write the word class on the chalkboard or form the word with letter cards. Say the word aloud and have children repeat it. Have them listen for the sounds /k/ and /l/ together at the beginning of the word. Then point out the first example with cl filled in.

Display the word drop. Say the word and have children repeat it. Ask them to listen for the two sounds at the beginning of the word (/d/ and /r/). Have them complete the second example.

Display the word trip and repeat the process above, having students listen for /t/ and /r/. Have them complete the third example.

Then display the words clap, track, and dress. Say the words and have children repeat them. Have children listen for /cl/, /tr/, or /dr/ in each word. Then have them complete the page.

Book 1.3
Greg's Mask 5 71

Name_____ Date_____

Words with Blends

Using the Word Study Steps

1. LOOK at the word.
2. SAY the word aloud.
3. STUDY the letters in the word.
4. WRITE the word.
5. CHECK the word.
   Did you spell the word right? If not, go back to step 1.

> **Spelling Tip**
>
> Use the dictionary to look up spellings of words.

Find and Circle

Where are the spelling words?

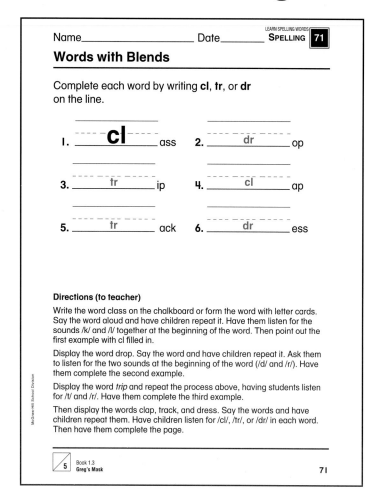

To Parents or Helpers:
Using the Word Study Steps above as your child comes across any new words will help him or her spell well. Review the steps as you both go over this week's spelling words.
Go over the Spelling Tip with your child. Help your child use the dictionary to look up spellings of words.
Help your child find and circle the spelling words in the puzzle.

72   Book 1.3
Greg's Mask 6

Name_____ Date_____

Words with Blends

Look at the spelling words in the box.

track dress class drop clap trip

Write the words that begin with **cl**.

1. class
2. clap

Write the words that begin with **tr**.

3. track
4. trip

Write the words that begin with **dr**.

5. drop
6. dress

Book 1.3
Greg's Mask 6 73

Name_____ Date_____

Words with Blends

Write a spelling word from the box to match each picture. Add **s** to each spelling word.

drop clap track trip

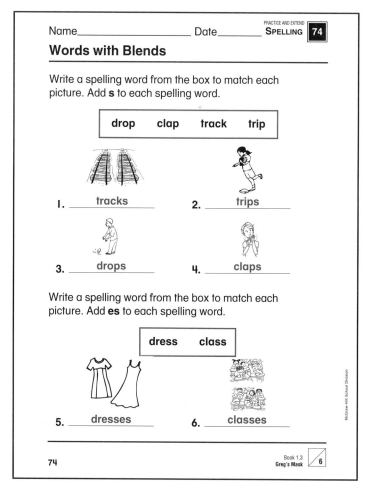

1. tracks
2. trips
3. drops
4. claps

Write a spelling word from the box to match each picture. Add **es** to each spelling word.

dress class

5. dresses
6. classes

74   Book 1.3
Greg's Mask 6

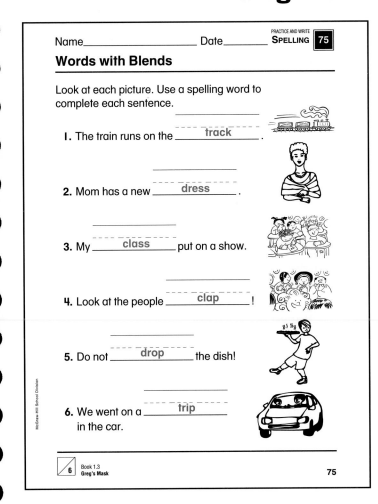

Words with Blends

Look at each picture. Use a spelling word to complete each sentence.

1. The train runs on the _____**track**_____.

2. Mom has a new _____**dress**_____.

3. My _____**class**_____ put on a show.

4. Look at the people _____**clap**_____!

5. Do not _____**drop**_____ the dish!

6. We went on a _____**trip**_____ in the car.

Book 1.3
Greg's Mask   75

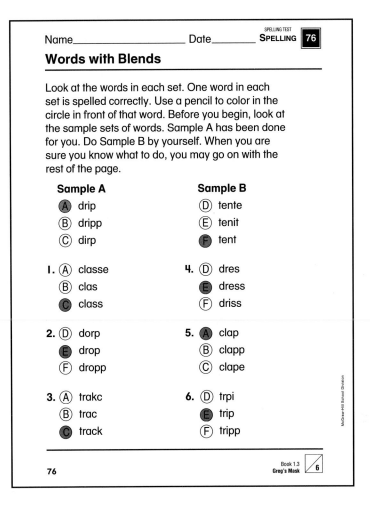

Words with Blends

Look at the words in each set. One word in each set is spelled correctly. Use a pencil to color in the circle in front of that word. Before you begin, look at the sample sets of words. Sample A has been done for you. Do Sample B by yourself. When you are sure you know what to do, you may go on with the rest of the page.

Sample A
- (A) drip
- (B) dripp
- (C) dirp

Sample B
- (D) tente
- (E) tenit
- (F) tent ⬤

1. (A) classe
   (B) clas
   (C) class ⬤

2. (D) dorp
   (E) drop ⬤
   (F) dropp

3. (A) trakc
   (B) trac
   (C) track ⬤

4. (D) dres
   (E) dress ⬤
   (F) driss

5. (A) clap ⬤
   (B) clapp
   (C) clape

6. (D) trpi
   (E) trip ⬤
   (F) tripp

76   Book 1.3
                  Greg's Mask

T27

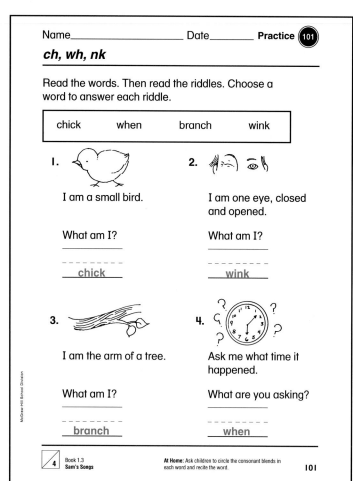

Name_____ Date_____ **Practice** 101

ch, wh, nk

Read the words. Then read the riddles. Choose a
word to answer each riddle.

| chick | when | branch | wink |

1.

I am a small bird.

What am I?

__chick__

2.

I am one eye, closed
and opened.

What am I?

__wink__

3.

I am the arm of a tree.

What am I?

__branch__

4.

Ask me what time it
happened.

What are you asking?

__when__

4 Book 1.3
Sam's Songs

At Home: Ask children to circle the consonant blends in
each word and recite the word.

101

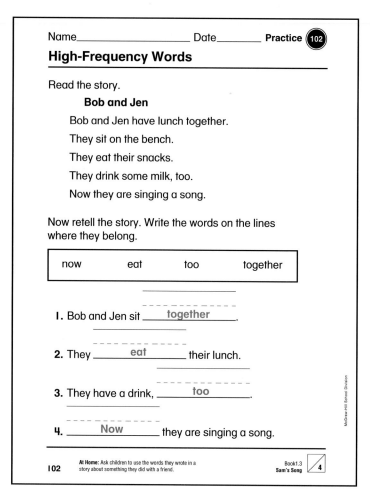

Name_____ Date_____ **Practice** 102

High-Frequency Words

Read the story.

Bob and Jen

Bob and Jen have lunch together.

They sit on the bench.

They eat their snacks.

They drink some milk, too.

Now they are singing a song.

Now retell the story. Write the words on the lines
where they belong.

| now | eat | too | together |

1. Bob and Jen sit _____ __together__ .

2. They _____ __eat__ _____ their lunch.

3. They have a drink, _____ __too__ .

4. _____ __Now__ _____ they are singing a song.

102

At Home: Ask children to use the words they wrote in a
story about something they did with a friend.

Book1.3
Sam's Song **4**

The Chomp Champs

The two men went to eat. Who
will be the champ? Chet ate a
ranch. Chet ate a bank. Hank
ate a bank. Chomp! Hank ate a bank.
Chomp! Chet could eat no more. Hank
could eat no more. Now they are
champs together.

At Home: Have children draw a picture that
illustrates this story.

4

102a

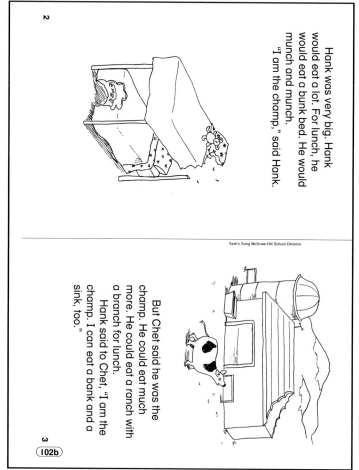

2

Hank was very big. Hank
would eat a lot. For lunch, he
would eat a bunk bed. He would
munch and munch.
"I am the champ," said Hank.

But Chet said he was the
champ. He could eat much
more. He could eat a ranch with
a branch for lunch.
Hank said to Chet, "I am the
champ. I can eat a bank and a
sink, too."

Sam's Song McGraw-Hill School Division

3

102b

Practice 103

Name_____ Date_____ Practice 103

Story Comprehension

Think about the story, "Sam's Song." Circle **true** if a statement is true. Circle **false** if it is not true.

1. Chuck is Sam's father.   true (false)

2. Chuck is Sam's brother.   (true) false

3. Chuck and Sam are owls.   (true) false

4. Sam is a baby owl.   (true) false

5. Sam has a big song.   true (false)

6. Mom, Dad, Chuck, and Sam like to sing.   (true) false

7. A small song is not a good song.   true (false)

8. Sam likes her own song.   (true) false

Book1.3 Sam's Song   **At Home:** Invite children to illustrate one of the true statements.   103

Practice 104

Name_____ Date_____ Practice 104

A Diagram

This **diagram** shows different sizes of dogs.

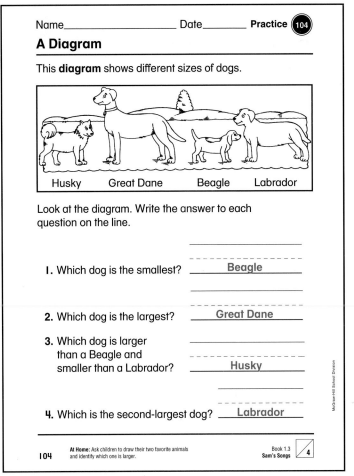

Husky   Great Dane   Beagle   Labrador

Look at the diagram. Write the answer to each question on the line.

1. Which dog is the smallest?   __Beagle__

2. Which dog is the largest?   __Great Dane__

3. Which dog is larger than a Beagle and smaller than a Labrador?   __Husky__

4. Which is the second-largest dog?   __Labrador__

104   **At Home:** Ask children to draw their two favorite animals and identify which one is larger.   Book 1.3 Sam's Songs   4

Practice 105

Name_____ Date_____ Practice 105

ch, wh, nk

Print the word on the line. Then circle the picture it names.

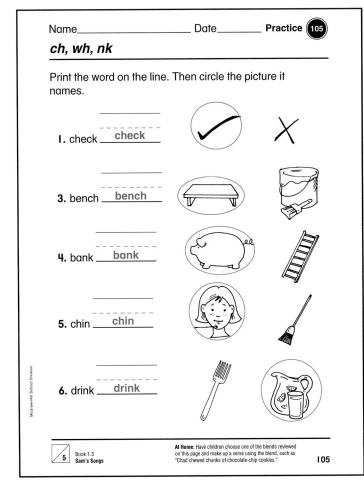

1. check __check__

3. bench __bench__

4. bank __bank__

5. chin __chin__

6. drink __drink__

Book 1.3 Sam's Songs 5   **At Home:** Have children choose one of the blends reviewed on this page and make up a verse using the blend, such as "Chad chewed chunks of chocolate-chip cookies."   105

Practice 106

Name_____ Date_____ Practice 106

ch, wh, nk; Blends

Circle the word that completes the sentence. Then write the word on the line.

1. The ship __sank__.
(sank) drank

2. I crunch on a __chip__.
chill (chip)

3. The cash is in the __bank__.
yank (bank)

4. She ate her __lunch__.
(lunch) branch

5. Do you play __chess__?
(chess) chin

6. I go home __when__ Dan does.
(when) whisk

106   **At Home:** Have children choose a sentence to illustrate.   Book 1.3 Sam's Song   6

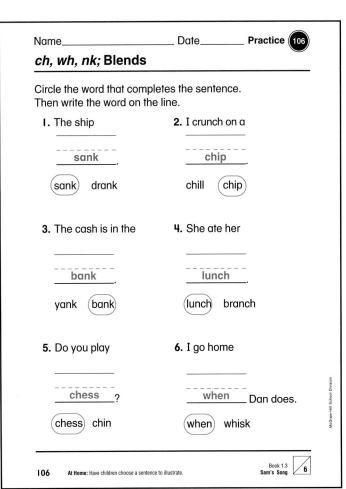

Sam's Song • PRACTICE

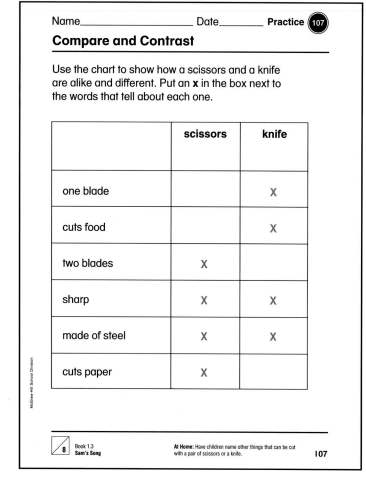

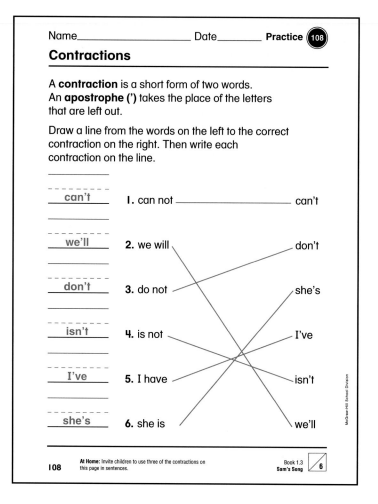

Sam's Song • RETEACH

Reteach 101

Name_____ Date_____ **Reteach** `101`

ch, wh, nk

Name each picture. Say the sound of the letters.
Notice the new sounds that **ch**, **wh**, and **nk**
make.

whale　　**ch**ick　　li**nk**

Circle the word that completes each sentence.
Then write the word.

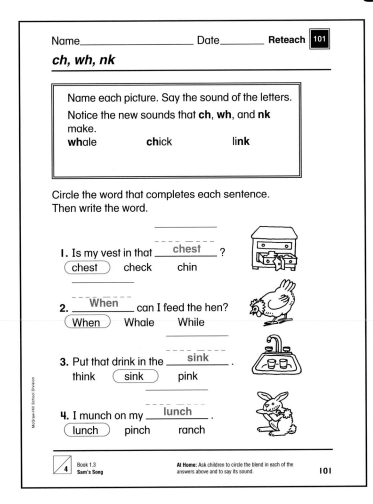

1. Is my vest in that ____chest____ ?
   (chest)　check　chin

2. ____When____ can I feed the hen?
   (When)　Whale　While

3. Put that drink in the ____sink____ .
   think　(sink)　pink

4. I munch on my ____lunch____ .
   (lunch)　pinch　ranch

4　Book 1.3
Sam's Song

At Home: Ask children to circle the blend in each of the
answers above and to say its sound.

101

Reteach 102

Name_____ Date_____ **Reteach** `102`

High-Frequency Words

| eat | together | too | now |

Write the word that fits best in each sentence.
Use each word once.

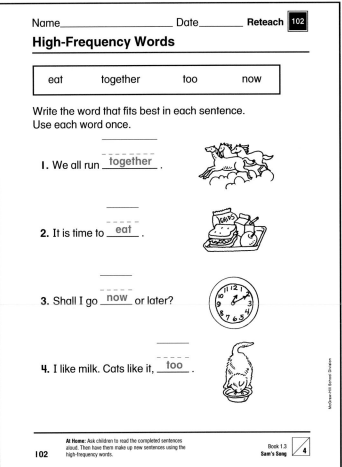

1. We all run ____together____ .

2. It is time to ____eat____ .

3. Shall I go ____now____ or later?

4. I like milk. Cats like it, ____too____ .

102

At Home: Ask children to read the completed sentences
aloud. Then have them make up new sentences using the
high-frequency words.

Book 1.3
Sam's Song
4

Reteach 103

Name_____ Date_____ **Reteach** `103`

Story Comprehension

Think about "Sam's Song." Then fill in the chart.

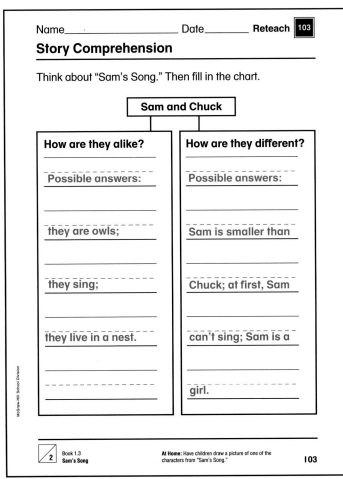

Sam and Chuck

How are they alike?	How are they different?
Possible answers:	Possible answers:
they are owls;	Sam is smaller than
they sing;	Chuck; at first, Sam
they live in a nest.	can't sing; Sam is a
	girl.

2　Book 1.3
Sam's Song

At Home: Have children draw a picture of one of the
characters from "Sam's Song."

103

Reteach 104

Name_____ Date_____ **Reteach** `104`

A Diagram

This **diagram** shows different sized fish.

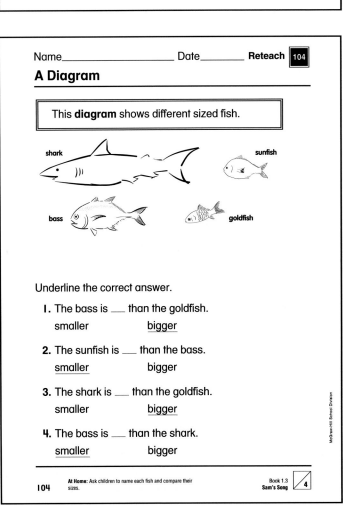

shark　　sunfish
bass　　goldfish

Underline the correct answer.

1. The bass is ___ than the goldfish.
   smaller　　　bigger

2. The sunfish is ___ than the bass.
   smaller　　　bigger

3. The shark is ___ than the goldfish.
   smaller　　　bigger

4. The bass is ___ than the shark.
   smaller　　　bigger

104

At Home: Ask children to name each fish and compare their
sizes.

Book 1.3
Sam's Song
4

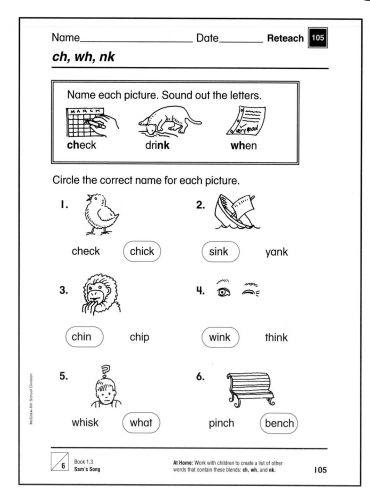

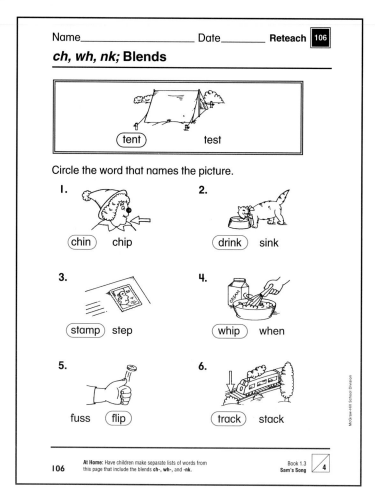

Name_____ Date_____ **Reteach** 105

ch, wh, nk

> Name each picture. Sound out the letters.
>
> **ch**eck   dri**nk**   **wh**en

Circle the correct name for each picture.

1. check   (chick)
2. (sink)   yank
3. (chin)   chip
4. (wink)   think
5. whisk   (what)
6. pinch   (bench)

Name_____ Date_____ **Reteach** 106

ch, wh, nk; Blends

> (tent)   test

Circle the word that names the picture.

1. (chin)   chip
2. (drink)   sink
3. (stamp)   step
4. (whip)   when
5. fuss   (flip)
6. (track)   stack

Name_____ Date_____ **Reteach** 107

Compare and Contrast

> When you **compare**, you tell how things are alike. When you **contrast**, you tell how things are different.

Look at the pictures. Then underline the answer to each question.

1. Which animal would make the best pet?

   <u>puppy</u>   giraffe   pig

2. Which animal says "oink"?

   puppy   giraffe   <u>pig</u>

3. Which animal has a long neck?

   puppy   <u>giraffe</u>   pig

4. Which animal barks?

   <u>puppy</u>   giraffe   pig

5. Which animal likes mud?

   puppy   giraffe   <u>pig</u>

Name_____ Date_____ **Reteach** 108

Contractions

> A **contraction** is a short form of two words.
> He did not hit the ball.
> He **didn't** hit the ball.

Write the contraction to replace the underlined words in each sentence.

| can't | she's | haven't | that's |

1. He <u>can not</u> see the box.

   He ____**can't**____ see the box.

2. I <u>have not</u> got the hat.

   I ____**haven't**____ got the hat.

3. I think <u>that is</u> a good plan.

   I think ____**that's**____ a good pan.

4. I hope <u>she is</u> at the bank.

   I hope ____**she's**____ at the bank.

Sam's Song • EXTEND

ch, wh, nk

Words with **ch**, **wh**, or **nk** are everywhere.
Look on the walls. Look in books. Look in
newspapers.
Write the words you find.
Answers will vary. Samples are shown.

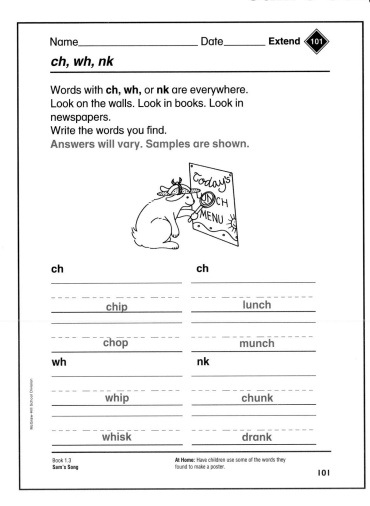

ch

_____
chip

_____
chop

wh

_____
whip

_____
whisk

ch

_____
lunch

_____
munch

nk

_____
chunk

_____
drank

Book 1.3
Sam's Song

At Home: Have children use some of the words they
found to make a poster.

101

High-Frequency Words

Look at the pictures.
Read the story.
Write words from the box.

| eat | now | too | together |

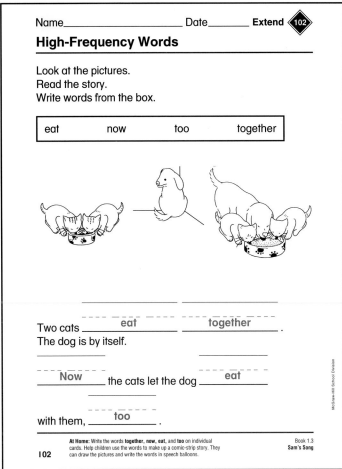

_____   _____

Two cats _____ _____ .
eat   together
The dog is by itself.

_____   _____

_____ the cats let the dog _____
Now   eat

_____

with them, _____ .
too

At Home: Write the words **together**, **now**, **eat**, and **too** on individual
cards. Help children use the words to make up a comic-strip story. They
can draw the pictures and write the words in speech balloons.

Book 1.3
Sam's Song

102

Story Comprehension

Pretend there is a new baby owl.
Draw a picture.
Show the other owls teaching the baby how to sing.

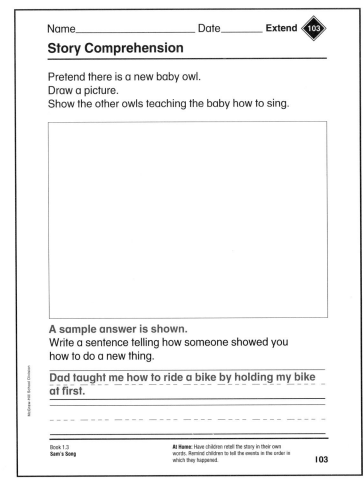

A sample answer is shown.
Write a sentence telling how someone showed you
how to do a new thing.

Dad taught me how to ride a bike by holding my bike
at first.
_____

Book 1.3
Sam's Song

At Home: Have children retell the story in their own
words. Remind children to tell the events in the order in
which they happened.

103

Use a Diagram

How many birds   do you know?

Cut out pictures of birds
Paste them on a big piece of paper.

Write the names of the birds   next to
them.

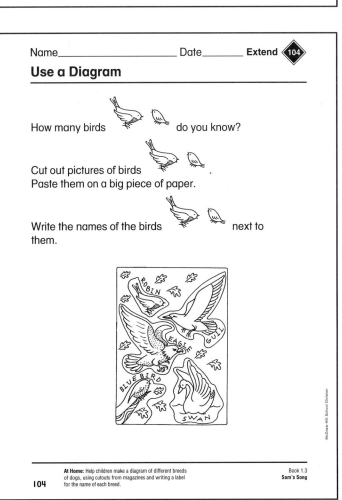

At Home: Help children make a diagram of different breeds
of dogs, using cutouts from magazines and writing a label
for the name of each breed.

Book 1.3
Sam's Song

104

Extend 105

Name_____ Date_____ **Extend** 105

ch, wh, nk

What is in the box? Look at the pictures.

Find the words. Circle them.

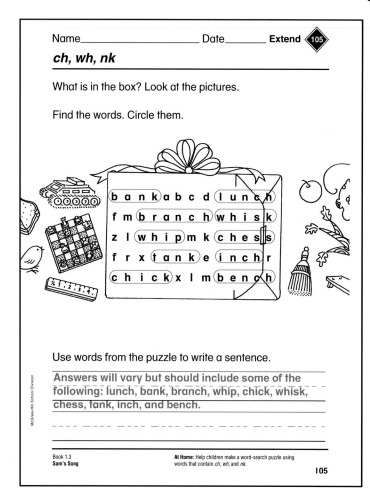

Use words from the puzzle to write a sentence.

Answers will vary but should include some of the following: lunch, bank, branch, whip, chick, whisk, chess, tank, inch, and bench.

Book 1.3
Sam's Song

At Home: Help children make a word-search puzzle using words that contain *ch, wh,* and *nk*.

105

Extend 106

Name_____ Date_____ **Extend** 106

ch, wh, nk; Blends

Play with a partner.

Toss a penny.

Move one space if you get heads.

Move two spaces if you get tails.

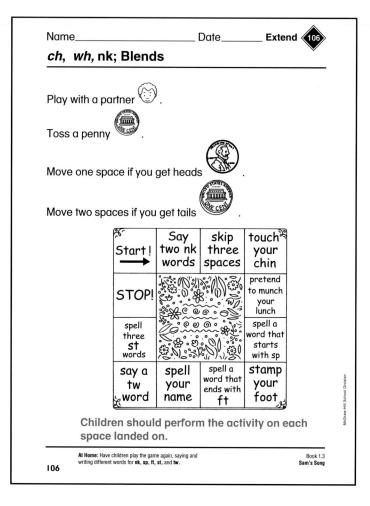

Children should perform the activity on each space landed on.

At Home: Have children play the game again, saying and writing different words for **nk, sp, ft, st,** and **tw**.

106

Book 1.3
Sam's Song

Extend 107

Name_____ Date_____ **Extend** 107

Compare and Contrast

Look at the pictures in each row.
Put an **X** on the one that does not belong.

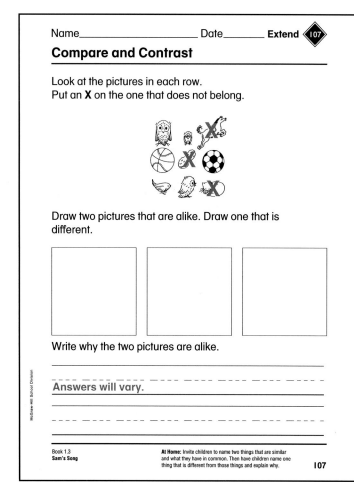

Draw two pictures that are alike. Draw one that is different.

Write why the two pictures are alike.

Answers will vary.

Book 1.3
Sam's Song

At Home: Invite children to name two things that are similar and what they have in common. Then have children name one thing that is different from those things and explain why.

107

Extend 108

Name_____ Date_____ **Extend** 108

Contractions

Cut out the contraction balloons at the bottom of the page. Paste each balloon on top of the balloons with words that match.

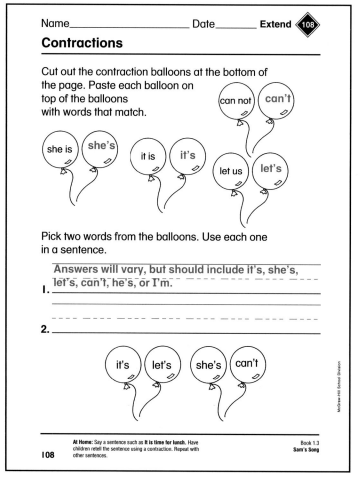

Pick two words from the balloons. Use each one in a sentence.

Answers will vary, but should include it's, she's, let's, can't, he's, or I'm.

1. _____

2. _____

At Home: Say a sentence such as **It is time for lunch.** Have children retell the sentence using a contraction. Repeat with other sentences.

108

Book 1.3
Sam's Song

Sam's Song • GRAMMAR

Past Tense

- Some verbs tell about actions that already happened.
- These verbs are in the **past tense**.
- Most verbs in the past tense end in **-ed**.
  The owls **watched** the sun.

Read the sentences. Circle the verbs that tell about actions that already happened.

1. The owls (watched) the sun.

2. The owls (looked) at Sam.

3. Sam (talked) to Mom and Pop.

4. Chuck (asked) the owls about the sun.

5. A star (winked) at Sam.

Past Tense

- Some verbs tell about actions in the past.
- Most verbs in the past end with **-ed**.
  Mom **talked** to Sam.

Read the sentences. Circle the verb that tells about past actions.

1. We ___ watch, (watched) ___ the owls.

2. Sam ___ want, (wanted) ___ to sing.

3. The star ___ wink, (winked) ___ at Sam.

4. The mouse crunch, (crunched) .

5. Mom and Pop ___ look, (looked) ___ at Sam.

Writing Past Tense Verbs

- Some verbs tell about actions that already happened.
- These verbs are in the past tense.
- Most verbs in the past tense end in **-ed**.
  The frog **jumped**.

Write a past tense verb that tells about the picture.
Find the verb in the box.

looked	hiked	wanted	liked	winked

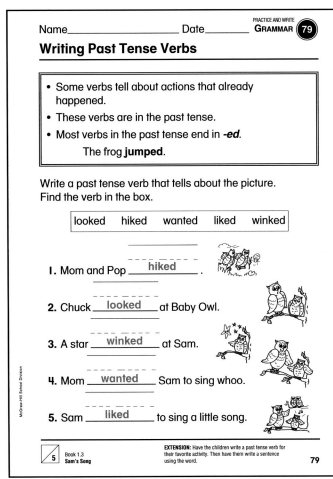

1. Mom and Pop __hiked__ .

2. Chuck __looked__ at Baby Owl.

3. A star __winked__ at Sam.

4. Mom __wanted__ Sam to sing whoo.

5. Sam __liked__ to sing a little song.

Names with Capital Letters

- The special name of a person or place begins with a capital letter.
  Jean lives in **New York**.

Write the sentences.
Begin each person's name with a capital letter.
Begin each place name with a capital letter.

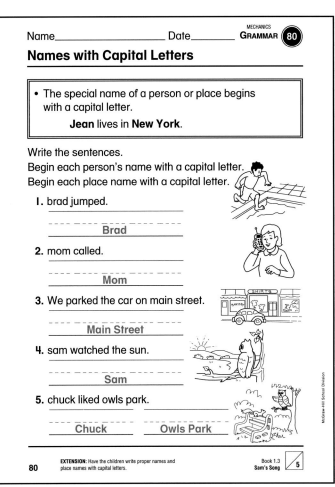

1. brad jumped.
   _____Brad_____

2. mom called.
   _____Mom_____

3. We parked the car on main street.
   _____Main Street_____

4. sam watched the sun.
   _____Sam_____

5. chuck liked owls park.
   _____Chuck_____ _____Owls Park_____

Sam's Song • GRAMMAR

Past Tense

Read each sentence. Look at the verb in ( ). Write
the verb in past tense to complete the sentence.

1. Mom _____watched_____ Sam. (watch)

2. The owls _____wanted_____ food. (want)

3. Pam _____looked_____ at Max. (look)

4. I _____wished_____ on a star. (wish)

5. Pop _____jumped_____ up. (jump)

More Practice with Past Tense

- Some verbs tell about actions that already happened.
- These verbs are in the **past tense**.
- Most verbs in the past tense end in **-ed**.

Circle the past tense verbs.

1. Mom and Pop (watched) Sam.

2. They (wanted) Sam to eat.

3. Sam (liked) to sing.

4. Mom, Pop, and Chuck (sang.)

5. Sam (wished) on a star.

Sam's Song • SPELLING

Page 77

Name_____ Date_____

Words with ch, wh, nk

1. **ch** in
2. wh en
3. si nk
4. ch ick
5. wi nk
6. thi nk

Directions (to teacher)

Review the digraph *ch* by explaining that the letters *ch* spell /ch/ as in the word *chin*. Write *chin* on the chalkboard or form the word with letter cards. Say the word aloud and have children repeat it. Have them listen for the sound /ch/ at the beginning of the word. Point out that *ch* has been filled in in the first example.

Display the word *when*. Say the word aloud and have children repeat it. Explain that the letters **wh** spell the sound /hw/. Have them listen for the sound /hw/ at the beginning of the word. Then have them complete the second example.

Display the word *sink*. Explain that the letters *nk* spell the sound /nk/ at the end of the word. Have children repeat the word and complete the third example.

Write the words *chick, wink,* and *think* on the chalkboard. Read the words aloud and have children repeat them. Then repeat each word and circle the letters that stand for the digraph *ch* at the beginning of the word or the digraph *nk* at the end of the word. Have children complete each word in the space provided.

5 Book 1.3
Sam's Song
77

Page 78

Name_____ Date_____

Words with Digraphs ch, wh, nk

Using the Word Study Steps

1. LOOK at the word.
2. SAY the word aloud.
3. STUDY the letters in the word.
4. WRITE the word.
5. CHECK the word.
   Did you spell the word right? If not, go back to step 1.

> **Spelling Tip**
>
> Use beginnings and endings of words you can spell to help you spell new words.
>
> **th**in + s**ink** = **think**

X the Word

In each row, put an X on the word that does not belong.

1.	chin	thin	rock
2.	when	hat	then
3.	lake	stop	rake
4.	chick	lick	went
5.	sink	red	blue
6.	ran	think	pink

To Parents or Helpers:
Using the Word Study Steps above as your child comes across any new words will help him or her spell well. Review the steps as you both go over this week's spelling words.
Go over the Spelling Tip with your child. Help your child write new words that use beginnings and endings of words he or she can spell.
Help your child complete the spelling activity.

78
Book 1.3
Sam's Song 6

Page 79

Name_____ Date_____

Words with ch, wh, nk

Look at the spelling words in the box.

> **chin   when   wink   chick   sink   think**

Name the pictures. Listen for the beginning sound. Write the spelling words that begin with the same sound.

1. when
2. chick
3. chin

Name the picture. Listen for the ending sound. Write the spelling words that end with the same sound.

4. sink
5. wink
6. think

6 Book 1.3
Sam's Song
79

Page 80

Name_____ Date_____

Words with ch, wh, nk

Read these poems. Complete each spelling word with the letters **ch**, **wh**, or **nk**.

Wh en the ship starts to si **nk**,

we go to help it, quick as a wi **nk**.

A **ch** ick is fat and small.

I thi **nk** it is a fuzzy ball.

A chick has a small **ch** in.
It has a mouth to put food in.

80
Book 1.3
Sam's Song 6

Sam's Song • SPELLING

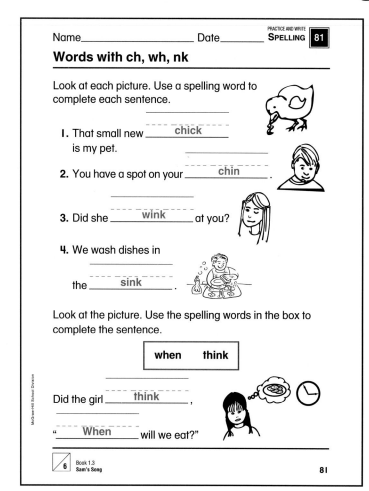

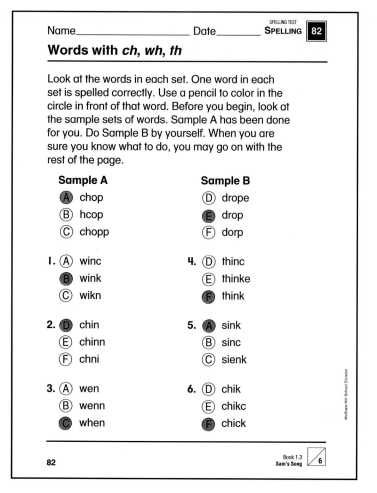

Words with *ch, wh, nk*

Look at each picture. Use a spelling word to complete each sentence.

1. That small new ___chick___ is my pet.

2. You have a spot on your ___chin___ .

3. Did she ___wink___ at you?

4. We wash dishes in the ___sink___ .

Look at the picture. Use the spelling words in the box to complete the sentence.

when	think

Did the girl ___think___ ,

" ___When___ will we eat?"

Words with *ch, wh, th*

Look at the words in each set. One word in each set is spelled correctly. Use a pencil to color in the circle in front of that word. Before you begin, look at the sample sets of words. Sample A has been done for you. Do Sample B by yourself. When you are sure you know what to do, you may go on with the rest of the page.

Sample A
- Ⓐ chop
- Ⓑ hcop
- Ⓒ chopp

Sample B
- Ⓓ drope
- Ⓔ drop
- Ⓕ dorp

1. Ⓐ winc
   Ⓑ wink
   Ⓒ wikn

4. Ⓓ thinc
   Ⓔ thinke
   Ⓕ think

2. Ⓓ chin
   Ⓔ chinn
   Ⓕ chni

5. Ⓐ sink
   Ⓑ sinc
   Ⓒ sienk

3. Ⓐ wen
   Ⓑ wenn
   Ⓒ when

6. Ⓓ chik
   Ⓔ chikc
   Ⓕ chick

Practice 109

Name_____ Date_____ Practice **109**

Long *a: a-e*

Read the words to yourself. Circle the correct word.
Then write it to complete each sentence.

1. Jake lives by a ___lake___.
   - lake
   - late

2. James has a pet ___snake___.
   - grape
   - snake

3. Jake can ___wade___.
   - wade
   - make

4. Jake can ___skate___.
   - case
   - skate

5. Jake will go to his ___cave___.
   - cave
   - cake

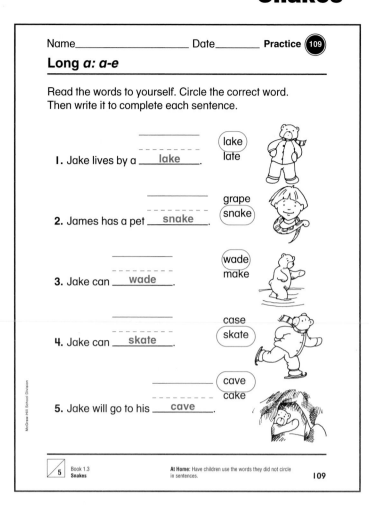

| 5 | Book 1.3 Snakes | **At Home:** Have children use the words they did not circle in sentences. | 109 |

Practice 110

Name_____ Date_____ Practice **110**

High-Frequency Words

Circle the word that completes each sentence.
Then write the word.

1. ___Where___ is the dog?
   - Where
   - Know

2. I ___know___ where he is.
   - why
   - know

3. The dog is ___under___ there.
   - where
   - under

4. ___Why___ is he hiding?
   - Why
   - Under

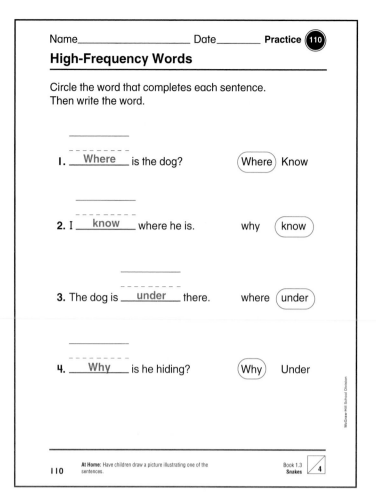

| 110 | **At Home:** Have children draw a picture illustrating one of the sentences. | Book 1.3 Snakes | 4 |

The Snake Cake

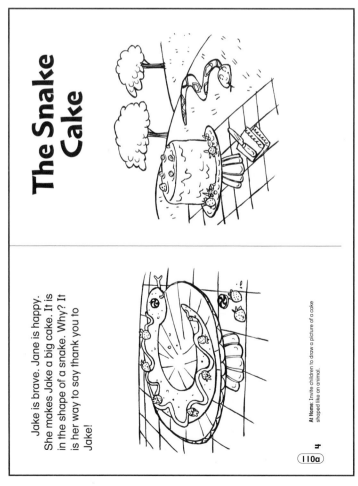

Jake is brave. Jane is happy. She makes Jake a big cake. It is in the shape of a snake. Why? It is her way to say thank you to Jake!

At Home: Invite children to draw a picture of a cake shaped like an animal.

110a

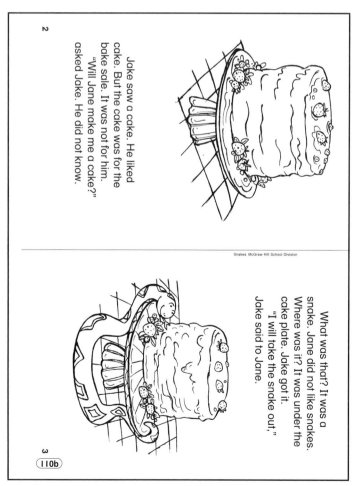

Jake saw a cake. He liked cake. But the cake was for the bake sale. It was not for him. "Will Jane make me a cake?" asked Jake. He did not know.

2

What was that? It was a snake. Jane did not like snakes. Where was it? It was under the cake plate. Jake got it. "I will take the snake out," Jake said to Jane.

3

110b

T39

Snakes • PRACTICE

Practice 111

Name_____ Date_____ Practice (111)

Story Comprehension

Think about what you have learned in "Snakes."
Draw a line to the word that completes each
sentence.

1. Snakes live in   rat

2. A snake can chomp a   pets

3. Snakes have no   slip

4. A snake can hang from a   legs

5. A snake can twist and   branch

6. Some snakes make good   lakes

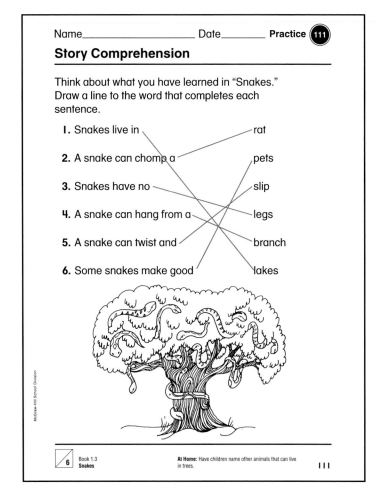

6 | Book 1.3
Snakes

At Home: Have children name other animals that can live in trees.

111

Practice 112

Name_____ Date_____ Practice (112)

A Diagram

The **diagram** shows different kinds of snakes.

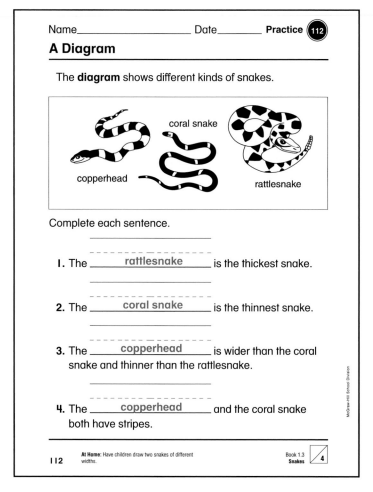

coral snake

copperhead

rattlesnake

Complete each sentence.

1. The _____rattlesnake_____ is the thickest snake.

2. The _____coral snake_____ is the thinnest snake.

3. The _____copperhead_____ is wider than the coral
snake and thinner than the rattlesnake.

4. The _____copperhead_____ and the coral snake
both have stripes.

112 | **At Home:** Have children draw two snakes of different widths.

Book 1.3
Snakes | 4

Practice 113

Name_____ Date_____ Practice (113)

Long *a: a-e*

Choose the word to complete each sentence.
Write the word on the line.

| make | safe | game | grade |

1. Shall we play a fun ____game____?

2. I want to ____make____ a cake.

3. I cross when it is ____safe____.

4. We are in first ____grade____.

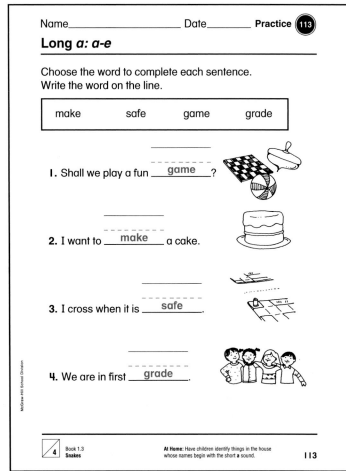

4 | Book 1.3
Snakes

At Home: Have children identify things in the house whose names begin with the short *a* sound.

113

Practice 114

Name_____ Date_____ Practice (114)

a-e; ch, wh, nk

Write the words to make each sentence tell about
the picture.

1. bake chase   cake rank

____bake____ a ____cake____

2. tape drink   lane punch

____drink____ some ____punch____

3. grapes drape   plate flame

____grapes____ on a ____plate____

4. When What   chip champ

____what____ a ____champ____

5. chick chill   tank bank

____chick____ in a ____tank____

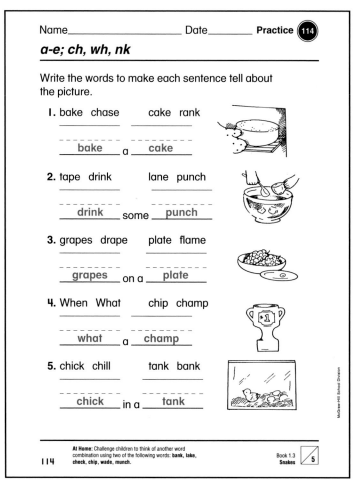

114 | **At Home:** Challenge children to think of another word combination using two of the following words: **bank, lake, check, chip, wade, munch.**

Book 1.3
Snakes | 5

T40 *Annotated Workbooks*

Name_____ Date_____ Practice **115**

Compare and Contrast

Look at the pictures. Write **snake** next to the pictures that tell about snakes. Write **me** next to the pictures that tell about people.

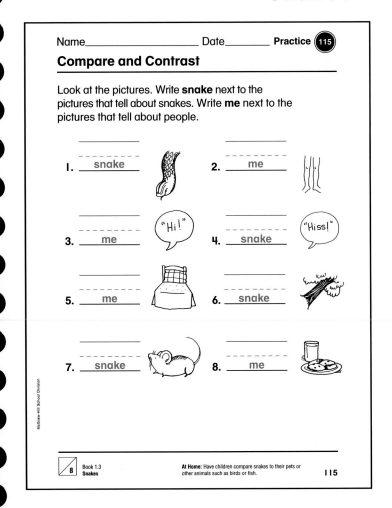

1. snake

2. me

3. me

4. snake

5. me

6. snake

7. snake

8. me

8 Book 1.3
Snakes

At Home: Have children compare snakes to their pets or other animals such as birds or fish.

115

Name_____ Date_____ Practice **116**

Contractions

A **contraction** is a short form of two words. An **apostrophe (')** takes the place of the letters that are left out.

Write the contraction for the underlined words in each sentence.

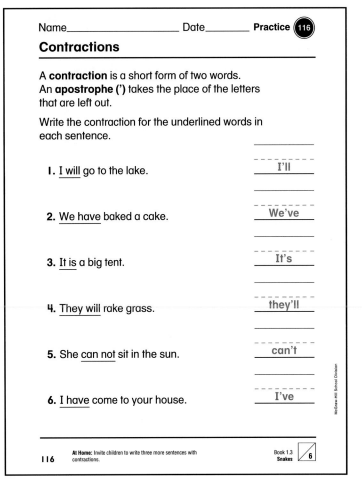

1. <u>I will</u> go to the lake. — I'll

2. <u>We have</u> baked a cake. — We've

3. <u>It is</u> a big tent. — It's

4. <u>They will</u> rake grass. — they'll

5. She <u>can not</u> sit in the sun. — can't

6. <u>I have</u> come to your house. — I've

116

At Home: Invite children to write three more sentences with contractions.

Book 1.3
Snakes 6

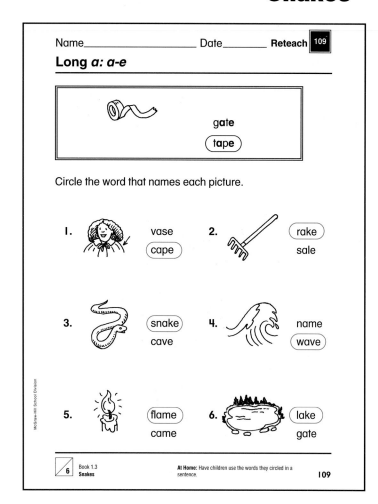

Name_____ Date_____ **Reteach** `109`

Long *a: a-e*

gate

(tape)

Circle the word that names each picture.

1. vase
   (cape)

2. (rake)
   sale

3. (snake)
   cave

4. name
   (wave)

5. (flame)
   came

6. (lake)
   gate

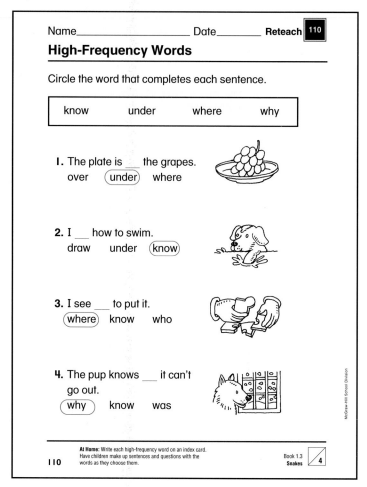

Name_____ Date_____ **Reteach** `110`

High-Frequency Words

Circle the word that completes each sentence.

| know | under | where | why |

1. The plate is ___ the grapes.
   over (under) where

2. I ___ how to swim.
   draw under (know)

3. I see ___ to put it.
   (where) know who

4. The pup knows ___ it can't go out.
   (why) know was

Name_____ Date_____ **Reteach** `111`

Story Comprehension

Use the sentences to fill in the chart.

1. Snakes can be pets.
2. Snakes can eat rats.
3. Some snakes have fangs.
4. Snakes have no legs.
5. Snakes can hiss.
6. Snakes can be very long.

What I knew.	What I learned.
Answers will vary, depending upon children's experience.	

Name_____ Date_____ **Reteach** `112`

A Diagram

The **diagram** on this page shows different kinds of snakes.

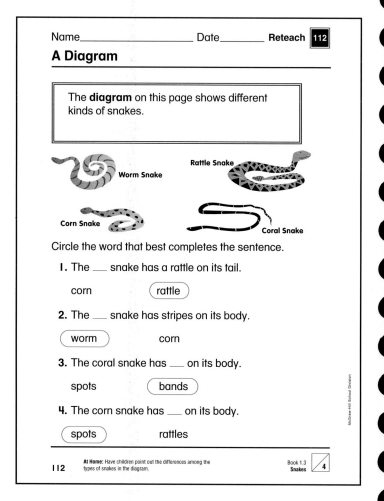

Worm Snake   Rattle Snake

Corn Snake   Coral Snake

Circle the word that best completes the sentence.

1. The ___ snake has a rattle on its tail.
   corn (rattle)

2. The ___ snake has stripes on its body.
   (worm) corn

3. The coral snake has ___ on its body.
   spots (bands)

4. The corn snake has ___ on its body.
   (spots) rattles

Page 113

Name_____ Date_____ Reteach **113**

Long *a: a-e*

Read these words. How are they different?

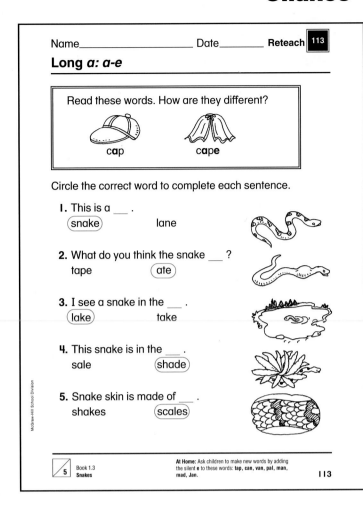

cap   cape

Circle the correct word to complete each sentence.

1. This is a ___ .
(snake)   lane

2. What do you think the snake ___ ?
tape   (ate)

3. I see a snake in the ___ .
(lake)   take

4. This snake is in the ___ .
sale   (shade)

5. Snake skin is made of ___ .
shakes   (scales)

5 | Book 1.3 **Snakes**   **At Home:** Ask children to make new words by adding the silent **e** to these words: **tap, can, van, pal, man, mad, Jan.**   113

Page 114

Name_____ Date_____ Reteach **114**

a-e; ch, wh, nk

I swim in the **lake** .

rake   (lake)

Underline then write the word that completes each sentence.

1. Let's bake a __cake__ .
brake   cake

2. We go __when__ the bell rings.
whisk   when

3. This is too __much__ to eat.
much   such

4. __Thank__ you for the gift.
Thank   Tank

114   **At Home:** Have children read a magazine article and find words that have the same middle sound as **game.**   Book 1.3 **Snakes** | 4

Page 115

Name_____ Date_____ Reteach **115**

Story Elements

To **compare** means to tell how things are alike.
To **contrast** means to tell how things are different.

The words in the center of the chart tell how people and snakes are alike. Circle one of these words. Then draw a picture in each circle to show how people and snakes do this thing differently.
Answers may vary.

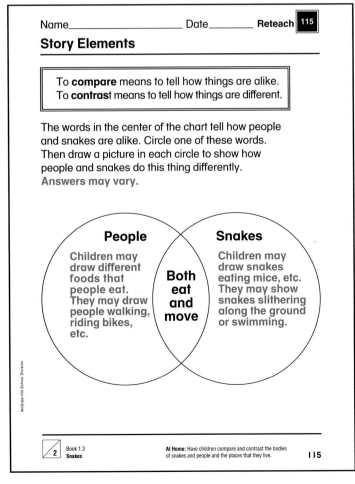

People
Children may draw different foods that people eat. They may draw people walking, riding bikes, etc.

Both eat and move

Snakes
Children may draw snakes eating mice, etc. They may show snakes slithering along the ground or swimming.

2 | Book 1.3 **Snakes**   **At Home:** Have children compare and contrast the bodies of snakes and people and the places that they live.   115

Page 116

Name_____ Date_____ Reteach **116**

Contractions

A **contraction** is a short form of two words.
An **apostrophe (')** takes the place of the letters that are left out.
She will make up the tale.
She'll make up the tale.

Underline the contraction in each sentence.

1. There's the vase.

2. "I'll be brave," Maria says.

3. Suki knows that it's time to go.

4. They'll chase the fox.

5. Jake doesn't like the snake.

6. Marco and Dan don't see the rake.

7. They've left a skate by the lake.

8. She's got a cape.

116   **At Home:** Have children make up other sentences that contain contractions.   Book 1.3 **Snakes** | 8

Snakes • EXTEND

Name_____ Date_____ **Extend** 109

Long *a: a-e*

Take 2 pieces of paper.
Fold them to make a book.
Do one activity on each page.

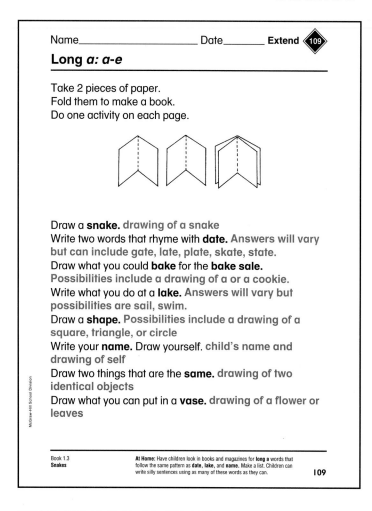

Draw a **snake.** drawing of a snake
Write two words that rhyme with **date. Answers will vary but can include gate, late, plate, skate, state.**
Draw what you could **bake** for the **bake sale. Possibilities include a drawing of a or a cookie.**
Write what you do at a **lake. Answers will vary but possibilities are sail, swim.**
Draw a **shape. Possibilities include a drawing of a square, triangle, or circle**
Write your **name. Draw yourself. child's name and drawing of self**
Draw two things that are the **same. drawing of two identical objects**
Draw what you can put in a **vase. drawing of a flower or leaves**

Book 1.3
Snakes

At Home: Have children look in books and magazines for **long a** words that follow the same pattern as **date, lake,** and **name.** Make a list. Children can write silly sentences using as many of these words as they can.

109

Name_____ Date_____ **Extend** 110

High-Frequency Words

Cut out the words.
Paste them in the sentences.

| Where | is the cat?

She is | under | the bed.

| Why | is she there?

I | know | ! She is with her baby.

| know | | Why | | under | | Where |

Be a detective. Ask questions to find out **where** and **why.** Write your questions here.

Questions will vary, but all should start with Where
or Why and end with a ?

Book 1.3
Snakes

At Home: Write a few questions using the words **where, why, know,** or **under.** Have children read each question and find out the answer.

110

Name_____ Date_____ **Extend** 111

Story Comprehension

Read the question.
Write **yes** or **no.**

Can you find snakes in hot lands?
_____
yes

Can a snake eat a rat?
_____
yes

Does a snake have ears?
_____
yes

Can you see a snake's ears?
_____
no

Draw a picture of a baby snake. Show the snake getting food.

Book 1.3
Snakes

At Home: Fold a piece of construction paper in half. Have children write a title and author and draw a picture on the cover. Encourage children to use facts about snakes they learned from the story as they write a snake book.

111

Name_____ Date_____ **Extend** 112

Use a Diagram

Long snakes. Short snakes.
Look in a book about snakes.
Find out how long some snakes are.
Draw the snakes here.
Write each snake's name.
Write how long each snake is.

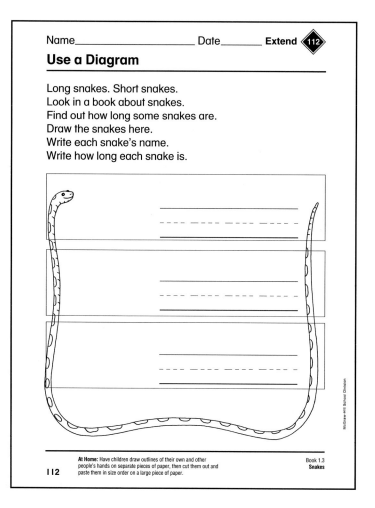

Book 1.3
Snakes

At Home: Have children draw outlines of their own and other people's hands on separate pieces of paper, then cut them out and paste them in size order on a large piece of paper.

112

T44 *Annotated Workbooks*

Long *a*: *a-e*

Name_____ Date_____ Extend ◆113◆

Play tic-tac-toe.
Make a word in each box.
Make three words in a row to win.

___ ___ ─── ─── ___ a ___ e	___ ___ ─── ─── ___ a ___ e	___ ___ ─── ─── ___ a ___ e
___ ___ ─── ─── ___ a ___ e	___ ___ ─── ─── ___ a ___ e	___ ___ ─── ─── ___ a ___ e
___ ___ ─── ─── ___ a ___ e	___ ___ ─── ─── ___ a ___ e	___ ___ ─── ─── ___ a ___ e

Children may form words such as fame, cake, tape, same, take, blame, flake, cape, and so on.

Book 1.3
Snakes

At Home: Have children make up a poem using words from the tic-tac-toe game.

113

---

a-e; ch, wh, nk

Name_____ Date_____ Extend ◆114◆

Take a trip to a far land to find snakes.
What will you pack? Choose from the box. Tell why.

cap	cape	case	can	lunch	chest	whip
game	tape	clock	skate	bank	tank	cane

Packing List

cap   to keep sun off my face

_____   _____
_____   _____
_____   _____
_____   _____
_____   _____
_____   _____
                       Answers will vary.
_____   _____

114

At Home: Play "I Spy" with the words above. Have children guess the word and use it in a sentence. Dialogue might include the following: "I spy with my little eye a word ending with **nk**." (bank)

Book 1.3
Snakes

Story Elements

Name_____ Date_____ Extend ◆115◆

Read the sentences. Put a ✔ if the sentence tells about the picture.

☑ The snake is in a hot land.
☐ The snake is in a cold land.
☑ The snake is on the rock.
☐ The snake is under the rock.
☑ It is day.
☐ It is night.

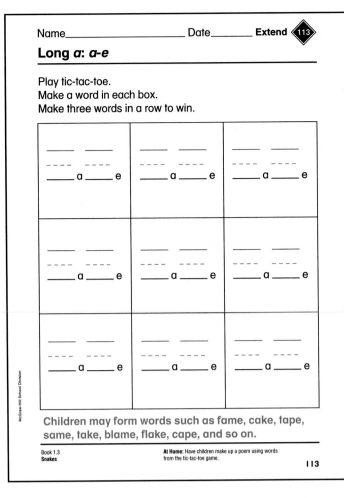

Answers will vary. Sample answers are shown.

Write another sentence about the picture.

_____
There is sand on the desert.
_____
What will the snake do next?

_____
The snake will look for food.

Book 1.3
Snakes

At Home: Invite children to retell part of a favorite story. Help children write several sentences describing the setting. Remind children to give details about both the time and place of the action.

115

Contractions

Name_____ Date_____ Extend ◆116◆

Say a sentence below.

Have a partner 🙂 say what you say.
Say "Simon Says" first.
Your partner uses a contraction to say what you say.

Like this:
You say: "I **can not** eat that cake."

🙂 says: "I **can't** eat that cake."
You say: "Simon says, 'I **would not** pet a snake.'"

🙂 says: "I **wouldn't** pet a snake."

Use these words to make other sentences.

we will	could not	do not	are not

You and your partner can take turns.

116

At Home: Encourage children to continue playing this game. Take turns. Keep score.

Book 1.3
Snakes

Snakes • GRAMMAR

Name_____ Date_____ **LEARN GRAMMAR 83**

Is and *Are*

- The words *is* and *are* are verbs that tell about the present.

> The snake <u>is</u> on the log.
>
> The big snakes <u>are</u> on the log.

Read the sentences. Draw a circle around the verbs *is* and *are*.

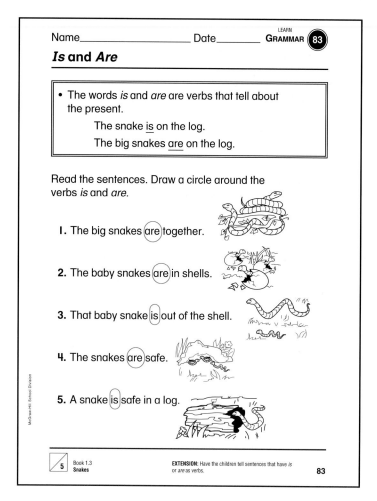

1. The big snakes (are) together.

2. The baby snakes (are) in shells.

3. That baby snake (is) out of the shell.

4. The snakes (are) safe.

5. A snake (is) safe in a log.

5 | Book 1.3 **Snakes**

EXTENSION: Have the children tell sentences that have *is* or *are* as verbs.

83

Name_____ Date_____ **LEARN AND PRACTICE GRAMMAR 84**

Is and *Are*

- The words *is* and *are* are verbs that tell about the present.
- The word *is* tells about one person, place, or thing.
- The word *are* tells about more than one person, place, or thing.

The snake **is** hungry.   The snakes **are** hungry.

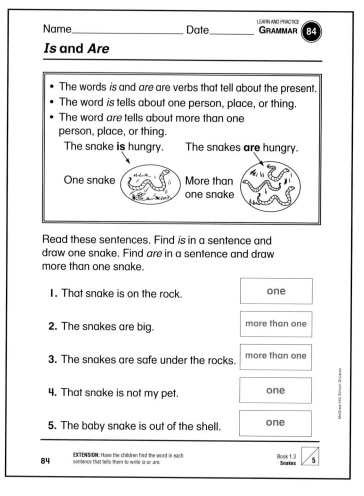

One snake   More than one snake

Read these sentences. Find *is* in a sentence and draw one snake. Find *are* in a sentence and draw more than one snake.

1. That snake is on the rock. | one

2. The snakes are big. | more than one

3. The snakes are safe under the rocks. | more than one

4. That snake is not my pet. | one

5. The baby snake is out of the shell. | one

84

EXTENSION: Have the children find the word in each sentence that tells them to write *is* or *are*.

Book 1.3 **Snakes** | 5

Name_____ Date_____ **PRACTICE AND WRITE GRAMMAR 85**

Is and *Are*

- The words *is* and *are* are verbs that tell about the present.
- The word *is* tells about one person, place, or thing.
- The word *are* tells about more than one person, place, or thing.

> This **is** a safe snake.
>
> These snakes **are** not safe.

Read the sentences.
Write *is* in the sentences that tell about one person, place, or thing.
Write *are* in the sentences that tell about more than one person, place, or thing.

1. There ___are___ a lot of snakes in the world.

2. The snakes ___are___ moving.

3. A snake's skin ___is___ made of scales.

4. The snake ___is___ safe in a log.

5. This snake ___is___ not safe.

5 | Book 1.3 **Snakes**

EXTENSION: Have the children draw pictures and *is* on the pictures of one and *are* on those that are more than one.

85

Name_____ Date_____ **MECHANICS GRAMMAR 86**

Correcting Sentences with *Is* and *Are*

- Begin every sentence with a capital letter.
- End a statement with a period.
- End an exclamation with an exclamation point.

Read the sentences. Circle the words that need to be capitalized. Write the correct end mark.

1. (the) snake is in a log .

2. (is) a snake in the tree ?

3. (look) at all those snakes !

4. (are) they safe snakes ?

5. (that) snake is in a hot land .

6. (where) are all the snakes ?

7. (look) out for the big snake !

8. (that) snake is not my pet .

86

EXTENSION: Have the children make the incorrect sentences correct.

Book 1.3 **Snakes** | 8

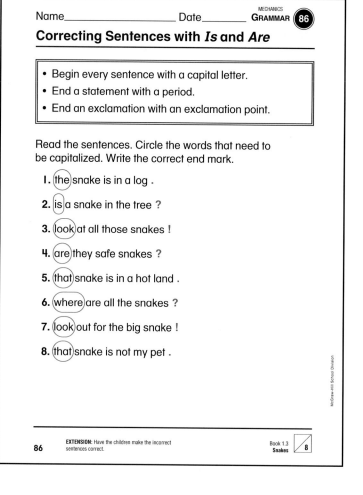

Snakes • GRAMMAR

Test

Read each sentence. Circle the correct verb.

1. There _____ a lot of snakes.

   (are)   is

2. There _____ big snakes and small snakes.

   (are)   is

3. One snake _____ in the log.

   are   (is)

4. One snake _____ in the damp land.

   are   (is)

5. That _____ a big rat!

   are   (is)

More Practice With *Is* And *Are*

- The verbs *is* and *are* tell about the present.
- The verb *is* tells about one person, place, or thing.
- The verb *are* tells about more than one person, place, or thing.

Read each sentence aloud. Write *is* and *are* where they belong.

1. Most snakes _____ are _____ safe.

2. But one snake _____ is _____ not safe.

3. One snake _____ is _____ on the log.

4. Some snakes _____ are _____ making their mouths big.

5. Where _____ is _____ a snake safe?

Worksheet 83

Words with Long a: a-e

1. sn **a** k **e**
2. m a d e
3. l a k e
4. c a m e
5. sh a d e
6. n a m e

Directions (to teacher)

Review the long *a* sound by explaining the silent *e* rule. Present the CVCe (consonant-vowel-consonant-e) pattern as in *snake*. Write *snake* on the chalkboard or form the word with letter cards. Say the word aloud and have children repeat it. Then have them look at the first example on the page. Point out that the letter *a* and the silent *e* have been filled in.

Write the words *lake, made, came, shade,* and *name* on the chalkboard. Read the words aloud and have children repeat them. Then repeat each word and circle the letters that stand for the long *a* sound (*a* and silent *e*). Have children complete each word in the spaces provided.

Worksheet 84

Words with long a: a-e

Using the Word Study Steps

1. LOOK at the word.
2. SAY the word aloud.
3. STUDY the letters in the word.
4. WRITE the word.
5. CHECK the word. Did you spell the word right? If not, go back to step 1.

> **Spelling Tip**
>
> Think of times when you have seen the word. Maybe you have read it in a book or on a sign. Try to remember how it looked. Write the word in different ways to see which one looks correct.
>
> ~~lak~~ ~~lacke~~ lake

Fill in the Blank

Write the spelling word that best fits each sentence.

1. There is no sun in the __shade__.
2. She __came__ to the park.
3. I saw a __snake__ at the zoo.
4. The __lake__ is blue.
5. I __made__ a cake.
6. What is your __name__?

To Parents or Helpers:

Using the Word Study Steps above as your child comes across any new words will help him or her spell well. Review the steps as you both go over this week's spelling words.

Go over the Spelling Tip with your child. Help your child write new words in different ways to see which one looks right.

Help your child complete the spelling activity.

Worksheet 85

Words with Long a : a-e

Look at the spelling words in the box.

| snake made lake came shade name |

Find the spelling words in the snake. Circle each spelling word.

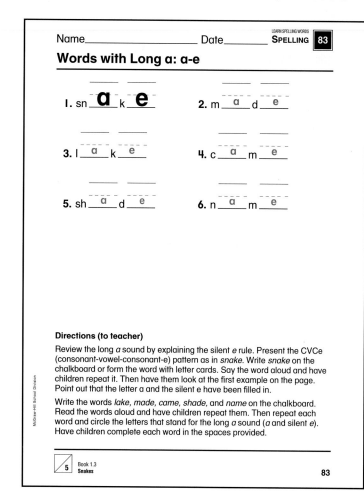

Write each spelling word under the correct snake.

Words with ending ade | Words with ending ame | Words with ending ake

1. made
2. shade
3. came
4. name
5. snake
6. lake

Worksheet 86

Words with Long a : a-e

Read the sentences. Complete each spelling word with **ade**, **ame**, or **ake**.

1. You can swim in a l____ake____.
2. My n____ame____ is Jake.
3. When it is hot, I sit in the sh____ade____.
4. A sn____ake____ is an animal that cannot run.
5. The baby snake c____ame____ out of its shell.
6. The snake m____ade____ a nest in the grass.

Name________________ Date________ PRACTICE AND WRITE SPELLING 87

Words with Long *a* : *a-e*

Read the story. Use the spelling words to complete the story.

My ___name___ is Sam. I am a baby ___snake___. I ___came___ out of a shell. I used my egg tooth to get out.

My Mom and Dad swim in a ___lake___ with the other snakes.

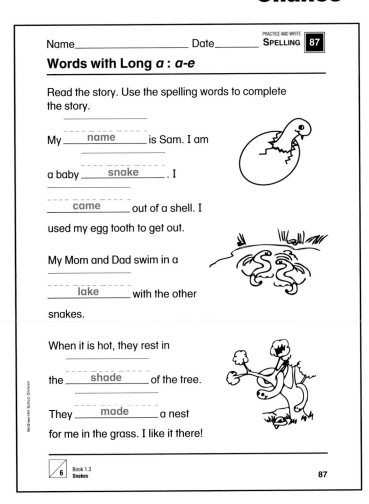

When it is hot, they rest in the ___shade___ of the tree. They ___made___ a nest for me in the grass. I like it there!

Name________________ Date________ SPELLING TEST SPELLING 88

Words with Long *a* : a-e

Look at the words in each set. One word in each set is spelled correctly. Use a pencil to color in the circle in front of that word. Before you begin, look at the sample sets of words. Sample A has been done for you. Do Sample B by yourself. When you are sure you know what to do, you may go on with the rest of the page.

Sample A
- **(A) make**
- (B) mak
- (C) maek

Sample B
- (D) sikn
- (E) singk
- **(F) sink**

1. (A) nam (B) naem **(C) name**
2. (D) lak **(E) lake** (F) laek
3. (A) sanke (B) snak **(C) snake**
4. **(D) made** (E) maed (F) madde
5. (A) caem **(B) came** (C) camme
6. **(D) shade** (E) shede (F) shead

Let's Camp Out! • PRACTICE

Name________________ Date________ **Practice 117**

a-e; ch, wh, nk; Blends

Use these words to answer the riddles.

chick	bank	stump	white	plane

1. You can fly in me. What am I? plane

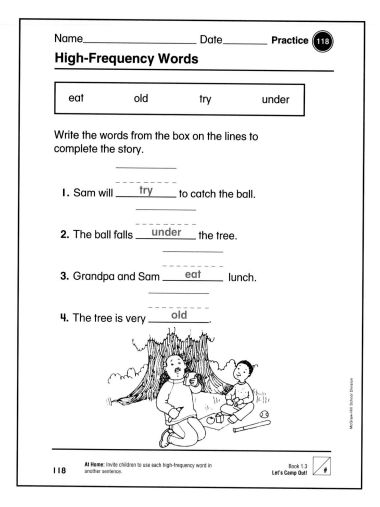

2. I am soft and yellow. I live on a farm.
   What am I? chick

3. I am the color of the clouds. white
   What am I?

4. Put your cash in me. I will save it.
   What am I? bank

5. Cut down a tree. I am all that is left.
   What am I? stump

McGraw-Hill School Division

At Home: Ask children to name four new words with these letter combinations: st, ch, mp, br

Name________________ Date________ **Practice 118**

High-Frequency Words

eat	old	try	under

Write the words from the box on the lines to complete the story.

1. Sam will try to catch the ball.
2. The ball falls under the tree.
3. Grandpa and Sam eat lunch.
4. The tree is very old.

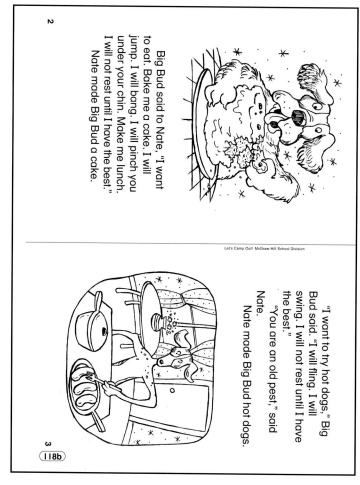

McGraw-Hill School Division

At Home: Invite children to use each high-frequency word in another sentence.

The Gum Trap

"What is that?" said Big Bud.
"It is gum," said Nate.
Big Bud chewed lots of gum.
He could not chat. He could not think.
"You will not rest! You are in a gum trap set by the best!" said Nate.

At Home: Encourage children to draw a picture of the story they read about Nate and Big Bud.

Big Bud said to Nate, "I want to eat. Bake me a cake. I will jump. I will bang. I will pinch you under your chin. Make me lunch. I will not rest until I have the best."
Nate made Big Bud a cake.

Let's Camp Out! McGraw-Hill School Division

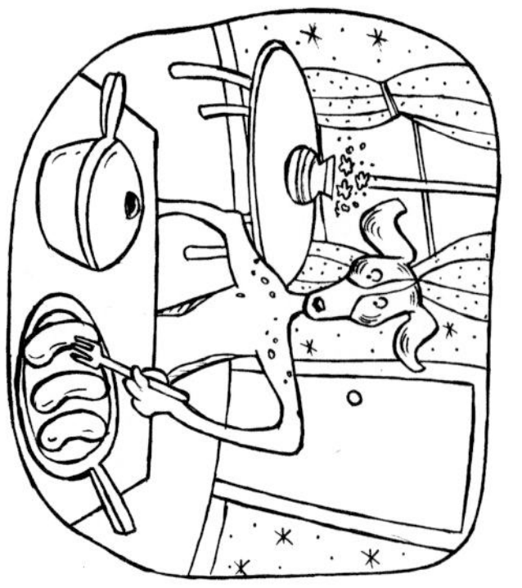

"I want to try hot dogs," Big Bud said. "I will fling. I will swing. I will not rest until I have the best."
"You are an old pest," said Nate.
Nate made Big Bud hot dogs.

Story Comprehension

Name_____ Date_____ Practice **119**

Read the statements. Underline the things you might do on a camping trip.

1. sleep in a tent

2. wade in a lake

3. shop for gifts

4. sit by a fire

5. look at the stars

6. put on a pack

7. chat on the phone

8. find a nest

9. sing songs

10. see a movie

11. see a frog

12. take a hike

At Home: Have children draw a picture of something they might see on a camping trip.

119

A Diagram

Name_____ Date_____ Practice **120**

This **diagram** shows how to make water safe when you are camping.

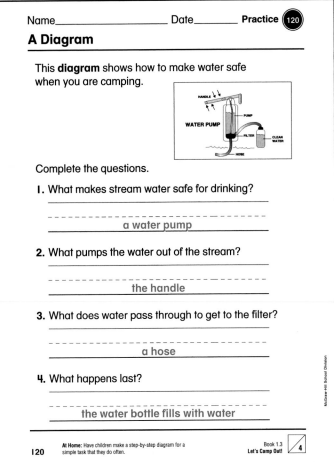

Complete the questions.

1. What makes stream water safe for drinking?

_____

a water pump

2. What pumps the water out of the stream?

_____

the handle

3. What does water pass through to get to the filter?

_____

a hose

4. What happens last?

_____

the water bottle fills with water

At Home: Have children make a step-by-step diagram for a simple task that they do often.

Book 1.3 Let's Camp Out! | 4

Compare and Contrast

Name_____ Date_____ Practice **121**

Read the sentences. If the sentence tells how things are alike, color the picture. If the sentence tells how things are different, circle the picture.

1. Jake and Pam sit in a hut.

2. Spot is small. Fluff is very big.

3. My socks are pink. My hat is pink.

4. We like to sing.

5. Sam bakes good cakes. My cakes are bad.

6. Now it is cold. Then it was hot.

At Home: Ask children to compare today's weather with yesterday's weather.

121

Story Elements

Name_____ Date_____ Practice **122**

The **setting** is where and when a story takes place.
Read the story.
Then circle the pictures that describe the **setting** of the park.

The Park
Brad lives in a big city.
There is a big park near him. It has lots of plants.
There are swings. Brad likes to run on the hills.
Then he sits on the bench. He likes to look at people.

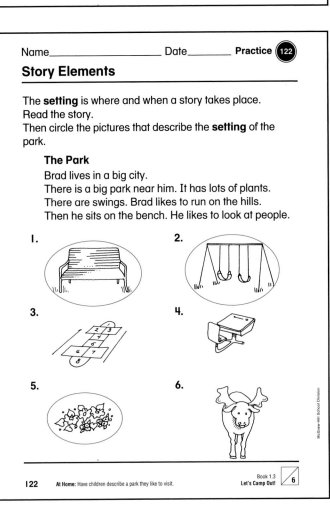

1.

2.

3.

4.

5.

6.

At Home: Have children describe a park they like to visit.

Book 1.3 Let's Camp Out! | 6

Let's Camp Out! • PRACTICE

Name_____ Date_____ **Practice** 123

Possessives

An **apostrophe (')** and the letter **s** at the end of someone's name mean that person or thing owns something.

Write the words to show who owns something. Remember to add **'s**.

1. Jake   tape _____ Jake's tape _____

2. bird   song _____ bird's song _____

3. Kate   chin _____ Kate's chin _____

4. snake   fangs _____ snake's fangs _____

5. Jane   vase _____ Jane's vase _____

6. Eric   brush _____ Eric's brush _____

McGraw-Hill School Division

6 Book 1.3 **Let's Camp Out!**

At Home: Help children to add three more examples to this list.

123

Name_____ Date_____ **Practice** 124

Contractions

A **contraction** is a short form of two words. Some letters are replaced by an **apostrophe (')**.

Draw a line from the words to the correct contraction.

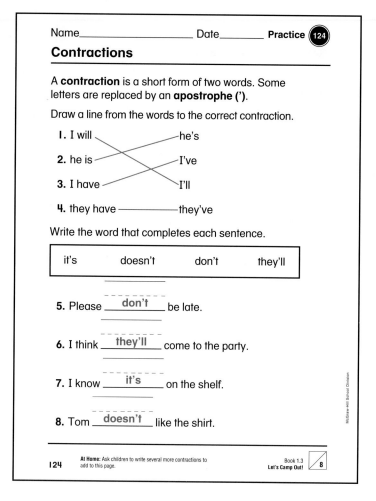

1. I will   he's

2. he is   I've

3. I have   I'll

4. they have ———————they've

Write the word that completes each sentence.

it's	doesn't	don't	they'll

5. Please ____ don't ____ be late.

6. I think ____ they'll ____ come to the party.

7. I know ____ it's ____ on the shelf.

8. Tom ____ doesn't ____ like the shirt.

McGraw-Hill School Division

124 **At Home:** Ask children to write several more contractions to add to this page.

Book 1.3 **Let's Camp Out!** 8

Let's Camp Out! • RETEACH

a-e; ch, wh, nk; Blends

Name_____ Date_____ **Reteach** 117

when

Circle the missing letters. Then write them to complete the words.

1. si **ng**   fl (**ng**)

2. te **nt**   (**nt**)   ng

3. sn **a** k **e**   a-a (**a-e**)

4. **tr** ap   (**tr**)   pl

5. **dr** ink   cl (**dr**)

6. **ch** in   (**ch**)   tw

Book 1.3
Let's Camp Out!   6
At Home: Have children think of words that begin with the consonant blend they did not circle.   117

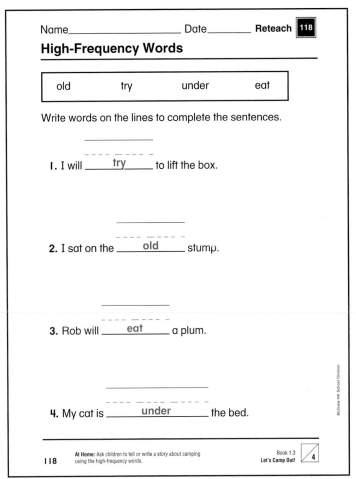

Name_____ Date_____ **Reteach** 118

High-Frequency Words

| old | try | under | eat |

Write words on the lines to complete the sentences.

1. I will _____**try**_____ to lift the box.

2. I sat on the _____**old**_____ stump.

3. Rob will _____**eat**_____ a plum.

4. My cat is _____**under**_____ the bed.

118   **At Home:** Ask children to tell or write a story about camping using the high-frequency words.   Book 1.3
Let's Camp Out!   4

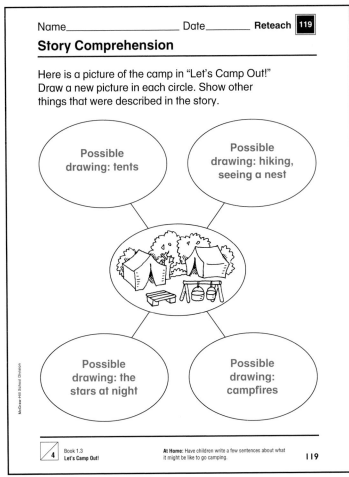

Name_____ Date_____ **Reteach** 119

Story Comprehension

Here is a picture of the camp in "Let's Camp Out!" Draw a new picture in each circle. Show other things that were described in the story.

Possible drawing: tents

Possible drawing: hiking, seeing a nest

Possible drawing: the stars at night

Possible drawing: campfires

Book 1.3
Let's Camp Out!   4
At Home: Have children write a few sentences about what it might be like to go camping.   119

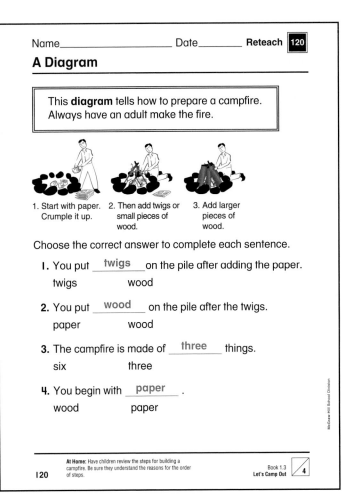

Name_____ Date_____ **Reteach** 120

A Diagram

This **diagram** tells how to prepare a campfire. Always have an adult make the fire.

1. Start with paper. Crumple it up.
2. Then add twigs or small pieces of wood.
3. Add larger pieces of wood.

Choose the correct answer to complete each sentence.

1. You put __**twigs**__ on the pile after adding the paper.
   twigs   wood

2. You put __**wood**__ on the pile after the twigs.
   paper   wood

3. The campfire is made of __**three**__ things.
   six   three

4. You begin with __**paper**__ .
   wood   paper

120   **At Home:** Have children review the steps for building a campfire. Be sure they understand the reasons for the order of steps.   Book 1.3
Let's Camp Out   4

Compare and Contrast

Name_____ Date_____ Reteach **121**

When you **compare** two things you see how they are the same. When you **contrast** two things you see how they are different.

Color the pictures that tell about your home. Circle the pictures that tell about camping.

1.
2.
3.
4.
5.
6.

At Home: Ask children to pick two household appliances to examine. Help them understand how the items are alike and different.

121

Story Elements

Name_____ Date_____ Reteach **122**

The **setting** is where and when a story happens.

Color the pictures that could be found in the setting of a circus.

1.
2.
3.
4.
5.
6.
7.
8.

122

At Home: Ask children to draw a picture of their favorite place. Ask them what kind of a story might be set there.

Possessives

Name_____ Date_____ Reteach **123**

An **apostrophe (')** and the letter **s** at the end of someone's name mean that person has or owns something.
the leg of Ted   =   Ted's leg

Write the underlined word and add **'s** to show who owns something.

1. the mud of the <u>pig</u>   _____pig's_____ mud

2. the cot of <u>Bonita</u>   _____Bonita's_____ cot

3. the log of the <u>dog</u>   _____dog's_____ log

4. the jet of the <u>men</u>   _____men's_____ jet

5. the skates of the <u>king</u>   _____king's_____ skates

6. the pet of <u>Kenya</u>   _____Kenya's_____ pet

At Home: Have children write other words that show ownership.

123

Contractions

Name_____ Date_____ Reteach **124**

A **contraction** is a short form of two words.
She is waving at me.
She's waving at me.

Circle the contraction in each sentence.

1. (I'll) take the pup.

2. I see that (they've) packed the box.

3. (She'll) look for the tent.

4. (Let's) eat lunch.

5. Jack (doesn't) like the snacks.

6. (Don't) rake the yard.

7. (We've) got to go home.

8. I (can't) eat these grapes.

124

At Home: Invite children to write a story about an outdoor adventure using some of the contractions on this page.

Let's Camp Out! • EXTEND

a-e; ch, wh, nk; Blends

Play with a partner 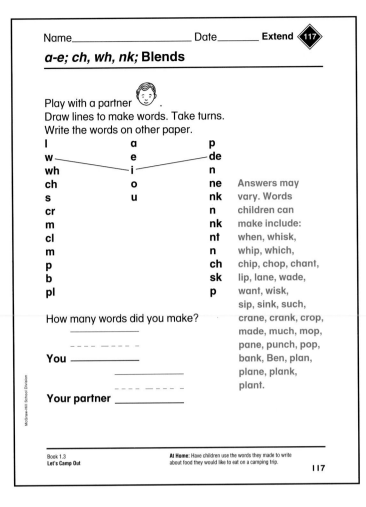.
Draw lines to make words. Take turns.
Write the words on other paper.

l	a	p
w	e	de
wh	i	n
ch	o	ne
s	u	nk
cr		n
m		nk
cl		nt
m		n
p		ch
b		sk
pl		p

Answers may vary. Words children can make include: when, whisk, whip, which, chip, chop, chant, lip, lane, wade, want, wisk, sip, sink, such, crane, crank, crop, made, much, mop, pane, punch, pop, bank, Ben, plan, plane, plank, plant.

How many words did you make?

_____

You _____

_____

Your partner _____

McGraw-Hill School Division

Book 1.3
Let's Camp Out

At Home: Have children use the words they made to write
about food they would like to eat on a camping trip.

117

High-Frequency Words

Play with a partner .
Act out a clue for a word in the box. Do not use words.
Have your partner write the word.
Take turns.

try	old
eat	under

Write the words here.

_____   _____

Order of answers will vary.

_____   _____

_____   _____

_____   _____

_____   _____

118

At Home: Take turns with children making up word clues,
such as "What word means **not over?**" for the words **try,
old, eat,** and **under.**

Book 1.3
Let's Camp Out

Story Comprehension

What would you do on a camping trip?
Make a postcard.
Write what you did. Draw a picture.
Write who you will send your card to.

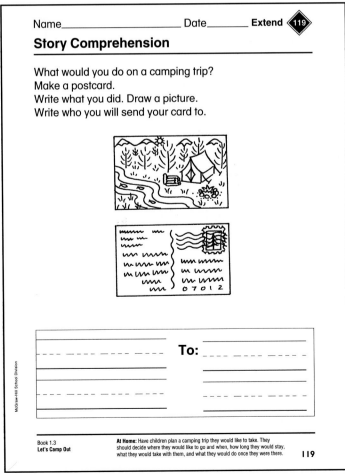

To: _____

_____

_____

McGraw-Hill School Division

Book 1.3
Let's Camp Out

At Home: Have children plan a camping trip they would like to take. They
should decide where they would like to go and when, how long they would stay,
what they would take with them, and what they would do once they were there.

119

Use a Diagram

Pack the backpack.
Write what goes in the backpack on the lines below.

Answers may vary. Likely possibilities include food, marshmallows, rope, pots.

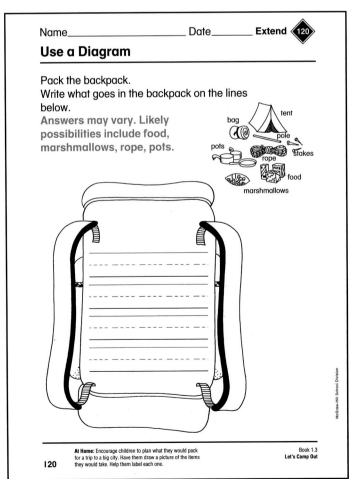

120

At Home: Encourage children to plan what they would pack
for a trip to a big city. Have them draw a picture of the items
they would take. Help them label each one.

Book 1.3
Let's Camp Out

T55

Compare and Contrast

Name_____ Date_____ Extend ◆121

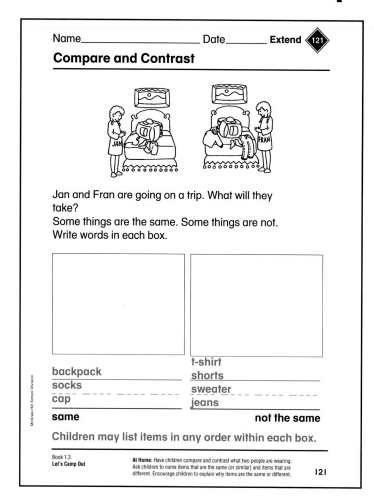

Jan and Fran are going on a trip. What will they take?
Some things are the same. Some things are not.
Write words in each box.

	t-shirt
backpack	shorts
socks	sweater
cap	jeans
same	**not the same**

Children may list items in any order within each box.

Book 1.3
Let's Camp Out

At Home: Have children compare and contrast what two people are wearing. Ask children to name items that are the same (or similar) and items that are different. Encourage children to explain why items are the same or different.

121

Story Elements

Name_____ Date_____ Extend ◆122

Circle words that tell about the picture.

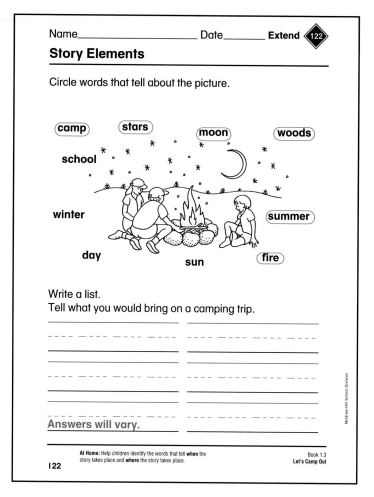

camp   stars   moon   woods

school

winter   summer

day   sun   fire

Write a list.
Tell what you would bring on a camping trip.

_____   _____
_____   _____
_____   _____
_____   _____
_____   _____
Answers will vary.

122

At Home: Help children identify the words that tell **when** the story takes place and **where** the story takes place.

Book 1.3
Let's Camp Out

Possessives

Name_____ Date_____ Extend ◆123

Do what the sentences tell you to do.
Make up a sentence of your own.

Draw a picture. Give it to a partner 🙂 to color.

Color the pig's face pink.

Color the cat's tail black.

Color the bird's beak yellow.

Color the dog's ears brown.

Color the **Sentence should follow the pattern of the previous sentences: Color the (animal's body part) (a color)**

Book 1.3
Let's Camp Out

At Home: Have children draw pictures of people and the things that belong to them. Help children label their pictures by writing words and phrases, such as **Jack** and **Jack's baseball,** and drawing arrows pointing to each.

123

Contractions

Name_____ Date_____ Extend ◆124

Cut on the dotted lines.
Slip the letter strip through the slits.
Pull it up and down to make new words.
How many words can you make?

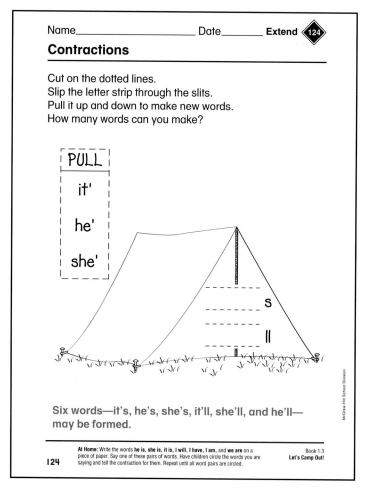

PULL
it'
he'
she'

s
ll

Six words—it's, he's, she's, it'll, she'll, and he'll—may be formed.

124

At Home: Write the words **he is, she is, it is, I will, I have, I am,** and **we are** on a piece of paper. Say one of these pairs of words. Have children circle the words you are saying and tell the contraction for them. Repeat until all word pairs are circled.

Book 1.3
Let's Camp Out!

Let's Camp Out! • GRAMMAR

Contractions with *Not*

- A **contraction** is a short form of two words.
  You <u>are not</u> going on a hike. — Long form
  You <u>aren't</u> going on a hike. — Short form

Read the sentences. Draw a circle around the short
form of two words.

1. Greg (isn't) packing for a trip.

2. They (aren't) packing for a trip.

3. You (aren't) a singer.

4. You are not a singer.

5. Pam is not getting her pack.

6. Pam (isn't) getting her pack.

6 Book 1.3
Let's Camp Out!
EXTENSION: Have the children think of sentences with
contractions. Write the contractions on a chart.
89

Contractions with *Not*

- A **contraction** is a short form of two words.
- An **apostrophe** (') takes the place of the
  letters that are left out.
      She is not picking up sticks. — is not
      She isn't picking up sticks. — isn't

Read the sentences. Draw a circle around the two
words that were joined in the contractions.

1. Pam isn't looking at the Big Dipper.
   (is not)   not at   Pam is

2. Max isn't a singer.
   (is not)   Max is   not a

3. They aren't packing.
   (are not)   They are   not packing

4. Greg isn't picking up sticks.
   Greg is   (is not)   not picking

5. They aren't warmed up.
   (are not)   They are   not warmed

90 EXTENSION: Have the children look for contractions in trade
books that have been read to them. Write the contractions
they find on a chart.
Book 1.3
Let's Camp Out! 5

Contractions with *Not*

- A **contraction** is a short form of two words.
- A **apostrophe** (') takes the place of the letters
  that are left out.

Write the contraction for the underlined words in
each sentence.

1. Cory <u>is not</u> picking up twigs.
   _____isn't_____

2. She <u>is not</u> seeing the Big Dipper.
   _____isn't_____

3. They <u>are not</u> finding the food.
   _____aren't_____

4. They <u>are not</u> hiking.
   _____aren't_____

5. She <u>is not</u> hiking.
   _____isn't_____

5 Book 1.3
Let's Camp Out!
EXTENSION: Have the children rewrite the sentences in
the long form with both words.
91

Contractions with *Not*

- A **contraction** is a short form of two words.
- A **contraction** is a way of saying two words as one.
- Two words are joined and a letter is left out.
- An **apostrophe** (') takes the place of the
  letters that are left out.
      You **are not** going on a hike.
      You **aren't** going on a hike.

Correct the contractions. Put in the apostrophe (').
Write the contraction.

1. That isnt our food.   _____isn't_____

2. They arent making a fire.   _____aren't_____

3. Greg isnt finding our tent.   _____isn't_____

4. Isnt that a big tent?   _____isn't_____

5. They arent sleeping.   _____aren't_____

92 EXTENSION: Have the children tell the two words that were
joined to make the contractions in this exercise.
Book 1.3
Let's Camp Out! 5

Name_____ Date_____

Contractions with *Not*

Circle the two words that make the contraction.

1. Greg isn't going on a trip.

   Greg (is not) going on a trip.

2. Greg isn't going to get a pack.

   Greg (is not) going to get a pack.

3. They aren't making a fire.

   They (are not) making a fire.

4. They aren't sleeping in a tent.

   They (are not) sleeping in a tent.

5. Greg isn't looking for the Big Dipper.

   Greg (is not) looking for the Big Dipper.

6. They aren't sleeping in a tent.

   They (are not) sleeping in a tent.

Name_____ Date_____

Contractions with *Not*

- A **contraction** is a short form of two words.
- An **apostrophe** (') takes the place of the letters that are left out.

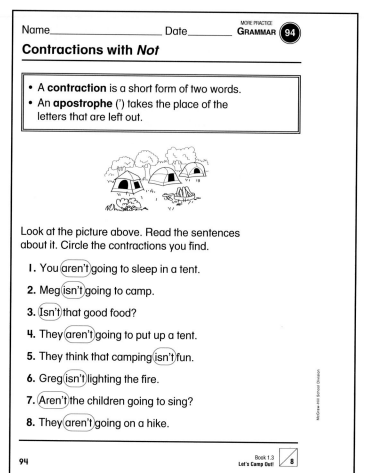

Look at the picture above. Read the sentences about it. Circle the contractions you find.

1. You (aren't) going to sleep in a tent.
2. Meg (isn't) going to camp.
3. (Isn't) that good food?
4. They (aren't) going to put up a tent.
5. They think that camping (isn't) fun.
6. Greg (isn't) lighting the fire.
7. (Aren't) the children going to sing?
8. They (aren't) going on a hike.

Let's Camp Out! • SPELLING

Words from Science

1. Sticks
2. sun
3. twigs
4. fire
5. snow
6. mud

Directions (to teacher)

Write the words *sticks, sun, twigs, fire, snow,* and *mud* on the chalkboard. Have children find the word sticks filled in on this page. Read the word aloud and have them repeat it.

Tell children they will be writing the other five words on this page. Read each word aloud. Have children repeat it and write it in the blank provided.

You may also wish to present the challenge words *try, old, eat,* and *under.*

6 Book 1.3 **Let's Camp Out** 89

Words from Science

Using the Word Study Steps

1. LOOK at the word.
2. SAY the word aloud.
3. STUDY the letters in the word.
4. WRITE the word.
5. CHECK the word.
   Did you spell the word right? If not, go back to step 1.

Spelling Tip

Add -s to most words to tell about more than one.
stick + **s** = stick**s**
fire + **s** = fire**s**

Find and Circle
Where are the spelling words?

s	s t i c k s	a	s u n
o	t w i g s	r	f i r e
r	c	s n o w	e	p	m u d

To Parents or Helpers:
Using the Word Study Steps above as your child comes across any new words will help him or her spell well. Review the steps as you both go over this week's spelling words.
Go over the Spelling Tip with your child. Help your child add -s to words to tell about more than one.
Help your child find and circle the spelling words in the puzzle.

90 Book 1.3 **Let's Camp Out** 6

Words from Science

Look at the spelling words in the box.

| sticks sun twigs fire snow mud |

Write each spelling word on the line where it belongs.

Write the spelling words with three letters.

1. sun
2. mud

Write the spelling words with four letters.

3. fire
4. snow

Write the spelling word with five letters.

5. twigs

Write the spelling word with six letters.

6. sticks

6 Book 1.3 **Let's Camp Out** 91

Words from Science

Look at each picture. Complete each sentence with a spelling word.

1. When the ____sun____ is out, it can be hot.

2. They make cakes out of ____mud____ just for fun.

3. We can make a man out of ____snow____.

4. A ____fire____ can make us warm.

Each spelling word below tells about more than one. Rewrite each word so that it tells about only one.

5. sticks ____stick____

6. twigs ____twig____

92 Book 1.3 **Let's Camp Out** 6

Let's Camp Out! • SPELLING

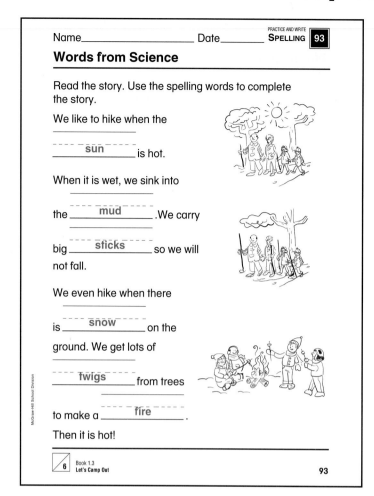

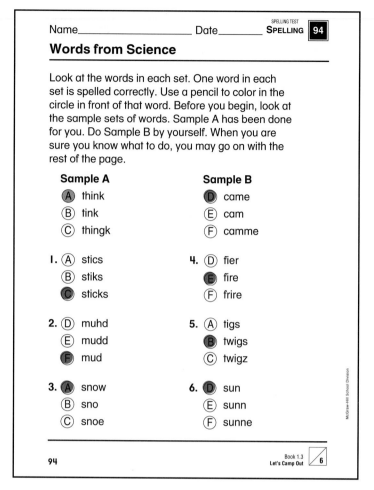

Unit 3 Review • PRACTICE and RETEACH

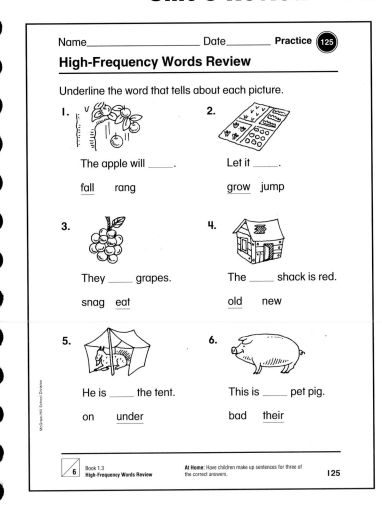

Name_____ Date_____ Practice 125

High-Frequency Words Review

Underline the word that tells about each picture.

1. The apple will _____.

   fall   rang

2. Let it _____.

   grow   jump

3. They _____ grapes.

   snag   eat

4. The _____ shack is red.

   old   new

5. He is _____ the tent.

   on   under

6. This is _____ pet pig.

   bad   their

Book 1.3
High-Frequency Words Review 6

At Home: Have children make up sentences for three of the correct answers.

125

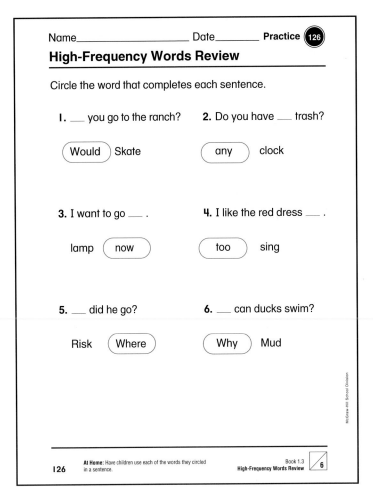

Name_____ Date_____ Practice 126

High-Frequency Words Review

Circle the word that completes each sentence.

1. ___ you go to the ranch?

   (Would)   Skate

2. Do you have ___ trash?

   (any)   clock

3. I want to go ___ .

   lamp   (now)

4. I like the red dress ___ .

   (too)   sing

5. ___ did he go?

   Risk   (Where)

6. ___ can ducks swim?

   (Why)   Mud

126 At Home: Have children use each of the words they circled in a sentence.

Book 1.3
High-Frequency Words Review 6

Name_____ Date_____ Reteach 125

High-Frequency Words Review

Circle the word that completes each sentence.

1. I have a ___ drum.

   not   (new)

2. Bob ___ corn.

   (grows)   grabs

3. The crab is ___ the dock.

   (under)   on

4. Are there ___ fish ?

   craft   (any)

5. We all ___ down.

   (fall)   nut

Book 1.3
5 High-Frequency Words Review

At Home: Have children draw another picture for one of the sentences.

125

Name_____ Date_____ Reteach 126

High-Frequency Words Review

Circle the words that tell about the picture.

1. (their dolls)

   his boat

2. (old king)

   old wing

3. went away

   (eats jam)

4. fox runs

   (frogs together)

5. (too big)

   black dog

6. hot water

   (try again)

126 At Home: Have children tell a story that starts with one of the pictures on this page.

Book 1.3
High-Frequency Words Review 6

T61

High-Frequency Words Review

Name_____ Date_____ Extend 125

Read the story. Draw a picture about the story.

"I want to **eat."** Max said.

Pam said, "Me **too!"**

"Do you **know where** we can get a snack?" Max asked Pam.

"I **grow** grapes. We can **try** to get a bunch," Pam said. They went to the lake. "There are the grapes!" they said **together.**

Max went to eat a grape.

"Do not eat a grape **now!**" Pam said.

"Why?" Max asked.

"I **would** wash them," Pam said.

Now write what happens next.

_____
_____
_____
_____
_____

Book 1.3
Let's Camp Out

At Home: Children can tell a story about what they like for a snack and where they get it.

125

High-Frequency Words Review

Name_____ Date_____ Extend 126

Rewritten sentences may vary. Samples are shown.
Read the sentence. Look at the picture. Circle **Yes** or **No**.
Write the **No** sentences to make them **Yes** sentences.

1. This shack is **new**.
   YES (NO)

   This shack is old.

2. Bob **eats** cake.
   YES (NO)

   Bob eats a cone.

3. She is **under** the cot.
   YES (NO)

   She is on the cot.

4. You can **fall** when you skate.
   (YES) NO

5. We can go on it **together**.
   (YES) NO

126

At Home: Take turns making up YES and NO sentences. Whoever guesses can reword the NO sentences to make them correct.

Book 1.3
Let's Camp Out

Verbs

Name_____ Date_____ REVIEW GRAMMAR 95

Read the sentences in the box. Look at the part with the line under it. What is the best way to say this part? Mark the letter for your answer.

Frog jumps. <u>Jumping Stan.</u> The others jump.
(1)

1. Ⓐ Stan jumps.
   Ⓑ Stan jumping.
   Ⓒ Stan jump.

Mom, Pop, and Chuck sing. <u>Sam with them.</u>
(2)

2. Ⓐ Sam with Chuck sing.
   Ⓑ Pop and Sam sings.
   Ⓒ Sam sings with them.

<u>Owl blink.</u> Stan watches Owl. Stan blinks like Owl.
(3)

3. Ⓐ Owl blinks.
   Ⓑ Blink Owl.
   Ⓒ Owl blinking.

Last night, I wanted to eat. <u>I look for pizza.</u>
(4)

4. Ⓐ I looks for Pizza
   Ⓑ I looked for pizza.
   Ⓒ Pizza for I look.

Book 1.3
Stories to Tell

Go on

95

Name_____ Date_____ REVIEW GRAMMAR 96

There are a lot of snakes. <u>One snake are on the log.</u> It is a big snake. (5)

5. Ⓐ One snake is on the log.
   Ⓑ One snakes are on the log.
   Ⓒ Snakes is on the log.

The stars are bright. Where are they? <u>The stars is in the sky.</u>
(6)

6. Ⓐ Stars in the sky.
   Ⓑ The star are in the sky.
   Ⓒ The stars are in the sky.

<u>Bat aren't in the tree.</u> Find Bat. Bat is inside the barn.
(7)

7. Ⓐ Bat are not in the tree.
   Ⓑ Bat isn't in the tree.
   Ⓒ Bat are in the tree.

<u>Greg and Tam isn't in school.</u> Greg is at home. Tam isn't in school. (8)

8. Ⓐ Greg and Tam is in school.
   Ⓑ Greg and Tam are in school.
   Ⓒ Greg and Tam aren't in school.

96

Book 1.3
Stories to Tell 8

Unit 3 Review • SPELLING

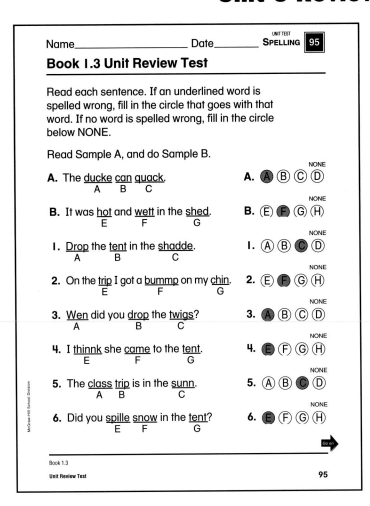

Book 1.3 Unit Review Test

Read each sentence. If an underlined word is spelled wrong, fill in the circle that goes with that word. If no word is spelled wrong, fill in the circle below NONE.

Read Sample A, and do Sample B.

A. The <u>ducke</u> <u>can</u> <u>quack</u>.
   A   B   C

A. Ⓐ Ⓑ Ⓒ Ⓓ NONE

B. It was <u>hot</u> and <u>wett</u> in the <u>shed</u>.
   E   F   G

B. Ⓔ Ⓕ Ⓖ Ⓗ NONE

1. <u>Drop</u> the <u>tent</u> in the <u>shadde</u>.
   A   B   C

1. Ⓐ Ⓑ Ⓒ Ⓓ NONE

2. On the <u>trip</u> I got a <u>bummp</u> on my <u>chin</u>.
   E   F   G

2. Ⓔ Ⓕ Ⓖ Ⓗ NONE

3. <u>Wen</u> did you <u>drop</u> the <u>twigs</u>?
   A   B   C

3. Ⓐ Ⓑ Ⓒ Ⓓ NONE

4. I <u>thinnk</u> she <u>came</u> to the <u>tent</u>.
   E   F   G

4. Ⓔ Ⓕ Ⓖ Ⓗ NONE

5. The <u>class</u> <u>trip</u> is in the <u>sunn</u>.
   A   B   C

5. Ⓐ Ⓑ Ⓒ Ⓓ NONE

6. Did you <u>spille</u> <u>snow</u> in the <u>tent</u>?
   E   F   G

6. Ⓔ Ⓕ Ⓖ Ⓗ NONE

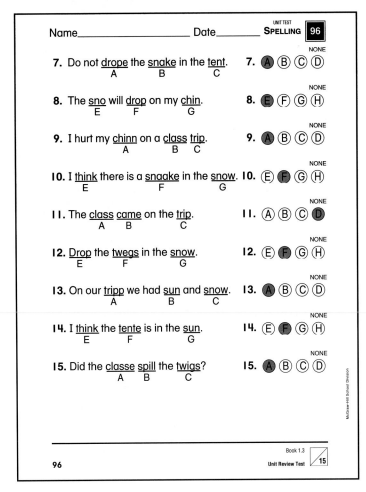

7. Do not <u>drope</u> the <u>snake</u> in the <u>tent</u>.
   A   B   C

7. Ⓐ Ⓑ Ⓒ Ⓓ NONE

8. The <u>sno</u> will <u>drop</u> on my <u>chin</u>.
   E   F   G

8. Ⓔ Ⓕ Ⓖ Ⓗ NONE

9. I hurt my <u>chinn</u> on a <u>class</u> <u>trip</u>.
   A   B   C

9. Ⓐ Ⓑ Ⓒ Ⓓ NONE

10. I <u>think</u> there is a <u>snaake</u> in the <u>snow</u>.
   E   F   G

10. Ⓔ Ⓕ Ⓖ Ⓗ NONE

11. The <u>class</u> <u>came</u> on the <u>trip</u>.
   A   B   C

11. Ⓐ Ⓑ Ⓒ Ⓓ NONE

12. <u>Drop</u> the <u>twegs</u> in the <u>snow</u>.
   E   F   G

12. Ⓔ Ⓕ Ⓖ Ⓗ NONE

13. On our <u>tripp</u> we had <u>sun</u> and <u>snow</u>.
   A   B   C

13. Ⓐ Ⓑ Ⓒ Ⓓ NONE

14. I <u>think</u> the <u>tente</u> is in the <u>sun</u>.
   E   F   G

14. Ⓔ Ⓕ Ⓖ Ⓗ NONE

15. Did the <u>classe</u> <u>spill</u> the <u>twigs</u>?
   A   B   C

15. Ⓐ Ⓑ Ⓒ Ⓓ NONE

T63

Phonological Awareness

 **OBJECTIVES** Children will blend sounds, segment sounds, and substitute beginning sounds.

Alternate Activities

Blend Sounds

SIMON SAYS

 GROUP This activity will help children blend sounds to form words.

- Play Simon Says with children, but use the segmented sounds to form words. For example, say, *Simon says, "/j/-/u/-/m/-/p/ in place."* (Children jump in place.) *Touch your /h/-/a/-/n/-/d/.* (Children don't touch their hand without hearing "Simon says.")

- Continue playing so that children blend sounds to decipher the directions Simon gives.

Segment Sounds

ARM TAP

 GROUP This activity will help children segment sounds.

- Segment the sounds in *spot* with the class, and clap as you say each sound. Invite children to clap the sounds of another word, such as *lift*.

- Then, show children how they can tap the sounds of a word in sequence on their arm. As you say each sound of a word, such as *shut,* tap your right wrist, elbow, and shoulder. (The children see the left-to-right progression as they watch you.)

- Invite the class to tap their right wrist, elbow, and shoulder as they segment a word. For words with four sounds, such as *stop,* have children touch their head as a fourth sound.

Substitute Sounds

SINGING NEW NAMES

 GROUP This activity will help children substitute beginning sounds in words.

- Sing the following to the tune of "Farmer in the Dell," substituting the initial sound in your children's names.

  Change the /b/ in *Bill.*
  Change the /b/ in *Bill.*
  Change the /b/ into a /h/,
  And *Bill* turns into *hill.*

- Continue the song, encouraging children to sing along, making silly names by substituting the initial sound in each child's name. Pause before the last word in the song, allowing children to substitute the sound and say the new word.

- Practice substituting sounds in other words by replacing the names with new words. For example, *Change the /b/ in bank. Change the /b/ into a /t/, and bank turns into tank.*

Blends

Alternate Activities

Visual

WORD SALAD

 Materials: blue and pink index cards
GROUP Use this activity to introduce the blends *st, sk, sp, ng, nt, nd, mp,* and *ft.*

- Use a pocket board or a bulletin board with thumbtacks for this activity.

- Make up blue cards with blends *st, sk, sp.*

- Make up pink cards with blends *ng, nt, nd, mp, ft.*

- Explain that the blue blends can be used at the beginning of words, and the pink blends can be used at the end of words.

- Place on the chalkboard these letters: *op, ar, ep, ip, in, it, ha, ba, wa, be, wi, bu, lu, li, la, ra.*

- Ask children to come up and place a pink card at the end of the two letters to form a word or a blue card at the beginning to form a word. (*stop, star, step, skip, skin, spin, spit, hang, bang, want, bent, hand, band, wind, bump, lump, limp, lamp, raft, lift.*) ▶**Logical/Mathematical**

Kinesthetic

ROLLING BALL WORD GAME

 Materials: blue and pink paper slips or
GROUP index cards, small ball

Have children practice using blends by adding other letters to blends to make words.

- Write *st, sk, sp* on blue slips.

- Write *ng, nt, nd, mp, ft* on pink slips.

- Each child should have one slip.

 Have each child come up with a word that
WRITING includes the blend on their slip, and ask them to write the missing letters on the slip.

- Once everyone has written a word on their slip, have children tape the slips to their shirts. Stand in a circle and throw a small ball back and forth. The student with the ball has to say his or her word and the word of the person to whom they are throwing the ball. ▶**Bodily/Kinesthetic**

Auditory

WORD FLAGS

 Materials: multicolored paper strips, tape or
GROUP staples

Have children work together in groups to suggest sentences containing words with blends.

- Divide the class into small groups. Give each group a list of words with blends: *stop, star, step, etc.*

 Ask groups to work together to first say and
WRITING then write sentences containing the words.

- Have children write the sentences on long strips of colored paper. Tape or staple the strips together to form a flag representing each group. ▶**Interpersonal**

See Reteach 85, 89, 90

Diagrams

 **OBJECTIVES** Children will learn to interpret diagrams.

Alternate Activities

Visual

WHERE DO YOU SIT?

 Materials: paper, markers

Allow children to work together in groups to create various diagrams based on classroom information.

- Organize the class into small groups. Ask each group to make a diagram that illustrates something about the classroom.

- Give each group markers and paper, and ask them to label the diagrams clearly.

- Have groups share the finished diagrams and post them in the classroom. ▶Spatial

Kinesthetic

LET'S PLAY STORE

Materials: large index cards, empty boxes and cans, markers

Give children further practice with diagrams by having them draw various coin combinations on diagrams they make.

- Make a grocery store in the classroom, and have children create signs telling how much the items on the shelves cost.

- Give each child one item to price and a large tag on which to make a diagram of the various coin combinations that could make that amount.

- In the center of the tag, have children write the cost, for example, 53 cents. Around the edges of that figure, have them draw the various coin combinations they could use to make 53 cents, for example, two quarters and three pennies. ▶Logical/Mathematical

Auditory

GETTING TO SCHOOL

Materials: paper and markers

Use this activity to help children learn how to diagram objects and how they work.

- Tell children that a diagram is a drawing that helps explain something by showing all of its parts or how it works.

- Show some examples of different types of diagrams so children can become familiar with the format. Point out and describe the features on each that are characteristic of diagrams.

- Ask children to work in small groups, making a diagram that will clearly show how something is put together or how something works. Remind them to label the parts of their diagrams clearly. Have children tell the features that characterize what they made as a diagram. ▶Spatial

See Reteach 88, 96, 104, 112, 120

Story Elements (Setting)

 **OBJECTIVES** Children will be introduced to the concept of setting as a story element.

Alternate Activities

Visual

WHERE ARE WE?

Materials: magazines, scissors

ONE Use this activity to introduce children to the concept of setting.

- Give each child a magazine that contains color photos of locations or settings.

- Have children choose a setting in which they think a story could take place.

WRITING Have children cut out the photo and label it with words or phrases that they would use if they were describing the setting in a story; for example, "a playground with swings and slides," or "a busy street with lots of cars and traffic lights."

- Have children share their settings with the class.

- Encourage children to create a drawing to illustrate their setting. ▶**Intrapersonal**

Kinesthetic

YOU ARE HERE

ONE Help children understand setting by having them describe various locations and objects around the classroom.

- Explain that the setting of a story is where and when the story happens.

- Ask: *If a story were to take place in a classroom, how might the author describe the classroom so that the reader could picture it?*

- Have children stand in various locations. Ask them to describe the location where they are standing. For example, a child might describe his or her location as follows: *The coat closets are made of brown wood. They are so full of jackets and coats that it is hard to close them.*

WRITING Have children return to their desks and write down their descriptions.

- Make a bulletin board called OUR CLASSROOM, and post the descriptions. ▶**Spatial**

Auditory

NAME THAT SETTING

Materials: songs that clearly demonstrate **ONE** different settings, paper, markers or crayons

Use music to help children understand setting.

- Play songs with specific settings, for example, a winter song ("Frosty the Snowman"), a summer song ("Summertime"), a song about water ("Sitting on the Dock of the Bay"). Include songs about specific locales (San Francisco, New York, etc.).

- Ask children to identify the setting and to list as many of the specifics about that setting as possible.

- Invite students to illustrate their settings. ▶**Musical**

See Reteach 91, 115, 122

Possessives

OBJECTIVES Children will learn that *'s* is added to a word to indicate the possessive. Children will practice making possessives by adding *'s* to the ends of words.

Alternate Activities

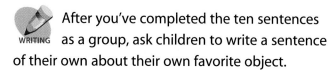

Visual

OUR FAVORITES

 Use this activity to introduce children to possessives.

- Write the names of ten children on the chalkboard.

- Ask those ten children to name their favorite toy or possession.

- Using the possessive form, write sentences about the ten children and their favorite objects.

- Start each sentence with the child's name, for example, *Jane's bicycle is red. Jim's comic book is funny.*

After you've completed the ten sentences as a group, ask children to write a sentence of their own about their own favorite object.

- Invite children to share their sentences with the group. ▶Linguistic

Kinesthetic

WHO DOES IT BELONG TO?

 Materials: common objects such as pencils, cups, books

Allow children to practice with possessives by using common objects and assigning them owners.

- Place five common objects on a table in the front of the classroom.

- Ask five children to come up and choose one of the objects to hold.

- Explain that the possessive form is a way of indicating who an object belongs to. Give examples of possessive form.

- Ask children to observe those children in front of the classroom and the objects the children are holding and to make statements about them using the possessive form. For example, they could say, *That is Jim's cup. Jim's cup is blue.*
▶Bodily/Kinesthetic

Auditory

CIRCLE THE *'S*

 Demonstrate how an apostrophe is used to show ownership.

- Read sentences that contain examples of possessive form, such as *Joe's pen is on the table.*

- Explain that the possessive form is a way of indicating who something belongs to. Demonstrate on the chalkboard how the apostrophe is used.

- Hand out duplicated sheets that contain the sentences you have just read, and ask children to circle the words that tell them who the object belongs to. Then say the sentences again. Children read along on their duplicated sheet and raise their hand when you say a possessive word. ▶Linguistic

See Reteach 92, 100, 123

Phonological Awareness

OBJECTIVES Children will blend sounds, segment sounds, and substitute ending sounds.

Alternate

Activities

Blend Sounds

TAP AND BLEND

GROUP This activity will help children blend sounds to form words.

- Say the individual sounds in a word, such as /t/-/r/-/a/-/p/. Ask children to use two fingers to tap their desk from right to left as they repeat each sound.

- Have children then go back to the first tap position and "sweep" their fingers on the desk as they blend the sounds together. Ask children to say the word as they make the hand motion.

- Use the following words: *truck, plan, camp,* and *twin.*

Segment Sounds

HOP TO IT

GROUP This activity will help children segment individual sounds in words.

- Have children spread out in a large, open space. Invite them to take a "bunny hop" for each sound they hear in the word. Have them say each sound aloud as they hop.

- Tell children to listen carefully to all the sounds. Begin with the word *clip.* Ask children how many hops they took. (four) Ask them to repeat the four sounds they heard as they hop back in place. (/c/-/l/-/i/-/p/)

- Continue with words such as: *block, trot, plug,* and *crib.*

Substitute Sounds

NEW ENDINGS

Materials: puppet

GROUP This activity will help children substitute ending sounds in words.

- Tell children that your puppet is confused. Each time you say a word, he repeats it with a new ending. For example, say, *When I say* cup, *the puppet says* cub. *When I say* tap, *the puppet says* tab. Ask children how the puppet is changing your words. (He's changing the /p/ to /b/.)

- Ask children to predict what the puppet will say when you say a word. Say, cap *(cab),* rip, *(rib).*

- Once children have practiced, have the puppet change the word endings to a new sound, such as /n/ to /t/. For example, man *(mat),* can *(cat).*

T69

Blends

BJECTIVES Children will be introduced to the blends *tr, pr, pl, cr, tw.*

Alternate Activities

Visual

MEMORY

Materials: index cards

PARTNERS Introduce the blends *tr, pr, pl, cr,* and *tw* by having children play a game of *Concentration.*

- Make up several complete sets of two index cards for each of the following words: *tray, tram, trap, prop, prod, prom, play, plan, plop, plum, crop, crab, cram, twin.*

- Pair children to play *Concentration* with the cards.

- Mix up the cards and place them face down on a tabletop. Each player turns up two cards in hopes of making a match. If the cards match, the player removes them and goes again. If there is no match, the player turns the cards face down again, and the next player tries to make a match.
  ▶**Logical/Mathematical**

Kinesthetic

WHAT SOUND ARE YOU?

Materials: small rubber ball

GROUP Have children work in a group to practice reading aloud words containing blends *tr, pr, pl, cr,* and *tw.*

- Assign each child one of the following blends: *tr, pr, pl, cr, tw.*

- Have children sit in a large circle and roll a ball from one player to another. Each time the ball is rolled, the child must say a word with his or her assigned blend.

- If a child is stumped for a word, have the group think of a word with the appropriate blend.
  ▶**Linguistic**

Auditory

TOUCH YOUR NOSE

Use this activity to help children practice lis-
GROUP tening for and recognizing the blends.

- Write on the chalkboard the following instructions:
  tr—raise your right hand
  pr—raise your left hand
  pl—touch your head
  cr—touch your nose
  tw—raise both hands

- Then read sentences that include the following words containing those blends: *tray, tram, trap, prop, prod, prom, play, plan, plop, plum, crop, crab, cram, twin.*

- Instruct children to listen carefully for one of the listed blends and do what the instructions say when they hear it. ▶**Kinesthetic**

 **CD-ROM**

See Reteach 93, 97, 98

Compare and Contrast

OBJECTIVES Children will learn how to compare and contrast information.

Alternate Activities

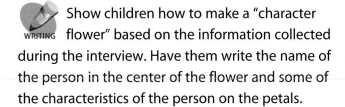

Visual

ALIKE AND DIFFERENT

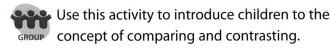

GROUP Use this activity to introduce children to the concept of comparing and contrasting.

- Read aloud a story that contains two very different characters, such as *Beauty and the Beast*.

- Ask children to compare and contrast the main characters.

- Ask, *In what way are these characters different from each other? Are there ways in which these two characters are alike?*

- Working as a group, create a Venn diagram that compares and contrasts the most striking attributes of the two characters. ▶**Spatial**

Kinesthetic

INTERVIEWS

PARTNERS **Materials:** colored paper, crayons and markers

Allow children to work in pairs to practice comparing and contrasting.

- Have children work in pairs. Ask them to interview one another, asking questions about the sorts of things they enjoy doing, their favorite food, color, TV show, and so on.

WRITING Show children how to make a "character flower" based on the information collected during the interview. Have them write the name of the person in the center of the flower and some of the characteristics of the person on the petals.

- When the flowers are complete, have children compare and contrast the information on the petals. ▶**Spatial**

Auditory

NAME THAT CHARACTER

GROUP Have children work in groups to practice comparing and contrasting characters from their favorite books.

WRITING Divide the class into small groups. Ask them to work together to write a character description for one of their favorite characters from a popular book or story. Encourage them to use as much detail as possible.

- When the descriptions are finished, read them aloud and have children guess who the characters are.

- Based on the descriptions, ask them to compare and contrast the characters. Ask: *Do you think this character would get along with that character—why or why not? What do they have in common—how are they different?* ▶**Logical/Mathematical**

See Reteach 99, 107, 121

Phonological Awareness

OBJECTIVES Children will blend sounds, segment sounds, and substitute middle sounds.

Alternate Activities

Blend Sounds

BLENDING STORY

GROUP This activity will help children blend sounds to form words.

- Explain to children you are going to tell them a story, but you need their help blending some of the words. Use the following story and questions: Mom made chocolate /ch/-/i/-/p/ cookies. What kind of cookies did she make? (chocolate chip).

  She found a crumb on my /ch/-/i/-/n/. Where was the crumb? (on my chin) /Ch/-/u/-/k/ shared some of my cookies. Who shared my cookies? (Chuck) He likes to /m/-/u/-/n/-/ch/ on the cookies. What does he like to do? (munch) We ate the cookies after /l/-/u/-/n/-/ch/. When did we eat the cookies? (after lunch)

Segment Sounds

DUCK, DUCK, GOOSE

GROUP This activity will help children segment individual sounds in words.

- Have children sit in a circle. Choose one child to be "It." Tell "It" a word, such as *chick,* and have him or her tap the head of each child as he or she says each sound in the word. For example, "It" says */ch/-/i/-/k/, /ch/-/i/-/k/, /ch/-/i/-/k/, Chick!*

- The last child tapped then chases "It" around the circle. If "It" is tagged, he or she sits in the middle of the circle. The new "It" continues the game with another word.

Substitute Sounds

WHAT'S IN THE MIDDLE?

GROUP This activity will help children substitute middle sounds in words.

- Assign two volunteers consonant sounds, such as /t/ and /k/, and ask them to stand in front of the class. Assign a short vowel sound to five other volunteers. Invite one of the children to stand in the middle of the volunteers with the consonant sounds.

- Ask the three children to say their sound in sequence, and have the class blend the sound to say the word. For example, /t/-/a/-/k/ (tack).

- Invite each of the other short vowel volunteers to take a turn in the middle. Have each child say his or her sound, and have the class blend the sounds to make a new word, such as /t/-/i/-/k/ (tick).

- Repeat the activity with other consonants sounds. Include blends by including one more volunteer. For example, /t/-/r/-/a/-/k/ (track), /t/-/r/-/u/-/k/ (truck), /t/-/r/-/i/-/k/ (trick).

Digraphs *ch, wh, nk*

OBJECTIVES Children will be introduced to the digraphs *ch, wh,* and *nk.*

Alternate Activities

Visual

KITES

 Materials: coat hangers, colored paper, staples, tape

Help children make kites containing words with the digraphs *ch, wh,* and *nk.*

- Bend three coat hangers into diamond shapes to make "kites." Label each kite with a digraph: *ch, wh,* or *nk.*

- Ask children to think of words that contain those sounds and write them on pieces of colored paper.

- Help children attach the words to the appropriate kite. Staple or tape them in a long line to make "tails" for the kites. ▶**Spatial**

Kinesthetic

PHONICS TRAIN

 Materials: construction paper, colored paper, glue or tape

Help children review the digraphs by constructing a Phonics Train.

- Make a Phonics Train. Draw a large picture of a train engine with the sound *ch, ch, ch* coming out of the smokestack.

- Leave room in the billow of smoke for children to paste *ch* words.

- Behind the engine, make two railroad cars—one labeled *wh* and one labeled *nk.*

 Have children write words that contain those digraphs on pieces of colored paper and paste them onto the appropriate cars. ▶**Spatial**

Auditory

LISTENING FOR SOUNDS

 Use this activity to further review the digraphs *ch, wh,* and *nk.*

- Say the following sentences aloud:
  I hope we get to <u>chat</u>.
  <u>When</u> are you coming over?
  The <u>bank</u> is closed.

- Ask children to identify the words that contain the letters that stand for the sounds *ch, wh,* and *nk.*

 Once they have identified the three words, ask them to write three of their own sentences using those words. Then have children share their sentences with others. Tell them to ask others to identify the words with digraphs in their sentences. ▶**Linguistic**

 **CD-ROM**

See Reteach 101, 105, 106, 114, 117

Contractions

OBJECTIVES Children will learn about contractions.

Alternate Activities

Visual

SMALLER WORDS

 Use this activity to introduce children to **GROUP** contractions.

- Explain that a contraction is a way of saying the same thing with fewer letters. Write the following sentences on the chalkboard:
  Jane <u>can not</u> come over.
  <u>Do not</u> eat that cookie, Sally.
  George <u>will not</u> answer the phone.
  <u>You have</u> got to get over here right away!

- Ask volunteers to replace the underlined words with the proper contractions. (*can't, Don't, won't, You've*)

- Write other sentences that contain contractions on the chalkboard. Ask children to name the contractions and identify the two smaller words that form each contraction. ▶**Linguistic**

Kinesthetic

WORD CARS

Materials: paper, markers, self-stick notes **ONE** Let children practice using contractions by pretending to be "word police officers."

- Have children draw cars on which they print the following words: *do not, can not, will not, you have, you will.*

- Give children self-stick notes with which they can "ticket" the cars for carrying too many words.

 Ask children to write on the tickets the **WRITING** contraction that corresponds to the two words printed on the cars. ▶**Spatial**

Auditory

FLASH CARDS

Materials: index cards, markers **PARTNERS** Have children work in pairs, quizzing each other with contraction flashcards.

- Have children work in pairs. Provide markers and index cards so that each pair can create flashcards for contractions.

- On one side of the card, have children write two words, for example *do not.* On the reverse side, have them write the corresponding contraction, *don't.*

- Have children take turns quizzing one another with additional words using both sides of the cards. ▶**Logical/Linguistic**

See Reteach 108, 116, 124

Phonological Awareness

 **OBJECTIVES** Children will blend sounds, segment sounds, and delete beginning and ending sounds.

Alternate Activities

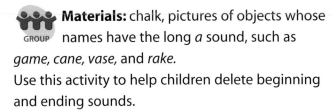

Blend Sounds

HOLD THAT SOUND

 ONE This activity will help children blend sounds to form words.

- Say the individual sounds in a word such as /f/-/l/-/ā/-/m/ (flame). Ask children to "hold each sound" as they blend them together.

- Tell them to speak as if they were a goat, extending each sound as they draw it out. For example, you say, /b/-/l/-/ā/-/z/, and children say, blllaaaazzze.

Segment Sounds

PIN IT

 ONE This activity will help children segment the individual sounds in words.

- Give each child an index card and a clothespin. Say a word, such as take, and ask children to say the first sound in the word, and attach the clothespin to the left side of the index card.

- Ask children what sound they hear next. Have them move the clothespin to the middle as they say the next sound. Continue as children say each sound, moving the clothespin from left to right.

Delete Sounds

TAKE IT AWAY

GROUP **Materials:** chalk, pictures of objects whose names have the long a sound, such as game, cane, vase, and rake.

Use this activity to help children delete beginning and ending sounds.

- Display the picture of the game on the chalkboard and a three-box grid beneath it. Ask the class to name the object. Have children name the three sounds in game. (/g/-/ā/-/m/)

- Erase the first box. Say, If I take away the beginning sound in game, what is left? (/ām/) What sound is missing? (/g/)

- Draw the first box again, and erase the last box. Say, If I take away the ending sound in game, what is left? (/gā/) What sound is missing? (/m/)

- Continue with other pictures, such as cane, vase, and rake.

Long *a: a–e*

 OBJECTIVES Children will be introduced to words containing the long *a* sound.

 Alternate **Activities**

Visual

TREASURE CHEST

 Materials: shoe box, construction paper, strips of white paper, and markers

Children will search through books they've read to find words with the long *a* sound.

- Cover a shoe box with construction paper so it looks like a treasure chest. Tell children they are going on a treasure hunt to search for words with long *a*.

- Provide books for children to look for words that contain the long *a* sound. Children will copy the words on strips of paper and place them in the treasure chest.

- At the end of the activity, have children open the treasure chest and review the words they tracked down. ▶**Intrapersonal**

Kinesthetic

TRADING CARDS

Materials: index cards, markers
Use this activity to give children more practice with words containing long *a* and silent *e*.

- Ask children to think of words that have a long *a* sound and end with a silent *e*.

 Once they have thought of the words, have children make four "trading cards"—index cards with the words written on them.

- Ask children to trade cards with each other until they have collected four cards that have four different words on them. ▶**Bodily/Kinesthetic**

Auditory

STORY LINES

Have children work with partners to write stories containing long *a* words.

- Have children work in pairs.

- To start, ask children to come up with six words that have the long *a* sound with a silent *e* on the end.

Once partners have decided on the words, have them work together to write a story six sentences long, each sentence containing one of the words.

- Invite pairs to share their stories and words with the class. Encourage the other children to listen carefully and raise their hand when they hear one of the *a–e* words chosen by the pair. ▶**Linguistic**

 **CD-ROM**

See Reteach 109, 113, 114, 117

Notes

Writing Readiness

Before children begin to write, fine motor skills need to be developed. Here are examples of activities that can be used:

- **Simon Says** Play Simon Says using just finger positions.
- **Finger Plays and Songs** Sing songs such as "Where Is Thumbkin" or "The Eensie, Weensie, Spider" or songs that use Signed English or American Sign Language.
- **Mazes** Use or create mazes, especially ones that require moving the writing instruments from left to right.

The Mechanics of Writing

POSTURE

- Chair height should allow for the feet to rest flat on the floor.
- Desk height should be two inches above the elbows.
- There should be an inch between the child and the desk.
- Children sit erect with the elbows resting on the desk.
- Letter models should be on the desk or at eye level.

PAPER POSITION

- **Right-handed children** should turn the paper so that the lower left-hand corner of the paper points to the abdomen.

- **Left-handed children** should turn the paper so that the lower right-hand corner of the paper points to the abdomen.

- The nondominant hand should anchor the paper near the top so that the paper doesn't slide.
- The paper should be moved up as the child nears the bottom of the paper. Many children won't think of this.

The Writing Instrument Grasp

For handwriting to be functional, the writing instrument must be held in a way that allows for fluid dynamic movement.

FUNCTIONAL GRASP PATTERNS

- **Tripod Grasp** The writing instrument is held with the tip of the thumb and the index finger and rests against the side of the third finger. The thumb and index finger form a circle.
- **Quadrupod Grasp** The writing instrument is held with the tip of the thumb and index finger and rests against the fourth finger. The thumb and index finger form a circle.

INCORRECT GRASP PATTERNS

- **Fisted Grasp** The writing instrument is held in a fisted hand.

- **Pronated Grasp** The instrument is held diagonally within the hand with the tips of the thumb and index finger but with no support from other fingers.

- **Five-Finger Grasp** The writing instrument is held with the tips of all five fingers.

- **Flexed or Hooked Wrist** Flexed or bent wrist is typically seen with left-handed writers but is also present in some right-handed writers.

- To correct wrist position, have children check their writing posture and paper placement.

TO CORRECT GRASPS

- Have children play counting games with an eye dropper and water.
- Have children pick up small objects with a tweezer.
- Do counting games with children picking up small coins using just the thumb and index finger.

Evaluation Checklist

Formation and Strokes

- ☑ Does the child begin letters at the top?
- ☑ Do circles close?
- ☑ Are the horizontal lines straight?
- ☑ Do circular shapes and extender and descender lines touch?
- ☑ Are the heights of all upper-case letters equal?
- ☑ Are the heights of all lower-case letters equal?
- ☑ Are the lengths of the extenders and descenders the same for all letters?

Directionality

- ☑ Do the children form letters starting at the top and moving to the bottom?
- ☑ Are letters formed from left to right?

Spacing

- ☑ Are the spaces between letters equidistant?
- ☑ Are the spaces between words equidistant?
- ☑ Do the letters rest on the line?
- ☑ Are the top, bottom and side margins on the paper even?

Write the Alphabet

Trace and write the letters.

A A A

A

a a a

a

B B B

B

b b b

b

Trace and write the letters.

C C C

C

c c c

c

D D D

D

d d d

d

Trace and write the letters.

E E E

E

e e e

e

F F F

F

f f f

f

Trace and write the letters.

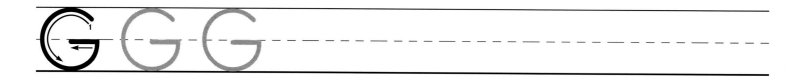

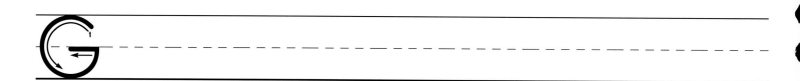

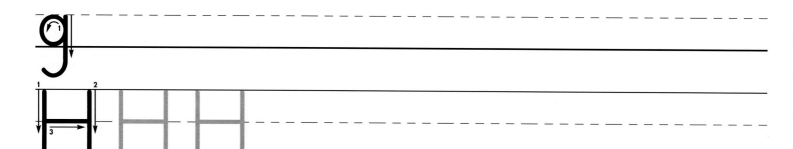

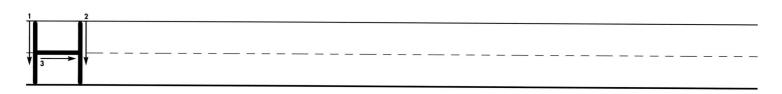

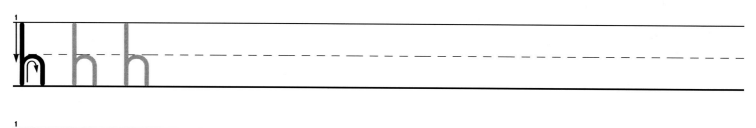

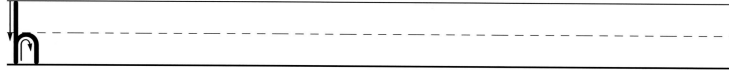

Trace and write the letters.

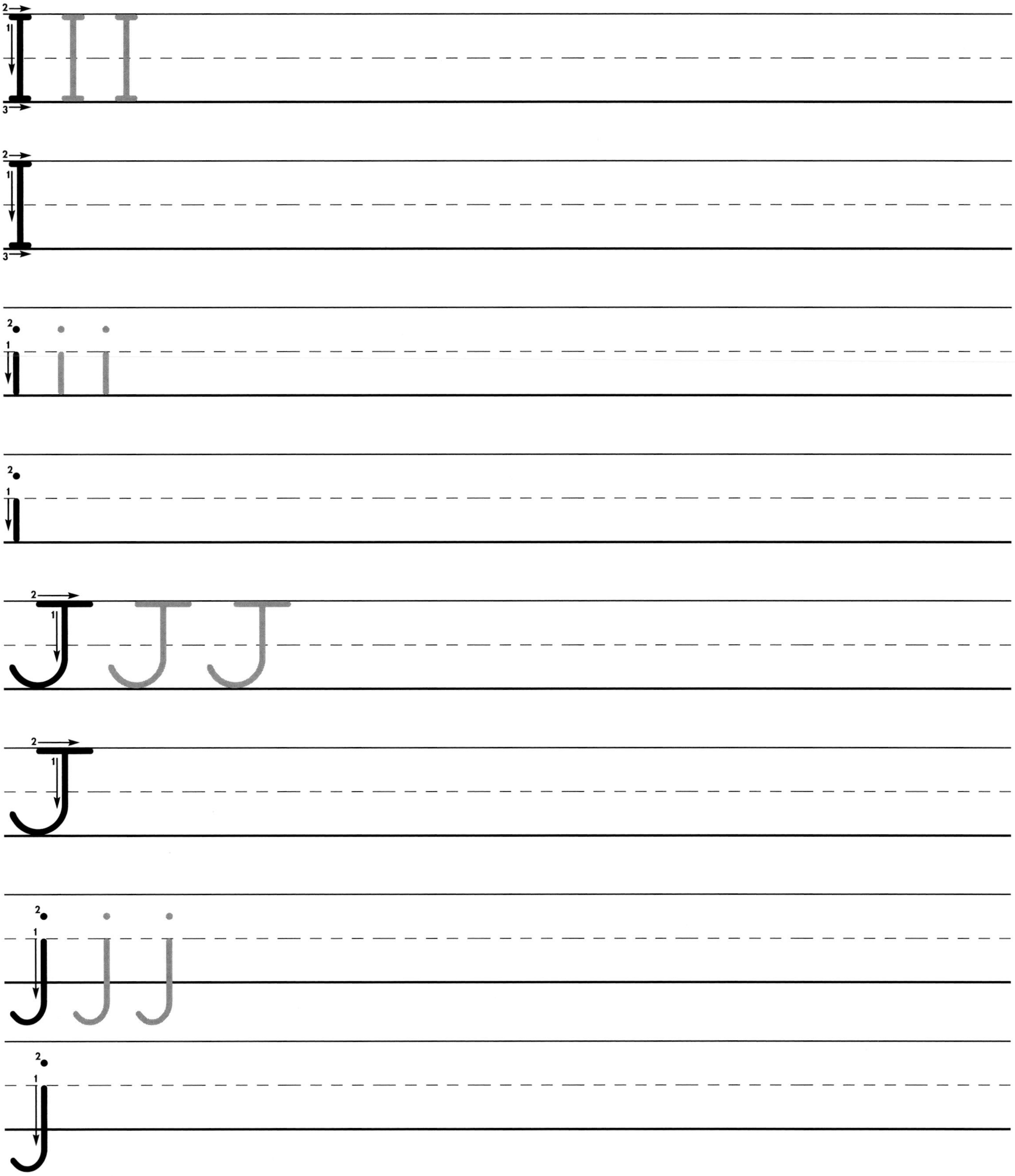

I I I

I

i i i

i

J J J J

J

j j j j

j

T83

Trace and write the letters.

Trace and write the letters.

M M M

M

m m m

m

N N N

N

n n n

n

Trace and write the letters.

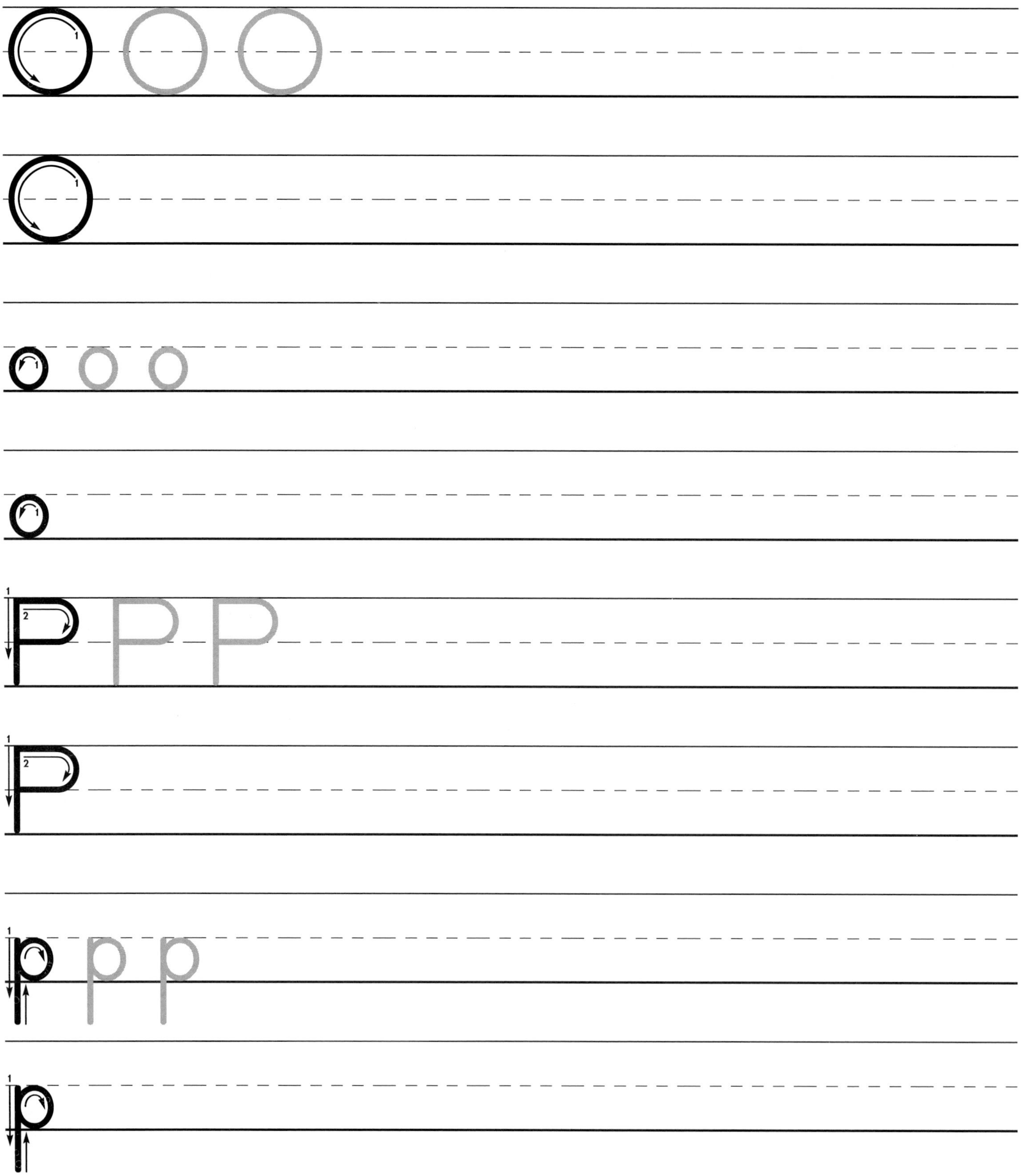

O O O

O

o o o

o

P P P

P

p p p

p

Trace and write the letters.

Trace and write the letters.

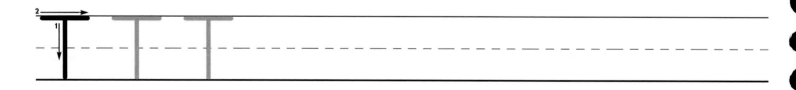

S S S

S

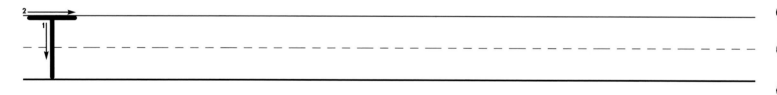

s s s

s

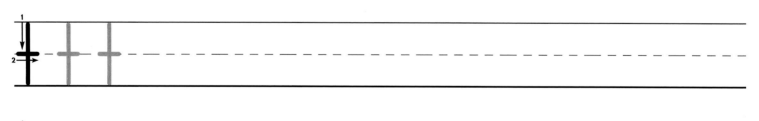

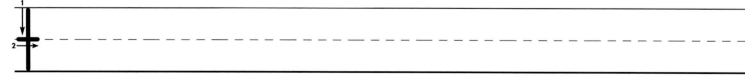

Trace and write the letters.

U U U

U

u u u

u

V V V

V

v v v

v

Trace and write the letters.

W W W W

W

w w w

w

X X X

X

x x x

x

Trace and write the letters.

Y Y Y

Y

y y y

y

Z Z Z

Z

Z Z Z

Z

Handwriting Models—Slant

A B C D E F G H

I J K L M N O P

Q R S T U V W

X Y Z

a b c d e f g h

i j k l m n o p

q r s t u v w

x y z

Handwriting Practice

Selection Titles | Honors, Prizes, and Awards

QUACK
Book 1, p. 30
by *Judy Barrett*

Author/Illustrator: *Judy Barrett*, winner of IRA-CBC Children's Choice Award (1978) for *Cloudy With a Chance of Meatballs*

WHAT DOES PIG DO?
Book 1, p. 50
by *Angela Shelf Medearis*
Illustrated by *Barbara Reid*

Author: *Angela Shelf Medearis*, winner of IRA-Teachers' Choice Award (1995) for *Our People*
Illustrator: *Barbara Reid,* winner of Canada Council Award (1985) for Children's Illustrations for *Have You Seen Birds?;* Ezra Jack Keats Award (1988); Mr. Christie Book Award (1991) for the *Zoe* series; ALA Notable (1994) for *Two By Two;* IBBY Honor List (1996) for *Gifts;* Governor General's Award for Illustration (1997) for *The Party*

A YEAR LATER
Book 1, p. 102
by *Mary Ann Hoberman*

Poet: *Mary Ann Hoberman*, winner of American Book Award Paper Picture Book Award (1983) for *A House Is a House for Me*

ONE GOOD PUP
Book 2, p. 10
by *Frank Asch*

Author/Illustrator: *Frank Asch*, winner of American Book Award Pick of the List Award (1997) for *Barnyard Animals*

WHAT BUG IS IT?
Book 2, p. 98
by *Pat Cummings*

Author/Illustrator: *Pat Cummings*, winner of Coretta Scott King Award (illustration; 1984) for *My Mama Needs Me;* National Council of Teachers of English Orbis Pictus Award, Boston Globe-Horn Book Award (1992), ALA Notable (1993) for *Talking with Artists;* ALA Notable (1996) for *Talking with Artists, Vol. 2*

Selection Titles	Honors, Prizes, and Awards
STAN'S STUNT Book 3, p. 10 by *Lynn Plourde* Illustrated by *Pam Levy*	**Illustrator:** *Pam Levy,* winner of 1996 Society of Children's Book Writers and Illustrators Magazine Merit Award for *Cricket* magazine
GREG'S MASK Book 3, p. 40 by *Ann McGovern*	**Author:** *Ann McGovern*, winner of Boston Globe-Horn Book Honor (1975) for *Scram Kids*
THE SHOPPING LIST Book 4, p. 10 by *Gary Apple* Illustrated by *Shirley Beckes*	**Illustrator:** *Shirley Beckes,* winner of The 39th Annual Book Exhibit, The Chicago Book Clinic Honor Book Certificate Award for *Irwin the Sock*
THE KNEE-HIGH MAN Book 4, p. 68 by *Ellen Dreyer* Illustrated by *Tim Raglin*	**Illustrator:** *Tim Raglin,* winner of Silver Medal by the Society Illustrators, 39th Exhibition

Selection Titles | Honors, Prizes, and Awards

 BABY CHICK
Book 5, p. 8
by *Aileen Fisher*

Poet: *Aileen Fisher*, winner of National Council of Teachers of English Award for Excellence in Poetry for Children (1978)

 SHRINKING MOUSE
Book 5, p. 48
by *Pat Hutchins*

Author/Illustrator: *Pat Hutchins*, winner of Boston Globe-Horn Book Honor (1968) for *Rosie's Walk;* New York Times Best Illustrated (1972) for *You'll Soon Grow Into Them, Titch;* IBBY Honor Award (1974); ALA Notable (1997) for *The Doorbell Rang*

 YOU CAN'T SMELL A FLOWER WITH YOUR EAR!
Book 5, p. 84
by *Joanna Cole*

Author: *Joanna Cole*, winner of ALA Notable (1983) for *Bony-Legs* and *Cars and How They Go;* ALA Notable, Golden Kite Honor Book (1984) for *How You Were Born;* Boston Globe-Horn Book Honor (1987) for *The Magic School at the Waterworks;* Texas Blue Bonnet Master List (1995) for *On the Bus with Joanna Cole;* IRA-CBC Children's Choice (1997) for *The Magic School Bus Blows Its Top: A Book About Volcanos*

 OWL AND THE MOON
Book 5, p. 120
by *Arnold Lobel*

Author/Illustrator: *Arnold Lobel*, Caldecott Honor (1970) for *Frog and Toad Are Friends,* (1972) for *Hildilid's Night;* Christopher Award (1972) for *On the Day Peter Stuyvesant Sailed Into Town;* Newbery Honor (1973) for *Frog and Toad Together;* Christopher Award (1977) for *Frog and Toad All Year;* Caldecott Medal (1981) for *Fables;* ALA Notable, Caldecott Honor (1982), Boston Globe-Horn Book Honor, New York Times Best Illustrated (1981) for *On Market Street;* Boston Globe-Horn Book Honor (1984) for *Rose in My Garden;* ALA Notable (1984) for *Book of Pigericks/Pig Limericks;* ALA Notable (1986) for *Three Day Hat;* Golden Kite Award Book (1987) for *The Devil and Mother Crump*

Selection Titles	Honors, Prizes, and Awards
NEW SHOES FOR SILVIA Book 5, p. 194 by *Johanna Hurwitz* Illustrated by *Jerry Pinkney*	**Author:** *Johanna Hurwitz*, winner of Texas Blue Bonnet Award (1987) for *The Hot and Cold Summer;* ALA Notable (1984) for *Rip-Roaring Russell;* Texas Blue Bonnet Master List (1996–97) for *Birthday Surprises: Ten Great Stories to Unwrap* **Illustrator:** *Jerry Pinkney,* winner of Coretta Scott King Award, ALA Notable, Christopher Award (1986) for *Patchwork Quilt;* Newbery Medal, Boston Globe-Horn Book Honor (1977) for *Roll of Thunder, Hear My Cry;* Boston Globe-Horn Book Honor (1980) *Childtimes: A Three Generation Memoir;* Coretta Scott King Award (1987) for *Half a Moon and One Whole Star;* ALA Notable (1988) for *Tales of Uncle Remus: The Adventures of Brer Rabbit;* ALA Notable, Caldecott Honor, Coretta Scott King Award (1989) for *Mirandy and Brother Wind;* ALA Notable, Caldecott Honor, Coretta Scott King Honor (1990) for *Talking Eggs: A Folktale for the American South;* Golden Kite Award Book (1990) for *Home Place;* ALA Notable (1991) for *Further Tales of Uncle Remus: The Misadventures of Brer Rabbit, Brer Fox …;* ALA Notable (1993) for *Back Home;* ALA Notable, Boston Globe-Horn Book Award, Caldecott Honor (1995) for *John Henry;* ALA Notable, Blue Ribbon (1997) for *Sam and the Tigers;* ALA Notable, Christopher Award, Coretta Scott King Award, Golden Kite Honor Book (1997) for *Minty: A Story of Young Harriet Tubman;* Aesop Prize (1997) for *The Hired Hand;* National Council for Social Studies Notable Children's Book Award (1998) for *The Hired Hand* and *Rikki-Tikki-Tavi;* Rip Van Winkle Award (1998); 1998 Hans Christian Andersen nominee
MY MAMI TAKES ME TO THE BAKERY Book 5, p. 304 by *Charlotte Pomerantz*	**Poet:** *Charlotte Pomerantz,* winner of Jane Addams Book Award (1975) for *Princess and the Admiral;* ALA Notable (1994) for *Outside Dog*

Trade Books

Additional fiction and nonfiction trade books related to each selection can be shared with children throughout the unit.

STAN'S STUNT

Bark, George
Jules Feiffer (HarperCollins, 1999)

When the vet has extracted various animals from George's belly, he can finally bark the way a dog should . . . or can he?

Little Lions
Jim Arnosky (G. P. Putnam's Sons, 1997)

Two baby mountain lions play and purr under the protection of their mother.

Red-Eyed Tree Frog
Joy Cowley, illustrated by Nic Bishop (Scholastic, 1999)

In bold, close-up pictures and simple but informative text, we follow a frog as it hunts for food through the night in a rainforest.

GREG'S MASK

Tidy Titch
Pat Hutchins (Greenwillow Books, 1991)

Titch helps his older brother and sister clean their rooms, resulting in an unexpected turn of events.

Follow the Leader
Erica Silverman, illustrated by G. Brian Karas (Farrar Straus & Giroux, 2000)

Two small boys play a game of follow the leader. Of course the bigger boy leads; that is, until the smaller boy wants his turn.

Sheila Rae, the Brave
Kevin Henkes (Greenwillow Books, 1987)

When brave Sheila, who generally takes care of her sister, gets lost one day, it is Sheila's sister Louise who helps her find her way.

Technology

 Multimedia resources can be used to enhance children's understanding of the selections.

 Sylvester and the Magic Pebble (Weston Woods) Video, filmstrip, or cassette, 11 min. Sylvester worries his family when he turns himself into a rock to escape a hungry lion.

 Wild Wonderful Animals in the Woods (National Geographic Educational Services) Video, 15 min. From bats and bears to slimy slugs, explore the ways some forest-dwelling animals live.

 Animals and How They Grow (National Geographic) CD-ROM Kit. Explores mammals, reptiles, amphibians, birds, and insects and how each grows and changes.

 Harold and the Purple Crayon (Weston Woods) Video, filmstrip, or cassette. Harold uses his imagination and his purple crayon to draw himself in and out of adventures.

 Me and You Series (National Geographic Educational Services) Videos. Five videos, Express Yourself, I Can Help, Too, I Can Make Friends, I Can Take Care of Myself, and Playing Fair teach children about respect.

 Jump Start Artist (Knowledge Adventure) CD-ROM, Macintosh and Windows. Children use interactive activities to draw, paint, quilt, and make puppets and collages.

SAM'S SONG

Goose
Molly Bang (Scholastic, 1996)

Having been adopted by wood-chucks at birth, Goose has to learn how to fly all by herself.

Little Louie, the Late Bloomer
Robert Kraus, illustrated by Jose Aruego and Ariane Dewey (HarperCollins, 1995)

Leo the tiger worries and wonders why his younger brother, Louie, can't do anything right.

Mole Music
David McPhail (Henry Holt & Co., 1999)

Mole practices the violin and dreams that his music will make the world a gentler place. As he fiddles, he thinks that his music isn't being heard, but he is mistaken.

SNAKES

Hide and Snake
Keith Baker (Harcourt Brace Jovanovich, 1991)

A brightly colored snake challenges the reader to find where it is hiding on each page.

The Day Jimmy's Boa Ate the Wash
Trinka Hakes Noble, illustrated by Steven Kellogg (Dial Press, 1980)

Jimmy's boa constrictor wreaks havoc on the class trip to a farm.

Verdi
Janell Cannon (Harcourt Brace Jovanovich, 1997)

A snake has a difficult time giving up his early years and growing older.

LET'S CAMP OUT!

Monk Camps Out
Emily Arnold McCully (Scholastic, 2000)

Monk's parents are nervous about his camping out in the backyard for the first time. Illustrations and text perfectly show both Monk's confidence and the concern of his Mom and Dad.

When I Go Camping with Grandma
Marion Dane Bauer, illustrated by Allen Garns (BridgeWater Books, 1995)

A young girl goes camping with her grandmother and enjoys the experience of kayaking, sleeping in a tent, and roasting marshmallows.

Arthur Goes to Camp
Marc Brown (Little, Brown, 1982)

Arthur isn't looking forward to camp Meadowcroak, and then mysterious things start happening there.

 Leo the Late Bloomer (Weston Woods) Filmstrip, 4 min. Leo the tiger learns to eat neatly, speak clearly, and read, all in good time.

 Titch (Weston Woods) Filmstrip, 4 min. Little Titch triumphs over his older siblings.

 Creepy Crawly Creatures in Your Backyard (National Geographic Educational Services) Video, 15 min. Children learn the importance of the work of all kinds of creepy critters, from tilling the soil to controlling dangerous pests.

Scary, Slithery Creatures in the Water (National Geographic Educational Services) Explains why jellyfish, sharks, and alligators don't always deserve their bad reputations.

 Imagination Express: Destination Rainforest (Edmark) CD-ROM, Macintosh and Windows. Interactive activities teach children about wildlife.

 Amazing North America (National Geographic Educational Services) Video, 45 min. Spectacular scenes reveal the natural wonders of the North American landscape.

 Seasons (National Geographic Society) CD-ROM, Macintosh and Windows. Animal and plant life change and evolve in each of the four seasons explored on this CD-ROM.

 Travel the World with Timmy (Edmark) CD-ROM, Macintosh and Windows. Children learn songs, compose stories, play games, and create arts and crafts as they visit the countries of Argentina, Japan, and Kenya.

Publishers Directory

Abdo & Daughters
4940 Viking Drive, Suite 622
Edina, MN 55435
(800) 800-1312 • www.abdopub.com

Aladdin Paperbacks
(Imprint of Simon & Schuster Children's Publishing)

Atheneum
(Imprint of Simon & Schuster Children's Publishing)

Bantam Doubleday Dell Books for Young Readers
(Imprint of Random House)

Blackbirch Press
260 Amity Road
Woodbridge, CT 06525
(203) 387-7525 • (800) 831-9183 •
www.blackbirch.com

Blue Sky Press
(Imprint of Scholastic)

Boyds Mills Press
815 Church Street
Honesdale, PA 18431
(570) 253-1164 • Fax (570) 253-0179 •
(800) 490-5111 • www.boydsmillspress.com

Bradbury Press
(Imprint of Simon & Schuster Children's Publishing)

BridgeWater Books
(Distributed by Penguin Putnam)

Candlewick Press
2067 Masssachusetts Avenue
Cambridge, MA 02140
(617) 661-3330 • Fax (617) 661-0565 •
www.candlewick.com

Carolrhoda Books
(Division of Lerner Publications Co.)

Children's Press (Division of Grolier, Inc.)
P.O. Box 1795
Danbury, CT 06816-1333
(800) 621-1115 • www.grolier.com

Child's World
P.O. Box 326
Chanhassen, MN 55317-0326
(612) 906-3939 • (800) 599-READ •
www.childsworld.com

Chronicle Books
85 Second Street, Sixth Floor
San Francisco, CA 94105
(415) 537-3730 • Fax (415) 537-4460•
(800) 722-6657 • www.chronbooks.com

Clarion Books
(Imprint of Houghton Mifflin, Inc.)
215 Park Avenue South
New York, NY 10003
(212) 420-5800 • (800) 225-3362 •
www.houghtonmifflinbooks.com/clarion

Crowell (Imprint of HarperCollins)

Crown Publishing Group
(Imprint of Random House)

Dial Books
(Imprint of Penguin Putnam Inc.)

Dorling Kindersley (DK Publishing)
95 Madison Avenue
New York, NY 10016
(212) 213-4800 • Fax (212) 213-5240 •
(888) 342-5357 • www.dk.com

Doubleday (Imprint of Random House)

E. P. Dutton Children's Books
(Imprint of Penguin Putnam Inc.)

Farrar Straus & Giroux
19 Union Square West
New York, NY 10003
(212) 741-6900 • Fax (212) 741-6973 •
(888) 330-8477

Four Winds Press
(Imprint of Macmillan, see Simon & Schuster Children's Publishing)

Greenwillow Books
(Imprint of William Morrow & Co, Inc.)

Grosset & Dunlap
(Imprint of Penguin Putnam, Inc.)

Harcourt Brace & Co.
6277 Sea Harbor Drive
Orlando, FL 32887
(407) 345-2000 • (800) 225-5425 •
www.harcourtbooks.com

Harper & Row (Imprint of HarperCollins)

HarperCollins Children's Books
1350 Avenue of the Americas
New York, NY 10019
(212) 261-6500 • Fax (212) 261-6689 •
(800) 242-7737 •
www.harperchildrens.com

Holiday House
425 Madison Avenue
New York, NY 10017
(212) 688-0085 • Fax (212) 421-6134

Henry Holt and Company
115 West 18th Street
New York, NY 10011
(212) 886-9200 • (212) 633-0748 • (888) 330-8477 • www.henryholt.com/byr/

Houghton Mifflin
222 Berkeley Street
Boston, MA 02116
(617) 351-5000 • Fax (617) 351-1125 •
(800) 225-3362 •
www.houghtonmifflinbooks.com

Hyperion Books
(Division of ABC, Inc.)
77 W. 66th Street, 11th Floor
New York, NY 10023
(212) 456-0100 • (800) 343-4204 •
www.disney.com

Ideals Children's Books
(Imprint of Hambleton-Hill Publishing, Inc.)
1501 County Hospital Road
Nashville, TN 37218
(615) 254-2451 • (800) 327-5113

Joy Street Books
(Imprint of Little, Brown & Co.)

Just Us Books
356 Glenwood Avenue
E. Orange, NJ 07017
(973) 672-7701 • Fax (973) 677-7570 •
www.justusbooks.com

Alfred A. Knopf
(Imprint of Random House)

Lee & Low Books
95 Madison Avenue, Room 606
New York, NY 10016
(212) 779-4400 • Fax (212) 683-1894

Lerner Publications Co.
241 First Avenue North
Minneapolis, MN 55401
(612) 332-3344 • Fax (612) 332-7615 •
(800) 328-4929 • www.lernerbooks.com

Little, Brown & Co.
3 Center Plaza
Boston, MA 02108
(617) 227-0730 • Fax (617) 263-2864 •
(800) 759-0190 • www.littlebrown.com

Lothrop Lee & Shepard
(Imprint of William Morrow & Co.)

Macmillan
(Imprint of Simon & Schuster Children's Publishing)

Marshall Cavendish
99 White Plains Road
Tarrytown, NY 10591
(914) 332-8888 • Fax (914) 332-1888 •
(800) 821-9881 •
www.marshallcavendish.com

Millbrook Press
2 Old New Milford Road
Brookfield, CT 06804
(203) 740-2220 • (800) 462-4703 •
Fax (203) 740-2526

William Morrow & Co.
(Imprint of HarperCollins)

Morrow Junior Books
(Imprint of HarperCollins)

Mulberry Books
(Imprint of HarperCollins)

National Geographic Society
1145 17th Street, NW
Washington, DC 20036
(202) 857-7345 • (800) 638-4077 •
www.nationalgeographic.com

Northland Publishing
(Division of Justin Industries)
P.O. Box 1389
Flagstaff, AZ 86002
(520) 774-5251 • Fax (800) 744-0592 •
(800) 346-3257 • www.northlandpub.com

North-South Books
1123 Broadway, Suite 800
New York, NY 10010
(212) 463-9736 • Fax (212) 633-1004 •
(800) 722-6657 • www.northsouth.com

Orchard Books (A Grolier Company)
95 Madison Avenue
New York, NY 10016
(212) 951-2600 • Fax (212) 213-6435 •
(800) 433-3411 • www.grolier.com

Owlet (Imprint of Henry Holt & Co.)

Penguin Putnam, Inc.
375 Hudson Street
New York, NY 10014
(212) 366-2000 • Fax (212) 366-2636 •
(800) 631-8571 •
www.penguinputnam.com

Willa Perlman Books
(Imprint of Simon & Schuster Children's Publishing)

Philomel Books
(Imprint of Penguin Putnam, Inc.)

Puffin Books
(Imprint of Penguin Putnam, Inc.)

G. P. Putnam's Sons Publishing
(Imprint of Penguin Putnam, Inc.)

Random House
1540 Broadway
New York, NY 10036
(212) 782-9000 • Fax (212) 302-7985 •
(800) 200-3552 •
www.randomhouse.com/kids

Scholastic
555 Broadway
New York, NY 10012
(212) 343-7500 • Fax (212) 965-7442 •
(800) SCHOLASTIC • www.scholastic.com

Charles Scribner's Sons
(Imprint of Simon & Schuster Children's Publishing)

Sierra Club Books for Children
85 Second Street, Second Floor
San Francisco, CA 94105-3441
(415) 977-5500 • Fax (415) 977-5793 •
(800) 935-1056 • www.sierraclub.org

Simon & Schuster Children's Books
1230 Avenue of the Americas
New York, NY 10020
(212) 698-7200 • (800) 223-2336 •
www.simonsayskids.com

Smith & Kraus
177 Lyme Road
Hanover, NH 03755
(603) 643-6431 • Fax (603) 643-1831 •
(800) 895-4331 • www.smithkraus.com

Teacher Ideas Press
(Division of Libraries Unlimited)
P.O. Box 6633
Englewood, CO 80155-6633
(303) 770-1220 • Fax (303) 220-8843 •
(800) 237-6124 • www.lu.com

Ticknor & Fields
(Imprint of Houghton Mifflin, Inc.)

Usborne (Imprint of EDC Publishing)
10302 E. 55th Place, Suite B
Tulsa, OK 74146-6515
(918) 622-4522 • (800) 475-4522 •
www.edcpub.com

Viking Children's Books
(Imprint of Penguin Putnam Inc.)

Walker & Co.
435 Hudson Street
New York, NY 10014
(212) 727-8300 • (212) 727-0984 •
(800) AT-WALKER

Watts Publishing
(Imprint of Grolier Publishing;
see Children's Press)

Whispering Coyote Press
300 Crescent Court, Suite 860
Dallas, TX 75201
(800) 929-6104 • Fax (214) 319-7298

Albert Whitman
6340 Oakton Street
Morton Grove, IL 60053-2723
(847) 581-0033 • Fax (847) 581-0039 •
(800) 255-7675 • www.awhitmanco.com

Workman Publishing Co., Inc.
708 Broadway
New York, NY 10003
(212) 254-5900 • Fax (800) 521-1832 •
(800) 722-7202 • www.workman.com

Multimedia Resources

AGC/United Learning
6633 West Howard Street
Niles, IL 60714-3389
(800) 424-0362 • www.unitedlearning.com

AIMS Multimedia
9710 DeSoto Avenue
Chatsworth, CA 91311-4409
(800) 367-2467 •
www.AIMS-multimedia.com

BFA Educational Media
(see Phoenix Learning Group)

Broderbund
(Parsons Technology;
also see The Learning Company)
500 Redwood Blvd
Novato, CA 94997
(800) 395-0277 • www.broderbund.com

Carousel Film and Video
260 Fifth Avenue, Suite 705
New York, NY 10001
(212) 683-1660 • e-mail:
carousel@pipeline.com

Cloud 9 Interactive
(888) 662-5683 • www.cloud9int.com

Computer Plus (see ESI)

Coronet/MTI
(see Phoenix Learning Group)

Crayola (Binney Smith)
1100 Church Lane
Easton, PA 18042
(800) 272-9652 • www.crayola.com

Davidson (see Knowledge Adventure)

Direct Cinema, Ltd.
P.O. Box 10003
Santa Monica, CA 90410-1003
(310) 636-8200

Disney Interactive
(800) 900-9234 •
www.disneyinteractive.com

DK Multimedia (Dorling Kindersley)
95 Madison Avenue
New York, NY 10016
(212) 213-4800 • Fax: (800) 774-6733 •
(888) 342-5357 • www.dk.com

Edmark Corp.
P.O. Box 97021
Redmond, WA 98073-9721
(800) 362-2890 • www.edmark.com

Encyclopaedia Britannica Educational Corp.
310 South Michigan Avenue
Chicago, IL 60604
(800) 522-8656 • www.eb.com

ESI/Educational Software
4213 S. 94th Street
Omaha, NE 68127
(800) 955-5570 • www.edsoft.com

GPN/Reading Rainbow
University of Nebraska-Lincoln
P.O. Box 80669
Lincoln, NE 68501-0669
(800) 228-4630 • www.gpn.unl.edu

Great Tapes for Kids
P.O. Box 954
Middlebury, VT 05753
(888) 543-8273 •
www.greattapes.com/cart/home.phtml

Hasbro Interactive
(800) 683-5847 • www.hasbro.com

Humongous
13110 NE 177th Pl., Suite B101, Box 180
Woodenville, WA 98072
(800) 499-8386 • www.humongous.com

IBM Corp.
1133 Westchester Ave.
White Plains, NY 10604
(770) 863-1234 • Fax (770) 863-3030 •
(888) 411-1932 •
www.pc.ibm.com/multimedia/crayola

ICE, Inc.
(Distributed by Arch Publishing)
12B W. Main St.
Elmsford, NY 10523
(914) 347-2464 • (800) 843-9497 •
www.educorp.com

Knowledge Adventure
19840 Pioneer Avenue
Torrence, CA 90503
(800) 542-4240 • (800) 545-7677 •
www.knowledgeadventure.com

The Learning Company
6160 Summit Drive North
Minneapolis, MN 55430
(800) 395-0277 • www.learningco.com

Listening Library
One Park Avenue
Greenwich, CT 06870-1727
(800) 733-3000 • www.listeninglib.com

Macmillan/McGraw-Hill
(see SRA/McGraw-Hill)

Maxis
2121 N. California Blvd
Walnut Creek, CA 94596-3572
(925) 933-5630 • Fax (925) 927-3736 •
(800) 245-4525 • www.maxis.com

MECC
(see the Learning Company)

Microsoft
One Microsoft Way
Redmond, WA 98052-6399
(800) 426-9400 • www.microsoft.com/kids

National Geographic Society Educational Services
P.O. Box 1041
Des Moines, IA 50340-0597
(800) 225-5647 •
www.nationalgeographic.com

National School Products
101 East Broadway
Maryville, TN 37804
(800) 251-9124 • www.ierc.com

PBS Video
1320 Braddock Place
Alexandria, VA 22314
(800) 344-3337 • www.pbs.org

Phoenix Films
(see Phoenix Learning Group)

Phoenix Learning Group
2348 Chaffee Drive
St. Louis, MO 63146
(800) 221-1274 • e-mail:
phoenixfilms@worldnet.att.net

Pied Piper (see AIMS Multimedia)

Scholastic New Media
555 Broadway
New York, NY 10003
(800) 724-6527 • www.scholastic.com

Simon & Schuster Interactive
(see Knowledge Adventure)

SRA/McGraw-Hill
220 East Danieldale Road
De Soto, TX 75115
(888) 772-4543 • www.sra4kids.com

SVE/Churchill Media
6677 North Northwest Highway
Chicago, IL 60631
(800) 829-1900 • www.svemedia.com

Tom Snyder Productions (also see ESI)
80 Coolidge Hill Rd.
Watertown, MA 02472
(800) 342-0236 • www.teachtsp.com

Troll Associates
100 Corporate Drive
Mahwah, NJ 07430
(888) 998-7655 • Fax (800) 979-8765 •
www.troll.com

Voyager (see ESI)

Weston Woods
12 Oakwood Avenue
Norwalk, CT 06850
(800) 243-5020 • Fax (203) 845-0498

Zenger Media
10200 Jefferson Blvd., Room 94,
P.O. Box 802
Culver City, CA 90232-0802
(800) 421-4246 • (800) 944-5432 •
www.Zengermedia.com

BOOK 1

	Decodable Words	Spelling	Vocabulary

MAX, THE CAT

Short *a*			Short *a*	High-Frequency Words
am	ham	**Pam**	bad	**give**
and	**has**	pan	**can**	**likes**
as	hat	pat	had	**one**
at	jam	rag	hat	**this**
bad	Jan	ran	**mat**	
bag	lap	**sad**	pan	
bat	**mad**	Sam		
cab	man	sat		
can	map	tag		
cap	**mat**	tan		
cat	**Max**	tap		
dad	nag	van		
Dan	Nan	wag		
fan	**nap**	wax		
fat	pad	yam		
had				

QUACK

Digraph *ck*			Digraph *ck*	High-Frequency Words
back	**pack**	rack	**back**	**on**
Jack	**packs**	sack	**pack**	**they**
Mack	**quack**	tack	**quack**	**what**
			rack	**your**
			sack	
			tack	

WHAT DOES PIG DO?

Short *i*			Short *i*	High-Frequency Words
bib	is	pin	**dig**	**does**
big	it	pit	**kick**	**her**
bin	jig	quick	**pick**	**look**
bit	Jim	quit	**pig**	**there**
Dick	**kick**	quiz	pin	
did	**kicks**	rib	win	
dig	kid	Rick		
digs	Kim	rip		
dip	kit	sick		
fin	lick	Sid		
fit	lid	sip		
fix	Lin	sit		
hid	lip	six		
him	mix	tick		
hip	Nick	Tim		
his	nip	tin		
hit	**pick**	tip		
if	**picks**	**wig**		
in	**pig**	win		

Boldfaced words appear in the selection.

BOOK 1

	Decodable Words			Spelling	Vocabulary
A PATH ON THE MAP	**Digraphs *sh, th***			**Digraphs *sh, th***	**High-Frequency Words**
	bath	math	that	dish	**be**
	cash	**path**	thick	**path**	**could**
	dash	rash	thin	**shack**	**down**
	dish	**shack**	**this**	that	**see**
	finish	shin	thrash	thin	
	fish	ship	wish	wish	
	mash	than	with		
TIME FOR KIDS: SHIPS	**Phonics Review**			**Words from Social Studies**	**Review High-Frequency Words**
				bus — map	**look** — **one**
				fast — **ship**	**this** — **what**
				go — stop	

BOOK 2

	Short *u*			Short *u*	High-Frequency Words
ONE GOOD PUP	**Short *u***			**Short *u***	**High-Frequency Words**
	buck	hum	shut	buck	**no**
	bud	hush	sub	**but**	**out**
	bug	hut	suck	cut	**ride**
	bun	jug	sum	duck	**small**
	bus	luck	sun	rug	
	but	mud	sup	**tug**	
	cub	mug	thud		
	cup	nut	**tub**		
	cut	**pup**	tuck		
	duck	rub	**tug**		
	dug	rug	up		
	fun	run	us		
	gum	rush	yum		
	hug	rut			
THE BUG BATH	**Short *o***			**Short *o***	**High-Frequency Words**
	Bob	job	pop	hop	**saw**
	box	jog	pot	**hot**	**two**
	cob	jot	rock	lock	**very**
	cot	lock	**rocked**	**not**	**want**
	dock	log	rod	rock	
	Don	lot	shock	**top**	
	dot	mom	sob		
	fog	mop	sock		
	fox	nod	tock		
	got	**not**	Tom		
	hog	**on**	**top**		
	hop	ox	tot		
	hot	pod			

BOOK 2

	Decodable Words	Spelling	Vocabulary

SPLASH!

Decodable Words — Short *e*

bed	led	**pets**
beg	leg	**red**
Ben	**legs**	Rex
bet	let	set
Beth	**Meg**	**shed**
Deb	men	Ted
deck	met	ten
den	**neck**	**them**
fed	Ned	**then**
get	net	vet
hem	peck	web
hen	peg	**wet**
Jen	pen	yes
jet	pet	yet
Ken		

Spelling — Short *e*

hen
pet
red
shed
then
wet

Vocabulary — High-Frequency Words

away
good
into
put

WHAT BUG IS IT?

Decodable Words — Blends and Double Consonants

bass	**hill**	**slim**
bell	hiss	slip
Bess	huff	slit
bill	hull	slob
buzz	ill	slop
cuff	**Jill**	slot
doll	kiss	slug
dull	lull	slush
fell	mass	**smack**
fill	mess	smash
flap	mill	smell
flash	**Miss**	smock
flat	muff	smug
flesh	**Nell**	snack
flick	**pass**	**snag**
flip	pill	**snap**
flock	puff	sniff
flop	quill	snip
fluff	ruff	snob
fresh	sell	snug
frill	sill	tell
frock	slam	thrill
frog	slap	till
fuss	slash	well
gill	slick	**will**
gull	slid	yell

Spelling — Blends and Double Consonants

doll
flat
miss
pass
puff
snap

Vocabulary — High-Frequency Words

about
again
around
use

TIME FOR KIDS: A VET

Decodable Words — Phonics Review

Spelling — Words from Social Studies

cat	job
help	pat
hog	**vet**

Vocabulary — Review High-Frequency Words

small	**good**
out	**want**

BOOK 3

Decodable Words			Spelling	Vocabulary

Blends

				Blends	High-Frequency Words
asked	melt	spend		**bump**	**fall**
bang	mend	spent		**jump**	**their**
belt	milk	spill		spell	**try**
bend	mint	spin		spill	**would**
bent	mist	splash		tent	
best	must	spot		**went**	
bump	nest	stab			
camp	pant	stack			
can't	past	staff			
damp	pest	stamp			
dent	pond	**Stan**			
dump	pump	**Stan's**			
dust	quilt	stand			
end	raft	stem			
fang	ramp	step			
fast	rang	stick			
felt	rent	stiff			
fist	rest	still			
fling	ring	sting			
flung	risk	stomp			
gang	rung	**stop**			
gasp	rust	stub			
gift	sand	stuck			
gust	sang	stuff			
hang	scab	stump			
held	scat	stung			
help	scuff	**stunt**			
hint	self	**stunts**			
hump	send	sung			
hung	sent	swift			
hunt	shelf	swim			
jest	shift	swing			
jump	sift	swung			
just	silk	task			
Kent	sing	tend			
king	skid	tent			
lamp	skill	test			
last	skimp	theft			
left	skin	**thing**			
lend	skip	thump			
lent	skit	tilt			
lift	skull	trust			
limp	slant	vent			
lint	soft	vest			
list	span	**went**			
loft	spat	west			
lump	speck	wilt			
lung	sped	wind			
mask	spell	wing			

BOOK 3

	Decodable Words	Spelling	Vocabulary

GREG'S MASK

Blends (Decodable Words)

black	clasp	drift	plot
blast	**class**	drill	plug
blend	click	**drip**	plum
blimp	cliff	**drop**	plump
blob	cling	drum	plus
block	**clip**	glad	press
blond	clock	glass	print
blot	clog	Glen	prop
bluff	club	**glob**	track
blush	cluck	grab	tramp
Brad	clump	grand	trap
brag	crab	grant	**trash**
brand	crack	grasp	trick
brass	craft	grass	trim
brick	cramp	**Greg**	trip
bring	crash	Greg's	trot
brisk	crib	grill	truck
brush	crisp	grip	trust
clack	crop	gruff	twig
clam	crush	grump	twin
clamp	crust	grunt	**twist**
clang	draft	plan	
clap	drag	plant	
clash	dress	plop	

Blends (Spelling)

clap
class
dress
drop
track
trip

High-Frequency Words (Vocabulary)

any
grow
new
old

SAM'S SONG

ch, wh, nk (Decodable Words)

bank	chip	link	stink
bench	chomp	lunch	such
blank	chop	**much**	sunk
branch	**Chuck**	munch	tank
brunch	chunk	pinch	thank
bunch	clank	pink	**think**
Chad	clunk	plank	trunk
champ	crank	**plink**	whack
chant	**crunch**	pluck	**when**
check	drank	**plunk**	**which**
chess	drink	prank	whip
chest	Frank	punch	**whish**
Chet	French	ranch	whisk
chick	Hank	rank	**wink**
chill	honk	**sank**	yank
chimp	hunk	**sink**	
chin	inch	spank	

ch, wh, nk (Spelling)

chick
chin
sink
think
when
wink

High-Frequency Words (Vocabulary)

eat
now
together
too

BOOK 3

	Decodable Words	Spelling	Vocabulary

SNAKES

Long *a: a-e*

bake	gate	save
base	gave	scale
blame	gaze	**scales**
brake	grade	shade
brave	grape	shake
cake	grate	shame
came	hate	shape
cane	Jake	shave
cape	Jane	skate
case	Kate	**snake**
cave	**lake**	**snake's**
chase	lane	state
crate	late	take
date	**made**	tale
Dave	**make**	tame
daze	mane	tape
drape	name	trade
fade	pane	vase
fake	plane	wade
fame	plate	wake
flake	rake	wave
flame	**safe**	whale
frame	sale	
game	same	

Long *a: a-e* (Spelling)

came
lake
made
name
shade
snake

High-Frequency Words

know
under
where
why

TIME FOR KIDS: LET'S CAMP OUT!

Phonics Review

Words from Science

fire	sticks
mud	**sun**
snow	**twigs**

Review High-Frequency Words

old
eat
together
under

BOOK 4

Decodable Words			Spelling	Vocabulary

THE SHOPPING LIST

Long *i: i-e*			Long *i: i-e*	High-Frequency Words
bike	lime	**smile**	bite	**after**
bite	line	**smiled**	hide	**always**
bribe	live	snipe	**smile**	**blue**
bride	**Mike**	spike	while	**were**
chime	**Mike's**	spine	**white**	**who**
chive	mile	stride	**wide**	
crime	mime	strike		
dime	mine	stripe		
dine	mite	swine		
dive	Nile	swipe		
drive	nine	tide		
file	pike	tile		
fine	pile	**time**		
fire	pine	tire		
five	pipe	tribe		
glide	pride	vile		
grime	prime	vine		
gripe	prize	while		
hide	quite	whine		
hike	ride	**white**		
hire	**ripe**	**wide**		
hive	shine	wife		
jive	side	wine		
kite	size	wipe		
life	slide	wire		
like	slime			

YASMIN'S DUCKS

Long *o: o-e*			Long *o: o-e*	High-Frequency Words
bone	home	rose	hole	**because**
broke	**hope**	scope	**home**	**buy**
choke	hose	shone	**hope**	**found**
chose	**hoses**	slope	nose	**some**
clone	**joke**	smoke	rope	**work**
close	mope	spoke	those	
clove	**nope**	stole		
code	nose	stone		
coke	note	stove		
cone	poke	strode		
cope	pope	stroke		
cove	pose	those		
dome	probe	throne		
dove	prone	tone		
drone	prose	vote		
drove	quote	woke		
globe	rode	yoke		
grove	**Rome's**	zone		
hole	rope			

BOOK 4

	Decodable Words	Spelling	Vocabulary
THE KNEE-HIGH MAN	Long *u: u-e* **brute** dune prune cube flute pure cure fume rude cute fuse **rule** dude **June** tube duke **mule** tune	Long *u: u-e* cute flute mule **rule** tube tune	High-Frequency Words **been** **carry** **clean** **done** **far**
JOHNNY APPLESEED	Long *a: ai, ay* bail **jays** sail bait laid **sailed** bay lay **say** braid maid snail brain mail Spain chain main sprain clay **May** spray **day** nail stain **days** paid stay drain pail strain **explained** pain stray fail pay sway faint plain tail frail play trail Gail praise train gay quail tray grain **quail's** vain **gray** raid wail **hail** rail wait hay **rain** **way** jail raise jay ray	Long *a: ai, ay* **day** **rain** say tail **wait** **way**	High-Frequency Words **how** **light** **little** **live** **pretty**
TIME FOR KIDS: RING! RING! RING! PUT OUT THE FIRE!	Phonics Review	Words from Social Studies **bell** **ring** **brave** **smoke** **pole** **truck**	Review High-Frequency Words **work** **always** **done**

BOOK 5, UNIT 1

	Decodable Words	Spelling	Vocabulary

SEVEN SILLIES

Decodable Words — Long *e: e, ee*

be	green	**sheep**
bee	greet	sheet
beef	he	sleep
beep	heel	sleet
beet	jeep	speech
bleed	keep	steel
cheek	Lee	steep
cheep	me	steer
creek	meet	street
creep	need	sweep
deed	peek	sweet
deep	peel	tee
deer	peep	teen
fee	queen	**three**
feed	reef	tree
feel	screech	tweet
feet	screen	we
flee	**see**	weed
fleet	seed	week
free	seek	weep
freed	seem	wheel
freeze	seen	
greed	she	

Spelling — Long *e: e, ee*

bee
she
sheep
three
tree
we

Vocabulary — High-Frequency Words

all
four
many
over
so

SHRINKING MOUSE

Decodable Words — Long *e: ie, ea*

beach	heal	sneak
bead	heat	speak
beak	Jean	squeak
bean	lead	steal
beast	leak	steam
beat	leap	streak
bleach	least	stream
cheat	meal	tea
chief	mean	teach
clean	meat	team
cream	neat	thief
deal	pea	weak
Dean	peach	yield
dream	peak	
each	reach	
east	**reached**	
eat	read	
feast	scream	
field	sea	
fields	seal	
flea	seat	
grief	shield	

Spelling — Long *e: ie, ea*

fields
leaf
piece
reached
read
sea

Vocabulary — High-Frequency Words

before
come
off
our
right

BOOK 5, UNIT 1

	Decodable Words	Spelling	Vocabulary

YOU CAN'T SMELL A FLOWER WITH YOUR EAR!

Decodable Words — Long o: o, oa, oe, ow

blow	glow	**opening**
blown	go	**pillow**
boat	goal	road
bold	goat	roast
both	**goes**	roll
bow	groan	row
bowl	grow	scold
coach	grown	show
coal	**hold**	shown
coast	**holding**	slow
coat	Joan	snow
cold	Joe	so
croak	load	soak
crow	loan	sold
don't	low	throat
float	moan	toad
flow	**moment**	toast
flown	most	toe
foal	mow	told
foam	no	toll
fold	oat	won't
follow	old	

Spelling — Long o: o, oa, oe, ow

boat
cold
goes
hold
road
show

Vocabulary — High-Frequency Words

by
find
kind
high
more

OWL AND THE MOON

Decodable Words — Long i: i, y, igh

blind	grind	sigh
bright	high	sight
by	**I**	**sky**
child	**kind**	slight
cry	**light**	sly
dry	might	tight
fight	mild	try
find	mind	why
flight	**my**	wild
fly	**night**	wind
fright	**right**	
fry	shy	

Spelling — Long i: i, y, igh

child
my
night
shy
sky
tight

Vocabulary — High-Frequency Words

everything
eyes
gone
head
room

TIME FOR KIDS: THE NIGHT ANIMALS

Decodable Words — Phonics Review

Spelling — Words from Science

bugs	**owl**
frog	pond
logs	**rat**

Vocabulary — Review High-Frequency Words

many
off
all

BOOK 5, UNIT 2

	Decodable Words	Spelling	Vocabulary

A FRIEND FOR LITTLE BEAR

Decodable Words — /ü/oo

bloom	fool	pool	spoon
boo	groom	proof	stool
boom	hoop	**roof**	stoop
boot	hoot	**room**	too
booth	loom	root	tool
broom	loop	scoop	tooth
cool	moo	shoot	troop
doom	mood	snoop	zoo
droop	moon	soon	zoom
food	noon	spool	

Spelling — /ü/oo

cool
fool
moon
roof
soon
zoo

Vocabulary — High-Frequency Words

called
friend
only
pulled
these

NEW SHOES FOR SILVIA

Decodable Words — /ä/ar

ark	chart	mark
arm	Clark	park
art	dark	part
bar	dart	shark
bark	**far**	sharp
barn	farm	spark
Bart	hard	star
car	harm	start
Carl	harp	tart
cart	Lark	yard
charm	march	yarn

Spelling — /ä/ar

bark
car
dark
park
part
star

Vocabulary — High-Frequency Words

every
morning
once
or
took

THE STORY OF A BLUE BIRD

Decodable Words — /ûr/ir, ur, er

bird	first	squirt
birds	fur	stir
birth	girl	**surprised**
burn	her	term
churn	herself	third
clerk	hurt	thirst
curb	jerk	turn
curl	shirt	twirl
dirt	sir	verb
fern	skirt	whirl
fir	stern	

Spelling — /ûr/ir, ur, er

bird
burn
first
girl
hurt
serve

Vocabulary — High-Frequency Words

brother
from
mother
sister
walked

BOOK 5, UNIT 2

Decodable Words	Spelling	Vocabulary

YOUNG AMELIA EARHART

Decodable Words
/ou/ou, ow; /oi/oi, oy

boil	fowl	our
bound	frown	out
bow	gown	plow
boy	grouch	point
boys	ground	pound
broil	growl	pout
brow	hound	proud
brown	**how**	prowl
cloud	howl	round
clown	**Howland**	Roy
coin	join	scout
couch	joint	soil
count	joy	sound
cow	loud	sour
crown	moist	south
down	mound	spoil
drown	mount	sprout
flour	mouth	town
foil	now	toy
found	oil	wound

Spelling
/ou/ou, ow;
/oi/oi, oy

boys	sound
mouse	town
noise	toy

Vocabulary
High-Frequency Words

father
horse
people
should
woman

TIME FOR KIDS: ON THE GO!

Phonics Review

Words from Math

feet	miles
five	sum
less	**ten**

Review High-Frequency Words

from	**or**
these	horse
called	people

Listening, Speaking, Viewing, Representing

☑ Tested Skill

☐ Tinted panels show skills, strategies, and other teaching opportunities

LISTENING	K	1	2	3	4	5	6
Learn the vocabulary of school (numbers, shapes, colors, directions, and categories)							
Identify the musical elements of literary language, such as rhymes, repetition, onomatopoeia, alliteration, assonance							
Determine purposes for listening (get information, solve problems, enjoy and appreciate)							
Understand and follow directions							
Listen critically and responsively; recognize barriers to effective listening							
Ask and answer relevant questions (for clarification; to follow up on ideas)							
Listen critically to interpret and evaluate							
Listen responsively to stories and other texts read aloud, including selections from classic and contemporary works							
Connect and compare own experiences, feelings, ideas, and traditions with those of others							
Apply comprehension strategies in listening activities							
Understand the major ideas and supporting evidence in spoken messages							
Participate in listening activities related to reading and writing (such as discussions, group activities, conferences)							
Listen to learn by taking notes, organizing, and summarizing spoken ideas							
Know personal listening preferences							

SPEAKING	K	1	2	3	4	5	6
Uses repetition, rhyme, and rhythm in oral texts (such as in reciting songs, poems, and stories with repeating patterns)							
Learn the vocabulary of school (numbers, shapes, colors, directions, and categories)							
Use appropriate language, grammar, and vocabulary learned to describe ideas, feelings, and experiences							
Ask and answer relevant questions (for clarification; to follow up on ideas)							
Communicate effectively in everyday situations (such as discussions, group activities, conferences, conversations)							
Demonstrate speaking skills (audience, purpose, occasion, clarity, volume, pitch, intonation, phrasing, rate, fluency)							
Clarify and support spoken messages and ideas with objects, charts, evidence, elaboration, examples							
Use verbal communication in effective ways when, for example, making announcements, giving directions, or making introductions							
Use nonverbal communication in effective ways such as eye contact, facial expressions, gestures							
Retell a story or a spoken message by summarizing or clarifying							
Connect and compare own experiences, ideas, and traditions with those of others							
Determine purposes for speaking (inform, entertain, compare, describe, give directions, persuade, express personal feelings and opinions)							
Recognize differences between formal and informal language							
Demonstrate skills of reporting and providing information							
Demonstrate skills of interviewing, requesting and providing information							
Apply composition strategies in speaking activities							
Monitor own understanding of spoken message and seek clarification as needed							

VIEWING	K	1	2	3	4	5	6
Demonstrate viewing skills (focus attention, organize information)							
Understand and use nonverbal cues							
Respond to audiovisual media in a variety of ways							
Participate in viewing activities related to reading and writing							
Apply comprehension strategies in viewing activities, including main idea and details							
Recognize artists' craft and techniques for conveying meaning							
Interpret information from various formats such as maps, charts, graphics, video segments, technology							
Knows various types of mass media (such as film, video, television, billboards, and newspapers)							
Evaluate purposes of various media, including mass media (information, appreciation, entertainment, directions, persuasion)							
Use media, including mass media, to compare ideas, information, and points of view							

REPRESENTING	K	1	2	3	4	5	6
Select, organize, or produce visuals to complement or extend meanings							
Produce communication using appropriate media to develop a class paper, multimedia or video reports							
Show how language, medium, and presentation contribute to the message							

Reading: Alphabetic Principle, Sounds/Symbols

☑ Tested Skill
☐ Tinted panels show skills, strategies, and other teaching opportunities

PRINT AWARENESS	K	1	2	3	4	5	6
Know the order of the alphabet							
Recognize that print represents spoken language and conveys meaning							
Understand directionality (tracking print from left to right; return sweep)							
Understand that written words and sentences are separated by spaces							
Know the difference between individual letters and printed words							
Understand that spoken words are represented in written language by specific sequence of letters							
Recognize that there are correct spellings for words							
Know the difference between capital and lowercase letters							
Recognize how readers use capitalization and punctuation to comprehend							
Recognize the distinguishing features of a letter, word, sentence, paragraph							
Understand appropriate book handling							
Recognize that parts of a book (such as cover/title page and table of contents) offer information							

PHONOLOGICAL AWARENESS	K	1	2	3	4	5	6
Listen for environmental sounds							
Identify spoken words and sentences							
Divide spoken sentence into individual words							
Produce rhyming words and distinguish rhyming words from nonrhyming words							
Identify, segment, and combine syllables within spoken words							
Blend and segment onsets and rimes							
Identify and isolate the initial, medial, and final sound of a spoken word							
Add, delete, or substitute sounds to change words (such as *cow* to *how*, *pan* to *fan*)							
Blend sounds to make spoken words							
Segment one-syllable spoken words into individual phonemes							

PHONICS AND DECODING	K	1	2	3	4	5	6
Alphabetic principle: Letter/sound correspondence	☑	☑	☑				
Blending CVC words	☑	☑					
Segmenting CVC words	☑						
Blending CVC, CVCe, CCVC, CVCC, CVVC words	☑	☑	☑				
Segmenting CVC, CVCe, CCVC, CVCC, CVVC words and sounds	☑	☑	☑				
Initial and final consonants: /n/n, /d/d, /s/s, /m/m, /t/t, /k/c, /f/f, /r/r, /p/p, /l/l, /k/k, /g/g, /b/b, /h/h, /w/w, /v/v, /ks/x, /kw/qu, /j/j, /y/y, /z/z	☑	☑					
Initial and medial short vowels: *a, i, u, o, e*	☑	☑	☑				
Long vowels: *a-e, i-e, o-e, u-e* (vowel-consonant-e)		☑	☑				
Long vowels, including *ay, ai; e, ee, ie, ea; o, oa, oe, ow; i, y, igh*		☑	☑				
Consonant Digraphs: *sh, th, ch, wh*		☑					
Consonant Blends: continuant/continuant, including *sl, sm, sn, fl, fr, ll, ss, ff*		☑					
Consonant Blends: continuant/stop, including *st, sk, sp, ng, nt, nd, mp, ft*		☑					
Consonant Blends: stop/continuant, including *tr, pr, pl, cr, tw*		☑					
Variant vowels: including /ù/oo; /ô/a, aw, au; /ü/ue, ew		☑	☑				
Diphthongs, including /ou/ou, ow; /oi/oi, oy		☑	☑				
r-controlled vowels, including /âr/are; /ôr/or, ore; /îr/ear			☑				
Soft *c* and soft *g*			☑				
nk		☑	☑				
Consonant Digraphs: *ck*	☑	☑					
Consonant Digraphs: *ph, tch, ch*			☑				
Short *e: ea*			☑				
Long *e: y, ey*			☑				
/ü/oo		☑	☑				
/är/ar; /ûr/ir, ur, er		☑	☑				
Silent letters: including *l, b, k, w, g, h, gh*			☑				
Schwa: /ər/er; /ən/en; /əl/le;			☑				
Reading/identifying multisyllabic words		☑	☑				
Using graphophonic cues							

Reading: Vocabulary/Word Identification

WORD STRUCTURE	K	1	2	3	4	5	6
Common spelling patterns							
Syllable patterns							
Plurals		✓					
Possessives		✓					
Contractions		✓					
Root, or base, words and inflectional endings (-s, -es, -ed, -ing)		✓	✓	✓		✓	
Compound Words		✓	✓	✓	✓	✓	✓
Prefixes and suffixes (such as un-, re-, dis-, non-; -ly, -y, -ful, -able, -tion)			✓	✓	✓	✓	✓
Root words and derivational endings				✓	✓	✓	✓

WORD MEANING	K	1	2	3	4	5	6
Develop vocabulary through concrete experiences, word walls, other people							
Develop vocabulary through selections read aloud							
Develop vocabulary through reading							
Cueing systems: syntactic, semantic, graphophonic							
Context clues, including semantic clues (word meaning), syntactical clues (word order), and graphophonic clues	✓	✓	✓	✓	✓	✓	✓
High-frequency words (such as the, a, and, said, was, where, is)	✓	✓					
Identify words that name persons, places, things, and actions							
Automatic reading of regular and irregular words							
Use resources and references (dictionary, glossary, thesaurus, synonym finder, technology and software, and context)							
Classify and categorize words							
Synonyms and antonyms			✓	✓	✓	✓	✓
Multiple-meaning words			✓		✓	✓	✓
Figurative language			✓	✓	✓	✓	✓
Decode derivatives (root words, such as like, pay, happy with affixes, such as dis-, pre-, un-)							
Systematic study of words across content areas and in current events							
Locate meanings, pronunciations, and derivations (including dictionaries, glossaries, and other sources)							
Denotation and connotation							✓
Word origins as aid to understanding historical influences on English word meanings							
Homophones, homographs							
Analogies							✓
Idioms							

Reading: Comprehension

PREREADING STRATEGIES	K	1	2	3	4	5	6
Preview and predict							
Use prior knowledge							
Set and adjust purposes for reading							
Build background							

MONITORING STRATEGIES	K	1	2	3	4	5	6
Adjust reading rate							
Reread, search for clues, ask questions, ask for help							
Visualize							
Read a portion aloud, use reference aids							
Use decoding and vocabulary strategies							
Paraphrase							
Create story maps, diagrams, charts, story props to help comprehend, analyze, synthesize and evaluate texts							

(continued on next page)

(Reading: Comprehension continued)

SKILLS AND STRATEGIES	K	1	2	3	4	5	6
Recall story details, including character and setting	☑	☑					
Use illustrations	☑	☑					
Distinguish reality and fantasy	☑	☑	☑				
Classify and categorize	☑						
Make predictions	☑	☑	☑	☑	☑	☑	☑
Recognize sequence of events (tell or act out)	☑	☑	☑	☑	☑	☑	☑
Recognize cause and effect	☑	☑	☑	☑	☑	☑	☑
Compare and contrast	☑	☑	☑	☑	☑	☑	☑
Summarize	☑	☑	☑	☑	☑	☑	☑
Make and explain inferences		☑	☑	☑	☑	☑	☑
Draw conclusions		☑	☑	☑	☑	☑	☑
Distinguish important and unimportant information				☑	☑	☑	☑
Recognize main idea and supporting details	☑	☑	☑	☑	☑	☑	☑
Form conclusions or generalizations and support with evidence from text			☑	☑	☑	☑	☑
Distinguish fact and opinion (including news stories and advertisements)				☑	☑	☑	☑
Recognize problem and solution				☑	☑	☑	☑
Recognize steps in a process		☑	☑	☑	☑	☑	☑
Make judgments and decisions				☑	☑	☑	☑
Distinguish fact and nonfact				☑	☑	☑	☑
Recognize techniques of persuasion and propaganda							☑
Evaluate evidence and sources of information, including checking other sources and asking experts							☑
Identify similarities and differences across texts (including topics, characters, problems, themes, cultural influences, treatment, scope, or organization)							
Practice various questions and tasks (test-like comprehension questions)							
Paraphrase and summarize to recall, inform, and organize							
Answer various types of questions (open-ended, literal, interpretative, test-like such as true-false, multiple choice, short-answer)							
Use study strategies to learn and recall (preview, question, reread, and record)							
LITERARY RESPONSE							
Listen to stories being read aloud							
React, speculate, join in, read along when predictable and patterned selections are read aloud							
Respond to a variety of stories and poems through talk, movement, music, art, drama, and writing							
Show understanding through writing, illustrating, developing demonstrations, and using technology							
Connect ideas and themes across texts							
Support responses by referring to relevant aspects of text and own experiences							
Offer observations, make connections, speculate, interpret, and raise questions in response to texts							
Interpret text ideas through journal writing, discussion, enactment, and media							
TEXT STRUCTURE/LITERARY CONCEPTS							
Distinguish forms and functions of texts (lists, newsletters, signs)							
Use text features to aid comprehension							
Understand story structure							
Identify narrative (for entertainment) and expository (for information)							
Distinguish fiction from nonfiction, including fact and fantasy							
Understand literary forms (stories, poems, plays, and informational books)							
Understand literary terms by distinguishing between roles of author and illustrator							
Understand title, author, and illustrator across a variety of texts							
Analyze character, character's motive, character's point of view, plot, setting, style, tone, mood		☑	☑	☑	☑	☑	☑
Compare communication in different forms							
Understand terms such as *title, author, illustrator, playwright, theater, stage, act, dialogue,* and *scene*							
Recognize stories, poems, songs, myths, legends, folktales, fables, tall tales, limericks, plays, biographies, autobiographies							
Judge internal logic of story text							
Recognize that authors organize information in specific ways							
Recognize author's purpose: to inform, influence, express, or entertain							
Describe how author's point of view affects text				☑	☑	☑	☑
Recognize biography, historical fiction, realistic fiction, modern fantasy, informational texts, and poetry							
Analyze ways authors present ideas (cause/effect, compare/contrast, inductively, deductively, chronologically)							
Recognize literary techniques such as imagery, repetition, flashback, foreshadowing, symbolism	☑						

(continued on next page)

(Reading: Comprehension continued)

VARIETY OF TEXT	K	1	2	3	4	5	6
Read a variety of genres and understand their distinguishing features							
Use expository and other informational texts to acquire information							
Read for a variety of purposes							
Select varied sources when reading for information or pleasure							
Know preferences for reading literary and nonfiction texts							
FLUENCY							
Read regularly in independent-level and instructional-level materials							
Read orally with fluency from familiar texts							
Self-select independent-level reading							
Read silently for increasing periods of time							
Demonstrate characteristics of fluent and effective reading							
Adjust reading rate to purpose							
Read aloud in selected texts, showing understanding of text and engaging the listener							
CULTURES							
Connect own experience with culture of others							
Compare experiences of characters across cultures							
Articulate and discuss themes and connections that cross cultures							
CRITICAL THINKING							
Experiences (comprehend, apply, analyze, synthesize, evaluate)							
Make connections (comprehend, apply, analyze, synthesize, evaluate)							
Expression (comprehend, apply, analyze, synthesize, evaluate)							
Inquiry (comprehend, apply, analyze, synthesize, evaluate)							
Problem solving (comprehend, apply, analyze, synthesize, evaluate)							
Making decisions (comprehend, apply, analyze, synthesize, evaluate)							

Study Skills

INQUIRY/RESEARCH AND STUDY STRATEGIES	K	1	2	3	4	5	6
Follow and give directions							
Use alphabetical order							
Use text features and formats to help understand text (such as boldface, italic, or highlighted text; captions; headings and subheadings; numbers or symbols)							
Use study strategies to help read text and to learn and recall information from text (such as preview text, set purposes, and ask questions; use SQRRR; adjust reading rate; skim and scan; use KWL)							
Identify/frame and revise questions for research							
Obtain, organize, and summarize information: classify, take notes, outline, web, diagram							
Evaluate research and raise new questions							
Use technology for research and/or to present information in various formats							
Follow accepted formats for writing research, including documenting sources							
Use test-taking strategies							
Use text organizers (book cover; title page—title, author, illustrator; contents; headings; glossary; index)		☑	☑	☑	☑	☑	☑
Use graphic aids, such as maps, diagrams, charts, graphs, schedules, calendars		☑	☑	☑	☑	☑	☑
Read and interpret varied texts, such as environmental print, signs, lists, encyclopedia, dictionary, glossary, newspaper, advertisement, magazine, calendar, directions, floor plans, online resources		☑	☑	☑	☑	☑	☑
Use print and online reference sources, such as glossary, dictionary, encyclopedia, telephone directory, technology resources, nonfiction books		☑	☑	☑	☑	☑	☑
Recognize Library/Media center resources, such as computerized references; catalog search—subject, author, title; encyclopedia index		☑	☑	☑	☑	☑	☑

Writing

☑ Tested Skill

Tinted panels show skills, strategies, and other teaching opportunities

MODES AND FORMS	K	1	2	3	4	5	6
Interactive writing							
Descriptive writing			☑				
Personal narrative			☑	☑	☑	☑	☑
Writing that compares		☑	☑	☑	☑	☑	☑
Explanatory writing			☑	☑	☑	☑	☑
Persuasive writing				☑	☑	☑	☑
Writing a story		☑	☑	☑	☑	☑	☑
Expository writing; research report	☑	☑	☑	☑	☑	☑	☑
Write using a variety of formats, such as advertisement, autobiography, biography, book report/report, comparison-contrast, critique/review/editorial, description, essay, how-to, interview, invitation, journal/log/notes, message/list, paragraph/multi-paragraph composition, picture book, play (scene), poem/rhyme, story, summary, note, letter							

PURPOSES/AUDIENCES	K	1	2	3	4	5	6
Dictate sentences and messages such as news and stories for others to write							
Write labels, notes, and captions for illustrations, possessions, charts, and centers							
Write to record, to discover and develop ideas, to inform, to influence, to entertain							
Exhibit an identifiable voice							
Use literary devices (suspense, dialogue, and figurative language)							
Produce written texts by organizing ideas, using effective transitions, and choosing precise wording							

PROCESSES	K	1	2	3	4	5	6
Generate ideas for self-selected and assigned topics using prewriting strategies							
Develop drafts							
Revise drafts for varied purposes, elaborate ideas							
Edit for appropriate grammar, spelling, punctuation, and features of published writings							
Proofread own writing and that of others							
Bring pieces to final form and "publish" them for audiences							
Use technology to compose, revise, and present text							
Select and use reference materials and resources for writing, revising, and editing final drafts							

SPELLING	K	1	2	3	4	5	6
Spell own name and write high-frequency words							
Words with short vowels (including CVC and one-syllable words with blends CCVC, CVCC, CCVCC)							
Words with long vowels (including CVCe)							
Words with digraphs, blends, consonant clusters, double consonants							
Words with diphthongs							
Words with variant vowels							
Words with r-controlled vowels							
Words with /ər/, /əl/, and /ən/							
Words with silent letters							
Words with soft c and soft g							
Inflectional endings (including plurals and past tense and words that drop the final e and double a consonant when adding -ing, -ed)							
Compound words							
Contractions							
Homonyms							
Suffixes such as -able, -ly, -ful, or -less, and prefixes such as dis-, re-, pre-, or un-							
Spell words ending in -tion and -sion, such as station and procession							
Accurate spelling of root or base words							
Orthographic patterns and rules such as keep/can; sack/book; out/now; oil/toy; match/speech; ledge/cage; consonant doubling, dropping e, changing y to i							
Multisyllabic words using regularly spelled phonogram patterns							
Syllable patterns (including closed, open, syllable boundary patterns)							
Synonyms and antonyms							
Words from Social Studies, Science, Math, and Physical Education							
Words derived from other languages and cultures							
Use resources to find correct spellings, synonyms, and replacement words							
Use conventional spelling of familiar words in writing assignments							
Spell accurately in final drafts							

(continued on next page)

T119

(Writing continued)

GRAMMAR AND USAGE	K	1	2	3	4	5	6
Understand sentence concepts (word order, statements, questions, exclamations, commands)							
Recognize complete and incomplete sentences							
Nouns (common, proper, singular, plural, irregular plural, possessives)							
Verbs (action, helping, linking, irregular)							
Verb tense (present, past, future, perfect, and progressive)							
Pronouns (possessive, subject and object, pronoun-verb agreement)							
Use objective case pronouns accurately							
Adjectives							
Adverbs that tell how, when, where							
Subjects, predicates							
Subject-verb agreement							
Sentence combining							
Recognize sentence structure (simple, compound, complex)							
Synonyms and antonyms							
Contractions							
Conjunctions							
Prepositions and prepositional phrases							

PENMANSHIP	K	1	2	3	4	5	6
Write each letter of alphabet (capital and lowercase) using correct formation, appropriate size and spacing							
Write own name and other important words							
Use phonological knowledge to map sounds to letters to write messages							
Write messages that move left to right, top to bottom							
Gain increasing control of penmanship, pencil grip, paper position, beginning stroke							
Use word and letter spacing and margins to make messages readable							
Write legibly by selecting cursive or manuscript as appropriate							

MECHANICS	K	1	2	3	4	5	6
Use capitalization in sentences, proper nouns, titles, abbreviations and the pronoun *I*							
Use end marks correctly (period, question mark, exclamation point)							
Use commas (in dates, in addresses, in a series, in letters, in direct address)							
Use apostrophes in contractions and possessives							
Use quotation marks							
Use hyphens, semicolons, colons							

EVALUATION	K	1	2	3	4	5	6
Identify the most effective features of a piece of writing using class/teacher-generated criteria							
Respond constructively to others' writing							
Determine how his/her own writing achieves its purpose							
Use published pieces as models for writing							
Review own written work to monitor growth as writer							

Activating and assessing prior knowledge, 10A, 37Q, 40A, 67Q, 70A, 97Q, 100A, 125Q, 128A, 139Q

Activities for anthology and leveled books, 37D, 67D, 97D, 125D, 139D

Additional phonics resources, 8J, 37F, 37H, 38J, 67F, 67H, 68J, 97F, 97H, 98J, 125F, 125H, 126J

Additional teacher resources, 8B, 38B, 68B, 98B, 126B

Alliteration, 21, 98G

Alphabetic principle, 8H, 8I–J, 8/9, 37E–F, 37G–H, 37Q–R, 38H, 38I–J, 38/39, 67E–F, 67G–H, 67Q–R, 68H, 68I–J, 68/69, 87E–F, 87G–H, 87Q–R, 98H, 98I–J, 98/99, 125E–F, 125G–H, 125Q–R, 126H, 126I–J, 126/127

Alternate teaching strategies, T64–76
   comprehension strategies, T67, T71
      compare and contrast, T71
      setting, T67
   phonics, T65, T70, T73
      blends, T65, T70
      continuant blends, T70
      ch, wh, nk, T73
   phonological awareness, T64, T69, T72
      blends, T64, T69
      ch, wh, nk, T72
   study skills, T64
      graphic aids: diagrams, T64
   vocabulary, T68, T74
      contractions, T74
      possessives, T68

Apostrophes, 37K–L, 67K–L, 97K–L, 112, 125K–L, 139I–J, 139K–L, 139M, 139O

Art link, 8D. *See also* Drawing, Viewing and representing.

Assessment
   assess/close 8J, 37F, 37H, 37J, 37L, 38J, 67F, 67H, 67J, 67L, 68J, 97F, 87H, 97J, 97L, 98J, 125F, 125H, 125J, 125L, 126J, 139F, 139H, 139J
   checklist, 6H
   follow–up, 6G, 33, 63, 93, 121, 135
   formal, 35, 65, 95, 123, 137
   informal, 8J, 33, 37F, 37H, 37J, 37L, 38J, 63, 67F, 67H, 67J, 67L, 68J, 93, 97F, 87H, 97J, 97L, 98J, 121, 125F, 125H, 125J, 125L, 126J, 135, 139F, 139H, 139J
   performance, 8G, 10A, 37D, 37L, 38G, 40A, 65D, 67L, 68G, 70A, 97D, 97L, 98G, 100A, 125D, 125L, 126G, 128A, 139D, 139L
   portfolio, 37N, 67N, 97N, 125N, 139N

reteaching, 37P, 37R, 67P, 67R, 97P, 97R, 125P, 125R, 139P, 139R
   standardized test practice, 37, 67, 97, 125, 139
   student self–assessment, 32, 62, 92, 120, 134
   unit resources for, 6E, 144A–C

Audience response, 37D, 67D, 97D, 125D, 139D

Auditory vocabulary activities, 10B, 40B, 70B, 100B, 128B

Authentic reading, 8B, 37C, 38B, 67C, 68B, 97C, 98B, 125C, 126B, 139C

Blending, 8C, 8I–J, 8/9, 10A, 10–33, 37A–H, 37Q–R, 38C, 38I–J, 38/39, 40A, 40–63, 67E–H, 67Q–R, 95, 97G–H, 98I–J, 123, 125E, 126I–J, 128A, 133. *See also* Minilessons, Phonics and decoding, Prevention/ intervention.

Book, concept of, 41, 71, 101
   author, 41, 71, 101
   illustrator, 41, 71, 101

Book, parts of, 67P

Brainstorming, 6I, 6J, 34, 51, 70A, 105, 125H, 125J, 140

Building background, 10A, 40A, 70A, 100A, 128A, 142A

Capitalization, 12, 37M, 42, 52, 67P, 74, 97M, 117

Capucilli, Alyssa Satin, 68A, 70

Cause and effect, analyzing, 49, 53, 111

Center activities, 8C–D, 38C–D, 68C–D, 98C–D, 126C–D
   art, 8D
   math, 98D
   phonics, 8C, 38C, 68C, 98C, 126C
   reading and listening, 8C, 38C, 68C, 98C, 126C
   science, 38D, 98D, 126D
   social studies, 8D, 38D, 68D, 126D
   working with words, 8D, 38D, 68D, 98D, 126D
   writing, 8C, 38C, 68C, 98C, 126C

Character, analyzing, 11, 37B, 37I–J, 45, 51, 54, 67D, 97B

Charts
   animal, 10A
   cause/effect, 53
   compare/contrast, 86, 101, 102, 103, 105, 108, 111, 120
   fantasy/reality, 140

predictions, 40, 63, 70, 93, 100, 121, 128, 135
   prewriting, 67M
   setting, 73
   story, 67M
   three column, 73, 128A, 139H
   two–column, 10A, 53, 67M, 70A, 86

Class and group discussions, 6I, 6J, 6, 7, 10A, 33, 34, 37A–C, 37D, 40A, 63, 64, 67A–C, 67D, 70A, 93, 94, 97A–C, 97D, 100A, 121, 122, 125A–C, 125D, 128A, 135, 136, 139A–C, 139D, 142A

Classroom management options, 8E–F, 38E–F, 68E–F, 98E–F, 126E–F

Comparison and contrast, 27, 51, 56, 58, 67I–J, 68G, 77, 78, 79, 81, 86, 87, 89, 90, 92, 93, 97A–C, 101, 102, 103, 105, 108, 111, 116, 121, 125A–C, T71

Comprehension strategies
   analyzing cause and effect, 49, 53, 113
   analyzing story elements, 37I–J, 41, 43, 45, 48, 51, 56, 58, 63, 67D, 73, 97B, 97C, 113, 125I–J, 126G, 129, 130, 131, 133, 134, 135, 139G–H, T67
      character, 11, 37B, 37I–J, 41, 45, 51, 67D, 97B, 97C, 126G
      plot, 11, 37B, 37C, 97B, 97C
      setting, 11, 37I–J, 41, 43, 45, 48, 52, 56, 58, 63, 67A, 67B, 67C, 73, 80, 89, 125I–J, 126G, 129, 130, 131, 133, 134, 135, 139G–H, T67
   comparing and contrasting, 27, 56, 58, 67I–J, 68G, 72, 77, 78, 79, 81, 86, 87, 89, 90, 92, 93, 97A, 97C, 97I–J, 101, 102, 103, 105, 108, 111, 116, 120, 121, 125A–C, 139E–F, T71
   distinguishing between fantasy and reality, 100
   drawing conclusions, 51, 53, 83, 108, 109, 118, 119, 130
   identifying main idea/supporting details, 31, 61, 91, 133
   making connections, 16, 47, 51, 92, 113
   making inferences, 13, 24, 27, 29, 30, 37A, 37B, 45, 48, 49, 51, 52, 53, 55, 57, 67A, 76, 79, 80, 81, 82, 83, 84, 85, 86, 87, 89, 92, 104, 105, 106, 109, 110
   making predictions, 10, 13, 18, 20, 21, 23, 26, 28, 29, 33, 37A–C, 40, 41, 54, 63, 67A–C, 70, 84, 93, 97A–C, 100, 101, 115, 116, 117, 118, 121, 125A–C, 128, 135, 139A–C
   oral, 8G, 38G, 68G, 98G, 126G
   sequence of events, 23, 26, 37C
   summarizing, 24, 32, 62, 92, 119, 120, 130, 136

using illustrations, 11, 13, 15, 17, 18, 21, 25, 37A, 37C, 41, 43, 45, 46, 47, 48, 49, 51, 55, 62, 67A, 67B, 67C, 71, 72, 76, 79, 102, 104, 108, 111, 113, 125C

using story props, 14, 17, 19, 22, 29, 43, 45, 52, 56, 62, 74, 77, 78, 81, 87, 92

Concepts of print, 13, 15, 25, 31, 42, 44, 48, 52, 57, 58, 67P, 74, 75, 76, 77, 82, 85, 86, 117

apostrophes, 37K–L, 67K–L, 97K–L, 112, 125K–L, 139I–J, 139K–L, 139M, 139O–P

capital letters, 12, 37M, 42, 52, 67P, 74, 97M, 117

commas, 24, 57, 72, 98/99

concept of a book, 41, 71, 101

directionality, 103

end punctuation, 13, 25, 31, 52, 56, 75, 76, 82, 85, 86, 98/99, 117, 125P

exclamation marks, 13, 25, 31, 37M, 75, 76, 85, 86, 90, 98/99

periods, 37M, 52, 82, 90, 98/99, 117

question marks, 37M, 90

quotation marks, 26, 31, 44, 48, 77, 87

sentences, 15, 51, 63, 82, 93, 117, 121, 135

spelling consistency, 37Q–R, 67Q–R, 97Q–R, 125Q–R, 139Q–R

tracking, 6, 12, 42, 47, 72, 76, 103, 126/127, 132

Conclusions, drawing, 83, 108, 109, 118

Connecting texts, 37D, 67D, 97D, 125D, 139D

Content–area reading, 100–121, 128–135, 142A, 142/143

Context clues, 15, 43, 55, 77, 131

Continuant stop blends, 8I–J, 37E–H, 67G–H, T64

Contractions, 97K–L, 125K–L, 139K–L, 139M, 139O–P

Conventions of language. *See* Grammar, mechanics and usage; Oral language development.

Critical thinking, 20, 30, 34, 37A–C, 64, 67A–C, 94, 97A–C, 106, 122, 125A–C, 136, 139A–C

Cross–curricular

art, 8D

language arts, 8G, 38G, 68G, 126G

math, 22, 58, 82, 98D, 104

music, 84

science, 10A, 20, 38D, 56, 68D, 70A, 86, 98D, 100A, 110

social studies, 8D, 16, 38D, 40A, 48, 68D, 78, 118, 126D, 128A

Cultural perspectives, 14, 50, 74, 114

Daily phonics routines, 8J, 10A, 35, 37F, 37H, 38J, 40A, 65, 67F, 67H, 68J, 70A, 95, 97F, 97H, 98J, 100A, 123, 125F, 125H, 126J, 128A, 137, 139F, 139H

Dakos, Kalli, 140–141

Decodable stories, 8/9, 38/39, 68/69, 98/99, 126/127

Decodable words, 10B, 40B, 70B, 100B, 128B

Decoding and phonics. *See* Phonics and decoding.

Diagrams, 36, 66, 96, 97I, 97J, 124, 138, 139E
Venn, 97I, 97J, 139E

Dictating and spelling, 8/9, 38/39, 68/69, 98/99, 126/127

Digraphs, 68I–J, 68/69, 70–93, 97E–F, 97G–H, 111, 125G–H, 126I–J, T72, T73
ch, wh, nk, 68/69, 70–97, 97E–F, 97G–H, 111, 125G–H, 126I–J, T72, T73

Double negatives, 125K, 139O

Drafting and drafting strategies, 37M, 67M, 97M, 125M, 139M

Drawing, 7, 8C, 8D, 10A, 28, 31, 33, 35, 37A, 37C, 37D, 37H, 37J, 37M, 37N, 38D, 38G, 40A, 41, 47, 61, 67C, 67J, 67M, 67N, 68C, 68G, 70A, 74, 78, 79, 97C, 97D, 97N, 98G, 105, 112, 125A, 125B, 125D, 125J, 125N, 128A, 139F, 139N, 142A. *See also* Art link, Viewing and representing.

Early intervention. *See* Prevention/ intervention.

English as a Second Language, 10A, 13, 17, 24, 27, 37E, 37F, 37J, 37K, 37N, 40A, 44, 46, 49, 55, 67F, 67K, 67L, 67N, 67O, 70A, 79, 83, 85, 87, 97N, 100A, 102, 105, 107, 115, 125N, 128A, 131, 133, 139N, 139O, 142A. *See also* Language support.

Extend activities. *See* Alternate teaching strategies, Meeting Individual Needs, Theme projects.

Fantasy and reality, distinguishing, 27, 100

First person, 6

Fluency

echo reading, 6

group reading, 12, 42, 52, 72

in phonics, 8J, 35, 38J, 67H, 68J, 97F, 98J, 125F, 126J, 137

reading dialogue, 87

reading with expression, 24, 62

rereading, 8/9, 32, 38/39, 62, 68/69, 92, 98/99, 120, 126/127, 134

shared reading, 90

taping and listening, 76

Formal assessment, 35, 65, 95, 123, 137

Genre, literary. *See* Literary genre.

Gifted and talented. *See* Meeting Individual Needs.

Grammar, mechanics and usage, 37O–P, 67O–P, 97O–P, 125O–P, 139O–P

book titles, 67P

contractions, 97K–L, 125K–L, 139K–L, 139M, 139O–P

nouns, 97M, 97P, 125M

parts of speech, 37O–P, 67O–P, 97O–P, 125O–P, 139O–P

possessives, 14, 37K–L, 67K–L, 80, 112, 139I–J, T67

singular possessive pronouns, 14

punctuation

apostrophes, 37K–L, 67K–L, 97K–L, 112, 125K–L, 139I–J, 139K–L, 139M, 139O

commas, 24

exclamation marks, 13, 25, 31, 37M, 75, 76, 85, 86, 90, 98/99, 125P

periods, 37M, 52, 82, 90, 98/99, 117

question marks, 37M, 90

quotation marks, 26, 31, 44, 48, 77, 87

verbs, 37O–P, 67O–P, 97O–P, 125O–P, 139O–P

contractions with *not,* 139O–P

is and *are,* 125O–P

past tense, 97O–P

present tense, 37M, 67M, 67O–P

recognizing, 37O–P

Grammar/spelling connections, 37M, 67M, 97M, 125M, 139M

Graphic aids/organizers

charts, 10A, 24, 40, 53, 63, 67M, 70A, 70, 73, 86, 93, 100, 101, 102, 103, 105, 108, 111, 120, 121, 128A, 128, 135, 139H, 140

diagram, 36, 66, 96, 97I, 97J, 124, 138, 139E, T66

timeline, 139M

webs, 40A, 97D, 100A, 125D, 129, 130, 131, 132, 134, 139D

character web, 97D, 139D

setting web, 129, 130, 131, 132, 134

word web, 40A, 100A

Graphophonic cues, 13, 15, 16, 17, 19, 21, 22, 42, 43, 45, 46, 50, 55, 60, 72, 80, 83, 84, 88, 89, 102, 106, 107, 110, 117, 130, 131, 132

Greg's Mask, 40–63

Group work, 6I, 6J, 6, 7, 8G, 8J, 32, 35, 37D, 37L, 37M, 38G, 40B, 42, 48, 61, 65, 67D, 67H, 67L, 68J, 68/69, 72, 92, 95, 97D, 97F, 97L, 100B, 123, 125D, 125F, 125J, 125N, 126G, 132, 134, 139D, 140, 141

Handwriting, 67M, 125M, T78–93

High–frequency words, 10B–C, 37A–B, 40B–C, 49, 67A–B, 70B–C, 79, 97A–B, 100B–C, 125A–B, 128B–C
  any, 40B–C, 67A–B
  eat, 70B–C, 97A–B, 128B–C
  fall, 10B–C, 37A–B
  grow, 40B–C, 67A–B
  know, 100B–C, 106, 125A–B
  new, 40B–C, 67A–B
  now, 70B–C, 97A–B
  old, 40B–C, 67A–B, 128B–C
  their, 10B–C, 37A–B
  together, 70B–C, 97A–B
  too, 70B–C, 97A–B
  try, 10B–C, 37A–B, 125A–B, 128B–C
  under, 100B–C, 125A–B
  where, 100B–C, 125A–B
  why, 100B–C, 125A–B
  would, 10B–C, 37A–B

High–utility vocabulary. *See* Vocabulary.

Homonyms, 10B

Imagery, 38G, 98G

Independent reading, 8B, 37B, 38B, 67B, 68B, 97B, 98B, 125B, 126B, 139D

Inferences, making, 13, 24, 27, 29, 30, 37A, 37B, 45, 48, 49, 51, 53, 55, 57, 67A, 76, 79, 80, 81, 84, 85, 86, 87, 89, 92, 104, 105, 106, 109, 110

Informal assessment. *See* Assessment.

Inquiry. *See* Research and inquiry.

Integrated language arts. *See* Cross–curricular.

Interactive writing activities, 37M–N, 67M–N, 97M–N, 125M–N, 139M–N
  drafting, 37M, 67M, 97M, 125M, 139M
  presentation ideas for, 37N, 67N, 97N, 125N, 139N
  prewriting, 37M, 67M, 97M, 125M, 139M
  publishing, 37M, 67M, 97M, 125M, 139M
  revising, 37M, 67M, 97M, 125M, 139M

Internet connection, 6J, 14, 35, 37D, 50, 65, 67D, 74, 84, 95, 97D, 104, 118, 123, 125D, 137, 139D

Intervention/prevention. *See* Prevention / intervention.

Journal writing, 8/9, 33, 37D, 37N, 37R, 38/39, 63, 67D, 67R, 68/69, 93, 97D, 97N, 97R, 98/99, 121, 125D, 125N, 125R, 126/127, 135, 139D, 139N, 139R

Language arts link, 8G, 38G, 68G, 126G

Language support, 10A, 13, 17, 24, 27, 37E, 37F, 37J, 37K, 37N, 40A, 44, 46, 49, 55, 67F, 67K, 67L, 67N, 67O, 70A, 79, 83, 85, 87, 97N, 100A, 102, 105, 107, 115, 125N, 128A, 131, 133, 139N, 139O, 142A

Learning styles
  analytical, 82, 86
  auditory, 10B, 40B, 70B, 84, 88, 100B, 126G, 128B, T64–T76
  kinesthetic, 8G, 8J, 10A, 20, 37L, 38J, 40A, 50, 58, 67H, 67L, 68J, 70A, 78, 97H, 98J, 100A, 110, 125F, 126G, 126J, T64–T76
  linguistic, 10A, 14, 37J, 37L, 38J, 40A, 48, 56, 67F, 67H, 67J, 67L, 70A, 74, 86, 88, 97F, 97L, 98J, 100A, 118, 125F, 125H, 125L, 126G, 128A, 139H, 139J, 139L
  logical, 56, 118, 139H
  spatial, 44, 97F
  visual, 8G, 10A, 14, 38G, 50, 58, 67F,67J, 68G, 68J, 74, 78, 82, 84, 97L, 98G, 104, 114, 125H, 125J, 125L, 128A, 139F, 139J, T64–T76

Let's Camp Out, 128–135

Leveled books, 8B, 37A–D, 38B, 68A–D, 68B, 97A–D, 98B, 125A–D, 126B, 139A–D

Limited English Proficiency. *See* Language support.

Listening and speaking activities, 6J, 6, 8G, 10A, 10B, 32, 33, 37D, 37L, 37N, 37O, 38G, 40A, 40B, 62, 63, 67D, 67L, 67N, 67O, 68G, 70A, 70B, 92, 93, 97D, 97L, 97N, 97O, 98G, 100A, 100B, 120, 121, 125D, 125L, 125N, 125O, 126G, 128A, 128B, 134, 135, 139D, 139L, 139N, 139O, 141. *See also* Speaking and listening activities.

Lists, making, 6I, 6J, 31R, 38J, 49, 51, 56, 63, 67I, 67R, 77, 97R, 125M, 125R, 139M, 139R, 140

Literacy support. *See* Language support.

Literary devices
  alliteration, 98G
  descriptive words, 98G
  first person, 6
  imagery, 38G, 98G
  repetition, 141
  rhyme, 7, 38G
  rhythm, 7, 38G
  See also Poetry, Rhyme, Writer's craft.

Literary genre, 8G, 10, 11, 38G, 38/39, 40, 41, 68G, 70, 71, 98G, 100, 101, 126G, 128
  fable, 8G
  fantasy, 140
  folktale, 68G
  informational story, 129
  poem, 6–7, 38G, 98G, 140–141
  narrative nonfiction, 101
  nonfiction article, 140
  story, 11, 41, 71, 126G

Literary practices, using, 8G

Literary response, 7, 33, 37A–C, 63, 67A–C, 93, 97A–C, 121, 123C, 125A–C, 135, 139A–C, 141

Long vowels and phonograms, 98I–J, 100–121, 125A–C, 125E–F, 125G–H, 126I–J, T75, T76
  long *a: a–e,* 98C, 98I–J, 100–121, 125A–C, 125E–F, 125G–H, 126I–J, T75, T76
  See also Phonics and decoding.

Main idea/supporting details, identifying, 31, 61, 91, 133. *See also* Comprehension strategies.

Margins, recognizing, 97M

Math link, 22, 58, 82, 98D, 104

McGovern, Ann, 38A, 40

Mechanics and usage, 37P, 67P, 97P, 125P, 139P
  apostrophes, 139P
  book titles, 67P
  capitalizing proper nouns, 97P
  letter punctuation, 37P
  sentence punctuation, 125P
  See also Grammar, mechanics and usage.

Media, reading and understanding, 142A, 142/143

Meeting Individual Needs
  for comprehension, 37J, 67J, 97J, 125J, 139F, 139H
  for phonics, 8J, 37F, 37H, 38J, 67F, 67H, 68J, 97F, 97H, 98J, 125F, 125H, 126J
  for study skills, 36, 66, 96, 124, 138
  for vocabulary, 37L, 40C, 67L, 70C, 97L, 100C, 125L, 128C, 139J, 139L
  for writing, 37N, 67N, 97N, 125N, 139N
  grouping suggestions for strategic reading, 10, 40, 70, 100, 128

leveled books, 8B, 37A–D, 38B, 67A–D, 68B, 97A–D, 98B, 125A–D, 126B, 139A–D

resources for, 6F, 8B, 38B, 68B, 98B, 126B

Minilessons, 13, 15, 23, 29, 31, 43, 47, 49, 51, 53, 59, 61, 77, 79, 81, 89, 91, 105, 109, 111, 113, 115, 119, 131, 133

blends, 23, 57

cause and effect, 53, 113

context clues, 15, 43, 77, 131

digraphs *ch,* 111

draw conclusions, 109

final consonants, 115

high-frequency words, 49, 79

main idea, 31, 61, 91, 133

making inferences, 13, 51, 81, 105

making predictions, 29

phonological awareness, 59

setting, 89

summarize, 119

use illustrations, 47

Minters, Frances, 98A, 100

Moral, of story, 8G

Multiple–meaning words, 73

Multisyllabic words, 8I–J, 38I

Music link, 84

Oral comprehension, 8G, 38G, 68G, 98G, 126G

Oral language development, 10A, 40A, 70A, 100A, 128A

Oral response to literature, 7, 33, 63, 93, 121, 135, 141

Organizing information. *See* Interactive writing activities, Summarizing, Theme projects.

Paragraphs, 67N

Partner work, 37N, 38/39, 38D, 62, 65, 67F, 67J, 67N, 70B, 82, 97A, 97N, 98D, 100B, 102, 104, 106, 120, 123, 125H, 125L, 125N, 126/127, 126C, 128B, 134, 139D, 139L, 141. *See also* Alternate teaching strategies

Peer conferencing. *See* Alternate teaching strategies, Group work, Interactive writing activities, Partner work, Theme projects.

Penmanship, 67M, 125M, T78–T93

Performance assessment opportunity. *See* Assessment.

Phonemic awareness, 8H, 38H, 68H, 98H, 126H

Phonics and decoding, 8H, 8I–J, 8/9, 37E–F, 37G–H, 37Q–R, 38H, 38I–J, 38/39, 67E–F, 67G–H, 67Q–R, 68H, 68I–J, 68/69, 97E–F, 97G–H, 97Q–R, 98H, 98I–J, 98/99, 125E–F, 125G–H, 125Q–R, 126H, 126I–J, 126/127, T64, T65, T69, T70, T72, T73, T75, T76

blends, 8I–J, 8/9, 23, 37E–H, 37Q–R, 38I–J, 38/39, 67E–H, 67Q–R, T64, T65, T69, T70

blending long a words, 98I–J, 125E–F

blending with short *a,* 25

bending with short *e,* 117

blending with short *u,* 106

continuant/stop blends, 8I–J, 37E–H, 67G–H, T64

stop/continuant blends, 38I–J, 67E–F, 67G–H, T70

CVCe pattern, 125G–H

decoding multisyllabic words, 8I–J

digraphs, 68I–J, 70–93, 97E–F, 97G–H, 111, 125G–H, 126I–J

ch, wh, nk, 68/69, 70–97, 97E–F, 97G–H, 111, 125G–H, 126I–J, T72, T73

double consonant words, 38I–J, 67G–H

final consonants, 37E–F, 37G–H

fluency in, 8J, 35, 38J, 67H, 68J, 97F, 98J, 125F, 126J, 137

initial consonants, 37E–F, 37G–H

letter sound correspondence, 8H, 8I–J, 8/9, 37E–F, 37G–H, 37Q–R, 38H, 38I–J, 38/39, 67E–F, 67G–H, 67Q–R, 68H, 68I–J, 68/69, 97E–F, 97G–H, 97Q–R, 98H, 98I–J, 98/99, 125E–F, 125G–H, 125Q–R, 126H, 126I–J, 126/127

letter substitution, 8J, 37H, 38J, 68J, 98J, 100A, 126J, 139H

long vowels and phonograms, 98I–J, 100–121, 125A–C, 125E–F, 125G–H, 126I–J, T75, T76

long *a: a–e,* 98C, 98I–J, 100–121, 125A–C, 125E–F, 125G–H, 126I–J, T75, T76

onset and rime, 8H, 38H, 68H, 98H, 126H

phonemic awareness, 8H, 38H, 68H, 98H, 126H

rhyming, 7, 8J, 8/9, 21, 38G, 38J, 38/39, 68/69, 98I, 98/99, 126J, 126/127, 139

segmenting, 8H, 8J, 38H, 68H, 98H, 126H, 126J, 126/127

short vowels, 8I–J, 25, 37E–H, 67E–H, 97G–H, 106, 117, 119

blending with short *a,* 25, 119

bending with short *e,* 117, 119

blending with short *u,* 106, 119

spelling and

words with blends, 37Q–R, 67Q–R

words with digraphs: *ch, wh, nk,* 97Q–R

words with long *a: a–e,* 125Q–R

words with silent *e,* 125Q–R

using words in context, 8I, 37E, 37G, 38I, 67E, 67G, 68I, 97E, 97H, 98I, 125E, 125G, 126I

word building, 8J, 37F, 37H, 38J, 67F, 67H, 68J, 97F, 97H, 98J, 125F, 125H, 126J

writing for, 8J, 37F, 38J, 68J, 97H, 98J, 125H, 126J, 139F

Phonics CD–ROM, 8J, 37F, 37H, 38J, 67F, 67H, 68J, 97F, 97H, 98J, 125F, 125H, 126J

Phonics daily routines. *See* Daily phonics routines.

Phonological awareness, 8H, 19, 29, 38H, 68H, 80, 91, 98H, 126H, T64, T69, T72, T75

Picture walk, 10, 37A–C, 40, 67A–C, 70, 97A–C, 100, 125A–C, 139A–C

Plourde, Lynn, 8A, 10

Poetry, 6–7, 8/9, 38G, 38/39, 68/69, 98G, 98/99, 126/127, 140–141

alliteration, 98G

descriptive words, 98G

first person, 6

imagery, 38G, 98G

reading for fluency, 8/9, 38/39, 68/69, 98/99, 126/127

repetition, 141

rhyme, 7, 38G

rhythm, 7, 38G

stanzas, 38G

Possessives, 14, 37K–L, 67K–L, 80, 112, 139I–J, T68

Predictions, making, 10, 13, 18, 20, 21, 23, 26, 28, 29, 33, 37A–C, 40, 41, 54, 63, 67A–C, 70, 84, 93, 97A–C, 100, 115, 116, 117, 118, 121, 125A–C, 128, 135, 139A–C

Prereading strategies. *See* Previewing literature.

Presentation ideas, 6J, 37D, 37N, 67D, 67N, 97D, 97N, 125D, 125N, 139D, 139N, 141

Prevention/intervention, 12, 15, 19, 21, 25, 29, 43, 45, 47, 51, 52, 60, 72, 73, 80, 90, 91, 103, 106, 112, 117, 119, 130, 132

blending, 25, 43, 45, 60, 106, 117

multiple-meaning words, 73

phonological awareness, 19, 29, 80, 91

punctuation, 90

rhyming words, 21

sentences, 15, 51, 117

short *a, e, i, o,* 119

tracking print, 12, 47, 72, 103, 132

Previewing literature, 10, 37A–C, 40, 67A–C, 70, 97A–C, 100, 125A–C, 128, 139A–C

Prewriting and prewriting strategies, 37M, 67M, 97M, 125M, 139M

Print, concepts of. *See* Concepts of print.

Publishing, 37M, 67M, 97M, 125M, 139M

Punctuation
apostrophes, 37K–L, 67K–L, 97K–L, 112, 125K–L, 139I–J, 139K–L, 139M, 139O
capital letters, 12, 37M, 42, 52, 67P, 74, 97M, 117
commas, 24, 57, 72, 98/99
end punctuation, 13, 25, 31, 37M, 52, 75, 76, 82, 85, 86, 98/99, 117, 125P
exclamation marks, 13, 25, 31, 37M, 75, 76, 85, 86, 90, 98/99
periods, 37M, 52, 82, 90, 117
question marks, 37M, 90
quotation marks, 26, 31, 44, 48, 77, 87

Quick write, 33, 63, 93, 121, 135

Read alouds, 6, 8G, 38G, 68G, 98G, 126G, 140

Reading comprehension. *See* Comprehension strategies.

Reading for information, 142A, 142/143
reading media, 142A, 142/143

Reading rate, 32, 62, 92, 120, 134

Realia. *See* Alternate teaching strategies, Cross–curricular, Cultural perspectives, Story activities, Theme projects.

Reference sources and resources, using.
See Research and inquiry.

Reluctant readers, 8B, 37A, 38B, 67A, 68B, 97A, 98B, 125A, 126B, 139A

Repetition, 141

Representing. *See* Drawing, Viewing and representing.

Rereading for fluency, 8/9, 32, 38/39, 62, 68/69, 92, 98/99, 120, 126/127, 134

Research and inquiry, 6J, 14, 16, 22, 35, 37D, 50, 56, 65, 67D, 78, 95, 97D, 104, 110, 118, 123, 125D, 137, 139D, 141
asking questions in, 6J, 141
creating presentations for, 6J, 141
drawing conclusions from, 141
identifying resources for, 6J

Research strategies, 6J

Responding to literature. *See* Literary response.

Retelling, 32, 37D, 62, 70, 70D, 91, 97D, 120, 125D, 130

Rhyme/rhythm, 7, 8J, 8/9, 21, 38G, 38J, 38/39, 60, 68/69, 98I, 98/99, 126J, 126/127, 140

Sam's Song, 70–93

Science link, 10A, 20, 38D, 56, 68D, 70A, 86, 98D, 100A, 110, 126D

Second–language support. *See* Language support.

Segmenting, 38/39, 68/69, 70B, 100B, 126/127, 128B

Selection summary, 8A, 38A, 68A, 98A, 126A

Self–assessment, 32, 62, 92, 120, 134

Self–monitoring strategies, 18, 53, 82, 110
ask questions, 53
picture clues, 82, 110
relate to personal experiences, 18
search for clues, 82, 110

Self–selected reading, 8C, 37I, 38C, 67I, 68C, 97I, 98C, 125I, 126C, 139I, T96–97

Semantic cues, 14, 73, 80, 112

Sentences, 15, 33, 51, 63, 67R, 82, 93, 117, 121, 125P, 125R, 135

Sequence of events, analyzing, 23, 26, 37C

Setting, analyzing, 11, 37I–J, 43, 45, 48, 52, 56, 58, 63, 67A, 67B, 67C, 73, 80, 89, 125I–J, 129, 130, 131, 133, 134, 135, 139G–H, T67

Setting purposes for reading, 10, 37A–C, 40, 67A–C, 70, 97A–C, 100, 125A–C, 128, 139A–C

Short vowels and phonograms, 25, 106, 117, 119
blending with short *a*, 25, 119
blending with short *e*, 117, 119
blending with short *u*, 106, 119

Sight words, 10B–C, 35A–C, 40B–C, 67A–C, 70B–C, 97A–C, 100B–C, 125A–C, 128B–C

Snakes, 100–121

Social studies link, 8D, 16, 38D, 40A, 48, 68D, 78, 118, 126D, 128A

"Something About Me," 6–7

Speaking and listening activities
act it out, 8D, 10A, 13, 17, 37N, 40B, 62, 65, 67N, 79, 95, 109, 113, 126G, 126/127, 134
asking and answering questions, 6J, 15, 17, 20, 32, 33, 40, 41, 44, 51, 52, 58, 61, 62, 63, 64, 67O, 70, 70C, 82, 86, 88, 92, 93, 94, 97A, 97C, 100, 107, 122, 128, 135, 141
class and group discussions, 6I, 6J, 6, 7, 10A, 33, 34, 37A–C, 37D, 40A, 48, 63, 64, 67A–C, 67D, 70A, 93, 94, 97A–C, 97D, 100A, 121, 122, 125A–C, 125D, 128A, 135, 136, 139A–C, 139D, 142A

conveying a message, 37N
explaining, 113, 139D
giving a class lesson, 97B
nonverbal responses, 24
pantomime, 14, 27, 67N, 88, 97Q, 114, 115
presentations, 6J, 33, 37D, 37N, 67D, 67N, 97D, 97N, 125D, 125N, 139D, 139N, 141
reading with expression, 12
retelling/summarizing, 10, 24, 32, 37D, 40, 55, 62, 70, 91, 97D, 120, 125D, 130
role play, 59, 67D
sharing ideas, experiences, 10A, 40A, 70A, 98D, 100A, 125J, 128A, 142A
sing–a–long, 97N, 137
speech, 125N
staying on topic, 67N
storytelling, 82, 125L, 139N
See also Listening and speaking activities, Speaking and listening strategies.

Speaking and listening strategies, 6J, 37D, 37N, 67D, 67N, 97D, 97N, 125D, 125N, 139D, 139N, 141

Spelling
assessing prior knowledge, 37Q, 67Q, 97Q, 125Q, 139Q
assessment, 37R, 67R, 97R, 125R, 139R
optional spelling test, 37R, 67R, 97R, 125R, 139R
patterns and sorting, 37Q–R, 67Q–R, 97Q–R, 125Q–R, 139Q–R
reteaching and, 37R, 67R, 97R, 125R, 139R
word meaning, 37R, 67R, 97R, 125R, 139R
words from science, 139Q–R
words with blends, 37Q–R, 67Q–R
words with digraphs: *ch, wh, nk,* 97Q–R
words with long *a: a–e,* 125Q–R
words with silent e, 125Q–R

Spelling/phonics connection, 37F, 67F, 97F, 125F, 139F

Spelling/vocabulary connection, 10B, 40B, 70B, 100B, 128B

Stan's Stunt, 10–37

Stop/continuant blends, 38I–J, 67E–F, 67G–H, T70

Story activities, 35, 37A–C, 65, 67A–C, 95, 97A–C, 123, 125A–C, 137, 139A–C

Story elements, analyzing, 31I, 34, 37I–J, 41, 43, 45, 48, 51, 54, 56, 58, 63, 67D, 73, 97B, 97C, 125I–J, 126G, 129, 130, 131, 133, 135, 139G–H, T67

Story patterns, 37M, 67M, 97M, 125M, 139M

Story props, using, 14, 17, 19, 22, 29, 45, 52, 62, 77, 78, 87, 92

Story questions, 34, 37A–C, 64, 67A–C, 94, 97A–C, 122, 125A–C, 136, 139A–C

Strategic reading, 10–37, 40–67, 70–97, 100–125, 128–139

Student self–assessment, 32, 62, 92, 120, 134

Study skills and information resources, 36, 66, 96, 124, 138
diagrams, 36, 66, 96, 124, 138, T66

Suggested lesson planner, 8E–F, 38E–F, 68E–F, 98E–F, 126E–F

Summarizing, 10, 31, 32, 37D, 40, 55, 62, 70, 91, 92, 97D, 119, 120, 125D, 130, 134, 136, 139N

Syntactic cues, 12, 15, 47, 52, 72, 90, 112, 132

Teaching tips
for decodable and high-frequency words, 10B, 40B, 70B, 100B, 128B
handwriting, 67M, 125M
instructional, 8I, 16, 21, 24, 26, 37K, 38I, 44, 54, 67I, 73, 83, 97I, 97K, 98I, 113, 125I, 125K, 126I, 130, 139G, 139O
management, 37I, 46, 56, 80, 139E

Technology resources. *See* Internet connection, Phonics CD–ROM, Technology tips.

Technology tips, 37M, 67M, 97M, 125M, 139M
margin setting, 97M
page breaks, 139M
proofreading on the screen, 37M
spell-checking, 67M
using the keyboard, 125M

Test–taking practice, 37, 67, 97, 125, 139

Text connections, 37D, 67D, 97D, 125D, 139D

Theme connections, 6I, 6J, 140, 141

Theme projects, 6J, 141

Time for Kids
Let's Camp Out, 128–135

Timelessness of literature, 68G

Transferring the strategy, 32, 62, 92, 120, 134

Usage. *See* Grammar, mechanics and usage.

Verbs 37O–P, 67O–P, 97O–P, 125O–P, 139O–P
contractions with *not,* 139O–P
is and *are,* 125O–P
past tense, 97O–P

present tense, 37M, 67M, 67O–P
recognizing, 37O–P.
See also Grammar, mechanics and usage.

Viewing and representing, 28, 37D, 37N, 67D, 67N, 97D, 97N, 125D, 125N, 139D, 139N

Viewing strategies, 37N, 97N, 125N

Visual literacy, 28

Vocabulary and vocabulary strategies, 10B–C, 37A–C, 37K–L, 40B–C, 67A–C, 67K–L, 70B–C, 97A–C, 97K–L, 100B–C, 125A–C, 125K–L, 128B–C, 139I–J, 139K–L
auditory activities for, 10B, 40B, 70B, 100B, 128B
context clues, 15, 43, 77, 131
contractions, 97K–L, 125K–L, 139K–L, 139O–P, T74
decodable words, 10B, 40B, 70B, 100B, 128B
high-frequency words, 10B–C, 37A–B, 40B–C, 49, 67A–B, 70B–C, 79, 97A–B, 100B–C, 125A–B, 128B–C
any, 40B–C, 67A–B
eat, 70B–C, 97A–B, 128B–C
fall, 10B–C, 37A–B
grow, 40B–C, 67A–B
know, 100B–C, 106, 125A–B
new, 40B–C, 67A–B
now, 70B–C, 97A–B
old, 40B–C, 67A–B, 128B–C
their, 10B–C, 37A–B
together, 70B–C, 97A–B
too, 70B–C, 97A–B
try, 10B–C, 37A–B, 125A–B, 128B–C
under, 100B–C, 125A–B
where, 100B–C, 125A–B
why, 100B–C, 125A–B
would, 10B–C, 37A–B
listening to words, 10B, 40B, 70B, 100B, 128B
multiple-meaning words, 73
possessives, 14, 37K–L, 67K–L, 80, 112, 139I–J, T67
synonyms, 107
using words in context, 8I, 37E, 37G, 38I, 67E, 67G, 68I, 97E, 97H, 98I, 125F, 125H, 126I
visual activities for, 10B, 40B, 70B, 100B, 128B
word building, 8J, 37F, 37H, 38J, 67F, 67H, 68J, 97F, 97H, 98J, 125F, 125H, 126J

Webs, 40A, 97D, 100A, 125D, 129, 130, 131, 132, 134, 139D

Word building, 8J, 37F, 37H, 38J, 67F, 67H, 68J, 97F, 97H, 98J, 125F, 125H, 126J

Word choice, 8G, 73, 83, 94, 98G

Word meaning, 37R, 67R, 97R, 125R, 139R

Word wall, 10C, 40C, 70C, 100C, 128C

Writer's Craft, 60
rhythms in writing, 60

Writing activities
address, 37M, 67A
billboard, 142/143
chart, 67M
class book, 37M
comparisons, 139F
drafting, 37M, 67M, 97M, 125M, 139M
facts, 123
field guide, 37M
instructions, 67N
invitations, 67N
journal, 8/9, 33, 37D, 37N, 37R, 38/39, 63, 67D, 67N, 67R, 68/69, 93, 97D, 97N, 97R, 98/99, 121, 125D, 125N, 125R, 126/127, 135, 139D, 139N, 139R
labels, 37H, 68D, 112, 139H
lists, 6I, 6J, 38J, 49, 51, 56, 63, 67I, 67R, 77, 97R, 125M, 125R, 139M, 139R, 140
mural, 125M
notes, 67A
number sentences, 82
personal identification, 67N
poster, 64
presentation ideas for, 37N, 67N, 97N, 125N, 139N
prewriting, 37M, 67M, 97M, 125M, 139M
publishing, 37M, 67M, 97M, 125M, 139M
quick write, 33, 63, 93, 121, 135
recording, 38D
responses, 13, 33, 37B, 37N, 63, 67C, 93, 121, 122, 125B, 135
revising, 37M, 67M, 97M, 125M, 139M
rhymes, 8J, 126J
riddles, 68J, 125R
sentences, 8C, 8D, 10B, 31, 37C, 37J, 37M, 38D, 38J, 61, 67M, 68C, 68D, 79, 97C, 98C, 98D, 100A, 122, 125C, 126D, 128B
song book, 97M
story, 37N, 67N, 97N, 125N, 139M, 139N
telephone number, 67N
words, 8D, 8J, 38C, 40A, 57, 97L, 98J, 125H, 126D

You're An Author Now, 140–141

The Scoring Chart is provided for your convenience in grading your students' work.

- Find the column that shows the total number of items.
- Find the row that matches the number of items answered correctly.
- The intersection of the two rows provides the percentage score.

TOTAL NUMBER OF ITEMS

NUMBER CORRECT	1	2	3	4	5	6	7	8	9	10	11	12	13	14	15	16	17	18	19	20	21	22	23	24	25	26	27	28	29	30
1	100	50	33	25	20	17	14	13	11	10	9	8	8	7	7	6	6	6	5	5	5	5	4	4	4	4	4	4	3	3
2		100	66	50	40	33	29	25	22	20	18	17	15	14	13	13	12	11	11	10	10	9	9	8	8	8	7	7	7	7
3			100	75	60	50	43	38	33	30	27	25	23	21	20	19	18	17	16	15	14	14	13	13	12	12	11	11	10	10
4				100	80	67	57	50	44	40	36	33	31	29	27	25	24	22	21	20	19	18	17	17	16	15	15	14	14	13
5					100	83	71	63	56	50	45	42	38	36	33	31	29	28	26	25	24	23	22	21	20	19	19	18	17	17
6						100	86	75	67	60	55	50	46	43	40	38	35	33	32	30	29	27	26	25	24	23	22	21	21	20
7							100	88	78	70	64	58	54	50	47	44	41	39	37	35	33	32	30	29	28	27	26	25	24	23
8								100	89	80	73	67	62	57	53	50	47	44	42	40	38	36	35	33	32	31	30	29	28	27
9									100	90	82	75	69	64	60	56	53	50	47	45	43	41	39	38	36	35	33	32	31	30
10										100	91	83	77	71	67	63	59	56	53	50	48	45	43	42	40	38	37	36	34	33
11											100	92	85	79	73	69	65	61	58	55	52	50	48	46	44	42	41	39	38	37
12												100	92	86	80	75	71	67	63	60	57	55	52	50	48	46	44	43	41	40
13													100	93	87	81	76	72	68	65	62	59	57	54	52	50	48	46	45	43
14														100	93	88	82	78	74	70	67	64	61	58	56	54	52	50	48	47
15															100	94	88	83	79	75	71	68	65	63	60	58	56	54	52	50
16																100	94	89	84	80	76	73	70	67	64	62	59	57	55	53
17																	100	94	89	85	81	77	74	71	68	65	63	61	59	57
18																		100	95	90	86	82	78	75	72	69	67	64	62	60
19																			100	95	90	86	83	79	76	73	70	68	66	63
20																				100	95	91	87	83	80	77	74	71	69	67
21																					100	95	91	88	84	81	78	75	72	70
22																						100	96	92	88	85	81	79	76	73
23																							100	96	92	88	85	82	79	77
24																								100	96	92	89	86	83	80
25																									100	96	93	89	86	83
26																										100	96	93	90	87
27																											100	96	93	90
28																												100	97	93
29																													100	97
30																														100